FACING FEARS

The Sourcebook for
Phobias, Fears, and Anxieties

FACING FEARS

The Sourcebook for Phobias, Fears, and Anxieties

Ada P. Kahn, Ph.D., and
Ronald M. Doctor, Ph.D.

Checkmark Books®

An imprint of Facts On File, Inc.

Facing Fears: The Sourcebook for Phobias, Fears, and Anxieties

Copyright © 2000 by Ada P. Kahn, Ph.D., and Ronald M. Doctor, Ph.D.

Checkmark Books
An imprint of Facts On File, Inc.
11 Penn Plaza
New York, NY 10001

Library of Congress Cataloging-in-Publication Data
Kahn, Ada P.
  Facing fears: The sourcebook for phobias, fears, and anxieties/by Ada P.
  Kahn and Ronald M. Doctor.
p. cm.—(Facts for life)
Includes bibliographical references and index.
ISBN 0-8160-3992-5 (acid-free paper)
1. Fear. 2. Phobias. 3. Anxiety. I. Doctor, Ronald M. (Ronald Manual) II. Title. III.
Series.
RC535 .K34 1999
616.85'22—dc21   99–048737

Text design by Evelyn Horovicz
Cover design by Cathy Rincon

Printed in the United States of America

MP FOF 10 9 8 7 6 5 4 3 2 1

This book is printed on acid-free paper.

CONTENTS

PART III: READING LIST AND RESOURCES

INTRODUCTION

Facing Fears is a timely resource, as public awareness of anxiety disorders is increasing. The first Surgeon General's report on mental health and mental illness, issued in December 1999, confirmed the prevalence of anxiety disorders in the United States. Anxiety disorders are the most common mental-health concern Americans face. Estimates indicate that more than 19 million Americans suffer from an anxiety disorder each year.

Those who struggle with anxieties, fears, and phobias in their daily lives often find their hearts racing and their bodies tense, frozen, and sweaty when faced with feared situations. If this experience sounds familiar, you may feel confused and intimidated because of the way you react to the things you fear. You may even be afraid that you might be "going crazy" or having a serious physical or mental-health problem. You may often go to extremes to avoid the things and situations that trigger your fears and unpleasant body sensations.

We hope this book will help educate you to put your situation in perspective, guide you toward your goals by providing resource information, and perhaps set you on your way toward recovery. By picking up this book, you have taken the first step toward helping yourself.

"THERE'S REALLY NOTHING TO BE AFRAID OF"

That famous line has been repeated for centuries and it hasn't done much to alleviate people's discomfort. But the truth is that facing your fears, instead of avoiding them, is a more appropriate way of proceeding. It is far better to confront difficult situations gradually, with effective strategies and skills that will help you overcome the anxiety associated with them.

This book can provide you with the knowledge you need to get started. You will find information that can help you identify your specific fears—in addition to helpful clues that will pinpoint specific anxiety triggers—so you can begin to take control. You will find skills to help you along your journey and a general plan for you and a support person, whether a trained therapist or a trusted friend, to systematically work toward reducing your fears. Once you begin the process of facing fears in the right way, you will experience progress and improved functioning. You will be less dependent on excuses, medication, and avoidance and start to feel better about yourself.

WHAT DO PEOPLE FEAR?

Everyone has fears. We are physiologically built and programmed to experience fear. This reaction has helped humanity survive and evolve. Unfortunately, fears are indiscriminant in that they can become attached to many everyday life situations, bodily reactions, and thoughts. This book will help you understand how fears develop as a result of these situations, and the differences and similarities between "fear" and "phobia."

You may have one or more social fears, which means that you have a lot of anxiety and tension in one or in many social situations, such as during interviews, parties, or when meeting new people. Your fears may be intense enough that you avoid these situations even though you would like to be able to enjoy them.

Or, you may have one or more specific fears, such as heights, darkness, insects, or snakes. Or you may be one of the 8–10 million Americans who suffer from agoraphobia and avoid going far from a safe place unless a family member or a trusted friend goes with you. There are also combinations of fear reactions and coexisting conditions such as depression and addictions that may cloud the picture and make it more difficult to overcome your fears.

Some individuals become obsessive and/or compulsive about certain situations. Fear is a component in their reactions. For example, if you fear contamination by germs, you may compulsively wash your hands very frequently to reduce this obsession-produced fear.

Individuals of all ages can develop fears because of traumatic experiences they have had or situations they have witnessed. Once considered synonymous with war and catastrophe-induced reactions, posttraumatic stress disorders now are known to develop from many forms of social, sexual and physical abuse that individually affect people.

Therapies for treating fears and phobias have progressed significantly during the last generation. Since the 1960s, researchers have advanced knowledge of behavior therapy as well as biological effects on phobias and depression. Many of these approaches are outlined in this book and, with support, can provide a starting place for improvement.

It's natural to look for quick solutions for overcoming fears that lead to anxiety reactions. However, many quick solutions have limited long-range effects and do not address the root of the problem.

Many factors may contribute to fears and anxiety reactions, including major life changes, allergies, sickness, isolation, and chemical changes in your body. Although it is important to try to work with these factors, it will be helpful to deal directly with the fears and anxiety reactions themselves. This will provide the greatest benefits for you. It is also important to understand that although anxiety disorders seem to come on quickly, they *diminish slowly.* Furthermore, it takes systematic or regular practice to change them, so don't expect "quick fixes." You can, however, expect to improve and feel and function better as soon as you start a regular program of intervention and self-help.

HOW THIS BOOK CAN HELP YOU

This book is a resource for people who suffer anxiety reactions of many types. It is not intended as a substitute for professional therapy. It is also not a "formula" program. If you are in therapy, it may support your therapeutic work and provide useful knowledge, direction, and skills to enhance therapy. If you are not in therapy, consider getting support and encouragement from people close to you who want to see you improve. But remember, the anxiety is not their problem, it is yours, and while support is essential, it is still just a supplement to your own desire to grow and blossom as a fully functional person.

The process of facing fears begins when you recognize your fear or phobia as a problem in your life. There are opportunities in this book for you to identify the type of anxiety you have, but openness and frankness are needed in making these assessments. Your level of motivation is also an important factor in working with anxiety reactions since it takes time, patience, practice, and skill building to see them diminish. The best motivation is to make changes because you care enough about yourself to work at feeling better, improving your functioning, and giving up avoidance as a way of coping. Once you begin to approach your problem in a systematic way, you will want to know the type of anxiety reaction you have, if it coexists with other conditions, and the specific triggers for these reactions. Overcoming fears usually requires practice over a period of time. Repetition and exposure are essential. It may be six weeks to a year or more until you feel you have mastered your fear reactions. Responses to specific fears are often the fastest to change. On the other hand, some disorders may take longer and will probably require professional help along the way.

Facing Fears is written in a straightforward and easy-to-understand style. To help you identify your general fear levels, there are some self-report questionnaires. There are also descriptions of the various types of anxiety reactions and charts of specific reactions, such as fear of flying and fears of dental procedures. General strategies for improvement are presented along with skill-building suggestions and tools. For convenience, we have incorporated a useful tool for change in a Three-Step Process that is fully presented in Chapter 2. If you choose to face your fears, the Three-Step Process will give you a place to start by helping you organize your efforts. While these are general procedures, they are useful in working with all types of anxiety disorders and should lead to progress. In some cases, these simple steps may be all that is needed to fully diminish the anxiety reaction.

You can obtain assistance from self-help and professional organizations listed under "Resources" to help you advance even further.

Extensive alphabetically arranged entries at the end of the book further explain many terms related to the text. A Reading List includes references to many books and journal articles that will give you additional specific information.

PART I

FACING FEARS

CHAPTER 1

GETTING ACQUAINTED WITH FEARS, PHOBIAS, AND OTHER ANXIETY DISORDERS

In this introductory chapter, you will become acquainted with various types of phobias and other anxiety disorders. You'll learn more about how extreme some reactions to phobias are and always have been.

Most people fear something but react in many different ways to those fears. Some of us feel just a little nervous in a fearful situation; others experience sudden, unpleasant "symptoms." For example, one individual can walk to the edge of a balcony and enjoy the view, but another will become drenched in sweat, shake, feel dizzy or faint, and pull back. These physiological reactions happen because what we perceive with these events affects what goes on in the body and vice versa. Many who have severe reactions to their fears tend to avoid the situations in which they experienced fear. Avoidance is a powerful coping skill or behavior because it results in immediate reduction or prevention of the aversive fear reaction. Avoidance also helps to make us unaware of the intensity of our fear reactions. Most people know they have certain fear reactions, but they do not understand the relationship between their fears, what triggers them, their thoughts, and their avoidance behaviors. Let's start to change that!

WHAT'S THE DIFFERENCE BETWEEN A FEAR AND A PHOBIA?

Who is a "worry wart," and who is truly phobic? When does a fear become a phobia? How can you tell the difference? *Natural* fears are those that most people share, such as fear of angry animals, dangerous snakes, or sudden loud noises. For most people, coming into contact with these triggers arouse fear reactions.

Fear

Fear is a natural reaction that most people in the same situation share, such as a feeling of sudden apprehension about being out on an exposed balcony. However, for the individual who retreats hastily and dizzily on hands and knees, the balcony situation is a phobia, and eventually that

3

person may completely avoid going to places that have high, exposed balconies.

There are many "prepared" fears, that is, reactions that humans *naturally* resort to with fear because these reactions have helped humanity survive. The most common prepared fears are of being stared at (eyes), heights (edges), small animals, snakes, angry people, closed places (trapped), blood and injury, and death. Fears vary in intensity and, under the right conditions, can lead to the development of a phobia. A great proportion of phobias actually develop out of these natural fear reactions.

Phobia

A *phobia* is an uncommon fear in which the reaction is out of proportion to the danger of the situation or the ongoing events. Others cannot reason away the person's fear of the given situation. Avoidance and escape are the first and most common modes of "coping" with these intense reactions. Unfortunately, these coping mechanisms often make the situation worse.

Phobias, fears, and other anxiety disorders are the most prevalent mental health disturbances in modern society. A large percentage of all adults have experienced at least one specific phobia at some time in their lives. Estimates are that from 5 to 11 percent of adults have fears that can be considered phobias. Of individuals who have specific phobias (fears of one thing), only about 6 percent seek treatment. Of agoraphobics (those who fear going out, particularly alone), fewer than 20 percent seek mental health treatment. Phobias are debilitating for many people. We hope this book will help direct some who do not seek treatment to embark on the self-help program and also to understand how professional assistance may help them.

What Are Some Types of Anxiety Disorders and Phobias?

Phobias are categorized by the American Psychiatric Association as anxiety disorders. There are three widely identified groups of phobias:

- specific phobias (formerly referred to as single or simple phobias)
- social phobias
- agoraphobia (with and without panic attacks)

Other types of anxiety disorders (which you will learn about in this book) include:

- generalized anxiety disorder (GAD)
- panic disorder (with or without agoraphobia)
- obsessive–compulsive disorder (OCD)
- posttraumatic stress disorder (PTSD)

What Are Some Specific Phobias?

The characteristic feature of a specific phobia is a persistent, uncommon fear of and compelling desire to avoid one specific object or situation. The category of specific phobias contains an endless list of fears—almost any object or situation can be phobic for a given individual—but a majority of phobias are related to the "prepared" fears discussed earlier.

If you have a specific phobia, you may experience physiological symptoms that are typical of many anxiety disorders, and these are important to identify. However, because a single fear is so specific, you may be able to avoid contact with the phobic object or situation, especially when the likelihood of confrontation with the feared object or situation, such as snakes, is low. On the other hand, individuals who fear common situations, such as elevators or heights, may not be able to avoid these stimuli so easily.

Specific phobias that many people experience include certain modes of transportation, such as automobiles, and such activities as driving across bridges, flying in an airplane, public speaking, and being atop heights. Other common phobic objects or situations include harmless animals such as dogs and cats, thunderstorms, darkness, or enclosed places.

Blood and injury phobias are special types of specific phobias. Interestingly, unlike other single phobias, which cause increased pulse and other physiological signs of arousal, blood and injury phobias usually produce a sudden lowering of pulse and blood pressure that can bring on fainting spells. Because of this unique "vasal-vagal" reaction, we have to approach these phobias in a different manner.

What About Social Phobias and Social Anxieties?

Do you experience undue anxiety in social situations such as parties, during interviews, at restaurants, or when making complaints or interacting with the opposite sex? You may fear situations in which you believe you are being observed and evaluated by others, such as while speaking in public, writing checks, using public restrooms, or eating. Of course, many people experience some degree of discomfort in these situations; however, when an individual begins to feel extremely anxious, becomes self-conscious, and avoids or escapes these situations they become clinically identified as phobias.

Social phobia may be associated with fears of negative criticism, humiliation, or embarrassment, such as making a fool of oneself, sweating, fainting, blushing, calling attention to oneself, or being rejected. Individuals who have these phobias usually avoid the specific situations they fear. Some individuals will participate in their feared activity only when they cannot be seen, for example, swimming in the dark. Often, social phobias are also accompanied by high levels of generalized anxiety.

The triggers in social phobias are usually the presence of others and self-consciousness. Images of embarrassment and humiliation are often present, and sometimes fears of not being able to "perform" correctly or adequately occur.

What Happens with Agoraphobia?

Agoraphobia may be the most serious of the phobias because it can be the most debilitating. Agoraphobics are afraid to leave a "safe place" such as home or a safe person such as a spouse or a close relative. Such separations cause intense anxiety and sometimes panic attacks. A small percentage of agoraphobics become housebound for periods of time. This disorder obviously interferes with working outside the home and with social interactions, travel, and normal activities and enjoyments.

Agoraphobics show a wide range of avoidance behaviors, including fear of entering public places, being in open spaces, traveling, and riding on public transportation; places where they may feel trapped and not able to return to their safe place at will. Agoraphobics often experience physiological symptoms, such as palpitations, lightness in the head, weakness, chest pain, and difficulty in breathing. Agoraphobics express fears of losing control, going insane, embarrassing themselves and others, fainting, and dying. Agoraphobia often begins with panic attacks, but these soon diminish in frequency; the *fear* of having a panic attack, however, persists, and body sensations are often triggers for intense anxiety and avoidance.

Panic, Panic Attacks, and Panic Disorder

A panic attack is not like the ordinary anxiety and nervousness that most people feel before a job interview or giving a speech. Panic and panic attacks are characterized by one or more of many discomforts, including an abrupt surge of terror and a feeling of impending doom that quickly peaks. Other symptoms of a panic attack can include rubbery legs, light headedness, dizziness, difficulty breathing, palpitating and "racing" heart, and choking and tingling or numb sensations. Panic may be brought about by particular stimuli or sometimes even by thinking about it. It may also appear to occur unpredictably and spontaneously without any cues, but often cues are thoughts, memories, or unnoticed body sensations. People who have experienced one panic attack usually fear that another one will occur.

A person can have panic attacks without having agoraphobia. Agoraphobia seems to be a special condition associated with panic attacks and is significantly more common in women.

Other Anxiety Disorders

Now here's an overview of other types of anxiety disorders that you will see in this book:

- generalized anxiety disorder (GAD)
- obsessive–compulsive disorder (OCD)
- Posttraumatic stress disorder (PTSD)

GENERALIZED ANXIETY DISORDER (GAD)

The National Institute of Mental Health defines generalized anxiety disorder (GAD) as always anticipating disaster; often worrying excessively about health, money, family, or work; and a more-or-less chronic state of anticipating dread or anxiety. Worry is the most common component. The worrier may experience physical symptoms, such as trembling, muscle tension, and nausea. Worry seems to be chronic and there is evidence that GAD begins in early life and more or less occurs through the life span of development.

Many individuals with GAD startle more easily than other people. They tend to feel tired, have trouble concentrating, and sometimes experience depression. They tend to catastrophize, which means anticipating that the worst scenarios will occur. The effects of GAD usually don't interfere with one's home, work, or social life. Unlike people who have phobias, people with GAD usually don't avoid certain situations because of their disorder. However, in severe cases, GAD can become very debilitating and make it difficult to carry out even the most ordinary of daily activities without the constant distraction of intrusive anxiety.

OBSESSIVE-COMPULSIVE DISORDER (OCD)

Most descriptions of OCD include some phobias, and many phobias include some obsessive-compulsive characteristics. Rituals performed to try to reduce anxiety about dreaded consequences are called compulsions. Sufferers of OCD experience no pleasure in carrying out the rituals they are drawn to, only temporary relief from the discomfort caused by the obsession. They are usually aware that the obsession is irrational, but its occurrence establishes a state where terminating or ignoring it is difficult (because it is overvalued).

Some people are obsessed with dirt or germs and wash their hands repeatedly. Some check things over and over again. Some touch things or count things. Many people can identify with having some of the symptoms of OCD, such as checking several times that they have turned off the coffeepot before leaving the house in the morning; others may check their pockets to be sure the car keys are there. However, OCD is diagnosed only when these activities consume a lot of time, are very distressing, and interfere in a major way with daily life.

About 1 in 50 people are afflicted with OCD. Adults with this condition recognize that what they are doing is senseless, but they feel they cannot control their obsessions and compulsions. Some people, particularly children who have OCD, may not recognize that their behavior is out of the ordinary.

You may remember that in the 1997 movie *As Good As It Gets* Jack Nicholson portrays a man who suffers from and later successfully faces and overcomes some of his obsessions and compulsions. He uses a new bar of soap each time he washes his hands. He must also eat at the same table in the same restaurant and be served by the same waitress, and he brings his own wrapped, plastic tableware. He avoids stepping on lines in the sidewalk. Although these behaviors provide comic relief in movies, OCD sufferers are at the mercy of their obsessions and find these distressing and tiring.

POSTTRAUMATIC STRESS DISORDER (PTSD)

Ordinary events can serve as reminders of a trauma or an incident that occurred and may trigger flashbacks or intrusive images. PTSD can occur in people who have been raped, witnessed a crime, survived a school shooting, been in a car accident, or fought on a battlefield. People who have PTSD have recurrent frightening thoughts and memories of their ordeal and may feel emotionally numb and vulnerable, especially with people they were once close to. PTSD was once referred to as shell shock or battle fatigue; it was thought to happen only to war veterans. Now it is known that PTSD can result from any number of traumatic occurrences. Trauma itself has immediate and long-range effects in people, but PTSD is a reaction that often shows up years later and carries with it numbing sensations, loss of stimulus discrimination, and impulse and anxiety problems.

Some people who have PTSD repeatedly relive the trauma in the form of nightmares and disturbing recollections during the day. They may also experience sleep problems and depression or may be easily startled. They may feel irritable and more aggressive than before. Seeing things that remind them of the incident may be distressing and may lead them to avoid certain places or situations that bring back those memories. Symptoms vary and, as mentioned, often begin much after the traumatic event. Diagnosis is difficult and requires a review of the person's life history as well as symptom patterns.

There is also a condition called Partial PTSD that consists of more limited symptoms of less severity. This will not be covered in this book. It is difficult to treat PTSD with self-help; professional help is recommended.

BEFORE YOU GO ON . . . SOME INTERESTING HISTORICAL FACTS ABOUT PHOBIAS

The term *phobia* derives from the Greek word *phobos,* which means fear, panic, terror, and flight. The word *phobos* comes from the name of the ancient Greek deity Phobos, who provoked fear and panic in enemies. The word *panic* is derived from the name for the god, known as Pan, whom the Greeks worshiped as their god of flocks, herds, pastures, and fields. The Greek word for "all" is also *pan.* People were dependent on Pan to make the flocks fertile; Pan himself was a lustful creature and known for an ability to reproduce. Pan's shape was that of a goat, which could traverse fields and dart through herds of cattle. Pan loved to scare people: he would dart out of the woods and frighten passersby, often in dark forests at night. The fright he created was known as panic.

Hippocrates (460 B.C.–377 B.C.) may have been one of the first who described phobias when he wrote about an individual who feared heights and precipices. If you have acrophobia (fear of heights), you may identify with this individual: "He would not go near a precipice, or over a bridge or beside even the shallowest ditch, and yet he could walk in the ditch itself."

William Shakespeare (1564–1616), in *The Merchant of Venice,* wrote of cat phobia, which is still a common phobia: "Some that are mad if they behold a cat."

In 1798, Benjamin Rush, American physician and author, published an article in which he gave his definition of phobia: ". . . a fear of an imaginary evil, or an undue fear of a real one." He then listed 18 species of fear named according to the object of excessive fear or aversion, such as dirt or rats.

FURTHER DEVELOPMENTS IN UNDERSTANDING PHOBIAS

In 1895, Henry Maudsley (1771–1831), British psychiatrist and author, included all phobias under the heading of *melancholia* and advised against the trend of giving a special name to each variety of phobic situation because many phobias often were noticed together or successively in the same individual. Researchers and therapists today recognize that one individual may have one or more phobias.

Sigmund Freud's writing and theorizing at the end of the 19th century further contributed to the stimulation of interest in the causes and treatment of anxieties and phobias. In 1895, Freud wrote *Obsessions and Phobias: Their Physical Mechanism and Their Aetiology.* In this paper, he distinguished the two by suggesting that with phobias the emotional state is always one of morbid anxiety, while in the obsessions other emotional states such as doubt or anger may occur.

Freud emphasized that the origin of phobias was anxiety that came from symbols of unconscious fantasies and conflicts. The anxiety was a "signal" that these unconscious energies might break through into consciousness. The symbolism always concerned an unacceptable aggressive or sexual impulse. Freud suggested that phobia relates to objects that have unconscious symbolic meanings and represent regressions to earlier infantile fears, usually centered around Oedipal conflicts. To him, the object always symbolized some sexual anxiety, and every phobia, therefore, included some element of sexual energy. This idea of an individual underlying cause in each phobia promoted the use of labels and the old view that each phobia had unique early causes.

MANY VIEWPOINTS ON UNDERSTANDING ANXIETY DISORDERS AND PHOBIAS

Developments in the latter half of the 20th century led to increased knowledge about anxiety and phobic disorders and new directions for treating them. Most therapeutic settings now focus on helping people cope with their individual phobic reactions. Also, phobias are seen as a large class of similar reactions learned by the same set of principles. In many settings, therapists use an integrated perspective. That means that no one viewpoint explains all the phenomena that various individuals experience. Although some psychiatrists suggest that phobias are maintained by unconscious conflicts remaining unconscious, other psychotherapists focus on the avoided behavior and thoughts of the individual, such as catastrophic misinterpretation of danger. These "behavioral" or "cognitive behavioral" approaches have proven to be the most effective for treating phobias and anxiety. We will concentrate on the principles of behavioral psychology to help you or your loved ones understand and cope with symptoms.

Some suggest that phobias are derived from conditioned experiences and that the phobic object may once have been part of a *traumatic* situation. On this basis, any object has an equal potential to become a phobic stimulus through association with traumatic conditions. Others say that certain phobic responses may be learned through imitating the reactions of others, or *vicarious learning*. Still another theory is that phobic reactions are learned by the positive consequences that follow (for example, soothing attention from a parent of a school-phobic child). This type of learning is called *operant conditioning*. Generally all three viewpoints affect the development of anxiety reactions.

We are just now beginning to understand the physiological mechanisms associated with anxieties, and this understanding has helped improve behavioral treatment. Furthermore, our biochemical and biological understanding have also improved and have led to improved medications that offer short-term relief from the effects of anxiety reactions.

EVOLUTION OF TREATMENTS

Psychoanalysis was used for many years as a treatment for anxiety disorders. However, in many cases, understanding the source of the anxiety did not make the anxieties and unwanted behaviors go away, so the effectiveness of psychoanalysis was questioned. Then, in the late 1950s and early 1960s, behavior therapy developed. Behavioral therapists believe that a phobia is a learned response and therefore can be unlearned. Behavioral therapists use techniques that involve gradually exposing the individual to whatever is feared. Exposure may take place in real life or in the person's imagination. For example, a person with a fear of heights may imagine himself over time higher and higher on a hill without anxiety; gradualness of exposure is an important factor.

Early behavior researchers speculated that effective results could follow from looking at an individual's symptoms, working with them, and systematically desensitizing them by gradual exposure. These methods proved to be much more highly effective than psychoanalytic or "talking" therapies. Thus, through a wide variety of behavior therapy techniques, thousands of individuals have learned that they do not have to be a victim of anxieties and phobias.

PHYSICAL EXAMINATIONS AND PHARMACOLOGY

In addition to behavior therapy, current treatment may include periodic examinations of cardiovascular, pulmonary, endocrine, or neurological functions, as well as pharmacological aspects. Also, the development of relatively safe, appropriate drugs in adjunct to working with therapists or with self-help has enabled many to overcome phobias, anxieties, panic disorders, and obsessive–compulsive behaviors. Drugs are most helpful as aids to support the person in working on functioning while anxiety situations are dealt with. Drugs have short-term benefits that over the long term become problems in and of themselves.

GETTING HELP FOR ANXIETY DISORDERS

In addition to self-help, such as following some of the suggestions in this book, if you or someone you know has serious symptoms of anxiety disorders, the best place to start may be your family physician. Your physician can help you determine whether your symptoms are due to some medical condition, an anxiety disorder, or both. Often, the next step may be a referral to a mental health professional. Those who can help include psychiatrists, psychologists, and social workers. Look for a professional who has specialized training in behavioral therapy or cognitive-behavioral therapy and who is open to the use of medications, should they be needed. It is also important that he or she have training and experience in treating anxiety disorders. You are free to ask them these questions.

If you embark on a therapy program, be sure to find a health care professional with whom you feel comfortable. You will work as a team to develop a plan to treat your anxiety disorder that may involve a variety of therapies.

New treatments for anxieties are being sought. The National Institute of Mental Health, for example, supports a sizable and multifaceted research program on the causes, diagnosis, treatment and prevention of anxiety disorders. This is part of an effort to overcome major mental disorders.

Now Take Three Steps: Move Forward in Your Life

In the next chapter, you'll learn about the Three-Step Process for beginning to face your fears. Face your fears and learn to control them. You'll take these steps one at a time. You may want to refer to the chapter several times as you continue to read the next chapters, which give more details about social phobias, specific phobias, panic attacks and agoraphobia, obsessive-compulsive disorder, posttraumatic stress disorder, depression, reducing fear of flying and sexual fears, and improving your self-esteem and feelings of well-being.

CHAPTER 2

TAKE THREE STEPS
TOWARD ANXIETY RELIEF

In this chapter, you'll read about getting started with the process of facing your fears and how you can make the most of the Three-Step Process.

This chapter is a roadmap of what the book is all about. Just as you follow a roadmap to get to another state, there are directions and guideposts to tell how far you are from various goals you set for yourself. You can go at any speed, can slow down, can even back off, stop, and pick up again. Sometimes you may be sidetracked, but your own guideposts will boost you back on track. You may even find other routes to take as you begin to understand your own personal fears.

The steps are described in ways that support your individualized *process of change* rather than the fear itself. For example, if you have a phobia, there are times when you suffer, and your *resistance* to facing the problem and your apprehension about dealing with your fear creates further suffering. Be aware that your resistance and apprehension about the fear are really separate from the problem itself. This is important to realize because the *fear problem* is much easier to diminish and change, whereas *resistance* and apprehension are deep attitudes that often stem from fears about our own abilities and efficacy in making changes in our lives. Resistance, unchecked and unchallenged, will keep us down, childlike, and doubtful about ourselves. Despair is the feeling associated with resistance. Hope and faith come from making the effort and being open to suggestions and ways to facilitate change. If you are ready to deal with your own resistance, this three-step plan can help you.

THE THREE-STEP PROCESS AND HOW IT
CAN WORK FOR YOU

Step 1: *Identify your fears through a process of self-diagnosis.*
Step 2: *Pinpoint what triggers your fears.*
Step 3: *Develop an individualized "exposure" program to help you face your fears.*

Step 1: Identify Your Fears Through a Process of Self-Diagnosis

Anxiety is always triggered by a stimulus. The process of self-diagnosis is to learn to identify stimuli that trigger anxiety. In general there are three sources of stimuli: *ideas-thoughts, body sensations,* and *perceptions* of the outside world (things we see, feel, smell, taste, or hear).

What makes you feel anxious? What do you fear and avoid? Specific things? Many things? Certain types of things or situations? To help you in your self-diagnosis process, a *Fear Self-Evaluation* that identifies common fear areas follows. There are no norms on this scale, but you can use it to measure progress in overcoming your anxiety and phobic concerns.

If you have a total score of 24 or better, chances are that you may have an active anxiety problem. Read on.

After you have identified your fears, the following chapters will help you identify and give a name to your disorder, such as generalized anxiety disorder, specific phobia, social phobia, agoraphobia, panic disorder, and so on.

Meanwhile, while you are taking the step to identify your fears, you can consider them on several levels: thoughts, perceptions, and body sensations.

Thoughts: Often, in situations where we don't understand our fear reactions, a thought (even subconscious) is producing the reaction. For example, many people become fearful when they encounter a sudden traffic jam. They feel "trapped." But what are they thinking? "Something horrible will happen to me and no one will respond." "I will never get out of here." "I'm going to have a heart attack and die." "People will see how fearful I am and laugh at me." *Overgeneralization* ("I always have bad luck") and *catastrophic thinking* (the what if?) are the major thought forms that cause anxiety and helplessness. What thoughts do you have that cause you to feel anxious? Write them down.

Perceptions: This involves sensing something that you associate with a fearful experience from the past. For example, many fearful flyers become apprehensive just driving to the airport (even if they are not traveling themselves) because the trip is associated with having flown (fearfully). Likewise, a smell, (e.g., medical odors), the look of a person (e.g., angry or disdainful people), hearing noises (e.g., while home alone), and other stimuli, can—if they have a history of association with fear—trigger anxiety. Perceptions as triggers are often subtle and require pausing as soon as apprehension starts to identify what was perceived or thought of that triggered the anxiety.

Body sensations: Body sensations are common anxiety triggers—particularly for the panic prone person whose body seems to react (panic) out of the blue. Body sensations are memories, stored in the body, of experiences we have had or of experiences we dread may happen. Body sensa-

---

FEAR SELF-EVALUATION

Here's how it works: Choose a number from 0 to 10 to show how much you avoid each of the situations listed because of fear or other unpleasant feelings.

0–1 = Would not avoid it, slight reaction

2–3 = Slightly want to avoid it, noticeable but not scary reactions

4–5 = Want to avoid it, discomfort, but could stay if required

6–7 = Definitely want to avoid it, marked discomfort, affects performance

8–10 = Always avoid it, panicky and unable to concentrate or perform

Write the number in the box opposite each situation.

1. Traveling alone (bus, train, car, or airplane)   _____

2. Being alone   _____

3. Going into situations where there are crowds of people   _____

4. Getting into situations where you feel trapped (left turn lanes, mid-aisle, center seats)   _____

5. Large open spaces   _____

6. Injections, seeing blood or injuries   _____

7. Hospitals, medical or dental procedures   _____

8. Small animals, insects   _____

9. Angry people, loud noises   _____

10. Closed spaces   _____

11. Eating or drinking with other people   _____

12. Being watched or stared at   _____

13. Talking to people in authority   _____

14. Being criticized, rejected   _____

15. Speaking or acting to an audience   _____

16. Other situations*   _____

Grand Total: _____

*Describe the main phobia you want to work on (for example, taking elevators; fluttering birds) and so on, and rank it.

---

tions will not harm you: they are the language of the body and they can tell us if arousal is occurring. Then begins the hunt for thoughts or perceptions that may trigger arousal. Or it may be that we are in a setting that itself causes arousal naturally, such as crowds, loud places, confusion, stimulants (e.g., caffeine or sugar, etc.) and *feelings*. Yes, feelings can produce body sensations—particularly if we are fearful or reluctant to show or to have feelings at all.

So get to know your body sensations. Put your attention on them in a positive way, and see if you can be aware of body arousal *as soon as it begins.* Make notes.

As you identify your fears, assess how serious your reactions are to your feared object or situation. You can use the following *Ten Point Fear Scale* for self-assessment. Knowing the intensity of your reactions to your fear at the outset of the process can serve as a guidepost for your progress. As you begin to improve, you can look back at the Ten-Point Scale again and see how you are moving from a possible 10 (panic attack and want to run) down to a 0 (feeling calm).

TEN-POINT FEAR SCALE

As you begin, think about which feelings apply to you. Try for achieving a feeling of relative comfort as your long-range goal with the Three-Step Process. Remember that everything under a 4 is tolerable and manageable, so let's set this as the place to work and not get so far into a situation that it triggers more than a 4.

(Possible reactions you may experience)

10	Panic: want to run, escape, desperate
9	Intense agitation, ready to bolt, shaky, heart pounding
8	Hyperventilation, numb, tingly, shaky (pulled inside)
7	Difficulty breathing, wanting to run; self is separating from the situation, barely tolerable
6	Dizziness, feeling separate, stomach pains, hyperventilation noticeable
5	Shakiness, worry about reaction, breathing more difficult, heart races
4	Perspiration, anxiety apparent but tolerable
3	Warmth starts to develop, tension, increased heart rate, more noticeable sensations
2	Increased hearbeat; some tension but does not preoccupy
1	Slight apprehensiveness, uneasy but no noticeable symptoms
0	Feeling of calm

Step 2: Pinpoint What Triggers Your Fears

Stimulation always has a trigger. Anxiety has a history. Consider your past history. What have your experiences been? Can you think of any ways in which you might have learned to become afraid and even filled with panic at certain situations? Where did reactions first occur? Do they occur over and over again in the same setting? Different settings?

Perceptions (External Triggers).   External triggers include natural-ly occurring fear areas such as heights, small animals, blood and injury, and angry people. Smells and kinesthetic reactions can also serve as trig-gers. Do you have an exaggerated fear reaction to these triggers that most people face at times? Remember that in Chapter 1 you learned that pho-bias are fears that are out of proportion to the real dangers of the situa-tion and that they are not shared by those around you. Often, just bring-ing a perception into your awareness will elicit some apprehension or slight anxiety. This is often a sure sign that the trigger is perceptual or external. Common external triggers are situations in which we project a catastrophic outcome in which injury or death could occur. Small animals that could bite, bees that could sting, planes that could fall out of the sky, etc. In other words our imagination is quite active.

What are the common factors present during your panic attacks or fear responses? For example, do they involve people? Do you fear being criticized or humiliated? You may have one or more social phobias or social anxiety disorders, as you'll read about in Chapter 4.

Is feeling trapped a common factor? For example, do you feel trapped while driving and trying to make a left turn when there is little seeming-ly safe opportunity to do so? Is it difficult to sit in the center seat at a restaurant, theater, or church?

Body Sensations (Internal Triggers).   Internal triggers include body sensations that become exaggerated and interpreted to mean that some-thing is going wrong with you. For example, a panic attack that "comes out of the blue" often begins with bodily sensations that are interpreted as dangerous. This escalates into fear. For example, if dizziness and heart palpitations come on, one may interpret these sensations as the beginning of a heart attack. But the sensation itself is not dangerous: the *interpreta-tion* or catastrophic, exaggerated thoughts are what lead to intense reac-tions. After all, wouldn't anyone be afraid if he or she thought that he or she was having a heart attack? On the other hand, if you knew your heartbeat was up and there was tension and a little light-headedness because you were rushing to get to the concert on time, you probably would not become fearful. Perhaps, you are becoming excited—it's your turn to bowl—and some of these body sensations represent excitement.

A fear of dying is often the basis for catastrophic thinking. Coming to terms with this eventual experience is important as well as coming to terms with the reality of being alone but having support.

Step 3: Develop an Individualized "Exposure" Program to Help You Face Your Fears

The key to following this plan successfully focuses on systematic exposure to the fear situations and/or triggers in a safe and non-fear-producing manner.

Start by imagining what your life would be like if you didn't have these problems. For example, you may give excuses for not being successful in business, but your real problem is a fear of elevators and, hence, an avoidance of taking a job in a high-rise building in a large city.

The first step in self-help exposure therapy is your imagination. If you weren't phobic about elevators, where would you like to be? Working in New York City? Working in another job in your own city?

> Ralph, a 29-year-old college graduate, feared riding in elevators and took a job with an insurance agency in his small midwestern town doing routine clerical and computer work in a ground-floor real estate office. He felt safe there. His was one of the few agencies with a ground-floor office. He often heard about job opportunities elsewhere but rejected even going to an interview because he feared taking an elevator. He identified his specific phobia and knew what set it off: even the thought of riding in an elevator.

Ralph decided to take charge of his feared situation, face it, and begin to make changes in his life. He planned his own exposure program. He went to a six-story building in town with his wife; she was very understanding of his problem and made him feel safe. They began by going to the building and watching people get on and off the elevator. He would imagine himself getting on and going to another floor to work. He would talk with his wife about how he felt while watching the people come and go. At first, just watching them made him feel arousal (4 or 5). However, after he learned about relaxation techniques, how to apply them, and how to breathe in fearful situations, he reduced his feelings to only apprehensiveness (on the Ten-Point Fear Scale). He could bring the arousal below a 3 and was now ready to approach closer to the feared stimulus.

When he felt more comfortable just watching other people come and go, he and his wife went to the building on Saturdays when the elevator wasn't crowded. He stepped inside it. Again, he felt his old feelings of increased heartbeat and shakiness come over him. They stepped out of the elevator, he practiced some easy deep breathing exercises, and they would reenter it. Finally he was able to push the button for the second floor. They rode up and got off. He repeated this exercise a few times. Occasionally, his arousal would jump up but would quickly subside. Pulling back also helped reduce his anxiety. Once down below 4, he would start to approach the situation again. His anxiety level was significantly less than it had been before he started practicing. One or more times he said, "I just can't do this," and backed out of the elevator. Another day he tried again and was able to progress. Floor by floor, he practiced going up to the sixth. The fact that other people weren't around on Saturdays helped him to feel in control. He could exit at any floor he wished to if his anxiety level mounted as the elevator ascended. The hardest part was waiting for the door to open. Counting helped because he knew from study that the door took about a count of four to six before opening, so he would count to 10 in order to give himself a few seconds before exiting.

The outcome of Ralph's life changes? After a few months of practice with this specific elevator, he and his wife would go to other buildings at even crowded times and ride the elevators. All along, Ralph was evaluating his reactions. Even in a crowd, when he couldn't push the button himself, he only experienced mild apprehensiveness. That was comfortable for him. Next, he graduated to riding alone (at first with his wife in the lobby and then gradually having her outside and then at home and, finally, riding when she was not available). Wow! His feelings about himself improved, and though there were "setbacks," he just went back to that point in practicing and went forward again until those ups and downs diminished.

He decided to take a major step. He answered several ads for jobs and was hired for a job he now loves in a 12-story building. He feels in control of his life and has improved his self-esteem. You can do that, too.

YOU CAN SUCCEED WITH THIS PLAN

Throughout the book, you'll be encouraged to plan your own goals according to the three steps, to follow the method, and not to leave steps out. As you take action to protect yourself from vulnerability, you'll probably see your self-confidence build as you see your fears and your reactions to them diminish.

Maybe you have kept your fears to yourself. Perhaps that's your secret: no one else knows about them. This book will help you realize that you can draw support from others, just as Ralph did from his wife. Sometimes one needs help from others with exposure.

As you start the plan, identify your fears and what triggers them, and plan your gradual exposure to your feared situation, realize that anxiety is a state of mind that affects everything you do. In an anxiety state, you can't think as rationally as you'd like. Being anxious is a difficult state because your normal senses don't feel right. As you are going through self-assessment and beginning to set goals and make explicit plans for exposure, write them down. That way you can review and revise them during moments when you are feeling like yourself. Take your written plan with you when you practice. It will help guide your exposure work. Do your notes to yourself look rational? Are your goals realistic? Make both short term (baby step) goals and longer term (life changes) as you practice.

UNDERSTANDING BEHAVIOR MODIFICATION (BEHAVIOR THERAPY)

Behavior therapy focuses on behaviors and responses rather than on "underlying causes." Instead of trying to alter the "personality" by probing into "unconscious" reasons that may motivate a person's behavior, behavior therapy focuses directly on the problematic behavior. After all, this is the problem. It is often used in conjunction with talking, understanding, and medication.

Therapists believe that behaviors are not inherited but are learned in response to the environment. Of course, our physiology and disposition affect our learning, but the specifics are shaped by our experiences. Behavior therapy can help you learn to relax and modulate feelings and undesirable behaviors such as avoidance and physiological reactions.

The goal of behavior modification is to help you develop self-control of behavior, affect and cognition, and to develop an increased number of rewarding and adaptive behaviors. You can define your own goals, perhaps in conjunction with a family member or friend. Feel encouraged to make choices about how and when to learn new behaviors. You may want to set your goals based on your own assessment of behaviors, such as frequency or intensity (for example, of ritualistic hand washing), and physiological responses (such as dizziness).

EXPOSURE THERAPY

Exposure therapy is also known as desensitization. Exposure therapy can help you reshape your responses to anxiety-producing situations. There are several forms of exposure therapy, including gradual exposure (such as Ralph's experience in the elevator), exposure at full intensity (or flooding and implosive therapy), and exposure with modification of thought processes (contextual therapy). As you saw in Ralph's case, gradual exposure to the anxiety producing situation at first and then some cognitive work or desensitization helped his progress. Note that relaxation is usually combined with exposure work.

MORE ABOUT SYSTEMATIC DESENSITIZATION

In 1958, Joseph Wolpe (1915–97), a U.S. psychiatrist born in South Africa, with a background in learning theory, began to treat adults with a variety of anxiety concerns, including phobic anxiety, reactive depression, and obsessive-compulsive disorder with a process he called systematic desensitization.

In this process, the individual is trained to achieve deep muscle relaxation. Then, while relaxed, imagine increasing degrees of anxiety-producing stimuli, and then eventually face these stimuli in vivo (in real life) until the maximum stimulus no longer causes great anxiety. Thus, an individual who fears sexual intercourse might place coitus at the top of the list of anxiety-producing stimuli; thinking about sitting with a date in a bar might rank at the bottom of the list. After going through a series of relaxation training exercises, one is asked to imagine, with as much detail as possible, the least anxiety-producing item from the list. While relaxing and imagining the situation, one tries to weaken the association between it and his or her anxieties. After becoming comfortable with imagining the least-threatening situation, one gradually moves up the fear hierarchy of anxiety-producing situations, progressing to the next item only after desensitization to the current item. Fear hierarchies typically contain 12 to 15 items graded on intensity of reactions.

HOW DOES FLOODING WORK?

Like desensitization, the technique known as flooding involves the individual imagining or experiencing stress-producing situations in real life at full intensity. This is a technique best used with the help of a therapist. The person is exposed directly to a maximum level of stress-producing stimulus *without* a graduated approach. The therapist, rather than the patient, controls when and which stressful scenarios are to be imagined. The therapist describes vivid scenes in an effort to make them as disturbing as possible to the patient, with no instructions for the patient to relax. Such prolonged and repeated exposure to feared situations helps eliminate the individual's anxiety-laden response and replace it with another that is more acceptable.

We don't recommend this for you because it has to be done with an experienced therapist guiding the procedure. It is too difficult and scary to do alone or even with a supportive other, and, if not used properly, it can sensitize or strengthen your fear reactions.

HOW DOES MODELING AND
COVERT MODELING WORK?

Modeling therapy is also known as social learning or observational learning. The anxious individual watches another person, often of the same sex and age, successfully carry out a particular anxiety-producing action, such as speaking in front of a group of people or being introduced to members of the opposite sex. (Ralph watched people coming and going in and out of the elevator.) In some cases, another person "models" the action. The improvement occurs when the person experiences vicarious extinction of his or her previously anxiety-filled and symptom producing responses. This occurs through observing a relaxed state or a reduction in anxiety for the model.

This model-mediated desensitization is very helpful in your own work in that you can observe others more relaxed or even desensitizing themselves in situations that bother you. This process is called *vicarious extinction.*

BREATHING

The primary role of breathing is to supply the body with oxygen, and to exhaust carbon dioxide. But breathing plays an important role in the management of anxieties. With increased awareness of how you breathe and the incorporation of certain controlled breathing techniques into relaxation practice, you can quiet thoughts, calm emotions, deepen relaxation, and control blood pressure as well as other physical functions.

The major functions of breathing are respiration and ventilation. Breathing *in* puts oxygen into body cells, and breathing *out* removes the excess carbon dioxide. But in breathing out we also build carbon dioxide in the blood, and this shift helps our body relax. Poor breathing habits diminish the flow of these gases to and from the body, making it harder to cope with anxiety-filled situations. Anxious people tend to have an imbalance of oxygen relative to carbon dioxide. Breathing properly helps restore a balance and thus reduce anxiety and increase alertness. The key to proper breathing is simply to take a long, full "out" breath.

Most people breathe in one of two patterns. One is chest or thoracic breathing; the other is abdominal or diaphragmatic breathing. Chest breathing can become restricted by tension associated with anxiety or other emotional distress. Chest breathing is usually shallow and often rapid and irregular. When air is inhaled, the chest expands and the shoulders rise to take in air. Anxious people may experience breath holding, hyperventilation or constricted out-breathing, shortness of breath, or fear of passing out. Shallow breathing does not allow sufficient buildup of carbon dioxide in the blood. *Proper breathing therefore involves long, slow out-breaths* in order to build carbon dioxide in the blood.

Breathing patterns change during different psychological states. For example, when one is calm and relaxed, breathing probably usually becomes slower, deeper, and more rhythmic. When one feels anxious, breathing is shallow and less regular and there is less outbreath volume. When one is frightened, one may even hold one's breath, not allowing for much out-breath. This is called hyperventilation. Hyperventilation doesn't necessarily produce symptoms unless it is intense and chronic (as it is usually in anxiety states). Breathing can be consciously controlled by changing one's patterns of breathing and can thus influence the body toward relaxation while interrupting the feelings of physiological arousal, such as dizziness and rapid heartbeat.

Many people who feel anxious also have breathing-related complaints. Some can't seem to catch their breath or get enough air. Others may frequently sigh or swallow. Some breathe too deeply but do not exhaust adequately. Symptoms associated with hyperventilation resemble those of panic disorder, and—vice versa—panic attacks normally involve hyperventilation. One researcher, for example, took panic sufferers and just taught them proper diaphragmatic breathing. People practiced several times a day and also used it to reduce low levels of anxiety (4 and less). After one year, none of the subjects had experienced another panic attack!

Some symptoms reported by anxiety sufferers are similar to symptoms of hyperventilation. These symptoms include dyspnea (inability to catch one's breath, choking sensation, feeling of suffocation, frequent sighing, chest heaving, lump in throat), tension, muscle ache, irritability, low frustration tolerance, anxiety, fatigue, tingling and numbness, insomnia, heart palpitations, depression, restlessness, dizzy spells, trembling, coldness of the hands and feet, inability to concentrate, and bloating.

BREATHING FOR ANXIETY SYMPTOM REDUCTION

- Lie comfortably on your back on a padded floor or a firm bed, with eyes closed, arms at your sides and not touching your body, palms up, legs straight out and slightly apart, and toes pointed comfortably outward. Use pillows under your knees and under your head to allow those areas to be comfortable.

- Focus attention on your breathing. Breathe through your nose. Place your hand on the area of your abdomen that seems to rise and fall the most as you inhale and exhale.

- Place both of your hands lightly on your abdomen just below your navel and slow your breathing. Become aware of how your abdomen rises with each inhalation and falls with each exhalation. Breathe out through your mouth. Count to four as you breathe in, hold it to a two count, and then exhale to a count of eight. Exhale completely.

- If you have difficulty breathing into your abdomen, press your hand down on your abdomen as you exhale and let your abdomen push your hand back up as you inhale.

- Observe how your chest moves; it should be moving in synchronization with your abdomen.

- This form of diaphragmatic breathing is 4–2–8 breathing. Practice it many times a day.

Deep, diaphragmatic breathing with extended full outbreaths is a cornerstone for many relaxation therapies. Many behavioral therapies incorporate control of breathing as a basis because the cycle of anxiety can be altered with breath control. If you can master these techniques, you may find that as soon as you are aware of an anxiety trigger, you can become aware of your breathing. Try to deepen and slow it down and produce a long, slow exhale. This will help calm you and often cut off the cycle toward greater anxiety. Practicing the methods described in the preceding table on a regular basis will help you develop a more relaxed state and reduce the probability of high anxiety. Breathing practice should be six to seven brief periods (four-five breaths) three to four months before control is achieved.

LEARN TO RELAX!

Relaxation is a feeling of freedom from anxiety and tension. Internal conflicts and disturbing feelings of anxiety are absent. Relaxation also refers to the return of a muscle to its normal state after a period of contraction. Typically, anxiety states (such as generalized panic, agoraphobia, etc.) result from a physiology that is "tuned up" or chronically activated. Relaxation training over months gradually restores the physiology to a more neutral, normal level. In this relaxed state, panic and intense anxiety is less likely to occur, and it is much easier to accomplish desensitization.

Relaxation techniques are methods to release muscular tension consciously and achieve a sense of mental calm. You have just learned about diaphragmatic breathing. Historically, early relaxation techniques included meditation, tai chi chuan, massage therapy, yoga, music, and aroma therapy. More recent developments include hypnosis and biofeedback.

Relaxation training programs are often used in conjunction with other forms of therapy for many chronic diseases. The mind/body connection between relaxation and ill health has been demonstrated. Some of the physiological changes that occur during relaxation include decreased oxygen consumption, decreased heart and respiratory rates, diminished muscle tension, and a shift toward slower brain wave patterns.

In the 1970s, Herbert Benson, M.D., a cardiologist at Harvard Medical School, studied the relationship between stress and hypertension. In stressful situations, the body undergoes several changes, including rise in blood pressure and pulse and faster breathing. Dr. Benson reasoned that if stress could bring about this reaction, another factor might be able to turn it off. He studied practitioners of transcendental meditation (TM) and found that once in their meditative states, some individuals could willfully reduce their pulse, blood pressure, and breathing rate. Dr. Benson named this the relaxation response. He explained this procedure in his book *The Relaxation Response* (1976).

Relaxation training can be particularly useful if you have "white-coat hypertension," which means that your blood pressure is high only when facing a certain specifically anxiety-producing situations, such as having a medical examination or visiting a dentist. Relaxation training can also help reduce hostility and anger, which in turn affects your body and your physical responses to anxiety, such as gastrointestinal problems and headaches.

In progressive relaxation training, individuals are instructed to move through the muscle groups of the body, making them tense and then completely relaxed. Through repetitions of this procedure, individuals learn how to be in voluntary control of their feelings of tension and relaxation. Some therapists provide individuals with instructional audio tapes that can be listened to for practice; other therapists go through the procedure repeatedly with their clients. Relaxation training can also be self-taught. The most effective relaxation procedures for muscles are called progressive relaxation. Try to find a relaxation tape of progressive relaxation involving tension and release exercises.

Meditation is a form of mental focus and relaxation. The 4-2-8 diaphragmatic breathing you learned about is a form of emotional calming.

OTHER SELF-CARE STEPS

Besides following the Three-Step Process and beginning to take control of your life, there are other ways you can take care of yourself. Here are a few tips:

- Don't be alone with your fears. Tell someone else, such as a spouse or trusted friend. That "support person" may be able to help you with the gradual exposure program you outline for yourself.
- Get enough sleep. Often, too much or too little sleep is a symptom of an anxiety disorder. Determine the routines that allow you to enable your sleep pattern.
- Consider your diet. Try to eat a well-balanced diet with lots of fruits, vegetables, and grains. Try not to skip breakfast.
- Get some exercise regularly, several times a week.

You are fortunate that you picked up this book and have chosen to follow the three steps toward facing your fears. Remember that 85–90 percent of people with anxieties and phobias don't take constructive steps to help themselves. In fact, many take self-destructive routes, such as using drugs or alcohol in an attempt to diminish fears. These routes only lead to ill health. Assess your fears. Know what triggers them. Develop your own plan for self-improvement. What you want is a feeling of well-being—and you can achieve it. Start working on it. You'll feel better. You deserve it.

CHAPTER 3

GENERALIZED
ANXIETY DISORDER (GAD)

Bill M. is 34 years old and constantly looks at his watch both at work and at home. He worries that he will be late for an appointment or late to turn on his favorite TV show. He startles easily when someone walks into his office or near him at home. He worries about being able to pay his bills even though he has incurred a credit card interest charge for late payment only once. He is extremely concerned about his high blood pressure and checks it with a self-monitoring device several times a day. He is irritable, doesn't sleep well, and has frequent headaches. He wrings his hands often. He has been diagnosed as having generalized anxiety disorder.

Generalized anxiety disorder is a condition characterized by excessive anxiety on most days from worry about events and activities. To be diagnosed with GAD, the individual must have had such days for at least six months. The anxiety from worry is accompanied by at least three additional symptoms from a list which includes restlessness, being easily fatigued, difficulty concentrating, muscle tension, and disturbed sleep.

Adults who have GAD often worry about everyday, routine life circumstances such as possible job responsibilities, finances, the health of family members, household chores, car repairs, or being late for appointments. Although individuals who have GAD may not always identify the worries as "excessive," they report subjective distress due to constant worry and have difficulty controlling the worrying or functioning. The intensity, duration, or frequency of the anxiety and worry is far out of proportion to the actual likelihood or impact of the feared event.

Individuals who have GAD may experience cold and clammy hands, dry mouth, sweating, nausea or diarrhea, urinary frequency, trouble swallowing ("lump in the throat"), and an exaggerated startle response. In some cases, depression also occurs. Other conditions that may be associated with stress, such as irritable bowel syndrome and headaches, often accompany GAD.

In this chapter you'll read about some topics that lead to anxiety, including worrying, catastrophizing thoughts, differences between cognitive and somatic anxiety and hyperventilation. You will have an opportunity to rate yourself on a self-report anxiety scale that measures various aspects of the anxiety response.

PEOPLE WHO HAVE GAD ARE USUALLY FREQUENT WORRIERS

Worry is a state of mental uneasiness, distress, or agitation due to concern for a past, impending, or anticipated stressful event, threat, or danger. Some degree of worrying is a common, everyday occurrence for most people. For some people, however, worrying becomes excessive and chronic. Individuals who have GAD and other anxiety disorders tend to worry more and more often than others. For example, people who have agoraphobia may worry that they will experience a panic attack if they go out of their homes, or people who are phobic may worry about what will happen if they encounter the phobic object or situation. GAD sufferers, however, tend to be chronic and often pervasive worriers.

Worrying is a form of negative imagery. The worrier focuses on negative images or worst-case scenarios (catastrophizes). Worrying to excess can be an unhealthy stressor because it causes the body to react: the heart pounds, breathing quickens, and sweating may occur. For some individuals, guided imagery techniques, through which they imagine themselves in a given situation with a positive and pleasant outcome, may be useful. Additionally, relaxation techniques, such as meditation and biofeedback, may be helpful because they help diminish mental activity and focus thought processes. In a relaxed state, individuals can think more constructively and in a more organized manner and worry cannot occur.

SYMPTOMS ASSOCIATED WITH GENERALIZED ANXIETY DISORDER

Motor tension
- Trembling, twitching, feeling shaky
- Muscle tension, aches, soreness
- Restlessness
- Easily tired

Autonomic hyperactivity
- Shortness of breath or smothering sensations
- Palpitations or accelerated heart rate
- Sweating; cold, clammy hands
- Dry mouth
- Dizziness, lightheadedness

- Nausea, diarrhea, other abdominal distress
- Flushes (hot flashes) or chills
- Frequent urination
- Trouble swallowing or "lump in the throat"

Hypervigilance
- Feeling keyed up or on edge
- Exaggerated startle response
- Difficulty concentrating or "mind going blank"
- Trouble falling asleep or staying asleep
- Irritability

CATASTROPHIZING

Typically, people who suffer from GAD have a habit of imagining that the worst-case scenario will happen. Many people who frequently catastrophize have little self-confidence, low self-esteem, and difficulties making positive and desirable life changes. Many also have social phobias.

An example of catastrophizing is saying to oneself, "If I go to the party, no one will know me and I won't have a good time," or "If I take this new job, I'll fail because I don't have the right computer skills."

Catastrophizing causes anxieties because it keeps people in situations they might really prefer to change, such as improving their social life, changing jobs, or moving to a new city. With positive self-talk and learned techniques to improve self-esteem, the habit of catastrophizing can be overcome. In severe cases, various psychotherapies may be helpful.

WHAT'S A "LUMP IN THE THROAT?"

A feeling of a "lump in the throat" (medically known as *globus hystericus*) is a very common symptom of anxiety. Most people, whether phobic or not, have experienced this sensation at one time or another. Some people experience it before a job interview or a public speech and fear that they will not have their usual strong voice. The "lump" may actually cause some difficulty in swallowing, although the sufferer usually can make enough effort to eat. The symptom, although unpleasant and uncomfortable, can usually be relieved with relaxation techniques and completion of the stressful event. Also, it is not threatening to one's health.

WHAT ARE THE DIFFERENCES BETWEEN COGNITIVE AND SOMATIC ANXIETY?

Symptoms of anxiety fall into three broad categories: *cognitive, somatic,* or *muscular and autonomic.* Cognitive symptoms of anxiety are thoughts in the anxious person's mind that lead to anxiety (such as catastrophizing). Such thoughts may be ideas of impending doom, as though a horrible event is at hand, but the source cannot be pinpointed. Other examples are racing thoughts, inability to concentrate, and runaway imaginations. The only way that cognitive anxiety can be measured is by the individual's own report.

However, somatic anxiety is easily measured by another person. Common symptoms of autonomic anxiety are increased heart rate and breathing, an increase in blood pressure, and feelings of nausea and dizziness. Sweating, muscle tension, headaches, stomachaches, jaw tension, and backaches are associated with muscle tension.

HOW TO WORRY LESS AND REDUCE ANXIETIES

- When you try not to worry about something, it is likely that you will worry about it more. It may be advantageous to stay with the worry and really concentrate on it because attention to it can lead to some control and to problem solution.

- Make a distinction between matters that you can do something about and those that you cannot. It may take practice, but it is important to differentiate these categories and to learn to accept those things that are out of your control.

- Instead of asking yourself repeatedly, "What if . . . ," write down a number of possible solutions to a specific problem and then list the advantages and disadvantages of each idea.

- Use a diversionary technique, such as going for a walk, doing some other form of exercise, playing a musical instrument, or listening to music. Doing so will help you organize your thoughts and come up with possible solutions. The best solutions may occur when you are not thinking about the immediate problem.

- Various forms of psychotherapy and self helps can relieve the stresses of excessive worrying for many people.

- Some people find it helpful to continue worrying in a specific place (like a particular chair) or at special times of the day, thus gaining some control and allowing time and place for nonworry thoughts. Remember, worry itself is the problem; the content is not important.

- Don't worry in bed. Get out of bed if you find yourself falling into a worry mode.

- Tell yourself to stop—or snap a rubber band on your wrist—if you fall into excessive or unnecessary worry.

People who have GAD mostly experience cognitive symptoms of anxiety. Even though these cognitive symptoms are prevalent, somatic reactions do occur but are often ignored.

HOW DOES SELF-REPORTING OF ANXIETY WORK?

Self-report is a way to evaluate your degree of anxiety. The *Self-Report of Responses to Anxiety* chart on page 30 is a typical example. This scale has no norms. However, there is a maximum score of 70 for each column (14 items; 5 is the top score/item). *A* refers to *autonomic symptoms, M* to *somatic or muscular systems,* and *C* to *cognitive responses.* Generally, total scores above 100 mean that the person is highly anxious. One of the most important factors is the relative values among the three categories, which tell the examiner and testee which system responds the greatest to stimulation and consequently which type of relaxation intervention might be

SELF-REPORT OF RESPONSES TO ANXIETY

This self-test suggests 39 different responses that you may have as reactions to anxiety. To determine your individualized and specific pattern, imagine that you are in a situation that causes you anxiety. Write a number from 0 to 5 (depending on how frequently you experience that particular effect) in the space after the question. If there are two sets of spaces, write the same number in both spaces. (The *A* column refers to autonomic symptoms, *M* to somatic symptoms, and *C* to central nervous system responses.)

    0 = Never have this reaction
    1 = Almost never have it
    2 = Seldom have it
    3 = Occasionally have it
    4 = Frequently have it
    5 = Always have it

	A	M	C
1. I tap my feet or fingers.		____	
2. My stomach flutters or feels full.	____		
3. I stutter or stammer.		____	
4. I clench my teeth or grind them.		____	
5. I kick my foot or bounce it.		____	
6. I bite my nails.		____	
7. I pick at things (hair, lint, etc.).		____	
8. I feel nausea.			____
9. I have tightness in my chest.	____		
10. My hand or head shakes or trembles.		____	
11. My hands feel cold.	____		
12. My hands sweat.	____		
13. My heart beats quickly and noticeably.	____		
14. I feel distant from my surroundings.			____
15. I continually have many of the same thoughts running through my head.			____
16. I move awkwardly, bump into things, or drop things.		____	

best suited to the individual. *A* responses do best with a breathing technique, *M* responses do best with muscle relaxation such as progressive relaxation, and *C* responses do best with mental relaxation such as meditation, thought stopping, and other techniques. GAD sufferers often score high on *C* responses.

The *A* (autonomic), *M* (muscular) and *C* (cognitive) scales should be scored by summing the scores of the individual items in each category.

	A	M	C
17. It is difficult to concentrate.		——	
18. I must be aware of everything around me to keep control.			——
19. My head or jaws ache.		——	
20. My head aches with a pounding either behind my eyes or on one side of my head.		——	
21. My forehead aches, or the back of my head aches with a kind of pulling ache.		——	
22. The muscles running from my shoulder blades across my shoulders to my neck ache on one side or both sides.		——	
23. My face flushes.	——		
24. I become dizzy.	——		
25. I want to be very close to someone.			——
26. I tend to have lapses of awareness.			——
27. I feel as if I want to smash something.	——		——
28. I have to go to the toilet often.	——		
29. I have difficulty eating or holding down food.	——		
30. My calves, thighs, or feet become tense.		——	
31. I breathe rapidly and shallowly.	——	——	
32. I have to check things again and again.			——
33. I keep forgetting things.			——
34. I want to retreat and sleep, safe at home.			——
35. I find myself putting everything in order.			——
36. I have to eat and eat.	——		
37. I produce gas (burp or other).	——		
38. My mouth becomes dry.	——		
39. I worry about many things.			——
Total:	A=	B=	C=

If one category is noticeably higher than the other two, then your anxiety reactions tend to be concentrated in that response system relative to the others. As mentioned, higher *A* scores are associated with autonomic (midbody) arousal—increased heart rate, difficulty eating, salivation reduction, hyperventilation, and so on. This is the core of the emotion of anxiety. The form of relaxation to concentrate on is diaphragmatic breathing, particularly the 4–2–8 pattern. This helps to calm autonomic arousal and will give you some control over these symptoms. If *M* is relatively higher, then anxiety symptoms are concentrated in the muscular responses and tension—shakiness, aches, ringing in the ears, headaches, need to move (difficulty sitting quietly), tension in back, shoulders and neck, and so on. The best form of relaxation here is progressive relaxation because it targets muscle groups. Because muscular tension is often the end product of autonomic arousal (but can become independent), breathing along with progressive relaxation is recommended. Breathing can be used prior to practicing the tension-release exercises.

If *C* is relatively higher then most symptoms are concentrated in thoughts and beliefs (often subconscious). Here, it is important to identify the thoughts that lead to fear reactions. "What am I thinking that makes me fearful or anxious in *this* situation?" Ask yourself this question. It might also be helpful to ask others if they have noticed what you might be thinking.

Meditation is helpful as a tool for quieting the thoughts and gaining some control over their automatic occurrence and their intensity. Meditation tapes and classes are places to start. Remember that it will take *months* before you notice improvements in *A, M,* or *C* systems. These reactions took years to develop, so there is no reason to believe they will diminish rapidly.

It is important to realize that these are just reactions in systems of functioning. These reactions developed as means to *cope* with stresses earlier in your life. The reactions have stayed on as coping mechanisms even though their origins have long past. The reactions protected you and helped you survive and cope. Now, however, they work against you and interfere with your functioning. Remember that *the reaction is not a disease;* it is a lifestyle habit that helped you in the past. We need to change it to help you in the future. Relaxation is the building block for change. It will not cure your problems (anxiety), but relaxation, once in place, will make it easier to make habit changes in emotional reactivity (automatic), tension (muscular), and catastrophic, self-defeating thoughts (cognitive).

Because the autonomic nervous system is always involved in anxiety, it may be helpful if you understand it in more detail. The autonomic nervous system has an arousal side (called the sympathetic) that produces anxiety symptoms and a calming or relaxation side (parasympathetic) that restores the body and brings it into a state of balance and presence.

Most people deal with sympathetic arousal by avoidance, using drugs, and self-medications. They will pull back or avoid situations that stimulate anxiety. Shopping, cleaning, watching television, napping, vacations, eating, distraction by massage, and so on are often activities to "relax." But do you actually relax? No, not physiologically. You calm or quiet the sympathetic system. You can bring it down so that symptoms are not so intense or noticeable, but technically you are not relaxing because the parasympathetic system is not engaged or activated to a sufficient degree. So how do you activate the "relaxation response" (parasympathetic arousal)? Simple. *Practice relaxation,* and eventually as you become proficient (after all you are just a *beginner* with parasympathetic arousal), the relaxation response will start to develop and will permeate your life and your activities. You will find that you can work without tension, relate without anxiety, and think without futurizing or catastrophizing. You will feel better, your body will be healthier, and your thinking will be more in the present and clearer. That is what we mean when we state that relaxation training is the *basis* for eventually making changes that will eliminate or reduce anxiety in your life.

HYPERVENTILATION AS A SYMPTOM OF ANXIETY

Hyperventilation means very rapid in-breaths, shallow and quick out-breaths, and a feeling of shortness of breath that can bring on high levels of anxiety. Hyperventilation causes a reduction in the carbon dioxide level relative to oxygen in the blood that in turn can lead to feelings of numbness, stomachaches, tingling of the hands, dizziness, muscle spasms, and fainting. Individuals who are anxious or aroused begin to breathe in a rapid deep manner with shallow exhalations. Gasping may occur. Although they have the sensation of shortness of breath, they are actually overbreathing. Sometimes this experience is accompanied by a feeling of constriction or pain in the chest.

The symptoms of hyperventilation and hyperventilation syndrome are frightening, and sufferers may fear that they are having a heart attack or that they will die. You cannot die from hyperventilation. Some agoraphobics experience hyperventilation when they attempt to leave home or even think of going out, particularly unaccompanied by a companion on whom they depend for security. Hyperventilation, or overbreathing, is also a common symptom among phobics when they face (or even think about) their phobic stimuli. For example, height phobics may hyperventilate when they even think about looking out from the top of a tall building.

Hyperventilation is more common in women than in men. Usually, hyperventilation occurs in individuals who have GAD, who are nervous or tense, or who are having an anxiety or panic attack. Usually anxiety sufferers are hyperventilating all the time but only notice it when they become symptomatic in particular situations. Once the individual recognizes that the hyperventilation syndrome is an anxiety reaction to a stimulus and not a disease itself, the attacks may become fewer or may stop because the panic component will be somewhat reduced.

One who hyperventilates can help himself or herself by understanding what happens during an attack. By voluntarily hyperventilating (about 50 deep breaths while lying down) and reproducing the symptoms felt during an anxiety attack, one will see that the symptoms do not indicate a heart attack or a "nervous breakdown." Once proper breathing is in place, the tendency to become anxious will diminish.

Warning: Hyperventilation may also be a response to severe pain, particularly abdominal pain. If there is any doubt about the cause of hyperventilation, you should be examined by a physician.

DEFENSE MECHANISMS AND ANXIETIES

Individuals who have GAD as well as other anxiety disorders express a wide variety of defense mechanisms ranging from projection, which is blaming someone else for one's situation, to rationalization, which is justifying questionable behavior by defending its propriety, to sublimation, which is using activities to distract oneself and use nervous energies. Denial is another defense mechanism. The presence of pathological denial (for example, of a drinking problem) is often seen in alcoholics or in people with substance abuse problems.

In follow-up studies of the Harvard University class of 1934, Dr. George Vaillant found that though virtually all of his subjects had significant life crises, those who overcame them tended to have "mature" defenses such as suppression (the capacity to focus on only the most important issue at the time, suppressing thought or worry about other problems until the one of high priority is solved) and *a good sense of humor.* Those who were overwhelmed by their anxieties and the stresses of life crises tended to employ the "less mature—more primitive" defense mechanism (blaming others) and denial (not admitting the presence of a problem to oneself). Denial is a frequently used defense mechanism in which individuals do not admit to themselves that a problem or event produces stress and anxiety. Additionally, a denial of a situation by some people can be a source of anxiety and stress to others.

USING THE THREE-STEP PROCESS FOR GAD

At the beginning of this chapter, you read about Bill and his anxious habits. When he learned that his collection of discomforts had a name, generalized anxiety disorder, he decided to take charge instead of letting his anxieties control him.

How Bill Took Step 1: Identifying Fear Areas

Bill identified his some of his fear areas by using the Self-Report of Responses to Fear table earlier in this chapter (see p. 30). He identified several of his responses to fear areas on which he wanted to work: worrying in general, headaches, and high blood pressure. He decided to tackle just these few areas at that time.

How Bill Took Step 2: What Triggered Bill's Anxieties?

Bill realized that overgeneralizing about certain things contributed to his anxieties: one was being on time and another was money. Once he had been late for a very important appointment, but now, most of the time, he was on time for appointments and TV watching. He realized it wasn't really worth worrying so much about that any more. Also, he once had a finance charge on a credit card, but lately he always paid his bills on time and realized that he would probably continue to do so. Now he could write that worry off his list.

Because these worries led to headaches and high blood pressure, reduction of worries helped both situations improve. As his own adaptation of Step 3, he chose to learn how to meditate and has been doing it twice a day for 15 minutes. He has also been practicing breathing exercises. He has had his blood pressure checked and it is lower.

Step 3: An Individualized "Exposure" Program

There was one more unwanted response Bill wanted to change: he is gradually exposing himself to being startled! He told his co-workers and family members that he is working on not reacting as intensely as he did before and has recruited their help. He has asked them to surprise him in different ways, and lately he is able to control his reactions.

With an increased feeling of control over some of his unwanted responses, Bill feels more relaxed, is less irritable, and sleeps more soundly. He plans to work on his old hand-wringing habit but believes in taking small steps toward improvement.

Everyday worries need not take over. You, too, can take small steps at a time, gain control over your anxieties, feel in control of your life, and feel better about yourself.

CHAPTER 4

SOCIAL PHOBIAS (SOCIAL ANXIETY DISORDER)

Jeff is 30 years old and has a desk job in a sales organization. He was hired at the same time as Pete, who has been promoted to sales manager. Jeff was offered the promotion before Pete, but Jeff turned it down. Jeff knew that being sales manager involved speaking in front of the sales force of 75 men and women. Jeff feels stuck but doesn't want to risk getting into a position in which public speaking is necessary. Jeff has a phobia shared by many people. It is a social phobia; it is fear of speaking in public.

Social phobias are the most common of all phobias.

What are some examples of common social phobias?

Aphephobia: Fear of being touched, affection, intimacy, standing close to others

Catagelophobia: Fear of ridicule, teasing, or mocking

Erythrophobia: Fear of blushing in front of others

Graphophobia, scriptophobia: Fear of writing in public, signing one's name (for example on credit card slips), writing checks

Kakorrhaphiophobia: Fear of failure, looking bad to others, taking tests

Xenophobia: Fear of strangers

Sociophobia: Fear of society in general

Fear of urinating or defecating in public rest rooms

Fear of being looked at by others: being stared at, for example, walking the aisle of an airplane

Fear of the opposite sex and fear of sexual relations

Many people have some social anxieties, such as wanting to be liked and accepted, to avoid criticism, to conform when conformity is desirable, and to be deemed competent. Social anxieties include a wide range of feelings, including worrying about what to wear for an occasion, about entering a roomful of strangers, or about eating in front of other people. When these situations become so difficult for an individual that he or she begins to avoid them, they are considered phobias.

Social phobia seems to be associated with fears of negative evaluation or embarrassing public behavior, such as making mistakes, being criticized, making a fool of oneself, sweating, fainting, blushing, speaking poorly, vomiting, or being rejected. Individuals with these phobias usually avoid the specific situations that they fear. Some individuals will participate in the activity only when they cannot be seen, for example, eating alone.

SHYNESS IS A FORM OF SOCIAL ANXIETY

Almost everyone experiences shyness at some time, especially "situational shyness," which arises in such uncomfortable social situations as meeting new people or going for a job interview. Extreme shyness is a symptom of social anxiety and is related to a fear of being unfavorably evaluated by others. It may also be related to a low sense of self-esteem. Shyness can be observed in several ways. Physically, the shy person may blush and perspire. Emotionally, he or she may feel anxious and insecure. The shy person may think that no one wants to talk to him or her or that no one likes him or her.

A shy person's behavior may actually help to discourage social interaction because shy people tend to keep their heads down and even avoid eye contact with others. Shyness may bring on a lack of social relationships or a distorted view of social relationships, causing the shy person to feel the anxieties of loneliness and emotional unfulfillment.

Shyness is often related to social phobia. People deal with shyness in different ways, depending on the individual's own personal system of defense mechanisms. Although it may cause some persons to withdraw and become quiet in social situations (introversion), shyness may encourage others to behave more aggressively in public, trying to cover up their shyness by being "the life of the party" (extroversion).

It is not uncommon for extroverted shy people to become performers or public figures, handling their shyness by keeping themselves in controlled, structured situations, performing well-rehearsed roles in familiar situations. (See the *Shyness Reactions* chart on page 38.)

HOW DO SOCIAL PHOBIAS DEVELOP?

Social anxiety and shyness often develop into a social phobia. Social phobias usually begin in late adolescence or early adulthood, although the age range for onset is usually from 15 to 30. Often social phobias are accompanied by heightened levels of generalized anxiety.

SHYNESS REACTIONS		
PHYSIOLOGICAL REACTIONS	OVERT BEHAVIORS	THOUGHTS AND FEELINGS
Blushing	Silence	Self-consciousness
Perspiring	Avoidance of others	Concern about impression on others
Increased pulse	No eye contact	
Heart pounding	Avoidance of action	Concern for social evaluation
Butterflies in stomach	Low speaking voice	Unpleasantness of situation

Some social phobias begin to develop over many months or years, but sometimes they are brought about by a precipitating traumatic event such as being neglected at a party or having said the wrong thing to an important person. Some social phobics attribute their fears to direct conditioning, some to vicarious factors, and some to instructional and informational factors. Direct negative learning experience may play an important role, but about half of social phobics are shy, always have been, and will always carry some aspects of the shyness throughout their lives. Others have been traumatized during childhood in social settings (ridiculed, criticized, humiliated, etc.). They may make greater progress if they can deal with the traumatic origins of their shyness, identifying them and processing them.

Parental behavior may have some influence on social phobias; for example, parents who have few friends and are socially anxious in the presence of others may influence their children to react in similar ways. Also, the presence of anxiety in children is often associated with verbal punishment and criticism by parents. Unlike specific or some single phobias, which tend to diminish as the individual grows into puberty and young adulthood, social phobias persist. Some have ongoing problems with generalized anxiety, dependence, and depression.

Social phobias often persist on a continuous basis, unlike agoraphobia, which tends to be episodic. Sometimes improving and sometimes worsening during periods of depression, social phobias also differ from the agoraphobic's fears of crowds. Social phobics fear observation by individuals; agoraphobics partly fear the masses of the crowds and the feelings that might occur in crowds, such as loneliness, separateness, or lack of identity.

Social phobias are equally common among men and women. Many agoraphobics have social phobias, and many social phobics have minor agoraphobic symptoms.

PERFORMANCE ANXIETY: A COMMON SOCIAL PHOBIA

Performance anxiety, or stage fright, is a common form of social phobia. Stage fright is also known as topophobia. It is a persistent, irrational, fear of exposure to scrutiny in certain situations, particularly in public speaking and in musical, dramatic, or other types of performances. This is a type of extreme fear that affects people in many kinds of situations where they are being evaluated, such as making a speech, playing a musical instrument, or performing in a chorus or a play.

Stage fright is related to a fear of making a mistake in front of others or of looking foolish. Actors, politicians, executives, and others who regularly are in the spotlight often are afflicted. Some anxiety is natural and may even enhance performance because anxiety pumps more adrenaline into the body's system, making one more alert and motivated. However, when the pressure becomes extreme, the effects on physical and emotional well-being can be destructive.

Symptoms may involve features of anxiety attacks, including dry mouth, lump in the throat, faintness, palpitations, rapid pulse, trembling, sweating, stomach upset, frequent urination, and inability to move. Migraine headaches, skin and gastrointestinal problems, hot and cold flashes, and hypertension can be typical reactions. As anxiety mounts, the individual may become increasing involved with overcoming it, which depletes energy to think, concentrate, and be creative. When the anxiety becomes worse, it becomes a phobia, and the phobic person may then avoid any performance situation that might provoke fears. However, many performers learn to overcome these feelings and go through with their performance.

WHAT HELPS OVERCOME PERFORMANCE ANXIETY?

Treatment includes positive thinking with the individual, for example, a musician who repeatedly tells himself or herself, "I know I'm good and have prepared well for this; I'll go on and make them sit up and notice me," "I've prepared properly, so even if I do lose concentration for a bit, my fingers can play the notes automatically," and "This concert is really going to be exciting."

Others use a mixed strategy, for example, thinking, "I will just concentrate on the music and ignore everything else," "I will just concentrate on staying relaxed," and "It's not the audience I worry about; it's my colleagues—if I mess it up they are sure to notice."

To overcome audience sensitivity, some individuals use cognitive coping statements such as: "I will pretend the audience is not there and that it is a rehearsal," and "I am in control; this tenseness I feel is an ally."

Leaning to cope with performance anxiety includes cognitive therapy and repeated exposure to an audience. Experience before an audience, for most performers, tends to reduce anxieties over time. However, it is difficult to determine whether the performances themselves enable people to be more comfortable or whether the most anxious performers, such as musicians, leave the field because of their anxieties.

PHARMACOLOGICAL TREATMENT FOR PERFORMANCE ANXIETY

Because many antianxiety drugs (such as benzodiazepines) can cause drowsiness, other medications have been used to combat performance anxiety. The class of drugs called beta blockers have been effective with many people. This class of drugs inhibits the activity of some neurotransmitters, which are often associated with producing the physical symptoms of anxiety. The drug most often used in studies has been propranolol (Inderal). It has been helpful for musicians, public speakers, students taking examinations, and athletes. However, some beta blockers are not safe for individuals who have asthma or other lung disorders, cardiovascular disease, diabetes, or hypothyroidism.

CATASTROPHIZING CAN BE RELATED TO PERFORMANCE ANXIETY

Some individuals experience performance anxiety in activities that are not scrutinized by the public, such as doing mechanical work or taking tests. Individuals who have this fear worry about doing something over which they might become embarrassed or humiliated. They tend to catastrophize, or worry about what might happen in the worst possible cases. Catastrophizing thoughts might include: "I think I'm going to faint," "I don't think I will be able to get through to the end without cracking up," "I'm almost sure to make a dreadful mistake, and that will ruin everything," "I don't feel in control of the situation; anything might happen," and "I think I'm going to be sick."

FEAR OF BLUSHING

It may surprise you that in this day and age, there are some people who are afraid that they will embarrass themselves by blushing in public. Fear of blushing is known as erythrophobia. This fear happens only when others are around. The phobic individual, more commonly a woman, is terrified that she will blush in the company of others and is convinced that in this state she will be very visible and consequently be the center of unwanted painful attention. If questioned, such an individual cannot say what is so dreadful about blushing, but most likely fear of disapproval from others is an important component of her anxiety.

A change of color may not be noticeable by an observer, despite the fact that the individual insists that she feels bright red; the force of this fear may lead the individual to a severe restriction of her social life.

Blushing involves an increase in blood volume to the face and head. It is part of the sympathetic nervous system arousal pattern of anxiety/excitement. External stimuli, such as the presence of other people, can become conditioned fairly easily.

FEAR OF SPEAKING AND SPEAKING OUT LOUD

Fear of speaking is known as laliophobia. This fear may be related to a fear of speaking aloud, fear of speaking over the telephone, and fear that one may use the wrong words, have an ineffective tone of voice, or sound powerless. Other fears related to speaking include hearing the sound of one's own voice and stuttering.

Fear of speaking aloud is known as phonophobia. This fear may be related to the fear of hearing one's own voice, of stuttering, or of having a poor voice quality. Muteness and aphonia (inability to speak louder than a whisper) may result as traces of avoidance.

FEAR OF SWEATING

Fear of sweating is a frequently occurring social phobia. Some individuals avoid crowds, being in close contact with others in elevators, and even eating in restaurants because they fear that they will sweat and look ridiculous. They may also worry about giving off an offensive odor and staining their clothing. They fear attracting attention to themselves.

Some women who suffer from hot flashes fear that others will notice that they are having a hot flash. Many individuals who have a low sense of self-esteem worry that others will hold them in even less regard if they sweat at an unpredictable time.

FEAR OF SWIMMING

Fear of swimming may be considered a social phobia in that many who fear swimming fear being seen in their bathing suits by others, fear criticism about their body shape, and fear that they may look ridiculous while swimming or approaching the pool or body of water where they are the object of attention.

Fear of swimming may also come from a fear of water or a fear of drowning (which would be considered a specific phobia). Some fear being out of control if a wave or the undertow overtakes them while swimming in an ocean or large lake. Some individuals are comfortable standing in a pool or a body of water but fear swimming; some can float or swim but fear putting their face in the water while they do so.

For many, a fear of swimming can be overcome by taking lessons and learning to use appropriate breathing techniques while in the water. For others, behavior modification techniques may be effective.

A typical treatment program gradually reintroduces phobics to stressful situations to help them gain confidence and develop skills one step at a time as they learn to deal with the situation. The starting point is wherever each individual feels comfortable.

APPEARANCE AND BEHAVIORS IN PERFORMANCE ANXIETY

Paces, sways, shuffles feet, knees tremble

Distracting arm and hand movements (swings, scratches)

Arms very rigid

Hands restrained (in pockets, behind back, always clasped)

Hand tremors

No eye contact

Face muscles tense (tics, grimaces)

Face pale or flushed

Moistens lips often; clears throat often

Perspires

Voice quivers or stammers

USING THE THREE-STEP PROCESS FOR SOCIAL PHOBIAS

How Jeff Took Step 1: His Fear Area Was Easy to Identify

It was easy for Jeff to identify his fear (see page 36). He didn't need any self-test. He knew that the few times he tried to speak in front of a group he felt extremely anxious, nauseated, dizzy, and sweaty. These symptoms made him very uncomfortable. He wanted to avoid them.

How Jeff Took Step 2: He Knew His Anxiety Triggers

Jeff knew that just getting up in front of his church group to make an announcement gave him his unwanted responses. The responses became magnified with a larger group. He decided to begin to make changes so that he would feel more comfortable speaking in public.

How Jeff Planned His "Exposure" Program: Step 3

Friends suggested to Jeff that if he practiced speaking in front of people more often, he might be able to overcome his fears, and, they said, if he planned ahead what to say and made some notes on a card, he might be more comfortable. That sounded good to him. He heard about Toastmasters, a club for people who want to improve their public speaking skills. He went to one meeting, just to try it out, and found that there were many people in the group who had been like him and had overcome their fears of speaking. Each week, he was asked to give a short speech. At first, his speeches were one or two minutes. The first few times, his anxiety responses began to take over. But knowing that he would be finished in less than a minute, he managed to keep on going. All the while, he practiced relaxation techniques, particularly breathing exercises because breathing helps to calm autonomic arousal. Gradually, he was able to give longer talks. This was his "exposure" therapy.

Jeff incorporated breathing techniques into his program. He felt that with better breathing, he was able to combat his dizziness and other reactions. He also learned about progressive muscle relaxation and practiced that both every day and again shortly before giving his talks. After six months of going to Toastmasters on a weekly basis, he rated his anxiety reaction as only "mildly apprehensive" and tolerable and felt in control of himself in front of a crowd. He was also willing to risk and to make mistakes as he learned a new skill of talking in front of others. Practice (exposure) and preparation (playing out the situation extensively) really helped him.

The best outcome of his taking these three steps was that within a year, he was promoted to district sales manager, and now he gives talks— up on a stage—on a fairly regular basis to the 75 people in his district.

Other social fears can be overcome with gradual exposure, too. Overcoming social fears can mean taking control of your life. Set realistic goals. Just functioning better in social situations is quite possible no matter how intense your reactions. If you set your goals too high, you will always be disappointed and discouraged; too low, and progress will seem trivial. Be realistic, and remember: you can always set new goals once you attain the ones you have now.

CHAPTER 5

SPECIFIC (SINGLE) PHOBIAS

> Martha is 22 years old and knows that whenever she sees a cat, she begins to feel shaky and sweaty, begins to breathe rapidly, and becomes slightly dizzy. Before accepting an invitation to anyone's home with which she is unfamiliar, she asks if there is a cat. If so, she avoids the invitation. If she sees a cat on the street, she crosses the street so that she does not have to see it or let it cross her path. She knows that cats (most) are harmless and that her fear is out of proportion to any danger involved. She does not react this way with dogs or birds. Martha has a phobia of cats.

Specific phobias are characterized by a marked and persistent fear that is excessive or unreasonable, brought on by the presence or anticipation of a specific object or situation (such as heights, seeing certain animals, or the sight of blood). The fear is individual; it is not shared by most others in the same situation. There is a history to this reaction, and, often, traumatic circumstances mark the onset. Exposure to the feared object or situation almost always provokes an immediate severe anxiety response. The person recognizes that the fear is excessive or unreasonable and tends to avoid the situation or endure it with intense distress. Virtually any object or situation can become a phobia for an individual. Examples of common specific phobias include driving across bridges, flying, harmless animals such as dogs and cats, heights, being in enclosed places, insects, snakes, bees, darkness, and thunderstorms.

Some people can live fairly securely with a specific phobia, such as the fear of snakes, because they are not likely to encounter them in large cities. However, a fear of elevators or escalators may interfere with one's occupational or academic functioning. Some phobias may interfere with one's social activities or relationships. Some individuals have marked distress about having a phobia. For most, having a phobia diminishes their self-esteem because they are unduly limited in what they can do or where they can go.

WHAT CAUSES PHOBIAS?

Direct or indirect learning experiences or exposure to negative instructions or vicarious experiences may lead to phobias in people. Many individuals who have specific phobias do not recall the origin of their fear, but often there is distress or trauma. Sometimes a phobia may appear gradu-

---

EXAMPLES OF TYPES OF SPECIFIC PHOBIAS

Animals

- Insects (entomophobia)
- Bees (Apiphobia; melisophobia)
- Spiders (arachneophobia)
- Frogs (batrachophobia)
- Horses (equinophobia)
- Fish (ichthyophobia)
- Mice (musephobia; murophobia)
- Snakes (opidiophobia)
- Birds (onithophobia)
- Animals (zoophobia)

Natural phenomena

- Night, darkness (acluophobia; nyctophobia)
- Heights (acrophobia)
- Wind (anemophobia)

- Lightning (astraphobia)
- Northern lights (aurophobia)
- Thunder (brontophobia; keraunophobia)
- Rain (ombrophobia)
- Rivers (potomophobia)
- Stars (siderophobia)

Miscellaneous

- Confinement (claustrophobia)
- Blushing or the color red (erythrophobia)
- Missiles (ballisphobia)
- Objects to the right (dextrophobia)
- Objects to the left (levophobia)
- Dolls (pediophobia)
- Hair (trichopathophobia; trichophobia)

---

ally or long after a traumatizing event. Treatment of the phobic symptom, however, does not have to wait until the origin is uncovered.

Some specific phobias do not last long and will improve as the individual grows older. Phobias in this category include doctors, injections, darkness, and strangers. However, fears of heights, storms, and enclosed places usually last longer. In children, fears of animals that are prevalent in children between the age of 9 and 11 remain with many girls after age 11 but disappear in most boys.

There are differences of opinions regarding the effects of family influences on specific fears. Although some experts believe that the majority of specific phobics come from families in which no other member of the family shares the same fear, some studies have found relatively strong associations between the fears of mothers and children. Many specific phobics have a tendency to become overly excited (anxious in specific situations). If reinforced within the family, they may develop sustained phobic reactions and avoidance. Home and peer groups undoubtedly contribute to the maintenance of phobic behavior.

BLOOD (AND BLOOD INJURY) PHOBIA

Many individuals are afraid of the sight of blood. This is a natural fear of humans. Fear of blood is known as hematophobia or hemophobia.

Although susceptible individuals may not say that they have a fear of blood, when faced with the sight of their own or another's blood, they may recoil, close their eyes, or even faint. A reaction may occur on hearing a description of blood and gore, such as a war scene, or even imagining seeing someone bleeding. Blood phobia is different from some other phobias in that the individual does not perceive danger of injury or death.

Blood phobics may experience more nausea, faintness, and disdain than fear or anxiety. Their reaction is atypical of the phobic in that *a vasovagal reaction* occurs (more on this below). They may avoid their phobic stimuli for fear of fainting, and this in turn can lead to anxiety. Women seem to be more fearful of the sight of blood than men.

With most phobias, the individual's pulse and breathing rate increase in response to the phobic stimulus. However, with blood and injury phobia (and related phobias, such as needles, injection, blood donation, medical odors, etc.), there is often a sharp drop in heart rate and blood pressure after arousal, which is called a diphasic cardiovascular pattern, or *vasovagal response*. Why some blood phobics lose consciousness when faced with the stimulus is not clearly understood, but one hypothesis is that it is a "protective" biological mechanism that, in the event of actual injury, prevents the individual from doing anything that might cause further blood loss. It could also protect humans from predatory animals because these animals will generally attack or continue to attack a fighting or moving subject. This reaction runs in families and appears to have a genetic basis.

Like phobias of animals, those of blood and injury often begin during childhood. It appears to be relatively common in minor forms and is excessive in very few instances. Epidemiological studies indicate that approximately 3.1 to 4.5 percent of the population report blood and blood-injury phobias. In a 1980 study, a high percentage of blood phobics (68 percent) reported that close relatives had the same fear.

Severe phobia of blood and injury can be seriously handicapping. For example, sufferers may avoid necessary medical and dental procedures or avoid attractive careers as medical professionals. Blood-injury phobic women may refuse to become pregnant to avoid medical examinations and the sight of blood. Having injections or having blood drawn, dental procedures—all medical care settings become triggering stimuli to blood and injury phobics.

Benjamin Rush (1745–1813), American physician and author, said of blood phobia:

> There is a native dread of the sight of blood in every human creature, implanted probably for the wise purpose of preventing our injuring or destroying ourselves, or others. Children cry oftener from seeing their blood, than from the pain occasioned by falls or blows. Valuable medicines are stamped with a disagreeable taste to prevent their becoming ineffectual from habit, by being used as condiments or articles of diet. In like manner, Blood-letting as a remedy, is defended from being used

improperly, by the terror which accompanies its use. This terror rises to such a degree as sometimes to produce paleness and faintness when it is prescribed as a remedy. However unpopular it may be, it is not contrary to nature, for she relieves herself when oppressed, by spontaneous discharges of blood from the nose, and other parts of the body. The objections to it therefore appear to be founded less in the judgments than in the *fears* of sick people.

EXAMPLE OF TYPES OF BLOOD-INJURY PHOBIAS

Blood (hematophobia; hemophobia)

Injury (traumatophobia)

Pain (algophobia; odynophobia)

Needles (belonephobia)

Skin lesions (dermatophobia)

Fever (pyrexeophobia; febriphobia)

Contamination (molysomophobia; mysophobia)

INTERNAL AND EXTERNAL STIMULI: HOW DO THEY INFLUENCE PHOBIAS?

Phobias of internal stimuli are within the individual; no external stimuli can be avoided to reduce fear. Examples are fear of cancer, heart disease, high blood pressure, venereal disease, and death. Fears of this type are often associated with depressive illnesses; in such cases, they improve when the depression improves. Illness phobias occur in both men and women. Some of these fears may be regarded as an extreme form of hypochondria.

Obsessive phobias are fears that are disproportionate to the threat of the situation, cannot be explained by the individual, and are beyond voluntary control. Examples are the fear of germs and fear of contamination, which lead to obsessive hand washing. Such phobias usually occur along with other obsessive-compulsive behaviors and are often pervasive, interfering with one's functioning.

CLAUSTROPHOBIA: PERHAPS THE MOST COMMON PHOBIA

Claustrophobia is an exaggerated fear of closed places, such as closets, subways, tunnels, telephone booths, elevators, small rooms, crowds, center-row seating, or other enclosed or confined spaces. More people may suffer from claustrophobia than any other exaggerated fear. The word is derived from the Latin word, *claustrum,* meaning "bolt" or "lock." Claustrophobia is a naturally occurring prepared fear.

Claustrophobia takes many forms. Some individuals fear being in a car or a room in which they cannot open a window or in which the door is closed or the shades drawn. Others fear sitting in the center of a row in a church, theater, or airplane. Some overcome their fears to some extent by sitting at the end of the row or at the aisle. Some claustrophobics fear and avoid flying because they do not like to be in an enclosed place.

Although most people dislike feeling hemmed in or trapped to any extent, claustrophobics react with severe anxiety reactions and possibly a panic attack and physiologic symptoms such as increased pulse when they feel closed in. Persons with this phobia often fear suffocation, panic and death.

Some whose phobias include being in tunnels may fear that the tunnel will cave in and they will be buried alive or be killed by the falling structure. Claustrophobics who are afraid of elevators must make many life choices so that they can avoid taking elevators. This may affect where they work and where they live. Some who fear elevators fear that the elevator will get stuck between floors, that the doors will not open, that they will be trapped, and that they may starve or suffocate to death. Some claustrophobics have similar fears about airplanes.

Many individuals who have agoraphobia also have claustrophobia. There is strong evidence that a claustrophobic tendency is an innate human potential that can become activated by (negative) experiences and become a conditioned response. Nevertheless, these reactions are avoidable, and improvement and recovery is possible with a proper treatment approach.

ANOTHER COMMON FEAR: ACROPHOBIA (HEIGHTS)

Fear of heights is known as acrophobia or hypsiphobia. This is one of the commonest phobias in the general population. Individuals who have acrophobia fear being on high floors of buildings or on the tops of hills or mountains. They usually feel anxious when approaching the edge of precipices such as bridges, rooftops, stairwells, railings, and overlooks. They usually fear falling and being injured. Some feel and fear an uncontrollable urge to jump. They may have fantasies and physical sensations of falling, losing balance or control, even when on firm ground. People who have height phobias generally try to avoid being in such places. The fear is automatic with exposure to edges. The fantasies and impulses come after the fear sensation itself.

Fear of elevators, escalators, balconies, and stairways are most often related to a fear of heights itself, as is sometimes a fear of flying or falling.

In severe cases involving heights, the individual cannot even stand on the lower steps of a ladder or staircase without experiencing some anxiety. Often, fear of driving on freeways or highways has an acrophobic component in that these roadways are often elevated (and sometimes have well-defined edges).

Treatment commonly involves exposure therapy in which graded exposure to heights is made while the subject is in a state of relative relaxation. For example, a person might start exposure with looking out the second-floor window until relaxation or comfort is achieved and then move on to third and subsequent floors in the same manner. In severe cases, a therapist or a trained support person may be necessary. Graded exposure is the key element. As each new grade is reached, the individual is ready to move on to the next level. Obviously, these levels or grades cannot be too large or too small or success, and motivation will wane.

FEAR OF FLYING

Fear of flying, known as aerophobia, represents one of the major fear categories for adults in the United States and probably throughout the world. Flying phobia is sometimes considered a specific phobia, but it also occurs as part of the agoraphobic syndrome. People who have the specific phobia avoid flying because they may fear crashes or other calamities. Those who have agoraphobia fear having a panic attack and its consequences.

The fear of flying itself has two points of origin—the anticipatory situation and the flying situation itself. Anticipatory anxiety occurs because a commitment has been made to fly (a reservation has been made, ticket purchased, people informed of trip, etc.). Anticipatory anxiety usually is experienced as feelings of dread, rapid pulse, total body sensations (tension, warmth, etc.), and fear-induced images and thoughts. Interestingly, the anticipatory fear is usually not of the airplane itself but of uncontrollable outcomes such as fear of losing control of oneself in the airplane and going crazy or embarrassing oneself in public, fear of separation from loved ones, fear of death, fear of relinquishing control to someone else, thoughts of falling from the sky and dying in a crash, and so on.

Fear in the plane itself may encompass many of the anticipatory fears just described but may also usually involve fear of being enclosed; fear of being alone or away from others on whom one depends; fears of feeling trapped and unable to leave at will; fear of social rejection due to the reaction; fear of the fear sensations; and sometimes feelings about the place or person the individual is leaving or about the place or person the individual may be seeing at the destination. Fear reactions are modulated by the degree of predictability and individual control in a sit-

---

WHAT LEADS TO FEAR OF FLYING?

Fear of experiencing a panic attack on the flight

Expectation of claustrophobic feelings on the flight

Media/verbal information about dangers inherent in flying

Vicarious acquisitions of the fear from other fearful passengers

Turbulent weather or expectation of bad weather

Delays in landing and feelings of being "trapped" in the air

Emotional reactions (e.g., grief) that are brought to the flight

---

uation. Neither prediction nor control (at least of the airplane) are present when flying.

News reports of air crashes, stories, and television and movie depictions can also provide stimuli for fear thoughts and reactions. It has also been pointed out that much of the common language used in the air travel industry has a fatalistic and fear engendering ring, such as *terminal, final boarding, final approach, departure lounge,* and so on; the fears engendered by terminology may be supplemented by insurance desks, oxygen masks, crash procedures, and a number of reminders of possible adverse consequences of flying. Many of these factors are external cues for anxiety; thoughts and sensations represent internal triggers to anxiety. Social anxiety can also intensify in the airplane in that the phobic individuals do not want to call attention to themselves, lest they be embarrassed.

Treatment for the fear of flying has varied from traditional therapies to hypnosis, flooding, and exposure therapies. The latter provide the best long-term success rate at about 75–80 percent. A "cue-controlled" relaxation procedure in which the phobic learns to produce relaxation on cue seems to offer promise as an effective technique. Success, of course, involves more than just being able to fly; the more rigorous criterion involves flying with progressively increased ease and comfort over a long-term series of trials. "Virtual" therapies are also being tried on an experimental basis.

USING THE THREE-STEP PROCESS FOR SPECIFIC PHOBIAS

How Martha Used Step 1: Identifying Her Fear of Cats

Like Jeff's fear of public speaking, Martha feared only one specific thing—cats—and she knew it.

HOW TO FLY WITH LESS ANXIETY

■ Make a commitment to fly when you choose to do so. Don't agree to fly with the idea that you will back out. See flying as an opportunity for you to become less fearful.

■ Prepare yourself far in advance. Practice relaxation so that you build skills in calming yourself. This will not prevent you from becoming anxious, but it will lessen the intensity, allow you to recover faster, and give you some control over the situation. Visualize yourself flying comfortably (as you would like to be able to fly) when you are relaxed.

■ Practice some desensitization. For example, go to the airport to relax yourself in that environment. Watch the planes take off and land, until you feel relaxed. Imagine being comfortable in an airplane that you are watching. This will help reduce the anticipatory buildup.

■ Take things with you to occupy yourself when flying. Also, make a tape for relaxation and to remind yourself of thoughts and ideas that will help you cope on the plane.

■ Remember: the fear will not go away without practice, preparation, and continued flying on a regular basis.

How Martha Used Step 2: Triggers of Her Fear of Cats

Martha knew that her fear responses were more intense the closer she got to a cat. She could tolerate a cat across the street but not when it came near her. Her most intense trigger was a cat, even a friend's, brushing up against her legs.

How Martha Used Step 3: Gradual Exposure to Cats

In her mind, Martha acknowledged that most cats would not harm her. She noticed other people petting cats and loving their pets with no fear. She decided that she wanted to rid herself of her fear because her extreme reactions made her feel out of control when they happened. She enlisted her older sister's help. They made an agreement that whenever Martha wanted to back off from the planned activity, she could do so without either judgment from her sister or self-criticism.

First, Martha looked at pictures of cats in encyclopedias and children's books. At first, even pictures caused fear reactions, but after a while, she was comfortable looking at pictures. Then she went to several pet shops and looked in through the windows. Later she was able to go inside and look at some cats in cages. She felt somewhat safe: they could not come out and rub against her. A few times she had to leave the pet shop and step outside when she felt some symptoms of anxiety coming on. During a period of two months, with several sessions each week, most often accompanied by her sister, she felt comfortable near the cats in the pet shop.

Martha decided to go to the home of a trusted friend who had a cat. When the cat came into the room, at first it didn't come near her. That was OK. She felt relaxed and comfortable and said to herself, "So what if the cat brushes up against my leg? It's not even a foot tall!"

Martha's successful program of self-planned exposure therapy is an example of what can be done to overcome many specific phobias. Use the Three-Step Process. Apply them to your own phobias. Let them help you face and reduce your levels of fear.

CHAPTER 6

PANIC ATTACKS AND AGORAPHOBIA

Jane S. is 22 years old. She was spending the weekend in a small midwestern town with her aunt and uncle, which she frequently did. She enjoyed walking in the early morning, and one day she decided to venture out alone for a 2-mile walk in an area she knew well. Nearly at the turnaround point, as she crossed over a small bridge, she felt a sudden wave of terror come over her for no apparent reason. Her knees felt rubbery, she felt dizzy and sweaty, and her heart was pounding. It was a terrifying experience. She knew that she had to return to the house as quickly as possible. That was Jane's first panic attack.

PANIC ATTACKS

Panic attacks are specific periods of sudden onset of intense terror and fearfulness, often associated with feelings of impending doom. During panic attacks there may be difficulty breathing (hyperventilation), palpitations, chest pain or discomfort, choking or smothering sensations, sweating, and a feeling of being detached. The feelings that accompany a panic attack cannot be controlled, and people often fear they are going crazy or going to die.

People who have panic attacks can learn to overcome them and, for most, to live panic free. Using cognitive behavioral therapies, people can learn ways to reduce anxiety and panic, using breathing exercises, techniques to refocus their attention, and cognitive changes. Exposure therapy, in which they are slowly exposed to the fearful situation, also helps restore functioning.

For diagnostic purposes, *panic disorder* is characterized by three panic attacks within a two-week span of time. Panic disorder affects between three and six million Americans, is twice as common in women as in men, and usually begins in young adulthood, although it can appear at any age.

USING THE THREE-STEP PROCESS TO FACE THE FEARS OF PANIC ATTACKS

At the beginning of this chapter, you read about Jane's first and only panic attack. She returned home and told her aunt and uncle about her terrify-

LOCATIONS OF FIRST PANIC ATTACKS*	
LOCATION	PERCENTAGE
Auto	15%
At work	9%
Home	8%
Public places	8%
Restaurant	8%
School	7%
Away from home	7%
Store	6%
Bridge	4%
Public transportation	4%
Street	4%

*Locations in which first panic attack occurred and percent of agoraphobics with first panic in these locations.

Source: Ronald M. Doctor, in *Phobia: Comprehensive Summary of Modern Treatment.* Edited by R. L. DuPont (New York: Brunner-Mazel, 1982).

ing experience. She was still nervous, shaky, and weak. She explained what had happened and how she felt when it happened. Although her uncle responded with "Don't worry about it. There's nothing to be afraid of," her aunt was more understanding. "Relax today and tomorrow, and the next time you are here, I will walk with you. I understand how anxious you are," her aunt said. Jane feared that she would have a panic attack again and did not go for any more walks that weekend.

Upon returning to her own city home, Jane thought about what to do to overcome her fear of having a panic attack. She knew that she enjoyed walking in the country and would want to walk there again when she visited.

How Jane Took Step 1: Identifying Her Fears

Jane feared having another panic attack because the feelings she experienced were so intensely unpleasant and upsetting. She feared walking alone, particularly in the country area or open space where her panic attack occurred.

How Jane Took Step 2: What Triggered Her Fears?

Jane didn't know what triggered her fear. Sometimes panic attacks have no specific triggers that can be identified except they occur under condi-

SYMPTOMS DURING A PANIC ATTACK
(FROM A STUDY OF 100 PATIENTS IN ENGLAND)

SYMPTOM	PERCENTAGE OF PEOPLE
Nervous and tense	93
Dizzy or faint	83
Agitated	80
Palpitations	74
Weak legs	73
Trembling/shaking	72
Feeling totally unable to cope	66
Stomach churning	65
Sweating/perspiring	65
Shortness of breath	59
Confused	58
Things not quite real	57
Loss of control	52
Tightness/pressure in the head	43
Blurred vision	36
Feeling of becoming paralyzed	19

Source: From Ronald M. Doctor, Ph.D., and Ada P. Kahn, Ph.D, *The Encyclopedia of Phobia, Fears, and Anxieties,* 2d ed. (New York: Facts On File, 2000).

tions of stress. However, in her mind, she remembered the smell the country air, the open space, and the feeling of the ground under her feet. She wanted to avoid those things and hoped to avoid having another panic attack. Also, any body sensations that mimic the panic—even if less intense—became frightening.

How Jane Took Step 3: An Individualized "Exposure" Program

Before going to the country again, Jane spoke with her aunt by phone and discussed her fears. Speaking with her aunt was important because the more secretive one is about a panic attack, the more dangerous the panic-attack-provoking scene may appear.

Jane asked her aunt to walk with her the next weekend, which they did. At first, they only went about a block from the house when Jane began to feel slightly anxious. They turned back and went out again later that day. That was wise because in recovery from fear, one should be willing to retreat when necessary and take small steps, preventing anxiety from growing too high. Meanwhile, Jane practiced some deep-breathing exercises. They went out several times over the weekend but never went as far as the bridge where the panic attack occurred.

Several weeks later, Jane visited again and went walking again. They repeated the previous activity, taking longer walks each time. Jane would describe her feelings of slight to moderate anxiety to her aunt. When the anxiety level became too high, they turned back until the sensation subsided, and then she turned around and walked again toward the bridge. Gradually, over several more weekends, Jane and her aunt walked as far as the bridge, crossed over the bridge, and walked back home again. Jane was only very mildly anxious around the bridge, to which she had attached so much anxiety. She was grateful that her aunt was so supportive.

Jane still has a slight fear that a panic attack will occur again somewhere else. However, she knows that she overcame her fear of the place where the first one occurred, and she feels confident that if she ever has one again, she will know what to do to overcome the fear associated with it.

Panic attacks need not control your life. *You* can be in control. By facing your fear and looking at your situation in a relaxed and systemic manner, you can take steps to cope in effective ways.

Panic attacks can lead to agoraphobia or avoidance of major activities away from a safe place. Here is some information on agoraphobia.

AGORAPHOBIA: SOME HISTORICAL NOTES

The term *agoraphobia* was introduced in 1872 in Otto Westphal's (1824–1902) classic paper describing three agoraphobic cases:

> . . . impossibility of walking through certain streets or squares or possibility of so doing with resultant dread of anxiety . . . no delusions to cause the strange fear . . . agony was increased at hours when streets dreaded were deserted and shops were closed. The subjects experienced great comfort from companionship of men or even an inanimate object, such as a vehicle or a cane. The use of beer or wine also allowed the patient to pass through the feared locality with comparative comfort. One man even sought, without immoral motives, the companionship of a prostitute as far as his own door. Another case also had a dislike to crossing a certain bridge. He feared he would fall into the water. . . .

Westphal labeled his cases *agoraphobia* because the fears expressed were characterized principally by an intense feeling of dread or "phobia" in open streets or public places, much like the *agora* (Greek word for "marketplace"). He commented that the thought of the feared situation frequently was as distressing as the situation itself. Within the next century, researchers and therapists recognized that *fear of fear* was a central concept in agoraphobia. Ironically though, all three of Westphal's cases were men. Today most people who seek treatment for agoraphobia are women.

THE CYCLE OF AGORAPHOBIA

ONGOING
CONFLICT

SERIES
OF
PANICS

ADDED
RELATIONSHIP
STRESSES

CONDITIONED
FEAR OF
BODY
SENSATIONS

ISOLATED
FEAR
DOMINATED
LIFE

SPREADING
FEAR
AND
AVOIDANCE
OF
PLACES

Source: From Dr. Alan Goldstein and Berry Stainback, *Overcoming Agoraphobia*. (New York: Viking Penguin, 1987), reprinted by permission.

Now the term *agoraphobia* is applied to many disabling fears, usually involving a group of fears centering around distance from "a safe place." Consequently, agoraphobics commonly fear going away from home; going into the street, into stores; occupying center seats in churches, theaters, or public transportation; crowded places; and large rooms where many people are gathered, or being far from help. Almost any situation in which the person feels trapped can trigger anticipatory fear reactions. The trapped situation, however, is not usually physical but social in that the person can leave but is embarrassed or reticent to call attention to himself or herself. Having a trusted companion along often allows the agoraphobic to venture much further.

Some agoraphobics are also claustrophobic, but claustrophobia is usually present before the agoraphobia develops. The common factor between the two phobias is that escape is blocked, at least temporarily.

Some people fear confinement in a barber's, beautician's, or dentist's chair; some fear taking a bath in the nude. Some individuals who are phobic about bridges fear them because long, narrow bridges with open sides high above a river offer no way out except to cross. Others fear tunnels and elevators for similar reasons. Fears of death and separation are almost universal with agoraphobics.

AGORAPHOBIA IS A DISABLING DISORDER

Agoraphobia a complex phobic disorder that affects mainly adults. It is also the most disabling. According to the National Institute of Mental Health (NIMH), about 1 adult in 20 suffers from agoraphobia. More than three-quarters of agoraphobics are women. According to the New York State Psychiatric Institute of the Columbia-Presbyterian Medical Center in New York City, 4 million Americans a year seek treatment for this disorder, which may represent only about 20 percent of all agoraphobics.

MAIN EFFECTS OF AGORAPHOBIA

MAIN EFFECTS OF AGORAPHOBIA ON SUBJECTS' LIVES			
112 MEN	%	818 WOMEN	%
Unable to work	42	Social restrictions	29
Lack of social contacts	29	Personal psychological effect	23
Personal psychological effect	11	Marital disharmony	14
Marital disharmony	9	Unable to work	14
Travel restrictions	4	Travel restrictions	11
Guilt about children	2	Guilt about children	6

Source: Reproduced from Isaac. M. Marks, *Fears, Phobias, and Rituals: An Interdisciplinary Perspective* (New York: Oxford University Press, 1987), reproduced by permission.

WHEN DOES AGORAPHOBIA BEGIN?

Agoraphobia usually begins with a panic attack or series of attacks followed by self-judgment, extreme sensitivity to physical sensations, helplessness, and social anxiety. These fears may lead to avoidance of certain situations and places. One then has secure feelings only in designated safe places such as home and car.

Most agoraphobia begins in early adulthood, between the ages of 18 and 35, with 24 years of age as the modal start. Many individuals who recognize their disorder do not seek treatment until about 10 years later. In this regard, agoraphobia differs from most specific phobias, which originate during childhood.

In most individuals, the agoraphobia is not triggered by a major life event. For example, some report relatively insignificant incidents at the onset of their agoraphobia, such as a minor fall on a slippery street, drug effects, being in traffic or a crowded restaurant, or being startled outdoors in the dark by a lamppost or dog. These attacks usually occur while the individual is under some major stress, such as marital conflict, situations associated with separation or commitment, pregnancy, bereavement, or physical illness. Emotional pressures are usually high.

Once the panic reaction happens a few times, a type of learning called *conditioning* occurs, and the anxiety tends to happen more frequently in places associated with the panic attack. Obviously, the original panic situation maintains an intense anxiety reaction from the start.

WHO DEVELOPS AGORAPHOBIA?

Agoraphobia often develops in outgoing, social, but anxious and shy people who often feel they need others around to function. Dependency and perfectionism can be associated with agoraphobia.

One theory about the cause of agoraphobia is that through their experience victims have come to regard the world as a dangerous place. Many agoraphobics have had at least one agoraphobic parent, and many have had at least one parent who is somewhat fearful. In some cases, they received mixed messages from their parents; although they were encouraged to achieve, they were not well prepared to deal with the world, either because they were overprotected—taught that home is the only safe place—or underprotected—having to take on too much responsibility at an early age and just cover over their anxieties.

MORE ABOUT COMMON SYMPTOMS OF AGORAPHOBIA

A common characteristic of agoraphobia is a history of panic attacks in which individuals experience symptoms of extreme terror, distortion of perceptions, and an overwhelming sense of imminent catastrophe, loss of control, or fear or public humiliation. A tendency to experience more fear and a fear of the fear then develops in which individuals begin to experience anxiety in anticipation of panic reaction. They begin to avoid feared situations, and generalization quickly occurs to similar situations. They may fear that they will lose control over their own reactions and that their fear may lead to a panic attack. Some are afraid of fainting, having a heart attack, dying among strangers, screaming, attacking someone, or otherwise attracting unwanted attention and causing embarrassment. In any event, their imagination is extreme and vivid.

Other symptoms of the feelings in agoraphobia may include many physical sensations that accompany other anxiety states, such as dry mouth, sweating, rapid heartbeat, hyperventilation, faintness, and dizziness.

Situations that bring on anxiety in agoraphobia have common themes involving distance from home or other safe places, crowds, confinement, and feeling trapped. Crowds and confinement bring on these anxieties because the individual often feels trapped and cannot leave easily, for example, waiting on line for a bus or train or being in a crowded department store.

Some agoraphobics develop ways to live more comfortably with their disorder. For example, those who go to movie theaters or churches may be less frightened in an aisle seat so that they can make a fast exit if they experience a panic attack. Having a telephone nearby is another comfort.

PERCENTAGE OF AGORAPHOBIC PEOPLE REPORTING CERTAIN SITUATIONS THAT RELIEVE ANXIETY	
SITUATION	%
Being accompanied by spouse	85
Sitting near the door in a hall or restaurant	76
Focusing my mind on something else	63
Taking dog, baby carriage, etc.	62
Being accompanied by a friend	60
Talking problems over with my doctor	62
Talking problems over with a friend	62
"Talking sense" to myself	52

Reprinted from Ronald M. Doctor, Ph.D., and Ada P. Kahn, Ph.D., *Encyclopedia of Phobias, Fears, and Anxieties*, 2d ed. (New York: Facts On File, 2000).

AGORAPHOBICS MAY ALSO HAVE DEPRESSION

Many agoraphobics have episodes of depression. The first episode may occur within weeks or months of the first panic attack. Individuals complain of feeling "blue," crying having spells, feeling hopeless, being irritable, lacking interest in work, and having difficulty in sleeping. Agoraphobia is often aggravated during a depressive episode. The increased anxiety may make individuals less motivated to work hard at tasks (such as going out) that they previously did with difficulty.

It is most important to realize that agoraphobia is usually not the result of depression or of a depressive episode. To the contrary, depression is usually the result of the agoraphobia because agoraphobics are restricted by their fears, and therefore cannot do or be the way they want. It is depressing to be restricted, to have to lie and make excuses, and to constantly pull oneself together.

AGORAPHOBIA CAN AFFECT
SOCIAL FUNCTIONING AND MARRIAGE

When individuals tend to avoid situations that provoke fear, their lives become restricted to varying extents. For example, they give up visiting homes of friends, shopping, and accompanying children to school. They become fearful even when anticipating these situations.

Many agoraphobics become socially disabled because they cannot travel to work, visit friends, or shop. They may refuse invitations and often make excuses for not going out. Various adjustments are necessary to compensate for the phobic's lack of participation in family life and activities outside the home. Sometimes these fears are hidden from their children in the hopes of avoiding passing them on in some way.

In most research projects involving agoraphobics, spouses seem to be fairly well adjusted and integrated individuals. In some cases, therapists assess the individual's perception of his or her marriage before and after treatment. Questions relate to categories of marital and sexual adjustment, orgasmic frequency, work and social adjustment, and "warmth" items. When agoraphobia improves with treatment, marriages usually remain stable or improve.

Agoraphobia may strain a marriage because the phobic person may ask the spouse to take over any chores that require going out, such as shopping, picking up children, and doing errands, and because spouses often must fulfill social obligations without the companionship of their mates. Spouses are additionally stressed by having to be "on call" in case anxiety attacks occur that require communication or a trip home to soothe the agoraphobic. Thus a couple that may have been happy may be driven apart by the disorder, with each blaming the other for a lack of understanding. However, in cases where the agoraphobic has an understanding, patient, and loving spouse, this support can be an asset in overcoming the agoraphobic condition. The spouse can attend training sessions with the therapist, attend group therapy sessions, and act as the "understanding companion" when the agoraphobic is ready to venture out.

IS THERE A BIOLOGICAL BASIS FOR AGORAPHOBIA?

Many autonomic and biochemical changes occur during agoraphobic attacks; these changes may be similar to those experienced during anxiety, depression, and sudden fright. Spontaneous panics are accompanied by physical changes including increased heart rate and elevated blood pressure.

Panic attacks associated with agoraphobia may be more likely to occur if the individual has hypoglycemia or mitral valve prolapse (MVP). MVP, which is more common in women than in men, is usually a benign condition in which a defect in the shape of a mitral heart valve may cause a sudden rapid, irregular heartbeat. Some studies have shown a higher incidence of these conditions among agoraphobics, but there are indications that although hypoglycemia (which is clinically quite rare) and mitral valve prolapse can produce body sensations that the individual reacts to with catastrophic thoughts and anxiety, they cannot cause agoraphobia. Treatment for these conditions does not cure the agoraphobia.

WHAT TREATMENTS ARE USED FOR AGORAPHOBIA?

Often, several kinds of therapies are combined. Most treatments are exposure based; that is, the major component involves exposing the agoraphobic to situations that are frightening and are also commonly avoided to demonstrate that there is no actual danger. Treatment may include direct exposure, such as having the individual walk or drive away from a safe place or a safe person or enter a crowded shopping center, in a structured way. Indirect exposure is also used; this may involve use of films with fear-arousing cues.

Exposure behavioral therapy has been used increasingly to treat agoraphobics. Facing the fearful situation with appropriate reinforcement can help the individual undo the *learned* fear. Some therapists develop a "contract" with the phobic individual and set up specific goals for each week, such as walking one block from home, then two and three, taking a bus, and progressing after each session. Many therapists accompany the phobic individuals as they venture forth into public places, particularly in the early stages of treatment. In some cases, therapists train spouses or family members to accompany the phobic individual.

Modification of cognitive distortions—such as a tendency to catastrophize, futurize, and overgeneralize—is important for long-term success. This can accompany the exposure work. *Catastrophizing* involves interpreting situations (such as body sensation) as dangerous and threatening when in fact they are not. *Futurizing* is to create an idea about how things could or might be in the future and imagining being stuck in that horrible situation. *Overgeneralization* is to take one situation (e.g., the freeway was crowded) and then assume that it is always crowded and therefore needs to be avoided.

Another treatment consideration is assertiveness training. This can be useful because often emotional reactions are suppressed with agoraphobia and, particularly as individuals become more relaxed and make progress with exposure, emotions begin to emerge. The emotional self must be allowed to open if long-term progress is going to occur.

PHARMACOLOGICAL THERAPY

Prescription medication is sometimes useful for agoraphobics, particularly those who have panic attacks, and it enhances the results of exposure-based treatments for many individuals, at least initially. Drugs are often used for three to six months and then discontinued once the individual has some control over bodily sensations, anxiety, and cognition. The treatment of choice today for agoraphobia involves use of behavioral exposure therapy and judicious use of medication, with the latter withdrawn as progress is made in behavioral therapy.

Drugs used in the treatment of panic attacks associated with agoraphobia include the tricyclic antidepressants and the monamine-oxidase inhibitors (MAOIs), which are also used to treat severe depression; alprazolam, an antianxiety drug; and the SSRI (specific serotonin reuptake inhibitor) antidepressants such as Zoloft and Prozac. Drugs such as tricyclic antidepressants are successful in reducing panic attacks in many individuals. Some antianxiety agents, such as Klonapin, Xanax, and Librium, reduce anticipatory fear but can lead to abuse as individuals take increasing doses to prevent panic attacks. There are also difficulties withdrawing from this class of drugs.

WORST FEARS DURING A PANIC ATTACK IN PATIENTS WITH AGORAPHOBIA		
WORST FEARS	1ST FEAR (%)	2ND FEAR (%)
Death	13	20
Fainting/collapsing	38	16
Heart attack	4	4
Becoming mentally ill	6	6
Causing a scene	6	7
Inability to get home/to place of safety	6	26
Losing control (becoming hysterical)	7	9
Other personal illness	10	7

Source: Adapted from Ronald M. Doctor, Ph.D., and Ada P. Kahn, Ph.D., *The Encyclopedia of Phobias, Fears, and Anxieties*, 2d ed. (New York: Facts On File, 2000).

INVOLVEMENT OF SPOUSES AND FAMILY MEMBERS IN TREATMENT AND SELF-HELP

Including spouses and/or family members may produce more effective and long lasting improvement than treatment involving the agoraphobic alone. The reason for greater improvement may be the motivation for continued "practice" in facing feared situations both between sessions and after treatment has ended.

Some support groups encourage agoraphobics to go out together and offer each other mutual support. In this way, individuals share common experiences, learn coping tips, and have an additional social outlet. Some agoraphobics get together for outings, help take children to and from school, arrange programs, and retrain themselves out of their phobias.

PANIC DISORDER WITHOUT AGORAPHOBIA

Panic disorder itself is more common than panic with agoraphobia. The exposure therapy approach described in the agoraphobia section is used to desensitize the panicked person to sensitized situations that they either avoid or enter with anxiety. Relaxation training is essential. There is evidence that proper use of diaphragmatic breathing (to eliminate subclinical hyperventilation) is highly effective in reducing anxiety and prepanic states so that panic attacks are eliminated or reduced considerably. Exposure work can then be used to desensitize conditioned anxiety. Judicious use of antianxiety medications along with practice in exposure and cognitive control can enhance the speed of improvement.

CHAPTER 7

ANOTHER RELATED ANXIETY DISORDER: OBSESSIVE-COMPULSIVE DISORDER (OCD)

Larry S. is 29 years old and has had trouble keeping a job. He has been so late for work so many times that he has been repeatedly fired for tardiness and absence. Larry gets up early enough in the morning but keeps going back into his apartment to check and recheck that the windows are closed and locked and that the door is double locked. He leaves his house, gets into his car, and returns to the apartment repeatedly, sometimes dozens of times. This makes him late for a job. Now he is reluctant to interview for another job because he knows that he will probably be late to report for work at this job, too. Larry has other compulsions, as well. He is a perfectionist and keeps certain things in his bathroom cabinets in exactly the same order. If something is out of order, he rearranges and rearranges over and over again. Larry has been diagnosed with Obsessive-Compulsive Disorder.

We are all fairly careful about locking doors, closing windows and turning off coffeepots. What's the line between careful and compulsive? How do you recognize signs of compulsive behavior in yourself and others? How do you know when rituals take over your life?

The American Psychiatric Association, in the *Diagnostic and Statistical Manual of Mental Disorders, Fourth Edition,* defines obsessive-compulsive disorder as recurrent obsessions or compulsions that are severe enough to be time consuming or to cause marked distress or significant impairment.

Obsessions are intrusive, unwanted thoughts. They may lead to the carrying out of ritualized, compulsive acts to undo the obsession and reduce anxiety aroused by it. Such obsession-ritual relationships are called obsessive-compulsive disorder or OCD. OCD is classified as an anxiety disorder because the obsessions, compulsions, or rituals are efforts to reduce or avoid anxiety in the individual's life.

WHAT ARE OBSESSIONS?

Obsessions are persistent, recurrent, ideas, thoughts, or impulses that one experiences as intrusive, unwanted, and inappropriate. The individual usually recognizes that the obsessive thought comes from his or her own mind, not on suggestion from anyone else. Obsessions come into the mind involuntarily. In some rare cases, the obsession is fully believed. They are often senseless, worrisome, and sometimes repugnant ideas, thoughts, images, that involuntarily invade consciousness. The automatic nature of these recurrent thoughts makes them difficult for the individual to ignore. In technical terms, obsessions are called "overvalued" ideation, meaning that they are thoughts that occur automatically and intensely so that some action is needed to resolve them.

WHAT ARE COMPULSIONS?

A compulsion is a persistent, uncontrollable impulse to perform an irrational act, such as washing the hands 50 times a day. The act serves an unconscious purpose, such as warding off anxiety, avoiding unacceptable impulses, or relieving a sense of guilt.

Washing, checking, and counting are the most common compulsions among people with OCD. Other types of rituals relate to fastidiousness and perfection, such as cleaning the house, showering, repeating names or phrases, hoarding, avoiding objects or specific items, and performing tasks extremely slowly and repeatedly, and doubting oneself.

Common compulsions also include fear of contamination by dirt or germs, concern that a disaster will occur if a task has not been completely done, or fear of acting on an embarrassing sexual impulse or dangerous aggressive urge. However, the compulsive act is not connected in a realistic way with what it is designed to produce or prevent, and the act is usually clearly excessive. Interestingly, although the individual may recognize the senselessness of the behavior, he or she does not derive pleasure from carrying out the ritual. Further, individuals are often in another state of being while engaged in the ritual and find it difficult to stop the ritual washing, checking, or counting. Decision making is difficult during obsessional times and this often results in a marked slowing of behavior and doubtfulness and indecision.

In OCD, obsessions increase anxiety and impulses to escape from the unwanted thoughts, and rituals reduce anxiety and, therefore, reinforce the obsessive thoughts and allow some relief.

The individual may recognize that the obsessions or compulsions are excessive or unreasonable and may make efforts to resist them. However, resisting them brings about increasing anxiety that may be relieved only by yielding to the temptation. Shame often accompanies the ritualistic compulsive behavior, which leads to secrecy and privacy in order to hide these from others.

OBSESSIVE-COMPULSIVE SELF-TEST

Many individuals who have obsessive–compulsive symptoms have difficulty with some of the following activities. Answer each question by writing the appropriate number next to it.

0   No problem with activity—takes me same time as average person, I do not need to repeat or avoid it.

1   Activity takes me twice as long as most people, or I have to repeat it twice, or I tend to avoid it.

2   Activity takes me three times as long as most people, or I have to repeat it three or more times, or I usually avoid it.

A high total score indicates the severity of the disorder.

Score	Activity	Score	Activity
——	Having a bath or shower	——	Visiting a hospital
——	Washing hands and face	——	Turning lights and tapes on or off
——	Care of hair (e.g., washing, combing, brushing)	——	Locking or closing doors or windows
——	Brushing teeth	——	Using electrical apparatus (e.g., heaters)
——	Dressing and undressing	——	Doing arithmetic or accounts
——	Using toilet to urinate	——	Getting to work
——	Using toilet to defecate	——	Doing own work
——	Touching people or being touched	——	Writing
——	Handling waste or waste bins	——	Form filling
——	Washing clothing	——	Posting letters
——	Washing dishes	——	Reading
——	Handling or cooking food	——	Walking down the street
——	Cleaning the house	——	Traveling by bus, train or car
——	Keeping things tidy	——	Looking after children
——	Bed making	——	Eating in restaurants
——	Cleaning shoes	——	Going to cinemas or theaters
——	Touching door handles	——	Going to public places
——	Touching own genitals, petting, or sexual intercourse	——	Keeping appointments
——	Throwing things away	——	Looking at and talking to people
——	Buying things in shops		
= —— Total		= —— Total	

Source: From Ronald M. Doctor, Ph.D., and Ada P. Kahn, Ph.D., *Encyclopedia of Phobias, Fears, and Anxieties,* 2d ed. (New York: Facts On File, 1989).

WHO GETS OCD?

A tendency for OCD is partly genetic and partly the result of environmental factors. Personality traits of orderliness and cleanliness may be related to OCD. There may be a genetically determined personality factor that makes some prone to develop obsessive-compulsive behavior. Compulsions quickly develop around obsessions. Generally, obsessive-compulsives indicate by scores on questionnaires that they have wide ranges of emotional changes and tendencies toward long periods of high arousal. With high arousal, there is a tendency toward narrowing the span of attention, which may partially explain the obsessive-compulsive's focus on one tiny aspect of his or her environment. An ability to distinguish between what is safe and what is unsafe breaks down under high levels of arousal, and the individual views all situations as potentially unsafe. Hence, the environment seems unsafe, and safe areas (such as one's house or apartment) become refuges from the external world. It is often in making the transition from outside (unsafe) to inside (safe) that OCD intensifies.

A major factor involved in OCD is that obsessive-compulsives fear loss of control. The obsessive-compulsive seems to need structure and rigidity more than others. He or she usually checks, filters, and censors all incoming and outgoing stimuli. Obsessive-compulsives rarely drink alcohol excessively because they fear becoming out of control while under the influence. Further, they try to extend their sense of control to their immediate environment, and some try to force family and close friends into ritualistic patterns.

In addition to fearing loss of control, obsessive-compulsives fear uncertainty. They are constantly in doubt about how their behaviors will influence their environment and activities, and they constantly ask for reassurance from others. Because of the fear of uncertainty and the need for reassurance, they are somewhat resistant to any form of medication. When they medicate, they resist the effects of a drug that takes more effort in control, with the net result that they may become more, not less anxious.

OCD may come on suddenly, often beginning in early childhood, as early as around age eight to 10. About two-thirds of those who have OCD have developed symptoms by the time they are 25 years old. Some OCD sufferers experience a chronic waxing and waning course of their disorder, which means that at times their symptoms are more in control than at other times.

The disorder seems to be about twice as prevalent in the general population as panic disorder. This disorder may affect as many as 2.4 million Americans and is a cause for anxiety for the sufferer as well as family members, co-workers, and friends.

WHAT CAUSES OCD?

Scientists have suggested that there may be a biological factor contributing to obsessive-compulsive disorders. There is some suggestive evidence that there may be an imbalance in the frontal lobes of the brains of obsessive-compulsives that prevents the two brain regions from working together to channel and control incoming sensations and perceptions. This speculation occurred after Positron Emission Tomography (PET) scans were used on groups of obsessive-compulsives, depressives, and those with no diagnoses. PET scanning devices transform quantitative measures of metabolic activity through the brain into color-coded pictures. Metabolic rates in the forward portion of the frontal cortex were different in obsessive-compulsive individuals and individuals with serious forms of depression. However, since symptoms of severe depression, as well as anxiety, often occur among obsessive-compulsives, diagnosing the disorder with certainty can be difficult. Also, if these results are reliable, we don't know if they reflect a cause or by-product of the OCD. Further studies on the range of environmental and physiological origins of obsessive-compulsive disorder are under way.

One interesting byproduct of this research is that behavioral treatments for OCD lead to a balance of the frontal cortex. It appears that behavioral changes produce physiological and perhaps anatomical changes in the brain that lead toward more normal functioning.

HOW IS OCD TREATED?

Pharmacological Therapies

Pharmacological approaches include use of prescription medications for some individuals. Researchers have learned that medications that affect the serotonergic system (such as clomipramine and fluoxetine) can be useful in relieving symptoms in some individuals. However, no medication seems to make OCD go away.

When the class of drugs known as monoamine oxidase inhibitors (MAOIs) were developed during the 1960s, treatment for obsessive-compulsive disorder began to include them. Currently accepted first line treatments for OCD include pharmacological therapy with clomipramine, a tricycle antidepressant that inhibits serotonin reuptake, or with one of the selective serotonin reuptake inhibitors (SSRIs). Unfortunately, according to researchers, up to 40 percent of patients with OCD fail to derive satisfactory response from initial therapies, and a high percentage are reluctant to start or sustain medication plans.*

Furthermore, as mentioned before, many OCD sufferers either undermedicate, stop medications, or refuse medications, leaving the percentage of failure much higher. Even those who are helped are not cured by medications alone. It appears that behavior therapy is a necessary part of any successful treatment program.

---

*Source: *Challenges in Clinical Practice*, 1998, p. 201.

BEHAVIOR THERAPY FOR OCD		
TECHNIQUE	ACTION EXPERIENCED	ANTICIPATED EFFECT
Prevention of response	Individual gradually delays performing ritual for longer intervals.	Helps reduce compulsion.
Thought stopping	Individual tries to voluntarily interrupt obsessive thoughts.	Helps decrease obsessions.
Imagery	Individual is encouraged to imagine being exposed to feared situation and prevent an unwanted response.	Helps decrease obsessions and anxiety.
Modeling	Therapist actively models response.	Alters patient's unwanted behaviors to more acceptable ones.
Exposure	Individual is gradually exposed to the feared thought or object.	Reduces anxiety; decreases obsessions and compulsions.

Other medications used for OCD include the SSRIs (fluoxetine, fluvoxamine, Sertaline, and paroxetine). Augmentation strategies may include Clonazepam, neuroroleptics, or buspirone. Alternative monotherapies may involve clonazepam, MAOIs, or Buspirone.*

Studies have also been under way to determine the possible use of other tricyclic antidepressant medications in treating obsessional disorders. It may be that individuals who are treated and cured of a clinical or subclinical depressive illness will be able to reduce their ritualistic behavior.

Behavior Therapy

Behavior therapy became popular as a treatment during the early 1960s, and there have been many advances since then. Now, behavior therapy is one of the most effective treatments for OCD.

In the course of research with obsessive-compulsives, scientists have found many differences between subgroups of obsessional-compulsive individuals; for example, researchers noted that those who have checking rituals differ from those with washing rituals, and that they respond differently to treatment. Also, differences were found between those who display overt compulsive behaviors and those who do not show such ritualistic behavior.

---

*Source: *Challenges in Clinical Practice*, 1998, p. 201.

What occurs during a session of behavior therapy? The person is exposed to situations that cause extreme stress and anxiety and provoke compulsive behaviors. The individual is not allowed to go through the usually performed rituals, such as excessive hand-washing after handling money. This technique works well for people whose compulsions focus on situations that can be easily recreated; for those who follow compulsive rituals because they fear catastrophic events that cannot be recreated, individuals must rely more on imagination.

WHY BEHAVIORAL INTERVENTIONS CAN BE EFFECTIVE

With behavioral therapy, individuals can practice a series of exercises alone or with the assistance of family members. Education of patients and members of their families is an important first step toward success with behavior therapy. Self-help books and patient-run support organizations also can be valuable.

Some people are reluctant to begin behavior therapy. In such cases, the therapist will try to correct misconceptions or catastrophic thoughts that may underlie the patient's fear of attempting the therapy. The most common reason for failure of behavior therapy in OCD is noncompliance. Treatment should only be initiated with patients who are motivated to carry out the therapist's treatment recommendations. Additionally, patients must understand that behavior therapy will not magically eliminate their symptoms of OCD overnight. Instead, improvement is a gradual process requiring hard work on sequential goals. However, progress should be apparent in the first few hours of practice.*

Exposure therapy involves the patient confronting a situation that triggers obsessive thoughts and/or a compulsive ritual; for example, one who fears contamination from germs is exposed to touching water faucets or doorknobs (if he or she typically avoids these objects). In addition to exposure therapy, a technique known as response prevention or ritual prevention is used. In the case of the person who will not touch a water faucet, the response prevention requires that the person resist urges to wash his or her hands for at least one hour after exposure or maybe longer and also to resist performing any other rituals that might reduce the discomfort resulting from exposure. The goal is to teach one's body that the only aversive consequence is anxiety and that this can be tolerated, managed, and diminished. The body learns to relax on its own.

Another example is a person who hoards certain items. Such an individual may be asked to throw objects into a trash can (exposure) without performing rituals such as staring at, checking, or shredding these objects

---

Source: *Challenges in Clinical Practice,* 1998, p. 209.

either while they are being thrown away or afterward (response prevention). Individuals are told that when they repeatedly expose themselves to situations that they have avoided without performing rituals to make themselves feel better, they will gradually get used to them through the process of habituation.

HOW IMAGERY IS USED IN TREATMENT

Imagery is an important part of obsessive-compulsive disorder and its treatment. Commonly, there are obsessional images, compulsive images, disaster images, and disruptive images. The disaster image has been well suited for a habituation-training approach. The disaster image is a secondary event arising from an obsession or a compulsive urge and serves to increase the anxiety and distress of the individual. In many cases, content of disaster images is of future disasters and catastrophes. Habituation training to these images may prove to be helpful in treating individuals whose symptoms include this particular type of image. Researchers have found that with some individuals, imagined exposure to feared disasters, when used in combination with response prevention procedures, leads to better long-term outcomes. Perhaps the fears of these individuals are the same as or closely associated with the disaster images others have.

IS OCD RELATED TO DEPRESSION?

Depression and anxiety are sometimes associated with obsessive-compulsive disorder (and vice versa). You'll read more about depression in the next chapter. Some individuals experience only OCD; others suffer from both OCD and depression. The link between OCD and depression is borne out by laboratory tests on patients who have the two illnesses. For example, obsessive-compulsives, like some people who have depression, do not stop producing dexamethasone, a steroid naturally produced in the body, during a dexamethasone-suppression test. When the steroid is injected into the body, the body should stop producing dexamethasone on its own. OCD patients continue to make the steroid. Also, obsessive-compulsives, like depressed people, show an abnormal lapse in the time it takes between first falling asleep and the first dream, normally from one to two hours. When researchers looked at the immediate family members of people suffering from OCD, they found a high percentage had depression or manic-depressive disorder. Many OCD sufferers have symptoms associated with depression, such as guilt, indecisiveness, low self-esteem, anxiety, and exhaustion. There is also situational depression from not being able to engage freely in activities of one's choosing.

HOW LARRY S. BEGAN TO CHANGE HIS COMPULSIVE BEHAVIORS WITH THE THREE-STEP PROCESS

At the beginning of this chapter, you read about Larry and his compulsions to check and recheck his door locks, window locks, and other situations. He realized that unless he brought his anxieties and compulsions under control, he would not be able to hold onto a job. His savings were running out. He worked on the three steps by himself and also consulted a behavior therapist who helped him work out a plan for improvement.

How Larry Took Step 1: Identifying His Fears and Anxieties

Larry made a short list of some of the situations that he constantly rechecked: doors, window locks, bathroom cabinets. He began to understand that he even experienced some physical symptoms until he performed the rituals of rechecking each time. He noticed shallow breathing, perspiration, and sometimes even headaches. As he performed the ritual, the symptoms were alleviated but only for a minute, and then he would go back to his apartment again and recheck again.

Step 2: What Triggered Larry's Compulsions and Rituals?

Larry realized that during the rest of the day, if he ever got past leaving his apartment and getting into his car and driving away (without going back home again and again), he could function. So he decided to concentrate on the few things that held him back from getting ahead with his everyday life.

Step 3: Larry's Individualized Exposure Program

With the help of a therapist, Larry learned to understand that his habit of rechecking things was out of proportion to any danger and that, once things were securely locked, no unwanted consequences would occur. At first he permitted himself to check things only three times. Then only two times. Then just once, understanding that the doors were locked and that the windows were closed and locked. Everything was OK, he convinced himself. Finally he was able to drive away from the apartment building. While practicing this exercise many times, sometimes with the therapist, and sometimes alone, Larry also employed breathing techniques that helped him relax. He practiced the breathing and relaxation techniques throughout the day so that he could count on them helping in moments of anxiety, such as when he had the urge to recheck. Eventually he interviewed successfully and was able to begin a job that required arriving on time each morning.

Compulsive behaviors can be overcome. Don't let the anxieties of compulsions stand in your way. You can face your fears and beat them.

CHAPTER 8

SIDE EFFECTS OF FEARS AND ANXIETY: LOW SELF-ESTEEM AND DEPRESSION

Now you've read about fears, phobias, anxieties, generalized anxiety disorder, social phobias, specific phobias, panic attacks, agoraphobia, and obsessive-compulsive disorder. Over the long run, fears and anxieties can take a toll on one's physical and mental well-being. Any or all of these conditions can reduce one's self-esteem, cause considerable stress, lead to depression, and affect overall health, vulnerability to disease, and chronic disorders.

HOW FEARS AND ANXIETIES CAN AFFECT SELF-ESTEEM

Self-esteem means accepting oneself, liking oneself, and appreciating one's self-worth. Self-esteem is built on accomplishment; that is, we feel good about ourselves when we can perform, accomplish, and act in ways that we value and desire to be. Anxiety tends to rob people of initiative and ability to take fulfilling action. People who have social or specific phobias, suffer panic attacks, or are plagued by obsessions and compulsions often have low self-esteem because they know that fears are holding them back from enjoying life fully. They can't be the way they want to be, and they can't do the things they would like to be able to do. For example, if it takes hours of rituals before one can go to bed, self-esteem is diminished; or if social situations are horrifying and avoided, if one can't fly to vacation sites, or if driving is as scary as moving through a minefield, then self-esteem suffers. A high degree of self-esteem is a major characteristic of successful coping with the anxieties and the stresses of everyday life. Individuals with high self-esteem feel confident and capable and get closer to fulfilling their essence.

WHAT LEADS TO LOW SELF-ESTEEM?

Although causes of low self-esteem vary between individuals, there are many common themes. Some have low self-esteem because of certain fears or concerns about themselves. Some are concerned about their physical appearance, for example, individuals who are overweight; this can be overcome by seeking counseling regarding a diet and exercise program. Some have prominent facial features, such as a misshapen nose or ear; with counseling and possibly cosmetic surgery, improvements can be made in both appearance and outlook.

Abuse is another common cause. Having been abused as a child, either sexually or psychologically, or being an abused spouse, or in a codependent relationship can have a lasting effect on a person's self-esteem. A sense of being violated develops in which intimacy is often shunned and personal worth and satisfaction are diminished.

Simple comments and criticism by teachers can cause anxiety for a child and lower self-esteem. For example, a child told that he or she cannot sing well and should just mouth the words may lose confidence in ever trying to sing again and actually develop a fear of being heard singing. A high school student who is criticized because of a tendency to stutter may become fearful of standing up and speaking in front of a crowd. In many cases, low self-esteem can lead to the anxieties of social fears and phobias. Almost anything that disrupts, colors, inhibits, or interferes with one's performance will affect self-esteem. This makes it all the more important to successfully deal with anxieties. There is a payoff in the end of improved self-esteem as well as with improved functioning!

FEARS, ANXIETIES, LOW SELF-ESTEEM, AND DEPRESSION

Fears, anxieties, and low self-esteem can and do lead to depression. Depression refers to a mood or affective disorder characterized by a wide range of symptoms including anxiety, hopelessness, helplessness, anxiety, personal devaluation, extreme sadness, and withdrawal from others. The person suffering from depression may be lethargic or agitated, lose appetite, or eat compulsively but shares this sense of sadness and hopelessness. There is usually an inability to concentrate or make decisions, exaggerated guilt feelings, a loss of sexual desire, and in serious cases, thoughts about suicide. *Help is necessary and help is available.*

Some depressed people are so disabled by their condition that they cannot call a friend or relative or seek medical help. If another person calls a doctor for them, they may refuse to go because they do not believe that they can be helped. Many depressed persons will not follow a doctor's advice and may refuse help and comfort. *Persistence on the part of family and friends is essential.*

UNDERSTANDING DEPRESSION

The term *depression* applies to a condition on a continuum of severity. We all feel "down in the dumps," or "blue" at times. Those feelings are at one end of the continuum. A clinical depression is at the other end. Depression can be a temporary mood fluctuation, a symptom associated with a number of mental and physical disorders, or a clinical syndrome encompassing many symptoms.

Clinical depression refers to a depression that lasts for more than a few weeks or includes symptoms that interfere with the ability to deal with everyday decisions and routine situations.

Seasonal mood disorder (seasonal affective disorder). Some individuals have mood symptoms related to changes of season, with depression occurring most frequently during winter months and improvement occurring in the spring. Many of these individuals experience periods of increased energy, productivity, and even euphoria in the spring and summer months.

WHEN DOES DEPRESSION BEGIN?

People of all ages can become depressed, although major depressive episodes peak at age 55–70 in men and at age 20–45 in women. About 20 percent of major depressions last two or more years, with an average of eight months. About half of those experiencing a major depression will have a recurrence within two years.

Some individuals may have only one episode of clinical depression during their lifetime; others have episodes that are separated by several years or suffer clusters of episodes over a short time span. Between episodes, such individuals function normally. However, 20 to 35 percent of sufferers have chronic depression that prevents them from functioning totally efficiently. For these people, depression is a recurrent disorder that may require maintenance on medication to prevent additional episodes.

ARE CAUSES OF DEPRESSION KNOWN?

Many factors can lead to depression, including a family history of depression, psychosocial stressors, diseases, alcohol, drugs, and anxiety disorders.

Psychosocial Factors

Depression can come from an individual's lack of confidence in his or her interpersonal skills, overdependency on others, the low self-esteem syndrome described above, perfectionism, unrealistic expectations, and psychosocial events, such as death of a spouse, loss of a job, and, for some, just the anxieties produced by urban living.

SIGNS AND SYMPTOMS OF DEPRESSION IN ADULTS

Psychological

- Loss of interest
- Unexplained anxiety
- Inappropriate feelings of guilt
- Loss of self-esteem
- Worthlessness
- Hopelessness
- Thoughts of death and suicide
- Tearfulness, irritability, brooding

Physical

- Headache, vague aches and pains
- Changes in appetite and changes in weight

- Sleep disturbances
- Loss of energy
- Psychomotor agitation or retardation
- Loss of libido
- Gastrointestinal disturbances

Intellectual

- Slowed thinking
- Indecisiveness
- Poor concentration
- Impaired memory

Environmental Influences

Researchers view depression as the result of interaction of environmental and biological factors. Historically, depression has been viewed as either internally caused (endogenous depression) or externally related to environmental events (exogenous or reactional influences). Major changes in the individual's environment, such as a move or job change, or any major loss, such as a divorce or death of a loved one, can bring on depression. Feeling depressed in response to these changes is normal, but when depression lasts for more than one month and interferes with effective functioning, treatment can be helpful.

Illness

Anxieties caused by serious illness can lead to depression. For example, depression may occur after one receives a diagnosis of a terminal disease. Also, certain illnesses that affect cerebral functioning and impair blood flow to the brain can produce depression. Such illnesses may include adrenal cortex, thyroid, and parathyroid dysfunctions, and many neurologic, metabolic, and nutritional disorders, as well as infectious diseases. Some medications can cause depression.

Social Learning Theory

Anxieties and fears can disrupt involvement with others, resulting in less-positive reinforcement, which in turn leads to more negative self-evaluation and a poor outlook for the future. Depressed people view themselves from their depressed state of being; this leads to a further sense of low self-worth, feelings of rejection, alienation, dependency, helplessness, and hopelessness. In social learning terms, activity and social contact reestablish reinforcers. Cognitive changes are an essential ingredient to moving out of the depressed state.

Cognitive Theory

Unrecognized negative attitudes toward oneself, the future, and the world can result in feelings of failure, helplessness, and depression. Especially under anxiety, such attitudes may activate a prolonged and deepening depressive state. Depressed people view events in their world in terms of failure and rejection, filled with loss and pessimism and helplessness. These are exaggerated beliefs and feelings. In cognitive therapy, depression is considered a cognitive problem not an emotional problem and is caused by negative thoughts that produce self-defeating emotions. Aaron Beck, a psychiatrist who has specialized in cognitive therapy, has identified 10 common cognitive distortions associated with depression. These are:

1. All-or none thinking (If it's not perfect, I am a failure.)
2. Overgeneralization (where a single negative event is seen as a never-ending pattern of defeat)
3. Mental filtering (seeing and dwelling on one small negative aspect)
4. Disqualification and discounting of the positive
5. Interpreting events as negative without evidence of such (for example, assuming you know what people are thinking)
6. Magnifying, catastrophizing, or minimizing one's positive qualities or accomplishments
7. Emotional reasoning (assuming that your negative emotions reflect reality)
8. "Should" statements that produce shame, guilt, and anger and are often unrealistic demands
9. Attaching negative labels to self and others (for example, "I'm a loser")
10. Personalization (seeing oneself as responsible for things that others are responsible for)

Modification of any of these distorted forms of thinking is important for relieving depression and preventing further occurrences.

Interpersonal Theory

This theory emphasizes the importance of social connections for effective functioning. An individual develops adaptive responses to the psychosocial environment at an early age. When early attachment bonds are disrupted or impaired, the individual may be vulnerable later on to depression. Social support is also essential to recovery from any of the disorders we have described.

Genetic Factors

Some individuals may be biologically predisposed to develop depression, based on genetic factors that researchers continue to investigate. There are genetic markers that indicate susceptibility to manic-depressive illness, and there has been considerable research at the end of the 20th century focused on understanding biochemical reactions influenced by these genes. There is some evidence that depression runs in families; among more severe depressives, family is a more significant factor. But remember that we don't inherit depression; we may inherit the biological mechanisms that can lead to depression, given the environmental conditions and lack of proper coping skills.

Neurotransmitter Theory

Research indicates that people who have depression have imbalances of neurotransmitters, natural biochemicals that enable brain cells to communicate with each another. Biochemicals that often are out of balance in depressed people include serotonin, norepinephrine, and dopamine. An imbalance of serotonin may cause anxiety, sleep problems, and irritability. An inadequate supply of norepinephrine, which regulates alertness and arousal, may contribute to fatigue and lack of motivation. Dopamine imbalances may relate to a loss of sexual interest and inability to experience pleasure.

There is, however, a "chicken-and-egg" problem here in that biochemical changes may just reflect the depression (state-related) or one's biochemistry may predispose them to develop depression (trait theory). From what we know and the fact that 80 percent of depressive episodes will diminish by themselves, depression is more a state problem and, for some, can have trait factors associated with it.

HOW PSYCHOTHERAPIES CAN HELP WITH DEPRESSION

Most depressed people can be effectively treated with a variety of types of therapies. In general, therapists use "talk" treatment to try to understand the individual's personal and social relationships that may have led to or contributed to the depression. Depression, in turn, may make these relationships more stressful.

Behavior and Cognitive Therapy

These therapies are based on the understanding that people's emotions are controlled by their views and opinions of themselves and their world. Empirically, these are the most effective forms of treatment for depression. Medication may accelerate improvement, but the focus on cognitive and behavioral changes is the essential ingredient in effective treatment. Therapists use techniques of talk therapy to help the individual replace negative beliefs and thought patterns. Behavioral changes such as increasing activity levels, exercise, and improvement in interpersonal functioning are also necessary.

Psychoanalysis

Treatment of depression with psychoanalysis is based on the theory that depression results from past conflicts that are pushed into the unconscious. In this therapy, loss is the primary cause of depression, and its roots stem back to childhood conflicts and traumas. Understanding childhood factors in the development of any disorder can be helpful and can give the person a sense of continuity and choice, but ultimately changes must occur in the present and this is the realm of the behavior therapies.

PHARMACEUTICAL APPROACH TO TREATING DEPRESSION

If psychotherapy is not helpful, or if the depression is so severe that one cannot work or function, or if there are ideas of suicide for one to three months, medications may be needed to accelerate the lifting of the depression in conjunction with an appropriate therapy.

How medications work depends on each individual's overall health, metabolism, and other unique characteristics. Results are usually not evident right away; antidepressant medications usually become fully effective in about 10 to 20 days after the individual begins to take them.

Here's a very brief overview of some of the major types of medications used to treat depression. They are tricyclic antidepressants, MAO inhibitors (MAOIs), lithium, and newer antidepressants, known as specific serotonin uptake inhibitors (SSRIs).

Tricyclic Antidepressants

These are often prescribed for individuals whose depressions are marked by feelings of hopelessness, helplessness, fatigue, inability to experience pleasure, and loss of appetite and resulting weight loss.

Monoamine Oxidase Inhibitors (MAOIs)

MAOIs are often prescribed for individuals whose depressions are characterized by anxiety, phobic and obsessive-compulsive symptoms, increased appetite and excessive sleepiness, or those who fail to improve on other antidepressant medications.

Lithium

Lithium is sometimes prescribed for people who have manic-depressive illness (a severe affective disorder characterized by a predominant mood of elation or depression, and in some cases an alternation between the two states). Sometimes it is prescribed for people who suffer from depression without mania.

Newer Antidepressants

During the 1980s and 1990s, more specifically active antidepressant drugs with fewer side effects were developed. Serotonin reuptake inhibitors (SRIs)—for example, fluoxetine (Prozac) and sertraline—are one class; buproprion (Wellbutrin) is another.

DEPRESSION IN ADOLESCENTS

Depression in teenagers may be somewhat different from that in adults. Teenagers may be depressed because of social fears or being in trouble. Their depression is sometimes linked to poor school performance, truancy, delinquency, alcohol and drug abuse, disobedience, self-destructive behavior, sexual promiscuity, rebelliousness, grief, and running away. Low performance in school can lead to a feeling of rejection, social expectations may be unrealistic, and conflicting messages from family may magnify their struggles for independence and assertiveness. They may feel a lack of support from family and other significant people and a decrease in their ability to cope effectively.

SELF-HELP FOR DEPRESSED INDIVIDUALS
AND THEIR FAMILIES

Self-help and support groups give individuals of all ages opportunities to share ideas for effective coping and self-care. Benefits of these groups include increasing contacts with other people, for example, participation in special interest groups, learning to cope with fears and exaggerated thoughts, and the following of regular exercise programs.

The National Depressive and Manic-Depressive Association is a national self-help organization with chapters throughout the country that meet locally to help members cope effectively with depression. (See Resources.)

The Depression and Related Affective Disorders Association (DRADA) is a nonprofit organization focusing on manic depressive illness and depression. DRADA helps organize support groups and provides leadership training programs and consultation for those groups. (See Resources.)

You'll read more about how anxieties and stress in your life can interfere with your good health in the next chapter. In the final chapter, you'll be asked to review the three steps outlined earlier in this book. You'll develop more understanding of the mind-body connection in overcoming fears and phobias, and have more of a basis for deciding on self-help or getting professional help.

Personal attitudes about one's efficacy or ability to take initiative, make changes, and seek positive outcomes develop early in life. Often, low self-esteem is associated with this belief. Change seems out of reach. Motivation is low and feelings of despair appear. Depression is often the emotional tone or expression of these beliefs. Fortunately, even small amounts of progress can help to change one's perception of self-efficacy and lift the depressive mood.

RECOGNIZING DEPRESSION IN ADOLESCENTS

- Sadness; feelings of helplessness or hopelessness
- Poor self-esteem and loss of confidence
- Overreaction to criticism
- Extreme fluctuations between boredom and talkativeness
- Sleep disturbances
- Anger, rage, and verbal sarcasm; guilt
- Intense ambivalence between dependence and independence
- Feelings of emptiness in life
- Restlessness and agitation
- Pessimism about the future
- Refusal to work in school or cooperate in general
- Increased or decreased appetite; severe weight gain or loss
- Death wishes, suicidal thoughts, suicide attempts

CHAPTER 9

OVERCOME FEARS AND
REDUCE STRESS IN YOUR LIFE

Stress is the most common underlying factor in the development of anxiety disorders; that is, the anxiety disorders usually develop under conditions of stress. Stress makes you vulnerable to experience anxiety, and once anxiety occurs, it quickly becomes attached to the situation that surrounds it.

Controlling stress is essential for wellness because continued exposure can lead to such symptoms as anxiety, headaches or more serious conditions, including high blood pressure and depression. But stress also makes it difficult to overcome the anxiety disorders. Successful treatment for anxiety requires, first, dealing with stressors in one's life. Research has shown that stress also affects the immune system and causes it to be less efficient in fighting off diseases.

UNDERSTANDING STRESS

Stress is an internal response to circumstances known as *stressors*. Stressors may be internal situations, such as your own fears, phobias, and feelings of insecurity or frustration, or external events, such as a bad review at work or cancellation of an airplane flight.

Stressors can also be reactions to happy events as well as to bad news and unhappy events; there are good stressors, derived from satisfying personal and professional events, as well as unpleasant ones. For example, happy personal stressors may include getting married, having a baby, or moving to a new house; happy work stressors may include landing a new job or being promoted. Stress caused by unpleasant effects has been termed *dis-stress*. Both types of stress cause physiological responses, including activation of the nervous system and of the "fight or flight" response. That is why during periods of anxiety or other stressful times, people may notice that they have faster heartbeats and sick feelings in their stomachs; it is difficult to work or function efficiently at such times. When negative stress (*dis*-tress) produces wear and tear on the body, positive stress or positive arousal can improve physiological functioning (for example, the immune system) and motivate or energize us toward taking action.

Chronic negative stress results in ongoing wear and tear on your body's organs and systems, making them more susceptible to illness. According to Herbert Benson, M.D., Harvard cardiologist and author of *The Relaxation Response,* more than 80 percent of visits to physicians' offices may result from stress in patients' lives. Physicians are aware of stress as a factor in diagnosing and treating many common health concerns. For example, many people seek help for gastrointestinal symptoms, an inability to sleep, headaches, and fatigue. Often, these are not symptoms of a disease but the byproducts of stress in their lives. The best treatment is to get at the cause of the stress. Physical problems, even if induced by stress, can interfere with the quality of one's work and the ability to meet the needs of family members.

SOURCES OF STRESS

Stress can come from one's own attitudes and perceptions, an individual's family, the workplace, or community connections. Stress within a family causes anxieties, tension and difficulties in communicating effectively. There may be intergenerational conflicts or situations arising from assisting elderly parents. In some cases, interpersonal anxieties and stresses develop when an adolescent has two simultaneous feelings, such as wanting to be independent during puberty and yet feeling dependent on parents. In a family, several people may be trying to cope with their own anxieties as well as the anxieties of others about whom they care; for example, when a father dies, the son tries to console his mother, even when struggling with his own sadness.

Stress that starts within the family can affect one's work; the reverse is also true. Family problems can make a person irritable on the job, distrustful of co-workers, and prone to make mistakes and get into accidents; likewise, a difficult day at the office can make a person short-tempered and hostile at home. Workplace factors that contribute to stress include lack of autonomy, lack of satisfaction, feeling bored, discriminated against, poor communication, bureaucracy, role conflicts, and feeling underpaid or overworked.

Many people feel stressed by demands made on them from their community or religious activities. Although these activities may add to one's social support system, some individuals take on too may responsibilities, feel that there is not enough time to accomplish their goals, and are asked to take on even more. Already feeling overwhelmed but wishing to maintain their reputation as a "doer," they agree. Learning when to say "no" is an important skill to practice.

Although stress can be physiologically devastating to many people, others find that stress actually raises their energy level and helps them focus their mind better on their work, family, or social activities. Some thrive on many kinds of stressors, such as competition and comparison with others. People who do are often attracted to high-stress occupations and professions or do well at competitive games and sports.

LEARNING TO MANAGE STRESS

Stressors cannot be eliminated, so our goal should be to control and manage stress. It is possible to neutralize the toxic effects of unrelenting stress. People who cope well with stress put their personal and professional lives into perspective. They learn to prioritize tasks and assignments. They may experience a constantly high level of pressure and unrealistic demands at work but develop their own ideals of conduct and test themselves by their own standards. They are able to prioritize their work and to enjoy family life as well as their chosen recreational activities.

Experiencing stress is part of human nature. In his book, *Why Zebras Don't Get Ulcers,* Robert M. Sapolsky looks at how wild animals process stress and explains what humans can learn from them. "The key thing with humans is, we're all going to have a bit of stress response. It's part of life." Sapolsky goes on, "Three minutes or three hours (of stress response) is no problem, but do it chronically, and you're up a creek. The stress response increases blood pressure, which can led to a stroke. It also shuts down digestion, which can lead to ulcers."

In explaining why zebras don't get ulcers, Sapolsky said: "Because they don't have computers, they don't worry about mortgages, blind dates, or Social Security. They worry about lions, and with lions, it's all taken care of in three minutes, or it's all over in three minutes. No stress."

RELIEVING STRESS: AN INDIVIDUAL MATTER

Avenues toward relieving stress are personal matters. However, if you are faced with an anxiety disorder or a mood disorder, dealing with stress in your life may be an essential prerequisite to overcoming the anxiety or mood problem. Many people find that regular physical workouts involving running, walking, exercising in a gym or a health club, or using gymnastic equipment at home helps them overcome their reactions to today's events and get ready to face tomorrow's challenges effectively. Using muscles is a way to use up some of the "fight or flight" readiness in the body. Exercise is also a very important activity while working on anxiety disorders because exercise not only helps process excess adrenaline but also helps you feel better, be less sensitized to body sensations that could trigger anxiety, and aids in self-confidence and willingness to face difficult issues and situations.

RECOGNIZE SIGNALS OF STRESS

Each person has unique sources of stress, as well as personal signals of stress. Sources of stress come from within oneself (personal), from family life, from the workplace, and from community activities. Some common sources of stress and personal signals are listed below.

SOURCES OF STRESS

Individual stressors

- Aging
- Feeling unattractive or insecure
- Achievement or success problems
- Change in habits
- Relationship concerns
- Inability to pay bills; mortgage worries

Family stressors

- Death, illness, or injury of a family member
- Divorce; remarriage
- Marital difficulties; sexual difficulties
- Holidays, vacations
- Problems with children
- Young adult leaving home or returning home
- Lack of privacy
- Not enough time

Workplace/community stressors

- Difficulties with boss or co-workers
- Threatened layoffs
- Boredom; not enough work
- Overwork; underpayment
- Lack of autonomy
- Automation in the workplace

Personal signals of stress

- Irritability or bad temper
- Headaches; stomachaches; digestive problems
- Inability to sleep
- Grinding teeth
- High blood pressure
- Lethargy; inability to work; finger-tapping
- Depression; panic or anxiety
- Fatigue; restlessness; accident proneness
- Sexual difficulties

A healthy diet with three meals a day is a basis for wellness and can also help prevent and relieve stress. Well-balanced meals provide a slow release of necessary nutrients throughout the day. For some people, too much caffeine causes additional stress by bringing on symptoms of anxiety. Crash diets or fad diets can lead to anxiety, depression, and an inability to maintain an appropriate weight. Acceptance of one's body image and a sense of good self-esteem may encourage maintainence of good nutrition as well as good health. The best antianxiety diet includes a large amount of protein, low sugar and refined carbohydrate intake, and the elimination of stimulants.

Hobbies help many people combat stress. Participating in an activity simply for the enjoyment of it reduces stress levels. Such hobbies may include playing a musical instrument, dancing, art and painting, sewing, building model trains or planes, or bird watching. Choices of hobbies are as diverse as human nature. Hobbies can help one focus the mind on tasks other than anxiety, worry, and self-devaluation.

A social support system is important, too. Many people find relief from stress in talking with their support groups. When they are able to talk about their issues, problems, and concerns and get feedback from trusted, objective family and friends, people receive an enlightened perspective that often helps them to lighten their stress load. *Recovery requires social support.*

WHAT IS STRESS MANAGEMENT?

Stress management refers to one's personal coping skills for dealing with stress. It also refers to a multibillion-dollar industry that includes programs, products, services, and techniques to help people reduce stress on an individual or group basis. For example, stress management programs offer help to people interested in overcoming stress-related disorders ranging from eating disorders to issues of self-esteem. Programs may include use of many alternative or complementary therapies.

All stress management approaches involve learning to relax. Learning to relax is an active process, more than just reducing sources of stimulation. Remember: the three types of relaxation are progressive muscle relaxation (for somatic/muscle tension), breathing (for autonomic arousal reduction), and mediation (for mental control). All three should be mastered for better functioning and as a prerequisite for resolving anxiety problems.

COMPLEMENTARY THERAPIES FOR STRESS RELIEF

Complementary or alternative therapies are a set of practices that may complement or compete with conventional medicine in the prevention and treatment of stress-related disorders as well as other diseases.

CHECKLIST: COPING WITH STRESS

- Identify external stress-producing factors over which you may have little or no control, such as on your job.
- Identify internal factors such as perfectionism and unrealistic self-expectations.
- Recognize your personal signs of stress, such as:

  Increased irritability with family members or co-workers

  Headaches; stomachaches; digestive disorders

  Overeating; increased alcohol consumption

  Sleeplessness; chronic fatigue

  Depression; feelings of hopelessness
- Separate your problems at home from your work concerns, and vice versa.
- Consider what you are saying to yourself that leads to exaggerated reactions. Often these are "have to," "must," or "should" statements.
- Be realistic in your daily outlook; don't expect too much of yourself or others.
- Prioritize your responsibilities; learn to say "no" occasionally to requests that you consider unreasonable or undoable.
- Pay attention to a healthy lifestyle, such as eating a well-balanced diet and exercising.
- Reduce your consumption of caffeinated beverages; cut down on coffee, tea, and cola, which can increase your heart rate and your irritability level.
- Develop a regular habit of exercising; a 20-minute walk each day can be effective in fighting muscle tension.
- Develop a sense of humor; increase your ability to see humor in sometimes intolerable situations.
- Learn some relaxation techniques that work for you, such as deep breathing or listening to your favorite music.
- Seek professional help if you feel overwhelmed.

People use many complementary therapies to relieve stress as well as anxieties. These include acupuncture, guided imagery, meditation, progressive muscle relaxation, and yoga. Some use massage therapy or listening to music as stress relievers. However, what allows one person to relax may actually cause stress for another. An example is noise level in the workplace or at home: Each individual should try to create an environment in which to work and live that is the least stressful to focus on reaching his or her peak performance and a feeling of well-being.

According to David Edelberg, M.D., writing in *The Internist* (September 1994), alternative medicine commonly refers to anything that historically has not been conventionally practiced or taught in medical school (although this trend began to change toward the end of the 1990s). In

1994, there were more than 200 fields of alternative medicine. Alternative fields can be divided into four broad categories: Traditional medicine, such as Chinese or Native American; hands-on bodywork; psychological or psychospiritual medicine; and many holdovers from the 19th century, such as chiropractic medicine and homeopathy.

Conventional medical practitioners adhere to scientific models and methodologies that many alternative medical practitioners believe focus too exclusively on reductionist and physiochemical explanations of biological phenomena. Proponents of alternative medicine suggest that this approach has limited understanding of health and disease and, in particular, of interactions between mind-body connections and the psychological, social, and biological factors that influence coping and adaptation to change.

Advocates of alternative approaches, in recent decades known also as holistic (or wholistic medicine), or complementary medicine, regard the influence of psychological factors and cognitive processes as equal to if not more powerful than the insights and methods of conventional medicine in coping with anxieties, stress, and disease and improving outcomes.

Keep in mind that alternative therapies are not subject to scientific scrutiny through controlled efficacy studies with placebo or comparisons of treatments. They are accepted and promoted as helping on the basis of "anecdotal evidence" stemming from individual reports of success. Some may be truly helpful; others may be useless or ineffectual with their use based on enthusiasm and strong belief.

Many individuals find relief of anxiety concerns from one or more or combinations of alternative therapies either along with or after seeking traditional care. However, as with other medical conditions, seriously troubled individuals should not overlook traditional mental-health treatments in favor of alternative therapies because they may be robbing themselves of valuable time as their condition progresses.

DECIDING ON COMPLEMENTARY THERAPIES

Individuals who decide to begin a complementary therapy should let their physician know what they are doing. The physician will need to take the effects of that treatment into account when evaluating care. Be wary of claims that a treatment works miracles. Watch out for contentions from proponents of a treatment that the medical community is trying to keep their "cure" a secret from the public. Also, be wary of any demands by the practitioner that an alternative treatment be substituted for a currently accepted practice. According to *Harvard Women's Health Watch* (June 1994), although there may be little harm in adding an alternative practice such as meditation or massage therapy to a therapeutic regimen, replacing a valid treatment with one that has no proven efficacy may have serious consequences.

Watch out for claims that the treatment is better than approved reme-dies just because it is "natural." Recently, the word *natural* has acquired a popular mystique. Natural products are not necessarily more benign than agents synthesized in a laboratory. A drug is any substance that alters the structure or function of the body, regardless of its source. Remember also that many plants contain toxic substances that can be harmful when taken in uncontrolled doses or in combination with other medications.

RELIEVING STRESS IN YOUR LIFE

Practice whatever stress-relieving techniques work for you. Understand that your fears and anxieties are sources of stress. Recognize your per-sonal signals of stress. Find new ways to cope with stress, such as being realistic about expectations of yourself and others, separating your home and work concerns, and following a healthy lifestyle that includes a good diet and time for exercise. You *can* manage stress.

In the final chapter of this book, you'll read more about the mind/body connection for overcoming fears and anxieties and your good health. You'll learn more about how what you think and the emotions you feel affect your body and your physical health.

CHAPTER 10

FACING FEARS:
THE MIND/BODY CONNECTION
AND FEELING BETTER

You've learned a good deal more about fears and phobias, anxiety and its manifestations, how stress works in your life, and how all of this can interfere with your good health.

Let's review the Three-Step Process and how to use it:

Identify your fears through a process of self-diagnosis.

Pinpoint what triggers your fears.

Develop an individualized exposure program.

Perhaps you've already started to use the three-step process to help you face your own fears. You may have overcome the resistance to making changes necessary to face your fears. You may be involved in the process of change and already see improvements. In using this book, you may want to review chapters to reinforce what you've already learned or to help a loved one cope with fears and anxieties. In any event, you should be congratulated for getting this far! Review of appropriate chapters will help reinforce your efforts. Keep up the good work!

Now we want to discuss the mind/body connection because understanding it will help you continue your plan of action. We also want to discuss finding the right therapist in case you need additional support and information.

WHAT'S THE MIND/BODY CONNECTION?

You've probably noticed that when you feel anxious, you feel certain physical sensations. Your body affects your mind; your mind affects your body. Research studies have demonstrated that psychological as well as physical stress has an effect on health. There are links between the brain and other organ systems, and vice versa. Increasingly, physicians are recognizing that behavioral therapies and complementary therapies such as relaxation training, biofeedback, and hypnotherapy are useful adjuncts in the comprehensive care of many people, many of whom have anxiety-related disorders.

The term *mind/body medicine* relates to a variety of treatments and approaches ranging from meditation and relaxation training to social support groups planned to engage the mind in improving physical as well as emotional well-being; in other words, our thoughts, beliefs, personalities, and attitudes have a profound influence on recovery and on the maintenance of anxiety.

According to Herbert Benson, M.D., author of *The Relaxation Response,* too often in the practice of modern medicine, the mind and body are considered to be separate and distinct, though it has become clear that they are not separate but one entity. Because of specialization, patients are no longer treated as whole persons. The body or physical being was considered autonomous and separate from the nonphysical mental, emotional, and psychological aspects of functioning, the latter being the subject matter of psychology. In fact, proper treatment has to include the whole person.

Many conditions have been found to respond to techniques used alone or in combination with standard medical and surgical treatments. These conditions include high blood pressure, coronary artery disease, cancer, chronic pain, temporomandibular joint syndrome (TMJ), headaches, eczema, psoriasis, irritable bowel syndrome, arthritis, rheumatic diseases, asthma, and diabetes. We hope you can see why we emphasized the body/physical aspects (such as diet, exercise, relaxation, etc.) along with the psychic/mental aspects (beliefs, cognition, resistance, etc.) in our Three-Step Process.

ADVANTAGES OF MIND/BODY PRACTICES

- They can be used along with standard medical practices.
- Financial cost of procedures is low.
- Physical and emotional risk is minimal; potential benefit is great.
- Many can be taught by paraprofessionals.
- There are no high-tech interventions.
- They may improve quality of life by reducing pain and symptoms for people who suffer from chronic diseases.
- They may help control or reverse certain underlying disease processes.
- They may help prevent disease from developing.

WHEN PROFESSIONAL HELP MAY BE NECESSARY

You know yourself better than anyone else knows you. That's why you are in the best position to decide whether you should pursue a course of self-help for your fears and anxieties or need professional help.

If you should decide that working with the three-step plan just isn't enough for you, professional assistance is available. Those who seek professional help to overcome effects of fears should not consider themselves weak. Seeking help is an intelligent way of using available tools to increase one's level of functioning. Counseling can assist in dealing with life situations requiring the input of a noninvolved, knowledgeable person. Death of a close relative or friend, divorce or remarriage, marital difficulties, sexual problems, or illness of one's own or a family member are common anxiety-producing occurrences. Financial problems, such as facing a large mortgage or accumulated bills, can happen to anyone. Individuals faced with these and other serious life stressors may feel out of control and that their worlds are caving in around them.

If you find yourself feeling totally overwhelmed and decide to seek professional help, how should you select a therapist and choose from a myriad of therapies? You may want to talk with a close relative, colleague, or friend who has experienced psychotherapy. However, if the issue of confidentiality is important to you, find a mental health professional or social worker in a hospital or community agency who can help direct you.

The therapist should be a person you like and respect and have values similar to yours; should understand and have treated your particular fears, anxieties, and stressors; should be active and behaviorally knowledgeable; should be open, communicative, and willing to provide direction; and should also be available by phone in case you need to make contact. Find a therapist who is multifaceted in his or her approach to problems and knowledgeable about many options available to treat particular problems. Look for one who is open to consulting with other professionals who have additional expertise.

CHOOSING A TYPE OF PSYCHOTHERAPY
AND A PSYCHOTHERAPIST

Psychotherapy refers to treatment of mental and emotional concerns by psychological methods. In psychotherapy, a therapeutic relationship between the patient and a therapist (psychotherapist) is established. The relationship focuses on the patient's symptoms. Patterns of behavior—anxiety reactions, mood swings, low self-esteem, and not being able to deal with stress—can benefit from this interaction between patient and therapist.

Do you need a medically trained physician? A psychiatrist? Guidelines for selecting a psychologist include:

The end of the stressful problem in sight, but the individual just can't get there by him- or herself.

The individual realizes that symptoms are of short duration and that the stress that brought the symptoms on can be identified.

Broad-based knowledge is necessary.

Knowledge of psychological principles (such as learning theory, social learning theory, and cognitive psychology) are necessary.

Experience with problems in living are needed.

Relationship factors contribute to the problem and must be dealt with.

The client does not want to use medications and would prefer to carry the responsibility for change himself or herself.

The client is looking specifically for a behavior therapist or a cognitive behavior therapist.

However, there are some reasons why a psychiatrist might be preferable:

MDs are the only mental health therapists who can prescribe medications.

For certain emotional illnesses, medications may be helpful.

The individual has incapacitating or debilitating symptoms that require hospital care.

The individual has other concurrent medical problems for which care and medications are being received.

There is a history of mental illness in the family—other family members may have been hospitalized for mental illness, or the individual him- or herself may require hospitalization for a mental problem.

GROUP THERAPY

Group therapy is treatment of emotional or psychological problems in groups of patients or in self-help support groups led by a mental health professional. Such groups attract individuals with similar concerns. For example, groups may work with recently widowed persons, divorced people, parents who have lost a child, or those concerned with obesity.

Please keep in mind, however, that unstructured groups are not helpful for anxiety problems. They tend to stir up anxiety and do not provide methods for alleviation. It is best to find a group program that is directed toward recovery, has a specific plan, helps you develop skills for anxiety reduction and elimination, and provides positive support.

GEROPSYCHIATRY

This is a specialized form of mental health care that addresses the complexities involved between mental and physical illness in the elderly. For example, an elderly patient who might appear to have mental symptoms may be experiencing symptoms of toxicity resulting from taking two or more incompatible drugs. Physicians specializing in geropsychiatry are located in community hospitals where they can provide a safe and secure environment and offer psychological evaluation in conjunction with medical testing and liaison services for elderly patients being treated for medical or surgical conditions.

FAMILY THERAPY

Family therapy is a form of psychotherapy that focuses on the family unit, or at least on the parent and child (in single-parent families). It is based on the theory that an individual who is troubled usually is seen in isolation from the family unit. Family members become aware of how they deal with each other and are encouraged to communicate more openly with each other.

Family therapy usually focuses on here-and-now anxieties and stresses and practical solutions. Family therapy might best be considered an adjunctive therapy because it does not deal directly with the anxiety problem. It can be helpful when at least one member has a relatively serious problem such as recurrent depression or needs ongoing assistance in coping with outbursts of anger and emotional withdrawal.

FACING FEARS

Now that you know more about facing fearful situations and about the help that is available, take charge. Now that you understand the connection between your mind and body, use that knowledge to help you overcome your fears.

You've learned how to self-diagnose the type of fears you have, to identify triggers for your fears, and to work systematically toward reducing those fears. Use the self-check charts in this book. Review the charts that list symptoms of anxiety and stress. See how your symptoms improve over time. Review the case histories; you may recognize some of your own anxieties in the brief stories about others.

If you are the spouse or parent of a fearful person, this book can help you understand what your loved one is facing, and the book can help you make choices between self-help and obtaining professional help to advance further in self-control. But remember: The Three-Step Process can be used in conjunction with professional therapy.

You can face your fears and take control of your life.

PART II

ENTRIES
A TO Z

acceptance The therapist displays a favorable attitude toward the phobic or anxious individual under treatment and conveys an implicit respect and regard for each client as an individual, without necessarily implying either approval of behavior or an emotional attachment toward the client. Acceptance has been defined as "valuing or prizing all aspects of the client including the parts that are hateful to himself or appear wrong in the eyes of society." The term *acceptance* is used interchangeably with UNCONDITIONAL POSITIVE REGARD by client-centered therapists. This nonjudgmental condition is seen as a necessary quality in any therapy.

accidents, fear of Those who fear having accidents fear behaving in any way that might result in injury to themselves or to other persons or in damage to property or the environment. Accident phobics associate certain factors with accidents and tend to avoid them: risky jobs, atmospheric conditions, a tiring work schedule, equipment failure, and the like. They also are fearful of personal factors such as inattention, errors of perception, risk taking, and decision making. Fear of accidents is related to a fear of decision making and a fear of errors. Some people who fear accidents also fear injury to themselves.

acculturation, fear of This process is associated with increased anxieties and fears. In situations where there are linguistic or cultural communication barriers or where an individual's expectations are not congruent with what takes place, anxieties can be heightened. The anxieties of the immigration experience is compounded particularly for individuals whose future residency status is in question.

Behavioral changes may include increasing alcohol and tobacco consumption, following immigration. When different family members become accustomed to the new culture at different rates, conflicts can arise between the generations, adding to the overall anxiety.

Increasingly, physicians are seeing immigrant patients from ethnic backgrounds that do not use the Western medical model. Some of these patients see Western medicine as one of many healing systems. Cultural expectations can cause anxieties for both physicians and patients.

acrophobia A fear of heights; also known as hypsosophobia, acrophobia is one of the commonest phobias in the general population. Treatment commonly involves exposure therapy in which graded exposure to heights is made while in a state of relative relaxation. For example, a person might start exposure with looking out the second-floor window until relaxation or comfort is achieved and then move on to third and subsequent floors in the same manner. In severe cases, a therapist or a trained support person may be necessary.

Acrophobics fear being on high floors of buildings or on the tops of hills or mountains, usually feel anxious approaching the edge of precipices such as BRIDGES, rooftops, stairwells, railings, and overlooks, and usually fear falling and being injured. Some feel and fear an uncontrollable urge to jump and may have fantasies and physical sensations of falling even when on firm ground.

Fear of elevators, escalators, balconies, and stairways are related to a fear of heights, as is sometimes a fear of flying or falling. In severe cases, the individual cannot even stand on the lower steps of a ladder without experiencing some anxiety. Often, fear of driving on freeways or highways has an acrophobic component in that these roadways are often elevated.

acupressure   Sometimes referred to as ACUPUNCTURE without needles, acupressure embraces the same concepts of energy flow and point stimulation as the original science but uses the pressure of the therapist's fingers for point stimulation. Used by many people for relief of physical symptoms as well as anxieties, acupressure is thought to combine the science of acupuncture with the power of the healing touch and has been most widely used for pain control.

In Oriental medicine, acupressure is helpful in conditions where the body's energy balance has been upset by a variety of physical and/or emotional stresses. Because it is an extremely gentle technique, acupressure is sometimes used by individuals who are fearful of needles.

acupuncture   This technique is used to relieve anxieties as well as pain. Acupuncture has been used for thousands of years as a component of Chinese medicine and is based on the theories about the body's "vital energy" (Chi), which is said to circulate through "meridians" along the surfaces of the body. The ancient theory holds that illness and disease result from imbalances in vital energy that can be remedied when therapy is applied to "acupuncture points" located along the meridians. The goal of acupuncture is to rebalance the flow of energy, promoting health and preventing future imbalance. The points are believed to have certain electrical properties, which, when stimulated, can alter chemical neurotransmitters in the body and bring about a healing response. Practitioners of acupuncture insert hair-thin stainless steel needles into body surfaces at acupuncture points. People who have needle phobias may find the procedure difficult to face.

In addition to reduction of anxieties and relaxation, acupuncture has been used to relieve osteoporosis, asthma, back pain, painful menstrual cycles, and migraine headaches.

addiction, fear of   Fear of dependence on a chemical substance can reach the extent that one establishes a physiologic need for it. Alcohol, tobacco, caffeine, narcotics, and some sedatives—many of which are prescribed by physicians for the treatment of anxiety—may produce addiction. Some individuals fear addiction and that their bodies will develop a physiological craving for the prescribed substance; thus, when the substance is removed or withdrawn, he or she develops withdrawal symptoms. Addiction is a physiological condition but has important psychological and social consequences. Some individuals fear that they may become so totally involved in their addiction that they might neglect or harm other people; others fear the loss of control implied by addiction.

Addiction to antianxiety medications is not a craving but is expressed in withdrawal reactions. Psychologic dependencies often occur. Even after discontinuing a medication, patients may carry the drug with them wherever they go (along with water, gum, and other soteria) because the mere possession of the drug is comforting.

adrenaline   The adrenaline hormone is secreted by the central, or medullary, portion of the adrenal glands that produce an increase in heart rate, a rise in blood pressure, and a contraction of abdominal blood vessels (often leading to "butterflies"). Anxiety and panic are the subjective reactions to these changes. These sympathetic changes can be reversed by activation of the parasympathetic system.

adverse drug reactions   Adverse drug reactions can be physical or mental reactions; they occur after self-administration of a drug and/or use of a drug for therapeutic purposes. How an individual reacts to drugs depends on many factors, including genetic susceptibility, general health, allergies, attitude in taking the drugs, medical history, tolerance to bodily changes, and other drugs or foods the individual has consumed. An example of an adverse drug reaction is extremely high blood pressure as a result of the combination of a drug in the monoamine oxidase (MAO) inhibitors category with wines, cheese, or other foods that contain tyramines. Adverse drug reactions may range from mild stomachaches to heart attacks, seizures, hallucinations, and even death. When one receives a presciption for any drug as part of therapy to help deal with a phobia or anxiety, one should ask the physician about any possible adverse reactions.

affective disorders   Affective disorders are also known as MOOD disorders and are often associated with anxiety. Affective disorders are so named because they involve changes in *affect*, a term that is roughly equivalent to emotion, or mood. In this disorders group, the individual experiences mood disturbances intense enough to warrant professional attention. An individual who has an affective, or mood, disorder may have feelings of extreme sadness or intense, unrealistic elation with disturbances in mood that are not due to any other physical or mental disorder. Some mood disorders have been thought to be related to ANXIETY; for example, AGORAPHOBIA is sometimes associated with depression, which may be a reaction to the demoralization that accompanies the phobic's feelings of incompetence, ineffectualness, and loss of self-respect. Some agoraphobics may feel disappointed and hopeless about themselves and are aware of their fearful dependency on their spouses or significant others. However, as phobics gain more mastery over their problems during the course of treatment, the depression that accompanies agoraphobia usually improves.

Mood disorders differ from thought disorders; schizophrenic and paranoid disorders are predominantly disturbances of thought, although individuals who have those disorders may also have some distortion of affect. A disorder of the thought processes is not a common feature in affective disorders; however, if the disorder reaches extreme intensity, there may be a change in thought pattern, but the change in thought will correspond to the extremes of emotion that the person is experiencing.

Affective disorders have been known throughout history. There are descriptions of mood disorders in the early writings of the Egyptians, the Greeks, the Hebrews, and the Chinese and in the works of Shakespeare, Dostoyevsky, Poe, and Hemingway. Many historical figures have suffered from recurrent depression, including Moses, Rousseau, Dostoyevsky, Queen Victoria, Lincoln, Tchaikovsky, and Freud.

Bipolar disorders and depressive disorders sometimes occur according to a seasonal pattern, with a regular cyclic relationship between the onset of the mood episodes and particular 60-day periods of the year.

A mood syndrome (depressive or manic) is a group of associated symptoms that occur together for a short duration; for example, *major depressive syndrome* is defined as a depressed mood or loss of interest of at least two weeks' duration, accompanied by several associated symptoms, such as weight loss and difficulty concentrating.

A mood episode (major depressive, manic, or hypomanic) is a mood syndrome that is not due to a known organic factor and is not part of a nonmood psychotic disorder such as schizophrenia, schizoaffective disorder, or delusional disorder. A mood disorder is diagnosed by the pattern of mood episodes; for example, the psychiatric diagnosis of major depression is made when there have been one or more major depressive episodes without a history of a manic or unequivocal hypomanic episode.

Manic episodes   Individuals who have manic episodes have distinct periods during which the predominant mood is either elevated, expansive, or irritable. They may have inflated self-esteem, decreased need for sleep, accelerated and loud speech, flight of ideas, risk taking, distractibility, grandiose delusions, or flamboyancy. The disturbance may cause marked impairment in their working or social activities or relationships; an episode may require hospitalization to prevent harm to themselves or others. They may experience rapid shifts of mood, with sudden changes to anger or depression.

The mean age for the onset of manic episodes is in the early 20s, but many new cases appear after age 50.

Hypomanic episodes   These mood disturbances are not severe enough to cause marked impairment in social or work activities or to require hospital care.

Major depressive episodes   Individuals who experience a major depressive episode have either depressed mood (in children or adolescents, irritable mood) or loss of interest or pleasure in all, or almost all, activities for at least two weeks. Their symptoms are persistent in that they occur for most of the day, nearly every day, during at least a two-week period. Associated symptoms may include appetite disturbance; change in weight; sleep disturbance; decreased energy; feelings of worthlessness or excessive or inappropriate guilt; difficulty concentrating; restlessness, such as an inability to sit still, pacing, hand-wringing, pulling or rubbing of hair; and recurrent thoughts of death or of attempting suicide. The average age of onset of depressive episodes is in the late 20s, but a major depressive episode may begin at any age. They are more common among females than among men.

Bipolar disorders   Bipolar disorders (episodes of mania and depression) are equally common in males and females and seem to occur at much higher rates in first-degree biologic relatives of people with bipolar disorder than in the general population.

Cyclothymia   This condition is characterized by numerous periods of hypomanic episodes and numerous periods of depressed mood or loss of interest or pleasure that are not severe enough to meet the criteria for a major depressive episode.

Dysthymia   This history of a depressed mood of at least two years' duration is not severe enough to meet the criteria for a major depressive episode.

aggression   A general term for a variety of hurtful or destructive behaviors that appear outside the range of what is socially and culturally acceptable, *anxiety* is often the outcome to the victim of aggressive acts. Fear of violence, aggression, or even confrontation are common triggers to anxiety.

Aggression includes extreme self-assertiveness, social dominance to the point of producing resentment in others, and a tendency toward hostility. Individuals who show aggression may do so for many reasons, including frustration, as a compensatory mechanism for low SELF-ESTEEM, lack of affection, hormonal changes, or illness. Aggression may be motivated by fears, anger, overcompetitiveness or may be directed toward harming or defeating others.

An individual with aggressive personality may behave unpredictably at times; for example, such an individual may argue inappropriately with friends or members of the family and may harangue them angrily. He or she may write letters of an angry nature to government officials or others with whom he or she has some quarrel.

The opposite of aggression is passivity.

The term *passive aggression* relates to behavior that seems to be compliant but where "errors, mistakes, or accidents" for which no direct responsibility is assumed results in difficulties or harm to others. Patterns of behaviors such as making "mistakes" that harm others is considered "passive aggressive." ("Gee, I'm sorry, I didn't mean to ruin all your work.")

agoraphobia   Agoraphobia, an anxiety disorder, is a stressful and complex syndrome characterized by extreme anxiety about being in places or situations from which escape might be difficult or embarrassing or in which help may not be available in the event of having a panic attack (see PANIC, PANIC ATTACKS, AND PANIC DISORDER). Agoraphobics have a fear that help will be unavailable in the event of development of embarrassing or incapacitating symptoms, such as dizziness or illness. This disorder involves fear of losing control of oneself, as in fainting or "going crazy."

ailurophobia   A fear of cats, this term is derived from the Greek word *ailouros*, meaning "cat." Fear of cats is also known as aelurophobia, galeophobia, gatophobia, and cat phobia. In its most intense form, this phobia may cause one to become virtually homebound or confined due to fear of encountering a cat in the street or even seeing one from a vehicle. The term *ailurophobia* also refers to a dread of being scratched or bitten in the genital area. Shakespeare grasps the cat phobic reaction in *The Merchant of Venice* when he says: "Some men there are love not a gaping pig; some, that are mad if they behold a cat."

alcoholism   Alcoholism is a physiological and psychological dependence on alcohol. Some fearful and anxious people become dependent on alcohol for relief of their symptoms. Because it exerts both mental and physical effects, alcohol becomes a major part of the dependent person's life. Many agoraphobics become alcoholics as a way of coping with their fears; because agoraphobic individuals do not go out, it is fairly easy for them to conceal their habit.

Factors that lead many individuals to alcohol dependence include fears, personality, environment, and the addictive nature of the drug alcohol. Many people become dependent on alcohol for relief of symptoms ranging from loneliness to ANXIETY and panic attacks (see PANIC, PANIC ATTACKS, AND PANIC DISORDERS.).

alone, fear of being   Fear of being alone is known as phobophobia and eremophobia. Fear of being alone sometimes relates to AGORAPHOBIA. Another term for the dread of solitude used by American physician and author Benjamin Rush (1745–1813) was *solo phobia*.

alprazolam   This is a generic name for a pharmaceutical produced marketed as Xanax. It is in a class of drugs known as triazolobenzodiazepine compounds with antianxiety and sedative-hypnotic actions. It is efficacious in agoraphobia and panic disorders and is also used to treat generalized anxiety disorder. Studies suggest that alprazolam also has antidepressant activity.

altophobia   Altophobia is a fear of heights.

Alzheimer's disease   A progressive, irreversible, neurological disorder, the development of this disease is feared by many people as they age. People who have Alzheimer's disease sufferers in their families cope with the anxieties of caregiving as well as the fears involved in watching the disease advance. Sufferers notice advancing stages of the disease often with increasing anxiety and fear.

The disease was named in 1907 by Alois Alzheimer (1864–1915) after diagnosing a 51-year-old patient. Although there is no cure (in the late 1990s), there are many research projects underway worldwide, and researchers increasingly understand more about the disease.

ambivalence   The simultaneous existence of two sometimes contradictory feelings, attitudes, values, goals, or directions, this term was introduced by Swiss psychiatrist Eugen Bleuler (1857–1939), to denote the simultaneous occurrence of two antagonistic emotions, such as hatred and love toward the same person or inclination and disinclination toward the same activity or goal. For example, some individuals have feelings of ambivalence toward parents who dole out both love and affection as well as punishment. Some individuals are ambivalent about work, marriage, and other major life issues. Ambivalence is common in PHOBIAS, including AGORAPHOBIA, as there is often a simultaneous approach-avoidance attitude toward potentially fearful situations.

amnesia, fear of   Fear of having amnesia is known as amnesiophobia. Amnesia is an inability to recall past experiences, or loss of memory. There are two basic types of amnesia that people fear: anterograde amnesia, or an inability to form new memories, in which the individual either does not consolidate what is perceived into permanent memory storage or cannot retrieve recent memories from storage; and retrograde amnesia, which is a loss of memory of events that occurred before the memory disturbance began. Episodic amnesia refers to a particular event or period in one's life that is forgotten. The episode may have been a significant one that may have led to the development of one or more phobias or anxieties. The fear of amnesia is now commonly related to the development of Alzheimer's disease.

amphetamines   Amphetamines, popularly referred to as speed, include dextroamphetamines, methamphetamines, and methylphenidates. Amphetamines are sometimes prescribed for depression and to give the user a sense of well-being and increased alertness. They are sometimes abused by individuals who have depression or anxieties and should be prescribed only for a limited time and for a specific purpose. All drugs in this group are associated with dependence, and all can produce one or more organic mental disorders, intoxication, delirium, delusional syndrome, or withdrawal syndrome. These drugs also act as appetite suppressants. Because of the possibility of developing dependency on amphetamines, many physicians have stopped prescribing them.

anger   An intense and basic emotional state in which one feels a high level of displeasure, frustration, and stress, anger's spectrum may range from slight irritation to explosive hostility. Anger is a source of energy that is discharged on others, objects, or oneself. Anger and anxiety are incompatible; anger is often used to counteract anxiety.

An individual who expresses extreme anxieties and angry feelings might be given three goals: first, to identify the feelings of anger, second, to use constructive release of the energy of anger through assertiveness or appropriate physical expression, and third, to identify thoughts and thought processes that lead to anger; for example, to identify feelings of anger, one might keep a diary of angry feelings and learn to recognize anger before losing control. The individual will learn to take responsibility for his or her own emotions and to stop blaming others for arousing the anger. In learning to use constructive release of the energy of anger, the individual may benefit from assertiveness training and may learn to express anger verbally to the appropriate source. Assertive techniques will help the individual increase feelings of self-esteem, demonstrate internal control over behavior, and harness energy generated by the anger in a nondestructive manner.

Anger can be tied to anxiety in that some people feel anxious whenever they begin to become angry and become distracted into anxiety, never really learning to express their feelings through appropriate assertive behavior.

Anger suppression is common in agoraphobia and responsible expression or assertion is usually part of the healing process.

angst   Loosely, anxiety, angst is a major concept of the existentialist approach to psychology which tries to understand the essence of human existence by emphasizing basic human values such as love, free will, and self-awareness. The word *angst* is derived from the German term meaning "fear, anxiety, anguish." U.S. psychoanalyst Rollo May (1909–   ) described angst as "the inward state of my becoming aware that my existence can become lost, that I can lose myself and my world, that I can become nothing." ANXIETY strikes at the center of an individual's existence, whereas fear, in contrast, is a threat to the periphery of physical survival.

anorexia nervosa   See EATING DISORDERS.

anniversary reaction   An anniversary reaction includes feelings of anxiety or other symptoms that arise around the anniversary of a significant event such as a divorce or the death of a family member or close friend. The reaction brings anxieties because it may involve the recall and reliving of the events. Some individuals experience dreams or minor illness at the same time each year. Anniversary reactions are often common when an individual has experienced a traumatic event.

anorgasmia (anorgasmy)   Anorgasmia is the inability to achieve orgasm or the absence of the orgasmic phase in the sexual reaction cycle. Anorgasmia may be caused by fears about sexual intercourse, incompatible sexual attitudes in the partners, anatomical and neurophysiological defects, fear of painful intercourse, or sociocultural conditioning.

antianxiety drugs   Used to reduce anxiety and tension, antianxiety drugs are prescribed to individuals during times of stress and in treatment of anxiety-related physical disorders under the supervision of a physician.

anxiety The word *anxiety* derives from a Greek root meaning "to press tight" or "to strangle." The Latin word *anxius* and its derivatives imply narrowness and constriction, usually with discomfort. Those words denoted distress, disquiet, and sadness rather than the uncertainty and fear denoted by the contemporary English word *anxious*.

Anxiety is an unpleasant feeling of generalized fear and apprehension, often of an unknown origin, accompanied by physiological symptoms; it may be triggered by the anticipation of danger, either from thoughts (internal) or from one's environmental (external).

Anxiety and fear have similarities and differences. Fear is sometimes defined as a response to a consciously recognized and usually external threat; in a general way, it *is* a response to a clear and present danger, whereas anxiety is a response to a situation, object, or person that the individual has come to fear through learning and experience. Anxiety, as noted by Danish existentialist philosopher Søren Kierkegaard (1813–55), is the full experience of fear in the absence of a known threat. In both fear and anxiety, however, the body mobilizes itself to meet the threat, and certain physiological phenomena occur. Muscles become tense, breathing is faster, the heart beats more rapidly, and there may be sweating or diarrhea. There may be shakiness, increased breathing and heart rate, and acute sensitivity to environmental stimuli (for example, an intense startle reaction). Some individuals may focus their anxiety on an object, situation, or activity about which they are phobic; for others, general or unknown stimuli may trigger what is known as free-floating anxiety. Some individuals may experience a sudden onset of anxiety and notice physical symptoms such as gastrointestinal upset, weakness, and faintness as precursors to a panic attack. Phobic anxiety is the anxiety that occurs only in contact with a particular situation or object.

anxiety attack The sudden onset of acute anxiety, sometimes starting with pounding of the heart, difficulty in breathing, excessive perspiration, and dizziness, anxiety attacks always begin in response to a stimulus that may be a bodily sensation, something seen or heard, a thought, or the imagining of any of these stimuli. Anxiety attacks are triggered by different stimuli for each individual, and each individual will show a different response to an anxiety attack; however, in most cases the main response systems at work are the cognitive (thought processes), the autonomic, and the muscular. In some individuals, an anxiety attack develops into a full-scale panic attack in which one experiences unbearable tension, fear of suffocation, and a feeling that one may die or that some unnamable disaster is going to occur.

anxiety drugs   Some individuals who have anxieties, fears, and phobias are advised by their physicians to take medication commonly known as anxiety drugs, antianxiety drugs, or anxiolytic drugs (anxiolytics). Usually these are prescribed in combination with some form of psychotherapy or exposure treatment. Use of the drugs usually makes the individual more receptive to the "talking therapy" that is used in many forms of psychotherapy and particularly to exposure therapy, which is effective in counteracting many forms of phobias.

Many drugs fall into the category of anxiety drugs. One widely used class of drugs is the BENZODIAZEPINES. The generic name of these drugs ends in *-pam*. Examples are diazepam (Valium®), ALPRAZOLAM (Xanax®), lorazepam, and exazepam. They usually begin to act within a half-hour and may reduce anxieties for a few hours. As the drug gradually passes out of one's body, anxiety is likely to return if its cause continues. Benzodiazepines are used to help individuals over a temporary circumstance that brings on anxiety. They are usually less helpful for chronic anxiety, and there is some risk of dependence on them. These drugs do not improve (on a lasting basis) phobias or compulsive rituals; exposure therapy is the recommended treatment. High doses of benzodiazepines may interfere with exposure therapy if the medications are taken up to four hours before or during exposure sessions. The chief side effects of these drugs are drowsiness, possibly confusion, and dependence if one takes them regularly for more than a few days. Use of benzodiazepines must be decreased slowly over days, weeks, or months, depending on how long one has been taking them.

Antidepressants are also sometimes referred to as anxiety drugs. Some individuals may not respond to one or more antidepressant drugs, and physicians will try one or more before setting up a regular regimen for an individual. Antidepressants fall into two broad classes. The first class is tricyclic antidepressants; examples are imipramine (Tofranil), amitriptyline (Tryptizol), doxepine (Sinequan), and dothiepin (Prothiaden). Chief side effects are drowsiness and dizziness, which improves after a few days, and dry mouth, blurred vision, constipation, and difficulty urinating. The second class is monoamine oxidase inhibitors (MAOIs); examples of these drugs include phenelzine (Nardil), isocarboxazid (Marplan), and tranlycypromine (Parnate). Individuals who take MAOIs must exclude certain foods from their diet. These foods contain tryptamine, a substance present in most cheeses, yeast extract, and alcohol. Use of these foods along with the drugs may cause a sudden, dangerous, rise in blood pressure.

Antidepressants, unlike benzodiazepines, may take up to three weeks before having a full effect. They may have to be taken regularly for many months (or years). When stopping the drugs, relapses are common.

Antidepressant drugs are useful for individuals who are anxious as well as depressed. Many phobics and ritualizers also experience moods of depression. Unlike benzodiazepines, high doses of antidepressants do not interfere with exposure therapy.

Beta-blockers are another group of drugs sometimes used to reduce some of the physical features of anxiety such as rapid heartbeat and palpitations. Commonly used drugs of this type include propranolol (Inderal), atenolol (Tenormin), and oxprenolol (Trasicor). Side effects may include drowsiness and dizziness.

anxiogenic   This term denotes drugs, substances, or activities that tend to raise anxiety levels. For example, in studies of panic disorder with or without agoraphobia, anxiety has been raised by caffeine, yohimbine, sodium lactate, or isoproterenol infusion; carbon dioxide inhalation; HYPERVENTILATION; and exercise. Certain stimuli, such as the sight of a dog (if one is dog phobic) or looking down from the top of a tall building (if one has a phobia of heights), may be anxiogenic.

apiphobia (or apiophobia)   Apiphobia is the fear of bees.

aquaphobia   Fear of water is termed *aquaphobia*.

arachnophobia (arachnephobia)   A fear of spiders, the word *arachnophobia* is derived from the Greek word *arachne*, meaning "spider." Also known as arachneophobia and spider phobia, it appears that spider fears may be a prepared fear. American psychologist Donald Kleinknecht (1942–   ), for example, found that of 71 spider-phobic people none had experienced direct fearful exposure but that 61 percent had become afraid through vicarious sources.

aromatherapy   Aromatherapy is the art and science of using essential oils from plant and flowers to reduce anxieties and enhance health. Practitioners of aromatherapy blend essential oils from around the world based on one's current physical, bioenergetic, and emotional condition and apply them with a specialized massage technique focusing on the nervous and lymphatic system. Aromatherapy massage has been used to treat conditions ranging from job anxieties, muscle soreness, acne, varicose veins, allergies, and other emotional conditions.

arrhythmia   Arrhythmia is an abnormal heart rhythm, usually detected by an electrocardiogram. When some individuals hear this diagnosis, they became anxious and find it a source of fear. It may or may not be of potential significance, and understanding its significance can relieve subsequent anxieties. Arrhythmias can be caused by several factors, such as coronary artery disease, heart valve problems, or hyperthyroidism. Individuals with this diagnosis should question their physician carefully about possible lifestyle changes, as well as possible need for medication.

assertiveness training   A behavior therapy technique in which individuals learn how to express both positive and negative feelings with other people responsibly and with a minimum of passivity, aggression, or guilt, assertiveness training is helpful in treating some agoraphobics, social phobics, speech phobias, and individuals with other phobias because it focuses on emotional expression which is incompatible with anxiety.

atelophobia   Fear of imperfection is termed *atelophobia*.

attention deficit and hyperactivity disorder (ADHD)   Attention deficit and hyperactivity disorder (ADHD) is a chronic condition that affects 7 percent of the population, more commonly in boys. Children who have ADHD are usually overactive, have symptoms of anxiety and impulsiveness, and are easily distracted. The disorder is usually noticed before age five. When ADHD is untreated in childhood, some children have behavioral and substance abuse problems later in life. The disorder causes anxieties for the parents and teachers because of the child's continuing complicated behavior.

Symptoms of ADHD are often accompanied by other problems, such as learning disabilities (although most of these children have normal intelligence), aggressive behavior, poor sleeping habits, and "difficult" temperaments. Some specialists believe that ADHD may have a genetic base. It was previously thought that the disorder was a result of brain damage.

Treatment includes medication and social skills therapy for the child, training for the parent, and recommendations for the teacher. Medical and psychological treatment can alleviate many of the symptoms. Stimulants, the most common medication for children with ADHD, act on the control mechanisms of the brain to normalize behavior and help the child sustain attention.

atychiphobia   Fear of failure is termed atychiphobia.

authority, fear of   Many individuals fear authority, some because the individual loses autonomy and feels dominated, and others when it loses its sense of legitimacy and becomes associated with coercion. Authority figures or groups within the family or government are feared when they are out of touch with the needs of their subordinates. A power structure that is opposed to social needs generally produces fear rather than cooperation and respect. A clash between two authority figures (e.g., two parents) is also disruptive and disturbing.

autogenic training   A form of psychotherapy that uses both body and mind to treat anxieties and other mental problems, autogenic training, which originated in Germany in the early 20th century, is a self-help as well as a therapeutic technique. It involves a variety of breathing and relaxation exercises and exploration of the subconscious, with or without the help of a therapist.

autohypnosis   This form of self-hypnosis is sometimes used with anxiety reactions to promote relaxation on cue in fearful situations. In general, autohypnosis by itself will not significantly relieve anxiety responses. It can, however, be used as a supplement to behavioral therapy to make images more vivid and to heighten one's ability to concentrate.

autoimmune disease   Autoimmune diseases are a diverse group of disorders in which the immune system mistakes parts of its own body for the enemy, causing symptoms that can lead to anxieties, fears, and symptoms of debilitating and long-term disease.

The main characteristic of these disorders is inflammation that varies from the merely irritating to the potentially deadly, as in diabetes. For example, in Type I diabetes, the immune system has damaged the body's insulin-producing capabilities.

Resulting autoimmune diseases can be either systemwide or specific to a particular body part. Rheumatoid arthritis and systemic lupus erythematosus are also autoimmune diseases.

autonomic nervous system   This part of the nervous system regulates involuntary functions and activates endocrine glands, smooth muscle, breathing, and heart muscle. The autonomic nervous system (ANS) is involved in the physiological changes that are part of expression and emotion; anxiety reactions are primarily those of the ANS. Increases in heart rate, perspiration on the face and palms of the hands, muscle tension, dry mouth, and queasy stomach result from activation of the ANS. Relaxation and calm reflect another side of the ANS.

The part of the ANS known as the sympathetic nervous system (SNS) prepares the body for meeting emergencies and to deal with threats to one's well-being. SNS changes include increased respiration, increased heartbeat, perspiration, and muscle tension. When an event is judged to be threatening, neural impulses are sent to the adrenal gland (the adrenal medulla), which in turn releases the hormones epinephrine (also known as adrenaline) and norepinephrine (noradrenaline) into the bloodstream, where they are circulated to various organ systems that they stimulate. The physical changes one perceives when anxious or frightened are partly a result of these hormones stimulating organs activated by the SNS.

Another branch of the ANS, called the parasympathetic nervous system (PNS), conserves energy and is most active when the individual is calm, quiet, and relaxed. The PNS helps to slow heart rate, reduce blood pressure, and facilitate digestion. In cases of extreme fright or shock and for some individuals who are fearful of blood or injury, there is a strong PNS response, which results in lowered blood pressure, dizziness, or fainting.

autonomic side effect   A disturbance of the autonomic nervous system, this effect may be a result of the use of antipsychotic and antianxiety drugs. The autonomic side effects include higher or lower blood pressure, blurred vision, nasal congestion, dryness of the mouth, dizziness, seizures, psychotic symptoms, depression, and reduced sexual drive.

autonomy   Autonomy is a feeling of being in CONTROL that is associated with attitudes of independence and freedom which may take many forms. An individual may express autonomy by making simple decisions for oneself. When one loses a sense of autonomy, one may experience anxieties, lose self-esteem, and become frustrated. In developing a sense of autonomy, peer groups play an important role. Children with good peer relationships generally acquire good feelings about themselves and develop confidence that others will like them. They will also develop the ability to realize what others expect of them and to make choices about meeting those expectations in a flexible way without anxieties.

For some individuals, particularly teenagers, peer groups may be destructive to autonomy. This may be the case with teenagers whose experiences with peers have not enabled them to develop self-confidence. Under these circumstances, anxieties and a desire for approval or acceptance may lead to drugs, smoking cigarettes, or other destructive behaviors that seems to make the individual feel part of the group.

autophobia   Fear of being alone or fear of oneself is termed autophobia.

aversions   An aversion is a preparatory response to fear and could lead to anxiety responses; for example, many people have strong dislikes (rather than fears) of touching, hearing, tasting, or smelling certain things that most people are indifferent to or even enjoy. An aversion is not a phobia because the feelings these people experience are somewhat different from fear; aversions make one uncomfortable and perhaps feel cold and clammy, short of breath, and nauseated, but not fearful. Fairly common aversions are the screechy sound of chalk against a blackboard, the scraping of a knife against a plate, the feel of fuzzy textures, wet wool or rubber, the feel of raw seafood, or the taste or smell of other foods. Aversions, while not as disabling as fears and phobias, can influence a person's life; for example, a person who has an aversion to the sound of chalk on the blackboard may give up an ambition to be a schoolteacher, and one who has an aversion to fuzzy textures may avoid touching the skin of fresh peaches and never eat fruits with fuzzy skins.

aversion therapy   This form of BEHAVIOR MODIFICATION seeks to help the individual avoid undesirable behaviors or stimuli by associating them with unpleasant or painful experiences; it is also known as *aversive therapy*. Aversion therapy has been used to treat alcoholism, nail biting, bed-wetting, smoking, fetishes, and many other "habit" problems, as well as obsessive thoughts and compulsive behavior. Its primary goal is to enable the individual to make a connection between the behavior and the aversive reaction and thereby reduce the frequency of the undesirable behavior. Secondarily, alternative, acceptable behavior must be shaped and reinforced.

Electrical and chemical techniques have been used to create aversions. With electrical therapy, the therapist administers a mildly painful shock to the patient whenever the undesirable behavior or its imagined equivalent is elicited; with chemical therapy, the individual is given a drug to produce nausea and is then exposed to the deviant stimulus or is required to carry out the deviant act at the time the drug produces its maximal effect. Unfortunately, the drug effect cannot be paired with deviant behavior as precisely as electrical stimulation. The chemical method has been used most widely in treatment of alcoholism; the electrical method has been used predominantly in the treatment of sexual disorders.

These are limitations to aversion therapy, which is based on Pavlov's classical conditioning theory, and therapists now place more importance on cognitive factors. A newer form of aversion therapy, based largely on modification of cognitive behavior, is known as covert sensitization. In this form of therapy, the patient is asked to imagine the deviant activity or stimulus and then to imagine some extremely undesirable consequence, such as nausea, shame, or pain.

aviatophobia (aviophobia)   Fear of flying is termed aviatophobia.

avoidance learning   This procedure is used to treat anxieties (see ANXIETY) and PHOBIAS by pairing a warning signal with an aversive event. After repetitions, the individual learns to respond to the signal alone and engages in avoidance behavior, whether the aversive event occurs or not. The behavior is then maintained by negative reinforcement (avoidance of aversive stimulation). Fear reduction can result from avoidance responses, and avoidance responses can continue after the feared event no longer occurs. Although avoidance behavior is motivated by fear, it is reinforced by the presence of a new stimulus, indicating that relief has been achieved.

avoidance response An observable behavior, avoidance response results from an anxiety-provoking situation. For example, a person who is fearful of elevators might walk up 15 floors rather than enter the elevator. Avoidance occurs in anticipation of aversive stimulation, whereas escape is a response to aversive (anxiety-producing) stimulation. Where avoidance is not possible, a phobic individual might exhibit escape behavior, such as running away from the situation. Both kinds of responses help to reduce the individual's anxiety.

avoidant personality disorder The essential feature of this disorder is a pervasive pattern of anxiety, social discomfort, fear of negative evaluation, and timidity, beginning in early adulthood and present in a variety of contexts. Individuals with avoidant personality disorder have anxiety, depression, and anger at themselves for failing to develop social relations. Some individuals have social phobia as a complication, and others who have this personality disorder also have specific phobias. Some individuals who are agoraphobic show relatively pervasive avoidant behavior, but this is usually due to a fear of being in places or situations where help may not be available, rather than being due to a personality disorder.

B

barbiturates Barbiturates consist of a group of more than 2,500 psychotropic substances that are used as antianxiety drugs, sedatives, anticonvulsants, and hypnotics. Derived from barbituric acid, these drugs act by depressing metabolic functions in several body systems, with the most profound effect on the central nervous system.

Shortly after the beginning of the 20th century, use of barbiturates replaced narcotics and other sleep-inducing drugs. Until benzodiazepines were available in the 1950s, barbiturates were the largest and most widely used group of sedatives and hypnotics. They produce increasing sedation with increased dosage, including poorer performance in vigilance tests, increased bodily unsteadiness, decreased intellectual performance, some loss of motor skills, and underestimation of time.

Because barbiturates induce sleep, chronic use may lead to tolerance and psychological and physical dependence. They are also one of the leading causes of fatal drug poisoning; for this reason, physicians generally prescribe only small quantities of these drugs.

The most commonly prescribed barbiturates for mild anxiety or insomnia are phenobarbital and butabarbital. Pentobarbital sodium is sometimes used during psychotherapy to help an individual relax and express himself or herself more freely.

Barbiturate addiction is the physical and psychological dependence on barbiturate drugs. Many phobia sufferers were prescribed barbiturates to diminish anxiety symptoms and became addicted and/or experienced extreme withdrawal effects.

bathophobia A fear of depths, bathophobia may be noticeable in situations such as looking into a dark room or boating or swimming in deep water. A person who fears depths may be comfortable when he or she can see the bottom of the lake but not in deeper water. Similarly, such an individual may not fear a dark space when he or she is aware of the size of the room.

bathroom phobia This is a fear of the bathroom or the toilet. Some children and some adults who have obsessive-compulsive disorders may be afraid of falling into the toilet, of being attacked by a monster coming from it, or of being infected. Bathroom phobia may also be related to a fear of dirt and germs, of using a toilet other than in one's own home, or of being seen or heard by others while urinating or defecating. Fears of urination or defecation in unfamiliar bathrooms are often not disclosed (or even assessed by surveys) but from clinical reports may be extensive. From the psychoanalytic viewpoint, bathroom phobia may involve ideas of castration.

battle fatigue   Also known as shell shock, a more recent term for this is *posttraumatic stress disorder.*

battle fear   Battle fear is also known as posttraumatic stress disorder.

bats, fear of   Some people fear bats because in folklore, myth, and art bats have become symbolic of black magic, darkness, madness, peril, and torment. The bat has been thought to be a ghost and also a witch's familiar, capable of transporting evil spirits into and out of the human body.

Some people believe in a superstition that bats are attracted to women's hair and that once entangled they can be cut out only by a man.

Most bats have gained their malevolent and fear-inducing reputation because of their ghastly appearance, their avoidance of light, and their ability to hunt in the dark; however, the vampire bats of Mexico, Central and South America deserve their bad name as they actually do feed on the blood of humans and animals, sometimes choosing favorite individuals to attack. The bat can draw blood from a sleeping victim because its saliva apparently contains an anesthetic substance that deadens the pain of the bite.

beards, fear of   Fear of beards or of persons who have beards is known as pogonophobia. In a classic study during the 1920s, American psychologist John Broadus Watson (1878–1958) was able to condition this fear in a young boy by classical conditioning methods. He found that the fear, first conditioned to a rabbit, generalized to other hairy objects such as beards, animals, and fur coats.

beauty shop, fear of   Some women fear going to a beauty shop because they fear going out (in the case of agoraphobics), that they will be judged unattractive by others in the shop (dysmorphophobia), or confinement in the beautician's chair. Some women fear being helpless during their visit to the beauty shop, that they may not be able to make a quick exit if they feel a need to leave the scene; others fear being at the mercy of another person, in this case the beautician. Another fear is that their appearance may be changed drastically by mistake, for example, too much hair cut off, their hair color changed unexpectedly, or the degree of curl not what they expected. There is also the fear of being seen by others in a vulnerable situation, such as while they are having their hair cut or colored. Fear of going to the beauty shop is related also to social phobia.

bed, fear of   Fear of beds, known as clinophobia, and of going to bed may be related to sleep phobias or sleep disorders. Persons who fear going to bed may do so because of unpleasant past experiences such as chronic insomnia, night terrors, sleepwalking episodes, or fear of bed-wetting. Others are afraid that they will not wake up; for some fear of going to bed is related to a fear of death.

bees, fear of   Fear of bees—apiphobia or melissophobia—which combines the anxiety of potential injury with a general fear of flying insects, often begins in the preschool or early school years. The fear may result from a child's own experience or from hearing frightening stories or seeing frightening movies. Bee phobics report that flying, stinging insects give the appearance of attacking them. The fact that fear of a tiny insect may seem ridiculous to others is often upsetting to the phobic but may be of assistance in treatment.

   The consequence of a fear of bees may mean restricted travel (so as to avoid seeing bees), driving with the windows of the car up at all times, or even staying indoors during daylight hours.

behavior analysis   A study of the relationship of problem behaviors and their consequences, behavior analysis is the first step in behavioral therapies, which are based on the principles of operant conditioning. During behavior analysis, the therapist will examine the interaction between stimulus, response, and consequence and plan a program according to the individual's needs. This ongoing process ends only when the treatment goals have been reached.

behaviorism   School of psychology associated with U.S. behavioral psychologist John Broadus Watson (1878–1958), who proposed that observable behavior, not consciousness, is the proper subject of psychology. OPERANT CONDITIONING evolved from this point of view, and the behavioristic approach led to many later techniques of behavior modification and methods for treating phobias. By this time, however, Watson had left psychology to pursue a career in advertising.

behavior modification   A type of psychotherapy used to treat phobias, behavior modification stresses the effect of learning on behavior, uses active therapist and client involvement and in vivo practices, outlines explicit goals and desired new behaviors, and evaluates progress toward those goals. This treatment does not rely on diagnostic labels and deemphasizes the importance of the past in determining current behavior.

behavior rehearsal   Behavior rehearsal is a behavior therapy technique in which the patient practices a new behavior in a controlled setting aided by the therapist. The therapist may use techniques of MODELING, coaching, feedback, positive REINFORCEMENT, and ROLE-PLAYING. Behavior rehearsal is useful in treating SOCIAL PHOBIAS. A widely used form of behavior rehearsal is assertiveness training, in which inhibited, submissive individuals learn to behave more assertively, to express anger, to respond to another's anger, and not to feel guilty or anxious in doing so.

behavior therapy   A form of psychological, emotional, and behavioral therapy that stresses learned responses, behavior therapy is also known as behavior modification. Behaviorial therapists work to modify an individual's undesirable or unwanted behavior, such as anxiety and avoidance, instead of trying to change the "personality" by probing into the individual's "unconscious" feelings. Unlike psychoanalysts, behavior therapists do not regard phobias as symptoms of unconsciously caused, "deeper" problems that require restructuring of the psyche, but they *do* regard panic, anxiety, and obsessive-compulsive behavior as something that has a learned component (as well as a biological component) and can be replaced with desirable behaviors. Behaviorists generally do not believe that other drastic symptoms will appear to replace the ones thus eliminated.

Behavior therapy is considered the most effective treatment for AGORAPHOBIA, SOCIAL PHOBIAS, and other specific phobias, as well as for obsessions, compulsions, certain sexual problems, and alcoholism. Many therapists used behavior therapy in conjunction with other forms of treatment to treat phobias.

Behavior therapy focuses on measurable aspects of observable behavior such as frequency or intensity of particular behaviors, such as compulsive hand-washing, physiological response, and verbal reports. Verbal reports by the patient and self-rating scales are commonly used to describe aspects of details of behavior. Specific treatment techniques are tailored by the therapist to the needs of the individual.

Treatment goals are defined by the therapist in conjunction with the patient and the patient's family. In behavior therapy, the therapist is seen as an instructor or coach, and the patient chooses whether to try to learn a new behavior. The goal generally is to develop self-controlled behaviors and an increased repertoire of new, more adaptive behaviors.

Behavior therapy includes many basic learning technique, such as reduction of anxiety, desensitization, flooding, classical conditioning, modeling, operant conditioning, aversive therapy, and reciprocal inhibition. Therapists often use techniques that gradually expose the phobic individual to the feared objects or situations. Such exposure may take place in real life or in the individuals's imagination. The gradualness of the exposure is considered important in making the treatment effective, combined with the simultaneous use of relaxation responses and cognitive changes.

A major development in the treatment of phobias was described in 1958 by behavioral psychiatrist Joseph Wolpe (1915–97), who had a background in learning theory. Wolpe reported excellent results in treating adults who had a variety of neuroses, including phobic anxiety, hysteria, reactive depression, and obsessive-compulsive disorder, with a procedure called systematic desensitization, adapted from a technique developed in the 1920s for helping children overcome animal phobias. Based on the principle of reciprocal inhibition, this technique trains the individual to relax the muscles, imagine increasing degrees of anxiety-producing stimuli, and then face increasing degrees of the fear-producing stimuli in vivo until the maximum stimulus no longer causes great anxiety.

Systematic desensitization requires the individual to learn deep-muscle relaxation and to rank situations that cause anxiety. For example, an individual who fears elevators might place at the top of the list of things that make him or her anxious riding to the top of a high building alone in an elevator; merely looking at the entrance to an elevator from the lobby of a building might rank at the bottom of the list of fear-producing stimuli.

After relaxing, the individual is then asked to imagine, in as much detail as possible, the least fear-producing item from the list. By relaxing while imagining the feared situation, the individual may weaken the association between the phobic situation and anxious feelings. Once he or she becomes comfortable imagining the least-threatening situation, he or she gradually moves up the hierarchy.

Some therapists believe that facing a feared situation in the imagination may be just as effective as facing it in reality. However, most therapists have found that there is a gap between imagination and reality. Once the individual has completed densensitization treatment and goes on to face the real fear, he or she is likely to regress slightly back down the list. For example, an individual who has learned to remain calm while riding an imaginary elevator to the top of a building may be able to enter an actual elevator but may not be comfortable riding in it right away. By taking a floor at a time, however, the individual will be able to master the fear and eventually ride to the top of the building alone.

During the late 1960s, another treatment for phobias was developed by Thomas Stampfl called implosion or implosive therapy. Implosion was a modification of a technique known as imaginal flooding, or just flooding.

Flooding Flooding, like desensitization, involves the individual's experiencing fear-provoking situations in his or her imagination or in vivo. In flooding, the individual is exposed directly to a maximum level of the fear-producing stimulus without any graduated approach.

However, in flooding, the therapist, rather than the individual, controls the timing and the content of the scenes to be imagined. The therapist describes such scenes with great vividness in a deliberate effort to make them as disturbing as possible to the phobic person. The individual is not instructed to relax; rather, the aim is for him or her to experience fears and anxieties with maximum intensity, which gradually diminishes. The prolonged experience with these feared objects or situations is designed to help the individual to experience "extinction" of the anxiety response.

Implosive therapy In this variation and extension of the flooding technique, the individual is repeatedly encouraged to imagine a fear-producing situation at maximum intensity to experience as intense anxiety as possible. Assuming that there is no actual danger in the situation, the anxiety reponse is not reinforced and thus becomes gradually reduced through extinction. However, the therapist also begins to weave fantasy-based images and thoughts drawn from psychoanalytic theory into the terrifying images, presumably also to extinguish these unconscious factors.

Like desensitization, both flooding and implosive techniques reduce phobic anxiety and behavior in persons with simple phobias, but desensitization appears to be more effective and more permanent. There is some evidence that small amounts of flooding are more effective with agoraphobics.

Exposure therapy This is a term used to describe a variety of behavioral therapies that have in common the use of gradual exposure to a feared situation (such as systematic desensitization), exposure at full intensity (flooding and implosive therapy) and exposure with cognitive modification (contextual therapy). Contextual therapy was developed by U.S. psychiatrist Manual Zane (1913–). The focus of contextual therapy is to keep the person rooted to the present situation and to work with the anxiety-producing internal cues of the person.

Modeling and covert modeling In this form of therapy, the phobic individual watches another person, often of the same sex and age as the phobic, successfully perform a particular feared action, such as crossing the street or taking an elevator. The phobic presumably experiences vicarious extinction of the feared response. Modeling is also called social learning or observational learning.

In "covert modeling" the phobic individual simply imagines that another individual is facing the same phobic situation without anxiety; there is no comment or reinforcement from the therapist in convert modeling.

Operant conditioning   This technique is based on the principle that individuals will either maintain or decrease the frequency of a particular behavior as a result of responses they receive from their environment. Thus, behavior that produces reinforcing consequences is strengthened, and behavior that produces aversive consequences is weakened. Avoidance and approach behavior to feared stimuli are often considered under operant control and are thus modifiable through operant shaping.

Hypnosis   Although hypnosis is not based on learning theory, it is classified as a behaviorial technique because the role of the therapist is active rather than passive, as it is in psychoanalysis. Hypnosis can be used to produce a hypnotic trance in which the individual becomes very receptive to suggestion. Through posthypnotic suggestion, an individual may learn to change behavior patterns, such as having phobic reactions to certain stimuli. Hypnosis by itself, however, it not an adequate form of treatment for phobias.

Biofeedback   Biofeedback, a technique to monitor psychophysiological events by electrical feedback, provides an anxious or phobic individual with a basis for self-regulation of certain processes, such as reaction to fearful situations. The technique is useful in many approaches to therapy for anxieties and phobias. It establishes a diagnostic baseline by noting physiological reactions to stressful events, enables therapists to relate this information to the individual's verbal reports, fills gaps in the individual's history, and encourages relaxation of the body part to which the biofeedback equipment is applied. Relaxation training is often suggested to assist the individual in controlling anxiety reactions.

being alone, fear of   Fear of being alone is known as autophobia. The term *taphephobia* is also used for being alone but usually refers to fear of being buried alive. Some agoraphobic individuals are also afraid of being alone, particularly when they leave the place where they feel secure. Infants and young children fear being alone, generally because they feel helpless and are afraid of being abandoned by their parents or other caretakers. Older people also fear being alone as they see others in their age group retiring and moving away or dying. A fear of being alone and a feeling of being far from anyone who cares about one may sometimes lead to depression.

For people of all ages, fears are usually greater when they are alone. Even though individuals who have SOCIAL PHOBIAS may avoid particular forms of social contact, they rarely like to be alone most of the time.

being enclosed, fear of   Fear of being enclosed in a very confined space is known as clithrophobia. Somewhat similar to claustrophobia, clithrophobia generally applies to a very small, well-defined space, whereas claustrophobia also can refer to fear of being in a large room without an easy or visible way out.

being locked in, fear of   Fear of being locked in is known as claustrophobia. The term *clithrophobia* might also apply if the space in which one is locked is very small as well as confining. Some individuals specifically fear being locked in an elevator, a closet, their car, or a room.

being looked at, fear of   Fear of being looked at or stared at is known as scopophobia. Fear of two staring eyes is common throughout the animal kingdom, including man. Particularly in individuals who have social fears, being looked at means being the object of another's attention and intention; the gaze of others thus may trigger acute discomfort in self-conscious persons. Many social phobics are afraid of being watched by others.

Realizing that eyes are looking at one may be instinctive. The eyes of another are one of the first figural entities perceived by the infant. Of all the features of the face, the eyes possess the greatest combination of those qualities that attract an infant's fixation—figure, color, movement, and light reflection. In human infants, two eyes are the minimal visual stimulus required to elicit the first human social response, the smile. The infant's smile and his or her fixation on the eyes of the person looking at him or her may be an instinctual response of the infant, which itself elicits further approach and caring behavior by the parent.

The effect of being looked at has been studied in animals; for example, when rhesus monkeys see a human face observing them in the laboratory, they show a change in behavior and in electrical activity in the brain stem. Many species of mammals use their eyes and eye markings to intimidate intruders, and eyes and conspicuous eyelike markings are used by birds and insects as defense against attack.

being touched, fear of   Fear of being touched is known as aphenphobia, haphephobia, and haptephobia. This fear may be a social phobia. In some cases, fear of being touched may relate to sexual fears. Some people fear being touched because they fear contamination.

belonophobia   Fear of needles and pins is known as belonophobia or belonephobia.

Benson, Herbert   Herbert Benson, M.D., (1935–) is the founding president of the Mind/Body Medical Institute; Associate Chief, Division of Behavioral Medicine, Harvard Medical School; and Chief, Division of Behavioral Medicine, New England Deaconess Hospital.

A cardiologist who discovered and described how the RELAXATION RESPONSE is a protective mechanism against overreaction to stress and anxieties, Dr. Benson is the author or coauthor of several books relating to relaxation and stress, including *The Relaxation Response* and *The Mind/Body Effect*. Hundreds of his articles have appeared in medical journals and popular magazines.

Dr. Benson discovered the relaxation response while studying people who practiced TRANSCENDENTAL MEDITATION. As a specialist in high blood pressure, his particular interests have included how the relaxation response can help people with high blood pressure and other health concerns. He warns that people with high blood pressure should not just give up their medication. What MEDITATION and the relaxation response do, he maintains, is improve on the benefit of the medication. He argues that "mindfulness" is needed to be healthy and productive.

benzodiazepine drugs   A group of prescription medications widely prescribed to help relieve symptoms of anxiety, benzodiazepine drugs also act as muscle relaxants, sedatives, and anticonvulsants. Different drugs in this class are approved for different conditions, such as panic disorder.

Benzodiazepine drugs have less toxicity and fewer drug interaction problems than barbiturates and nonbarbiturate sedative-hypnotic drugs. They also have a lower risk of cardiovascular and respiratory depression compared with barbiturates and are often used before general anesthesia.

Persons taking benzodiazepine drugs should avoid alcohol because interaction may result in depression of the central nervous system.

bereavement, phobia following   Phobias occurring after the loss of a loved one may be related to separation anxiety. In some individuals, such a loss brings back unresolved feelings from childhood caused by separation from one's parents.

beta adrenergic blocking agents   More commonly referred to simply as beta-blockers, these drugs have been used to assist in relief of anxiety. Primarily, beta-blockers tend to have a calming effect on the heart, reducing heart rate and force of contraction. When used long term, they usually result in lowered blood pressure. More recently, they are being used to help relieve some symptoms of anxiety such as shakiness and heart palpitations. Beta-blockers seem to cause an overall reduction in anxiety. The drugs atenolol and propranol are examples of beta-blockers.

bibliotherapy   Books as relief from anxieties is termed *bibliotherapy.*

biofeedback   A technique to monitor psychophysiological events by electrical feedback, biofeedback is useful in many approaches to therapy for anxieties and phobias. It provides an anxious or phobic individual with a basis for self-regulation of certain processes, such as autonomic system reaction to fearful situations. Biofeedback establishes a diagnostic baseline by noting physiological reactions to stressful events, enables therapists to relate this information to the individual's reports, fills gaps in the individual's history, and encourages relaxation in the part of the individual's body to which the biofeedback equipment is applied. Relaxation training is often suggested to assist the individual in controlling anxiety reactions.

biorhythms   Physiological functions, such as menstrual cycles, that follow a regular temporal pattern, these biological rhythms regulate psychological as well as physiological functions in the individual: energy level, hunger, sleep, and elimination can all be affected. These rhythms vary considerably from person to person and within a single individual at different times. Such external factors as changing travel and time zones or routines in unpredictable and unfamiliar ways affect one's biorhythms. Anxiety can result from bodily sensations produced by disruption of biorhythms and can lead to anxieties.

To deal with the anxieties caused by disruptions in biorhythms, individuals develop their own techniques; for example, one traveling through time zones may prepare by waking earlier for several days before the trip or by resting more upon return. Some develop particular dietary patterns that they find helpful, such as eating small meals oftener and drinking lots of water.

birds, fear of   Fear of birds is known as ornithophobia. Some bird phobics believe that the sudden, unpredictable movements of birds constitute an attack. Phobics commonly fear the swooping motions of birds and the sound and sight of flapping wings in an enclosed space. Other phobics mention the beady eyes and claws of birds as being particularly frightening. Pigeons are the phobic objects for many individuals, as pigeons gravitate toward buildings and people more than other birds do. Some individuals fear only the sight of a dead bird. Some bird phobics are less frightened by the sight of birds in the open and even may be fascinated by them in this situation. Alfred Hitchcock played on the duality of attraction to and revulsion by birds in his film *The Birds*.

This phobia, like many animal and common stimuli phobias, often severely limits the individual's functioning; for example, fear of birds in moderate to severe intensities limits the person's range of movement outside, often restricting one to areas of few birds or to travel at night. Also, travel is accompanied by ANXIETY or dread at the possibility of seeing birds; windows must be tightly closed, and walking in open spaces is impossible. The individual may not even be able even to look outside.

bisexuality   Some individuals fear bisexuality, the existence of the qualities of both sexes in the same person. An adult person who engages in bisexual behavior is one who is sexually attracted to and has contact with members of both sexes. Sigmund Freud (1856–1937) suggested that, both biologically and psychologically, the sexes differentiated from a common core, that differentiation between the sexes was relative rather than absolute, and that regression to the common core occurs to varying degrees in both normal and abnormal conditions.

black cats, fear of   Some individuals fear black cats because they are associated with witchcraft and superstition: they will avoid letting a black cat cross their path out of superstitious fear of future misfortune. Some fear black cats but not cats of other colors; other individuals fear only lighter-colored cats.

blood (and blood-injury) phobia   Many individuals are afraid of the sight of blood. Fear of blood is known as hematophobia or hemophobia. Although susceptible individuals may not say that they have a fear of blood, when faced with the sight of their own or another's blood, they may recoil, close their eyes, or even faint. A reaction may occur on hearing a description of blood and gore, such as a war scene, or even on imagining the sight of someone bleeding. Blood phobia is different from some other phobias in that the individual does not perceive danger of injury or death.

Blood phobics may experience more nausea and faintness than fear or anxiety. They may avoid their phobic stimuli because they fear fainting, and their fear of fainting in turn can cause them anxiety. Women seem to be more fearful of the sight of blood than men are.

With most phobias, the individual's pulse and breathing rate increase in response to the phobic stimulus. However, with blood phobia, (and related blood-injury phobias, such as phobia of needles, injection, blood donation, etc.) there is often a sharp drop in heart rate and blood pressure, which is called a diphasic cardiovascular pattern. Why some blood phobics lose consciousness when faced with the stimulus is not clearly understood, but one hypothesis is that it is a "protective" biological mechanism that, in the event of actual injury, prevents the individual from doing anything that might cause further blood loss.

Like phobias of animals, those of blood and injury often begin during childhood. It appears to be relatively common in minor forms and is excessive in very few instances. Epidemiological studies indicate that approximately 3.1–4.5 percent of the population report blood and blood injury phobias. In one 1980 study, a high percentage of blood phobics (68 percent) reported that close relatives had the same fear.

Severe phobia of blood and injury can be seriously handicapping; for example, sufferers may avoid necessary medical procedures or avoid attractive careers as medical professionals. Blood-injury phobic women may even avoid becoming pregnant to avoid medical examinations and the sight of blood.

blood transfusions, fear of During the 1980s, fear of blood transfusion became widespread when it was recognized that the human immunodeficiency virus (HIV), which is known to carry the dreaded autoimmune deficiency syndrome (AIDS), can be spread through blood transfusions. Others fear blood transfusions because the procedure involves use of needles or tubes placed in the body. Still others who have blood phobia fear seeing blood or blood components being fed into their bodies.

Although blood transfusions are feared by many, they are lifesaving for many others. Transfusions are given after great loss of blood in an accident or in a surgical operation to treat the systemic shock and fluid loss caused by severe burns, to replace the blood of an Rh-positive newborn infant, and to treat severe anemias.

Since the rapid spread of certain types of hepatitis and AIDS from blood transfusions, the blood of donors is tested before it is drawn and is tested again before it is transfused into a recipient. An understanding of how this is done will allay many fears.

blushing, fear of Fear of blushing, or erythrophobia, can be a painful and difficult symptom for therapists to treat. Fear of blushing is manifest only when other people are present. The phobic individual, most commonly a woman, is terrified that she will blush in the company of others and is convinced that is this state she will be very visible and consequently the center of unwanted, painful attention. If questioned, such an individual cannot say what is so dreadful about blushing, but it is often evident that shame (fear of disapproval of others) is an important component of her anxiety. A change in color may not be at all evident to the observer, despite the fact that the individual insists that she feels bright red; the force of her fear often leads the individual to a severe restriction of her social life.

Blushing represents an increase in blood volume to the face and head. It is part of the sympathetic nervous system arousal pattern of anxiety/excitement. As with any emotional response, external stimuli, such as the presence of other people, can become conditioned quite easily.

body image, fear of   Body image, the mental picture one has of one's body at any moment, is derived from internal sensations, postural changes, emotional experiences, fantasies, and feedback from others. Fear of deformity of one's own body is known as dysmorphophobia. Some individuals have fears relating to their body image and fear that one or more parts of their body are unattractive and noticeable to others.

A misperception of one's body image can lead to eating disorders, such as ANOREXIA NERVOSA or bulimia, in an effort to make oneself thinner.

body odor, fear of   Fear of body odors is known as osphreisiophobia or bromidrosiphobia. Some individuals fear their own body and have an unfounded fear that others will notice it. Such individuals may avoid going into crowded places where they must be close to others; may use deodorants and antiperspirants excessively; may bathe, shower or change clothes excessively; and may seek constant reassurance from family members that they cannot detect any odor. Fear of one's own body odor is considered a SOCIAL PHOBIA and usually responds to appropriate treatment.

body therapies   This group of therapies emphasizes the role of physical factors in anxieties and phobias and the resolution of those anxieties and phobias by relaxation, breathing, body manipulation, massage, and changes in posture and position of body parts. Body therapies are used in holistic therapies, which recognize relationships between mind and body in helping individuals overcome anxieties and phobias.

Body therapies encompass ancient Eastern traditions of spirituality and cosmology along with contemporary Western neuromuscular and myofascial systems of skeletostructural and neuroskeletal reorganization. They postulate that the body holds memory of trauma and that therapy must address body sensations. In fact, all proven theories for trauma focus extensively on body sensations.

Ancient disciplines in the category of body therapies include YOGA, TAI CHI CHUAN, Zen, Taoism, Tantra, and Samurai. In the 20th century, Austrian psychoanalyst Wilhelm Reich (1897–1957) observed that clinical patients with emotional disturbances all demonstrated severe postural distortions. This observation helped to uncover more connections between the body and its psyche and led to the development of the Reichian school of body therapy.

Another modern pioneer in the field was Moshe Feldenkrais (1904–84), who postulated that the human organism began its process of growth and learning with one built-in response, the fear of falling. All other physical and emotional responses were learned as the human organism grew and explored. To attain the full potential of the bodymind-emotions-spirit, there must be, according to Feldenkrais, "reeducation of the kinesthetic sense and resetting of it to the normal course of self-adjusting improvement of all muscular activity." This would "directly improve breathing, digestion, and the sympathetic and parasympathetic balance, as well as the sexual function, all linked together with the emotional experience." Feldenkrais believed that reeducation of the body and its functions was the essence of creating unity of the being. His method has helped many people with problems of back pain, whiplash, and lack of coordination. The method is also used to help people who have temporomandibular joint syndrome (TMJ), which is a collection of symptoms, including pain, that affect the jaw, face, and head, often brought about by anxieties, stress and tension.

Four systems of body therapies   Although many systems overlap and encompass aspects of the others, body therapies can be divided into four general categories, based on their methods.

Physical manipulation systems include the connective tissue work of the Ida Rolf (1896–1979) school (Rolfing) and the deep tissues release systems such myofascial release used by U.S. physical therapist John Barnes.

Energy balancing systems include Chinese ACUPUNCTURE and ACUPRESSURE.

Emotional release systems include bioenergetics, primal therapy, and rebirthing.

Movement awareness systems include those of Aston, Feldenkrais, Trager, and Aguado.

books as anxiety relief   Bibliotherapy is an interdisciplinary field that combines the skills of psychotherapists, librarians, and educators. In the course of a bibliotherapy program, books are selected to promote normal development and to change disturbed patterns of behavior. The books may be directly concerned with mental health or may be fiction or nonfiction works relating to and interpreting the readers' problems and concerns. It has been suggested that reading about a disturbing subject such as death, divorce, or aging gives the reader a sense of control over problems, a way of working them out in his or her mind. Use of selected books with children may alleviate fears by clearing up misconceptions and giving information about the unknown. Reading may also give the child the conforming knowledge that others share these fears and may promote communication with parents.

borderline personality disorder   This personality disorder is characterized by anxiety and by unstable moods, behaviors, self-image, and interpersonal relationships. Moods may shift from normal to depressed, and the individual often shows inappropriate intense anger or lack of control of anger. There may be impulsive moods, particularly with regard to activities that are potentially self-damaging, such as shopping sprees, psychoactive substance abuse, reckless driving, casual sex, shoplifting, and binge eating. In those who suffer from a borderline personality disorder, there may be an identity disturbance that is noticeable because of uncertainty about self-image, gender identity, long-term goals, or values. The individual may be chronically bored, and during periods of extreme stress, there may also be symptoms of depersonalization. This disorder is more common in females than in males.

boredom, fear of   Boredom is characterized by slow reactions, lack of productivity, wandering attention, and lessened emotional response; in extreme form, it may produce depression and hallucination. Boredom is a uniquely individual psychological condition in that what may be fascinating or soothing to one person may be boring or even anxiety arousing to another. It has been held responsible for ANXIETY that leads to vandalism, violence, educational and vocational dropping out, marital unhappiness, and even suicide (see SUICIDE, FEAR OF).

Participants in an experiment using an artificial sensory deprivation environment dropped out in spite of the fact that they were being paid well for doing nothing. Boredom is actually a type of punishment. Solitary confinement for prisoners is a dreaded condition.

Boredom, or lack of stimulation, can be a triggering stimulus for anxiety, particularly with agoraphobics; for example, many agoraphobics fear being alone, which is a state of too little social stimulation. Likewise, quietness, open spaces, and empty rooms are common anxiety triggers characterized by lack of stimulation.

An essential fact of boredom is that it is almost always the creation of the person who is bored. Things are only boring if someone judges them as boring. Some people seem bored with everything; others are bored with nothing. For some people, boredom is a self-imposed prison that keeps them from trying new things or having new, life-enriching experiences. This form of ennui often comes to individuals who thrive on excessive stimulation; it is not a function of environmental or social causes but the reduction in stimulation.

bradycardia   Extremely slow heart rate characterizes bradycardia; its opposite is tachycardia (rapid heart rate). In many blood-injury phobics, bradycardia occurs as a secondary reaction, following an initial phase of rapid heartbeat. Bradycardia can lead to fainting.

bridges, fear of   Fear of bridges is related to fear of being trapped, similar to the fear of being stopped in traffic and unable to turn around, and to fear of heights and narrow spaces. According to some sources, bridge fear may be considered a fear of childbirth. "The Angel of the Bridge," a short story by John Cheever, contains an excellent description of panic-attack symptoms on a bridge:

> The seizure came with a rush. The strength went out of my legs. I gasped for breath, and felt the terrifying loss of sight. I was, at the same time, determined to conceal these symptoms. . . . I felt the sense of reality ebbing. . . . The loneliness of my predicament was harrowing.

brief psychotherapy   In this form of therapy, sessions are limited to 10 to 15 in number, and during them the therapist uses active and goal-directive techniques and procedures. Brief psychotherapy has been used in individual and group settings to treat phobias and anxieties, but it is not the treatment of choice for these disorders. However, it has been effective in crisis management situations.

breathing   The major features of breathing are respiration and ventilation. Respiration puts oxygen into body cells, and ventilation removes the excess carbon dioxide. Poor breathing habits diminish the flow of gases to and from the body, making it harder for individuals to cope with fearful situations or situations that produce anxieties.

Deep, diaphragmatic breathing is a cornerstone for many relaxation therapies. Many therapeutic techniques (many known as alternative therapies) and behavior therapies incorporate control of breathing as a basis because the cycle of stress can be altered with breath control. Individuals who have mastered these techniques find that as soon as they are aware of a stressor, they become aware of their breathing and try to control their stress by deep, slow breaths. By contrast, holding the breath, as well as shallow, irregular breathing, can initiate as well as augment many stressful feelings and physiological responses. Posture can also affect breathing. Keeping the body in alignment allows greater lung capacity.

butterflies, fear of   Individuals who fear butterflies, moths, and other flying insects fear that the flying insect may attack them. Some phobics avoid enclosed areas out of fear that they may be trapped with the insect. Some phobics actually have accidents while trying to avoid butterflies and moths.

"butterflies in the stomach"   The feeling of uneasiness in the stomach is often referred to as "butterflies." Caused by a contraction of the abdominal blood vessels, this is a common experience among those who must make a speech in public, perform before an audience, appear for a job interview, or participate in any other type of activity that causes feelings of nervousness or apprehension.

C

catastrophic anxiety   Another term for panic or anxiety produced by overwhelming, frightening events, sometimes *catastrophic anxiety* is used to denote catastrophic thinking or a preoccupation with potentially disastrous events, such as crashing in an airplane.

catastrophize   To catastrophize is the habit of imagining that the worst-case scenario will happen. People who frequently catastrophize have little self-confidence, low SELF-ESTEEM, and difficulties making positive and desirable life changes. Many also have SOCIAL PHOBIAS.

An example of catastrophizing is saying to oneself, "If I go to the party, no one will know me and I won't have a good time," or "If I take this new job, I'll fail because I don't have the right computer skills."

Catastrophizing causes anxieties because it keeps people in situations they might really prefer to change, such as improving their social life, changing jobs, or moving to a new city. With positive self-talk and learned techniques to improve self-esteem, the habit of catastrophizing can be overcome. In severe cases, various psychotherapies (see PSYCHOTHERAPY) may be helpful, particularly cognitive behavioral therapies.

chiropractic medicine   Chiropractic medicine deals with the relationship between the skeleton and the nervous system and the role of this relationship in restoring and maintaining health. Many people visit chiropractors to relieve anxieties and stress as well as physical discomforts.

According to chiropractic philosophy, the body is a self-healing organism, and all bodily function is controlled by the nervous system. Abnormal bodily function may be caused by interference with nerve transmission and expression. This interference can be caused by pressure, strain, or tension on the spinal cord, spinal nerves, or peripheral nerves as a result of a displacement of the spinal segments or other skeletal structures.

chronic fatigue syndrome (CFS)   This illness is characterized by fatigue that occurs suddenly, improves, and relapses, bringing on debilitating tiredness or easy fatigability in an individual who has no apparent reason for feeling this way. It causes anxieties for the sufferer because the profound weakness caused by CFS does not go away with a few good nights of sleep but instead steals a person's vigor over months and years. Anxiety often occurs because of loss of income and vitality in relationships. Because many individuals who have CFS experience frustration both before being diagnosed and on learning that there is no cure, depression often accompanies the disease.

Although the illness strikes children, teenagers, and people in their 50s, 60s, and 70s, it is most likely to strike adults from their mid-20s to their late 40s. Women are afflicted about twice to three times as often as men; the vast majority of those who suffer this illness are white. Because young urban professionals were most afflicted during the 1980s, the name *yuppie flu* was attached to CFS. However, individuals regarded this name as trivializing their illness.

CFS symptoms   CFS can affect virtually all the body's major systems: neurological, immunological, hormonal, gastrointestinal, and musculoskeletal. According to the National Institutes of Health, CFS leaves many people bedridden or with headaches, muscular and joint pain, sore throat, balance disorders, sensitivity to light, an inability to concentrate, and inexplicable body aches. Secondary depression, which follows from the disease rather than causing it, is just as disabling. However, knowing that there is a chemical basis for mood swings and that they are directly related to illness can be reassuring.

Symptoms wax and wane in severity and linger for months and sometimes years. Some individuals respond to treatment; others must function at a reduced level for a long time. However, for all sufferers, the cumulative effect is the same, namely, transforming ordinary activities into tremendous stressful challenges. They cannot tolerate the least bit of exercise, their cognitive functions become impaired, and their memory, verbal fluency, response time, and ability to perform calculations and to reason show a marked decrease.

Disruption of sleep patterns cause the CFS sufferer additional stress. Despite constant exhaustion and desire for sleep, they rarely sleep uninterruptedly and awake feeling refreshed. Some have severe INSOMNIA, while others have difficulty maintaining sleep. There is often not enough rapid-eye movement (REM) sleep, which is considered necessary for a good night's rest.

Many CFS sufferers experience stressful disorders of balance or of the vestibular system, which is modulated by the inner ear. They sometimes feel dizzy, lightheaded, or nauseous. Even walking can be difficult, with sufferers tilting off balance or stumbling for no apparent reason. Some individuals who have balance disorders develop PHOBIAS, such as a fear of falling. Some who have this fear even become housebound.

CFS causes anxieties for sufferers, family, and friends. Those in their support circles can reduce their stress by being helpful, understanding, and available to listen. Sufferers are likely to feel estranged from some of their friends because they believe that no one really understands their feelings of emotional and physical exhaustion. This belief is exacerbated

because many sufferers think that others do not take their illness seriously. In addition, some friends and family members may fear that CFS is
contagious and try to maintain a distance from the sufferer. (Medical
opinion seems to indicate that CFS is not contagious). Spouses face the
issue of reduced sexual activity, although both partners can satisfy their
needs by engaging in sexual activity during peak periods of energy.

chronic illness   Chronic illness describes a disorder or set of symptoms
that has persisted for a long time with progressive deterioration. In addition to the anxieties and stresses of physical pain, chronic illness often
brings with it emotional consequences that can be more far reaching than
the illness itself. These effect not only the patient but also cause anxieties
for the immediate caregivers. Some, particularly close family members, let
illness-related anxieties take over their lives, and their depression arises
from COPING with illness and the threat of possible long-term disability or
death of a loved one.

Reactions to illness are similar to the stages of grief (see GRIEF REACTION)
after the death of a loved one. First, there is the patient's shock and a feeling of many losses, of CONTROL, or AUTONOMY, and of the way things used to
be. In addition, they experience physical losses ranging from having to give
up their job or favorite sport to impaired speech or vision. Stress and symptoms of depression may follow, including hopelessness, self-blame, shat-
tered self-esteem, or withdrawal. Some ill persons may develop many
fears: they may fear exercise and being active again. Others may deny the
realities of their condition and overdo activities too soon.

The anxieties of pain and fears about disability and death lead some
people who are ill to substance abuse as a form of escape. Anger, denial, or
perceived helplessness lead others to abandon medical treatment or assume
a "why me" attitude that gives them a pessimistic view of their world.

How individuals coped with life stress before the illness will determine how well they respond when illness occurs. However, even when
symptoms of illness go into remission or people have adjusted to their illness, a whole new set of external stressors may arise or family dynamics
can change dramatically.

Some individuals feel certain "benefits" from being chronically ill.
Such motivations are referred to as "secondary gains" and increase the
likelihood of their continuing to be ill or to have symptoms. Common
"benefits" of illness include receiving permission to get out of dealing with
a troublesome problem, situation, or responsibility of life; getting attention, care, or nurturing; and not having to meet their own or others'
expectations.

Every area of a person's life is affected by ill health, including marriage, family, work, financial affairs, and future plans. Professional coun-

seling can help individuals and their families adapt to stresses brought on by chronic illness. Counseling may also help individuals who feel a need to hide their illness, increase their use of drugs or alcohol, fail to follow treatment recommendations, or exhibit fear of resuming their activities. It can help those who have insomnia and disrupted sleep, experience prolonged depression, show negative personality changes, and have obsessive anxiety or preoccupation with death.

claustrophobia   An exaggerated fear of closed places, such as closets, subways, tunnels, telephone booths, elevators, small rooms, crowds, or other enclosed spaces, the word *claustrophobia* is derived from the Latin word, *claustrum*, meaning bolt or lock. More people may suffer from claustrophobia than any other exaggerated fear.

Persons with this phobia often fear suffocation and suffer increased heartbeat and severe panic when faced with being in an enclosed or very crowded space.

Claustrophobia takes many forms. Some individuals fear being in a car or room in which they cannot open a window. They cannot bear to be in a room with the door closed or the shades drawn. Others fear sitting in the center of a row in a church, theater, or airplane. Some overcome their fears, to some extent, by sitting at the aisle.

codependency   Codependency is a relationship in which the participants have a strong need to be needed, as well as to create mutual needs in a detrimental, weakening manner. Such as an interplay of needs is required to preserve the dependent relationship. Codependent relationships bring about anxieties for at least one or both of the partners. In many cases, an individual would like to eliminate the anxieties caused by the codependent relationship but is too addicted to the situation to change.

An example of a codependent relationship is one in which the husband covers up for his wife's alcoholism or supports her agoraphobia because it keeps her dependent on him. He does the household chores, drives the children to their activities, and explains her problem as an "illness."

There are many kinds of codependent relationships: examples include a parent who continues to support an adult child who should be responsible for himself because the parent wants the child to feel dependent on him or her, and a husband who does all the household chores, shopping, and driving children to activities, explaining that his agoraphobic wife is "not feeling well." Such a husband is an enabler to his wife; it is difficult for an individual to live with AGORAPHOBIA without an enabler. Many alcoholics and drug addicts also have enablers.

When a parent continues to compensate for or cover up a child's difficulties in school or with the law, thinking that he or she is protecting the child, a codependent relationship is established. It is often interpreted that this behavior persists because preserving the child's flaws and immature behavior will keep him or her forever dependent on the parent. Because codependency is viewed as a type of addiction, advocates of the codependent theory feel that these tendencies can be overcome with a process similar to the recovery process used by Alcoholics Anonymous.

cognitive behavior therapy   A type of therapy based on learning theory, cognitive behavior therapy is used to help some individuals who have anxieties and phobias by examining the irrational exaggerated thoughts that lead to anxiety reactions; for example, if a person feels that "everyone" criticizes him or her, he or she will experience resultant anxiety. The individual's own statements are stimuli.

Cognitive-behavior therapy includes self-instructional training, stress inoculation, and COPING skills interventions. Three prominent innovators in this field are Albert Ellis (b. 1913), Donald Meichenbaum (b. 1940), and Aaron Beck (b. 1921).

combat fatigue, battle fatigue, combat neurosis   These anxieties occur after the extreme stresses of war or battles. The term has been replaced in contemporary usage with POSTTRAUMATIC STRESS DISORDER (PTSD). Veterans of World War I were said to have "combat fatigue," while Vietnam veterans with the same symptoms have PTSD.

competition   One of the many dichotomies present in American life today that induces anxieties, competition encourages individual achievement and the need to win. As such, it is the extreme opposite of another American concept—teamwork—which teaches us to respect others, appreciate their strengths and weaknesses, share our skills and knowledge, and help others meet their goals.

Early in life, children on the playing field experience the contradiction of competition and teamwork. Thus begins a source of stress that we carry through much of our adulthood. Competition encourages comparisons between ourselves and others, both on a social and economic level; this in turn affects our feeling of self-esteem.

conflict resolution   This concept deals with the ability of people to come out of an encounter respecting and liking each other. This a win-win situation in which the anxiety of anger and confrontation are minimized and those involved are able to be heard and to express their position and their needs.

TECHNIQUES TO AVOID ANXIETIES IN CONFLICT RESOLUTION

- Think before you speak.
- Say what you mean and mean what you say.
- Listen carefully to the other person.
- Do not put words in the other person's mouth.
- Stick to the problem at hand.
- Refrain from faultfinding.
- Apply the same rules to handling personal and business conflicts.

---

control   A feeling of control over people's lives means that the controllers are directing the outcomes of their everyday events. While life is going well, most people do not consciously think about their level of control. However, when that sense of control is threatened, they become aware, and this loss of control leads to ANXIETY, ANGER, and FRUSTRATION. Lack of control and lack of predictability almost always produce anxiety reactions.

Issues of loss of control involve situations in which people who could help themselves do not do so. They may lose motivation because of previous failures or may be experiencing what psychologist Martin Seligman (1942–   ) called LEARNED HELPLESSNESS. They feel that whatever they do will not make any difference. Their learned response is to not try to gain control over their lives, but they continue to feel the stress of the anger, frustration, and hostility that may lead to physical problems.

The anxities in some people's job is caused by no control over the pace of work, the work environment, or decision making. People who live in institutions or other such situations are frustrated because they can't change their environments and feel that things are being done to them or for them. An example is patients in hospitals who feel that their sense of control and autonomy has been taken away from them because of the hospital routine. Other people do not recognize their own options for making decisions and feel trapped by invisible forces; people who always try to please others in an effort to gain validation and self-esteem are an example of this. Those who fear flying do so because when they put themselves in the hands of the pilot, they feel totally out of control.

Although individuals cannot always control all events happening around them, they can learn healthier responses to these stressful situations. RELAXATION, BREATHING, or BIOFEEDBACK techniques can help a person gain a feeling of control.

coping   Coping consists of the psychological and the practical solutions that people must find for anxiety-producing, as well as everyday situations. Examples of these situations are dealing with cancer, caring for an aging relative, readjusting after the death of a loved one, facing unemployment, and dealing with random nuisances. Different individuals develop different ways of coping and learn to adapt their responses and reduce their stress and anxieties.

To some, coping means getting on with life and letting things happen as they may; to others, it is consciously using the skills they have learned in the past when facing problem situations. Coping can mean anticipating situations, or it can mean meeting problem situations head on: for examples, managers who are able to handle employees in everyday situations become nervous and jittery just anticipating giving a public speech; in a serious medical crisis, some people cannot cope with their own illness but manage to muster strength when they need to care for a loved one.

Individuals can learn new coping skills from psychotherapists as well as those who practice such alternative or complementary therapies as meditation and RELAXATION training. Relaxation and deep BREATHING techniques can help overcome the stress involved in a difficult situation.

Better coping for better health   When Hans Selye (1907–82), an Austrian-born Canadian endocrinologist and psychologist, wrote his landmark book *The Stress of Life,* he described the GENERAL ADAPTATION SYNDROME. The secret of health, he said, was in successful adjustment to ever-changing conditions.

Research studies have shown that people who cope well with life's stresses are healthier than those who have maladaptive coping mechanisms. In his book, *Adaptation to Life,* George Vaillant (1901–45), a Harvard psychologist, summarized some insights about relationships between good coping skills and health. He found that individuals who typically handle the trials and pressures of life in an immature way also tend to become ill four times as often as those who cope well.

Authors Arthur A. Stone and Laura S. Porter, in their article "Psychological Coping: Its Importance for Treating Medical Problems" *Mind/Body Medicine* 1, no. 1 (March 1995), reported that coping efforts may have direct effects on symptom perception and may have indirect effects on physiological changes and disease processes, mood changes, compliance with physician's instructions, and physician-patient communication.

counseling   Varied professional services—counseling—are available to individuals who seek help in some area of their life, such as anxiety concerns. These services may range from those of a trained social worker to a psychiatrist. Individuals, couples, and families can find appropriate counseling services, which may be provided in situations such as a school, the workplace, a hospital or a clinic, or a community center.

To seek counseling assistance, call a local hospital or look in the yellow pages of the telephone directory under psychologists or psychiatrists. Some listings have the heading *counselors*. There are also many community self-help and support groups in which members share their experiences; for participants in these groups, sharing means that they are not alone with their problems. They learn from one another to problem-solve.

Before beginning therapy with any counselors, ask what their credentials are and whether they are certified by any state agency or professional board. As with any other professional, some may meet an individual's needs better than others; individuals should not be afraid to change counselors if they are not meeting their needs. Generally, counselors have less training than social workers, psychologists, or psychiatrists.

covert rehearsal   Covert rehearsal is an imagery technique in which an individual in therapy is asked to imagine himself or herself effectively doing a task that produces anxiety or tasks that are counter to anxiety. Often, this rehearsal is done in hierarchical fashion so as not to desensitize the client. The individual may repeat the visualization many times and consider different alternatives. This procedure often follows covert modeling, in which the individual imagines or observes another person successfully performing a behavior or action. The goal of covert rehearsal is to motivate the individual to believe that he or she can face the situation or do the task at a reduced level of anxiety.

crisis   A crisis can be turning point for better or worse in an acute disease or mental illness, or it can be an emotionally significant event or a radical change in status in a person's life. The anxiety involved in a crisis situation may result from a combination of the individual's perception of an event as well as his or her ability or inability to cope with it. Some people will cope with a crisis situation better than others.

D

dance therapy   A form of therapy that permits release of anxieties and expression of emotion through body movement, dance therapy can be used effectively with a wide variety of individuals, from those who have mild anxiety symptoms to those who have severe mental health disorders. Many individuals who will not speak about their anxieties will indicate something about them with movement. Movement also helps the client be "in touch" with their body and release tensions stored in the body.

Therapists who use this technique are usually trained in dance and body movement as well as psychology. Dance therapy alone does not relieve symptoms associated with anxiety disorders but may be used in conjunction with other therapies or medication.

deadlines   Most people have experienced anxieties in meeting or failing to meet a date or time something must be done. Once they have fallen behind, it is difficult to catch up. They find that rushing tends to add to the anxiety level and decrease effectiveness. Ineffectiveness leads to frustration. Some people become moody and emotional and blame themselves or others for the deadline failure.

The key to avoiding anxieties produced by deadlines is setting realistic time schedules, enlisting the help needed when deadlines go awry, and negotiating new deadlines when it appears that for one reason or another, deadlines are going to be missed. For individuals to keep a positive outlook, they should break deadlines down to a series of small steps. As each step is completed, they will feel some success, and that success, in turn, will keep them motivated toward their final goal.

dental anxiety   Dental anxiety, or fear of dentists and dentistry, is sometimes referred to as dentophobia. A morbid fear of dental treatment is often traceable to at least one traumatic dental experience in childhood but also may be associated in many cases with a lower-than-normal pain threshhold and in some cases with strong personality factors that affect the situation. Dental anxiety ranges from a mild fear of dental treatment to extreme ANXIETY that leads an individual to avoid contact with a dentist entirely. Mild to high dental anxiety may surface as a mild queasy feeling in the stomach, a dryness in the mouth, an increased pulse, sweaty palms, or trembling hands. Persons with extreme dental anxiety may experience difficulty in breathing, dizziness or lightheadedness, choking, chest pain, diarrhea, and panic attacks (see PANIC, PANIC ATTACKS, AND PANIC DISORDER);

some even bolt from the chair during a dental procedure. Most frequently cited fears are the sight of the anesthetic needle (see NEEDLES, FEAR OF) and the sight and sound of the dentist's drill. Dental anxiety often occurs on its own, but it may also be associated with more general fears of blood, injury, pain, and doctors and hospitals (see BLOOD (AND BLOOD-INJURY) PHOBIA; PAIN, FEAR OF; and HOSPITALS, FEAR OF). Although many advances in dentistry during the latter part of the 20th century have greatly reduced the anxieties most people have about dentistry, there are still many fearful individuals.

Diagnostic and Statistical Manual of Mental Disorders (DSM IV-R)

This categorical guide for classification of mental disorders was published by the American Psychiatric Association in 1994. Mental disorders are groups into 16 major diagnostic classes, for example, anxiety disorders and mood disorders. The book is used for clinical, research, and educational purposes. It is used by psychiatrists, other physicians, psychologists, social workers, nurses, occupational and rehabilitation therapists, counselors, and other health and mental health professionals who wish to base a diagnosis of mental disorders, including anxieties and phobias, on standardized criteria. It was planned to be usable across settings including inpatient, outpatient, partial hospital, consultation-liaison, clinic, private practice, and primary care, and with community populations.

depression   See AFFECTIVE DISORDERS.

dis-stress   Hans Selye (1907–82), an Austrian-born Canadian endocrinologist and psychologist, differentiated between the unpleasant or harmful variety of stress called *dis-tress* (from the Latin *dis*="bad," as in dissonance, disagreement), and *eustress* (from the Greek *eu*= "good," as in *euphonia, euphoria*). During both distress and eustress, the body undergoes virtually the same nonspecific responses to various stimuli acting upon it. However, certain emotional factors, such as frustration and hostility, are particularly likely to turn stress into distress. Anxieties and fear reactions are also likely to be associated with feelings of dis-stress. Ironically, Selye preferred the term *strain* to describe what we have come to call the "stress" reaction, but his translation skills were not sufficient to recognize this subtle difference in meaning.

dizziness   A feeling of being unsteady, lightheaded, or faint and a sensation of spinning, turning, falling in space, or of standing still while objects around are moving. During a phobic reaction or a panic attack (see PANIC, PANIC ATTACKS, AND PANIC DISORDER), an individual may hyperventilate (breathe more than they need to; See HYPERVENTILATION). This results in a drop in the carbon dioxide in the blood, causing constriction of blood vessels in the brain, leading to dizziness or fainting. Hyperventilation is sometimes caused by a physical condition but is often the result of stress, anxiety, worry, or panic attacks. Chronic jaw tension can also cause dizziness.

Dizziness also may accompany seasickness. Some sailors advise keeping one's eyes on the horizon to give one a steady spot to watch. In most cases, dizziness disappears when the individual sets foot on land. Dizziness as a result of intoxication with alcohol usually subsides after a period of sleep.

There are prescription drugs as well some over-the-counter remedies available to help control dizziness. When dizziness occurs often, a physician should be consulted, as it may be a symptom of a condition in need of medical treatment.

dysfunctional family   This term indicates that the developmental and emotional needs of one or more members of a family are not being met and lead to anxieties for all concerned.

Research has shown that people raised in dysfunctional families— where alcohol or drug abuse, emotional or physical abuse, neglect, incest, marital conflict, or severe workaholism were present—carry varying vestiges of these problems well into adulthood. These issues generally surface in intimate relationships and on the job; because these are places where other kinds of anxieties and stress can be found, unresolved family issues can compound the mental health issues.

People from dysfunctional families usually are excellent employees. They are hard workers, dependable, resourceful, loyal, kind—attributes that have helped them survive their earlier experiences. However, because people from dysfunctional families have often not learned to feel good about themselves, they may have poor SELF-ESTEEM, may compensate by working longer hours than others, may try for perfection, and may take on more than they can handle. This leads to even more stress that impacts their job performance and physical health.

E

eating disorders This compulsive misuse of food to achieve some desired physical and/or mental state, is characterized by a person's intense fear of being fat and a resultant severe weight loss. It also may result in ill health and psychological impairments. In some cases, eating disorders may be related to a fear of body shape, or dysmorphophobia.

People who have eating disorders may be experiencing anxieties in some aspect of their lives that they think will be improved by dieting in excess. There is low SELF-ESTEEM and a mortal fear of fatness. When sufferers acknowledge their compulsive behavior, their stress is often expressed in feelings of depression and a wish to commit suicide (see SUICIDE, FEAR OF). Sufferers typically hide their illness; when family, friends, or co-workers discover their illness, they try to help. Typically, people with eating disorders feel they don't deserve to be helped, and this creates a great deal of anxieties for all concerned.

Eating disorders share common addictive features with alcohol and drug abuse, but unlike alcohol and drugs, food is essential to human life, and proper use of food is a central element of recovery.

Anorexia nervosa Anorexia nervosa is a syndrome of self-starvation in which people willfully restrict intake of food out of fear of becoming fat, resulting in life-threatening weight loss. Anorexics (people who suffer from anorexia nervosa) "feel fat" even when they are at normal weight or when emaciated, deny their illness, and develop an active disgust for food. Deaths from anorexia nervosa are higher than from any other psychiatric illness.

Causes of anorexia vary widely. Many anorexics are part of a close family and have special relationships with their parents. They are highly conforming, anxious to please, and may be obsessional in their habits. There is speculation that girls who refrain from eating wish to remain "thin as a boy" in an effort to escape the burdens of growing up and assuming a female sexual and marital role. Another contribution to the increase in anorexia is contemporary society's emphasis on slimness as it relates to beauty; this is particularly prevalent in the fashion industry with its overly thin models. Most women diet at some time, particularly athletes and dancers, who seem more prone to the disorder than other women. In some cases, anorexia nervosa is a symptom of depression, personality disorder, or even schizophrenia.

Symptoms include severe weight loss, wasting (cachexia), food preoccupation and rituals, amenorrhea (cessation of the menstrual period), and hyperactivity (constant exercising to lose weight). The anorexic may suffer from tiredness and fatigue, sensitivity to cold, and complain of hair loss.

Eating disorders sometimes result in other mental health disorders as well as depression. Individuals may suffer from withdrawal, mood swings, and feelings of shame and guilt. Both anorexics and bulimics develop rituals regarding eating and exercise. They often are perfectionists in habits, such as clothes and personal appearance, and have an "all or nothing" attitude about life.

Bulimia   Bulimia is characterized by recurrent episodes of binge eating followed by self-induced vomiting, vigorous exercise, and/or laxative and diuretic abuse to prevent weight gain. Most people view vomiting as a disagreeable experience, but to a bulimic, it is a means toward a desired goal.

Another eating disorder is *bulimarexia,* which is characterized by features of both anorexia nervosa and bulimia. Some individuals vacillate between anorexic and bulimic behaviors. After months and perhaps years of eating sparsely, the anorexic may crave food and begin to binge, but the fear of becoming overly fat leads her/him to vomit.

Bulimics may be of normal weight, slightly underweight, or extremely thin. Bingeing and vomiting may occur as much as several times a day. In severe cases, it may lead to dehydration and potassium loss causing weakness and cramps.

A cycle of addiction   Behaviors of anorexics and bulimics are driven by the cycle of addiction. There is an emotional emptiness that in turn leads to the psychological pain of low self-esteem. The individual looks for a way to dull the pain using addictive agents (starvation or bingeing), which usually result in the need to purge or medical problems. Finally, suffering from guilt, shame, and self-hate, the individual goes back to a routine of starvation and/or bingeing and purging.

**TRAITS ASSOCIATED WITH DEVELOPMENT
OF EATING DISORDERS**

Poor sense of body image	Unstable moods
Low self-esteem	Perfectionism
Social phobias	Difficulty controlling impulses

---

ego   Ego is a Freudian term that describes the part of the personality that deals with the external world and practical demands. According to Sigmund Freud (1856–1939), there are three structural parts to the psychic apparatus: the ego, the id, and the superego. The ego constitutes executive function and enables the individual to perceive, reason, solve problems, test reality, delay drive discharge, and adjust instinctual impulses (the id) according to the demands of reality through the individual's conscience (the superego). Most of the functions of the ego are automatic. The most important function of the ego is adaptation to reality. This is accomplished by delaying drives until acceptable behaviors are carried out, instituting defense mechanisms as safeguards against release of unacceptable impulses, and conducting executive functions such as memory, planning, and thought. Anxiety arises from the ego as a signal that unacceptable unconscious material is building toward conscious discharge.

Ego defense mechanisms   These are unconscious strategies that an individual uses to protect the ego from threatening impulses and conflicts. The most common ego defenses are repression, projection, sublimation, and displacement.

Ego integrity   The last of Erikson's first eight stages of man, *ego integrity* seems to mean "the serenity of old age," the looking back on one's life with completeness and satisfaction and the acceptance of one's own death without fear as natural and as part of the life cycle. Without ego integrity, the individual may look back in despair, seeing his life as a series of mistakes and missed opportunities; depression may result.

employee assistance programs (EAPs)   EAPs are designed to provide employees with help for anxiety problems they face on or off the job; having an EAP in one's company is an important employee benefit. From the employer's point-of-view, whatever EAPs can do to help reduce fears and anxieties for the employee helps with the stress of running a business. EAPs also can make referrals to experts in anxiety treatment.

Employee assistance programs (EAPs) have been in existence for the past 50 years. Most authors trace the origin of EAPs to the founding of Alcoholics Anonymous in 1935. In the 1960s and 1970s the scope of EAPs began to include help for employee problems such as depression and other mental health concerns, drug abuse, DIVORCE, and other family difficulties. At the end of the 1990s, these programs had been expanded to include issues such as environmental stress, corporate culture, managing rapid technological change, and retraining.

How EAPs work   There are two types of EAPs: internal and external. The majority of EAPs use independent companies that provide EAP services under a contract with the employer.

Although the programs are geared to identifying employees whose personal problems may adversely affect their job performance, they also take a proactive stance in helping employees avoid problems before they occur; for example, companies are offering their employees seminars on stress reduction, parenting, adolescents and drugs, exercise, health, and diet.

EAPs provide referrals to appropriate professional services for employees and their immediate families. Confidentiality is assured; most employees would not use an EAP if they thought their problems would be revealed.

empty nest syndrome   A situation in which children have grown up and left home is a source of anxiety experienced by many middle-aged parents. Typically, the syndrome seems to affect women more than men, particularly women whose lives have focused on their children at the expense of engaging in activities for themselves. For these women, the empty nest syndrome can be a mild form of depression that occurs after the children have left. Such women (and men, too, to some extent) no longer feel needed and feel a void in their life.

On the other hand, there are many middle-aged couples who view their children leaving home with a sense of relief and fulfillment of having accomplished a major life task. Many empty nesters, particularly women, return to work, take on volunteer activities in their community, enroll in classes, or engage in new hobbies for which they previously had no time.

envy   A sense that something that others have is lacking in one's life, envy is an anxiety-producing emotion to which people usually are unwilling to admit.

Envy can spring from many types of relationships. However, it is the situations close at hand involving friends, relatives, neighbors, or colleagues that are generally more intense and generate envy. An ability to imagine or identify with an admired person's strengths is an intellectual asset that may enable individuals to progress and better themselves. However, it becomes negative when the envious person remains fixated on another person's life and does not try to better his own life in a constructive way. Low SELF-ESTEEM produces envy that often does not improve by the attainment of material things, status symbols, or fame. Healthy self-esteem makes envy unlikely and allows for creative identification with admired traits in others.

Because feelings of envy imply that someone is in a superior position and because most religions regard envy as a sinful, people develop various ways of masking or suppressing it. To avoid expressing envy, some people develop superior and snobbish attitudes and gossip, criticize, or imply that the person to be envied is really the envious one.

eustress   The term *eustress*, referring to "good stress," was coined by Hans Selye (1907–82), pioneer researcher in the field of stress. During eustress and dis-stress (bad stress), the body undergoes virtually the same nonspecific responses to the various positive or negative stimuli acting upon it. However, Selye explained, the fact that eustress causes much less damage than distress demonstrates that "how you take it" determines whether one can adapt successfully to change.

Examples of "good stress" include starting a new romance, marrying, having a baby, buying a house, beginning a new job, or earning a raise at work. All these situations, as well as others, demand adaptations on the part of the individual. Both *eustress* and *dis-stress* are part of the GENERAL ADAPTATION SYNDROME (G.A.S.) that Selye described as being the controlling factor in how people cope with stresses in their lives.

Later researchers (Thomas H. Holmes, an American neuropsychiatrist (b. 1918–   ), and Richard H. Rahe, long affiliated with the Nevada Stress Center of the University of Nevada School of Medicine) included several "good stress" situations in their Social Readjustment Rating Scale, which was designed to be a predictor of ill health. Sources of good stress included marriage, marital reconciliation, retirement, pregnancy, buying a house, and outstanding personal achievement.

F

faith healing   The essence of faith healing, for those who believe in it, is the strong conviction of mind over matter. For some people, belief in faith healing contributes to relief of anxieties and fears.

Historically, some faith healing takes place with the assistance of a "healer" who places hands on the individual who is then healed; for example, faith healing was and still is an accepted phenomenon of Roman Catholicism where certain saints have been thought to have healing powers. The Catholic shrine at Lourdes has gained the reputation for causing miraculous recoveries. Native American religious practice includes rituals intended to promote healing of mental and physical ills. Faith healing is a central doctrine of Christian Scientists who actively discourage reliance on doctors and conventional medicine. Today, there is a renewed interest on faith healing brought about by the resurgence of the fundamental and Pentecostal religious movements. Some of the movements' ministers seem able to cure their congregants' afflictions by arousing in them a religious fervor or hysterical response.

Psychosomatic illnesses are thought to lend themselves best to the faith healing process. To counter the claim that faith healing has succeeded where conventional medical treatments have failed, some skeptics take the position that patients resort to faith healing only when desperate. Feeling that something must work, a person gets into a state of mind in which psychosomatic symptoms disappear, or if the problem is genuinely physical, at least the person feels better.

Research methods are difficult to apply to faith healing in part because of the questionable psychosomatic aspects of many diseases. Also, many spontaneous remissions or recoveries from serious or hopeless conditions without benefit of the faith healing process have been recorded. A psychological study of individuals who had a physical stress condition that was relieved by faith healing showed that, although there was little indication of mental illness, they had strong denial mechanisms. These denial mechanisms could keep them from recognizing continuing symptoms of their stress.

flying, fear of   Fear of flying, known as aeroacrophobia, represents one of the major fear categories for adults in the United States and probably throughout the world. Flying phobia is sometimes considered a specific phobia, but it also occurs as part of the agoraphobic syndrome. People with the specific phobia avoid flying because they may fear crashes or other calamities. Those who have agoraphobia fear having a panic attack and its consequences.

The fear of flying itself has two points of origin—the anticipatory situation and the flying situation itself. Anticipatory anxiety occurs because a commitment has been made to fly (a reservation has been made, ticket purchased, people informed of trip, etc.). Anticipatory anxiety usually is experienced as feelings of dread, rapid pulse, total body sensations (tension, warmth, etc.), and fear inducing images and thoughts. Interestingly, the anticipatory fear is usually not of the airplane itself but of uncontrollable outcomes such as fear of losing control of oneself in the airplane and going crazy or embarrassing oneself in public, fear of separation from loved ones, fear of death, fears of relinquishing control to someone else, thoughts of falling from the sky and dying in a crash, and so on. Fear in the plane itself may encompass many of the anticipatory fears just described but also usually involve fears of being enclosed, of being alone or away from others one depends on, of feeling trapped and unable to leave at will, of social rejection due to the reaction, of the fear sensations, and sometimes of the place or person the individual is leaving or the place or person the individual may be seeing at the destination.

Treatment for the fear of flying has varied from traditional therapies to hypnosis, flooding, and exposure therapies. The latter provide the best long-term success rate at about 75–80 percent. A "cue-controlled" relaxation procedure in which the phobic learns to produce relaxation on cue seems to offer promise as an effective technique. Success, of course, involves more than just being able to fly. The more rigorous criterion involves flying with progressively increased ease and comfort over a long-term series of trials. Unfortunately, there are very few experimental studies to date that demonstrate comparative therapy effects.

The most commonly used drug for the fear of flying is probably alcohol. Unfortunately, although alcohol reduces autonomic arousal, it tends to produce anxietylike sensations (such as dizziness, loss of balance, mental confusion, lack of control of perceptual-motor functions, and so on) which, in turn, can trigger an anxiety response. PROPRANOLOL and ALPRA-ZOLAM are two drugs commonly used for fear of flying. They are both fast acting and produce relatively few side effects. Triazolam has also been used on a more experimental basis.

Efforts to identify personality qualities associated with the fear of flying have not been fruitful. Interestingly, family trauma associated with flying (such as loss of or injury to a family member—even a distant one— in an aircraft accident) is a significant predictor of phobic reaction. This would support a modeling theory of acquisition. Also, multiphobics or individuals suffering from panic disorders have a higher incidence of aerophobia than uniphobics and seem to be much more difficult to treat than the latter.

Some members of the military suffer a fear of flying as a symptom of POSTTRAUMATIC STRESS DISORDER.

food fears   Fear of food, or certain foods, is known as sitophobia, sitiophobia, and cibophobia. Some individuals fear eating certain foods, such as meat. For some, the fear is related to religious taboos. For example, many Hindus are vegetarian, and Muslims and Jews are forbidden to eat pork. If a religious individual eats a forbidden food by mistake or coercion, he or she may feel various reactions and may vomit or feel nauseous for days.

Food aversions   Many people strongly dislike certain foods, often because they associate them with nausea and vomiting. Most food aversions are taste aversions, but individuals may also dislike its sight, smell, or symbolic aspects. Many people avoid new foods. Individuals decide which foods are acceptable based on cultural and individual rearing patterns. Some, who mistakenly eat a taboo food, may become terrified of imagined consequences.

forgetting   An inability to retrieve stored long- or short-term memories, forgetting is a common occurrence and a source of anxiety for many people. Most people forget short-term as well as long-term memories, particularly the elderly who experience memory loss as they grow older. But forgetting is not just a sign of old age; many people consciously block out stressful memories and many are simply forgetful. They may forget recently made appointments, forget what their boss told them earlier in the day, or forget occurrences that happened in childhood.

Scientific studies have concentrated primarily on two factors, inhibition and loss of retrieval clues. Inhibition is the theory that similar kinds of learning, either before or after the event to be remembered, interfere with later recall of that event. Loss of retrieval clues is based on the theory that recall is easier when the individual is dealing with familiar people, things, and situations. Other theories hold that individuals have selective memories and may forget events or situations previously encountered that were unpleasant, stressful, or even traumatic. This concept is related to repression, which suggests that forgetting is a COPING mechanism.

Many individuals have fears of developing ALZHEIMER'S DISEASE when they begin to experience symptoms of forgetting.

friends   Friends are unique among human relationships. Although individuals have little or no choice in family or neighbors, they can choose their friends. Some friendships evolve from shared interests or values, some simply from a shared history, and some from compatible personalities. Qualities most appreciated in friends include loyalty, trust, and an ability to keep a confidence. People want to feel that they can rely on their friends and that they can have an open and honest friendship during good as well as anxious and stressful times.

When friends are supportive, they help relieve anxieties during periods of turmoil or crisis. Individuals who experience depression often report a lack of friends, although having a wide circle of friends is not a preventive factor for depression. Some reports have indicated that individuals who have many friends may be healthier and actually live longer than those who do not.

Friends can also be a source of anxiety because they may challenge or be challenged by other relationships in the individual's life. For examples, a friendship may be broken or changed when one friend marries; a friend of the opposite sex frequently is unsettling to a spouse or lover. Friends who do not meet with parents' approval can be a source of family conflict. Friends who decide to share housing or enter into a business partnership sometimes discover undesirable facets of the other person's personality that could be ignored when the relationship was less formal. In the workplace, a friendship may dissolve when two people are vying for the same promotion.

frustration   Frustration is the interference with an individual's impulses or desired actions by internal or external forces. Internal forces are inhibitions and anxieties, and external forces can come from a parent, teachers, friends, as well as the rules of the society. There are deep feelings of discontent and tension because of unresolved problems, unfulfilled needs, or roadblocks to personal goals. Regardless of the cause, frustration causes anxiety for most people.

Modern life is filled with frustrations from birth to old age. Crying babies may be frustrated because of hunger, school-age children may be frustrated by high expectations of their parents, parents may be frustrated by their jobs, and the elderly may be frustrated by their increasing lack of independence.

People who constantly feel anxious because of frustrations respond in many ways. A person who is mentally healthy usually deals with frustration in an acceptable way, sometimes with humor (see HUMOR, USE IN THERAPY). Others react with ANGER, hostility, AGGRESSION, or depression, while still others become withdrawn and passive. Many children and adults who are constantly frustrated show regressive behavior—going back to childlike behavior, particularly aggression or depression—and may become unable to cope with problems on their own.

G

gagging, hypersensitive   The feeling that one will gag or choke is often a symptom of anxiety. A fear of gagging is related to the feeling of a lump in the throat that one cannot seem to swallow. Those who are hypersensitive gaggers cannot tolerate foreign objects in their mouths, such as those objects used during dental treatment. In some cases, individuals may gag, retch, or vomit if they even hear or think about dentistry or smell an odor associated with dental procedures.

Gagging is a normal protective reflex for the oropharynx; the sensitivity and trigger area is greater in some individuals than others. In mild cases, gagging can be triggered just by touching near the back of the mouth with the tongue or being touched by a dental instrument. In more severe cases, the trigger can be touching the front of the mouth, the face, and the front of the neck; certain smells or sights associated with unpleasant oral experiences such as dentistry; or becoming ill due to certain foods.

Some hypersensitive gaggers swallow with their teeth clenched and thus have difficulty during dental procedures. Such individuals have particular difficulty in swallowing with their teeth apart.

There are several ways that individuals who experience gagging can be helped. General relaxation techniques are beneficial. Communicating one's fears to the dentist before a procedure is important. Use of a rating scale on which the patient indicates the types of procedures that are likeliest to induce the most gagging will improve communications between patient and dentist. During dental procedures, hypersentitive gaggers can be taught to signal (with a raised hand) whenever gagging is about to occur.

Hypersensitive gaggers can learn to modify their swallowing pattern, for example, swallowing with the teeth slightly apart and the tongue further back in the mouth. When sharp teeth make the tongue hypersentitive, the teeth can be smoothed down somewhat. Some dentists give anxious patients such homework assignments as learning to hold buttons under the tongue and rolling them around in the mouth so that they become accustomed to having foreign objects in their mouth without gagging.

gambling, fear of; compulsion   Individuals who fear gambling usually prefer secure situations to situations involving risks. They may be fearful of losing or of making errors, or they may be fearful of what they regard as sin or wrongdoing. They may not feel comfortable when they relinquish a certain amount of control over their circumstances, which is usually involved in gambling. Individuals who feel that they are compulsive gamblers—unable to stop once they start—may actually fear gambling because of what they perceive as "its" control over them and the ensuing detrimental effects on their lives. Those who have had bad experiences with gambling may fear it more than those who have never gambled before.

garlic, fear of   Fear of garlic is known as alliumphobia. This fear may extend to a variety of plants characterized by their pungent odor, including the onion, leek, chive, and shallot.

gender identity disorder   This type of psychosexual disorder occurs when an individual's gender identity is incongruent with his or her anatomical sex. When an individual believes that he or she is a man or a woman in the body of the other sex, anxieties often result. Some individuals who have these feelings relieve their anxieties by having a sex change operation.

gender role   The set of behaviors and attitudes that are socially associated with being male or female. These attitudes may be expressed to varying degrees by the individual. Historically, in Western cultures, gender role for many women was passive and submissive, which led to many anxieties (see ANXIETY) and frustrations, until the women's liberation movement and the sexual revolution in westernized countries during the latter half of the 20th century. As a result of many societal changes, gender roles have also changed significantly; for example, child care is no longer exclusively the woman's role, and earning the larger part of the family income is no longer exclusively the man's role. However, changes in gender roles have led to many contemporary anxieties, such as women's feelings of conflict between motherhood and career and men's fears of inferiority when the wife advances rapidly in her career and out-earns the husband.

general adaptation syndrome (G.A.S.)   A term that we now know as stress, general adaptation syndrome was coined by Hans Selye (1907–82), an Austrian-born Canadian endocrinologist and psychologist, in his landmark book, *The Stress of Life* (1956). The G.A.S. is the manifestation of stress in the whole body as it develops over time. It is through the G.A.S. that various internal organs, especially the endocrine glands and the nervous system, help individuals adjust to constant changes occurring in and around them and to "navigate a steady course toward whatever they consider a worthwhile goal."

Dr. Selye was a pioneer in an area that has continued to look at stress as a threat to wellness. The secret of health, he contended, was in successful adjustment to ever-changing conditions. Life, he said, is largely a process of adaptation to the circumstances in which we exist. He viewed many nervous and emotional disturbances, such as high blood pressure and some cardiovascular problems, gastric and duodenal ulcers, and certain types of allergic problems, as essentially diseases of adaptation.

Selye called his concept the general adaptation syndrome because it is produced only by agents which have a *general* effect on large portions of the body. He called it *adaptive* because it stimulates defense mechanisms. He used the term *syndrome* because individual manifestations are coordinated and interdependent on each other.

There are three stages in the G.A.S, Selye said. Individuals go through the stages many times each day as well as throughout life. Whatever demands are made on us, we progress through the sequence. The first is an alarm reaction, or the bodily expression of a generalized call for our defensive forces. We experience surprise and anxiety because of our inexperience in dealing with a new situation. The second stage, resistance, occurs when we have learned to cope with the new situation efficiently. The third stage is exhaustion or a depletion of our energy reserves, which leads to fatigue. Adaptability, Selye continued, was a finite amount of vitality (thought of as capital) with which we are born. We can withdraw from it throughout life but cannot add to it.

generalized anxiety disorders (GADs)   Excessive anxiety levels and apprehension often are the main characteristics of GAD. Other symptoms associated with the disorder can be categorized as motor tension, autonomic hyperactivity, and hypervigilance.

generational anxiety   The anxieties faced by millions of middle-aged individuals who care for aging relatives in addition to raising children, holding a job, and trying to live their own lives is sometimes referred to as generational or sandwich generation anxiety. As the numbers of people above age 65, 75, and even 85 increase dramatically and 95 percent of older people live outside of nursing homes, responsibility for their care falls increasingly to the middle-aged people, and in most cases, women. As these middle-generation individuals see their children entering and finishing college and becoming involved in a career and marriage, they may feel "trapped" by another long-term burden that they may view as more demanding than that of raising school-age children.

Many midlife individuals find that their love of parents turns toward anger as their own lives are pulled in three or four different directions. Many must give up their own time, interests, and relaxation to become caregivers. Thus the "women (or men) in the middle" are three times more likely to suffer depression and more likely to become dependent on prescription drugs and alcohol and to become physically ill. Their spouses and children also suffer restrictions on social and leisure activities, disruption of household routines, and added financial burdens.

To relieve generational anxieties, individuals in the middle might analyze their situations carefully and consider whether they can fully cope with these demands. A family conference can be called to apprise everyone involved of the burdens and to build realistic shared responsibilities, if at all possible. Community support groups for children of aging parents can be helpful. Having a single physician for the entire family may be helpful in tying together all the medical care the aging parent needs and, at the same time, providing emotional support and encouragement for those in the middle.

gephyrophobia   Fear of bridges is termed gephyrophobia.

germs, fear of   Fear of germs is known as bacillophobia or mikrophobia. The term *germs* commonly refers to any microorganism that can cause disease. Germs, although a nonspecific term, for the purpose of causing anxieties and phobias, can include the many types of bacteria, molds, yeasts, and viruses. Fears of germs can lead to other behaviors, such as OBSESSIVE-COMPULSIVE DISORDER, in which an individual may constantly wash his or her hands, or specific disease phobias, such as tubercolophobia.

gestalt therapy   A type of psychotherapy, gestalt is one of many therapies useful in treating individuals who have phobias and anxieties. It emphasizes treatment of the person as a whole, including biological aspects and their organic functioning, perceptions, and interrelationships with the outside world, and focuses on the sensory awareness of the individual's here-and-now experiences rather than on past recollections or future expectations. It can be used in individual or group therapy settings because gestalt therapy uses role-playing, acting out anger or fright, reliving traumatic experiences, and other techniques such as the "empty chair" to elicit spontaneous feelings and self-awareness, promote personality growth, and help the individual develop his full potential. Gestalt therapy was developed by Frederic S. Perls, a German-born U.S. psychotherapist (1893–1970).

ghosts, fear of   Fear of ghosts is known as phasmophobia or daemonophobia. A ghost may be the spirit of a dead person, which haunts living persons or former habitats, or it may be a returning or haunting memory or image.

The fear of ghosts may have been planted in the minds of primitive peoples because of concern about the afterlife of deceased relatives. Dead ancestors, who were worshiped in many early cultures as gods or near gods, were thought to be easily angered. Gifts and ceremonies were necessary to sustain their good will and to decrease hostilities that the dead were believed to bear toward the living.

Belief in and fear of ghosts was furthered by desires for a pleasant afterlife, a heaven or Elysian fields, accessible to some but not all spirits. Criminals and witches were condemned to walk the earth rather than enter a restful existence after death. The spirits of murder victims or individuals who had been buried improperly could not rest in peace until the wrong had been righted. Burial customs and rituals indicate a desire to keep the spirits of the dead away from the living.

Ghosts have assumed many appearances: some materialize in healthy physical form; others show signs of their cause of death. In some cases, only a disembodied head or other fragment of the body appears. Ghosts may appear as skeletons, corpses, or in the burial shroud. Ghost animals, ships, and trains have also been sighted. Mysterious moving lights can indicate a ghostly presence. Ghosts may appear for a variety of purposes, including to convey information from the beyond, to right a wrong, or to finish some business interrupted by their death. There have been reports of living persons appearing as apparitions across impossible barriers of time and space at a moment of crisis. The least lively type of ghost is the haunt, a spectral figure that appears to be on patrol, covering the same place with the same actions at the same time on a regular basis and having no interaction with the living. Haunted houses and castles are a particularly British phenomenon.

Psychical researchers have offered several explanations for ghostly appearances by those in the field of psychical research. Mental telepathy and the possibility that everything in existence has a mysterious double have been suggested. Sigmund Freud (1856–1939) and Swiss psychologist Carl Gustav Jung (1875–1961) took ghosts seriously but indicated that they felt that a scientific explanation could be found for them. On the universality of ghost beliefs, psychologist William James (1842–1910) commented: "So few are explained away it is a bad method to ignore them."

U.S. physician and author Benjamin Rush (1745–1813) had this to say about the ghost phobia:

> This distemper is most common among servants and children. It manifests itself chiefly in passing by graveyards, and old empty houses. I have heard of a few instances of grown people, and of men of cultivated understandings, who have been afflicted with this species of Phobia.

Physicians who have sacrificed the lives of their patients through carelessness, rashness, or ignorance; as also witnesses who have convicted by their evidence—judges who have condemned by their influence—and kings and governors who have executed by their power, innocent persons, through prejudice or resentment, are all deeply affected with the Ghost Phobia. Generals of armies and military butchers, who make war only to gratify ambition or avarice, are likewise subject to paroxysms of this disorder. The late King of Prussia, upon a certain occasion, abused his guards most intemperately, for conducting him from a review through a graveyard. The reflection on the number of men whom his power and sword had consigned to the mansions of death, produced in his majesty, this Ghost Phobia in all its horrors.

globus hystericus   Globus hystericus is the feeling that one has a lump or mass in the throat when nothing is there. The individual usually experiences difficulty in swallowing. This can be a symptom of anxiety arousal.

goal   The object or end toward which therapy for anxieties or phobia is aimed. In different types of therapy there are different types of goals: for example, in BEHAVIOR THERAPY, a goal for an individual who has a specific phobia might be to face the phobic item or situation without fear; in PSYCHOANALYSIS, the treatment goal is to make unconscious material conscious; in family therapy, the goal is to restructure the family system and bring about a better functioning family group. Goals should be specific, measurable, and attainable. There may be many goals for one individual, and goals may change during the course of therapy; for example, an elevator phobic's first goal might be to face an elevator without fear. A later goal would be to enter the elevator and then ride up in it.

goblins, fear of   Some people fear the small, grotesque spirits known as goblins, considered by some to be a type of fairy. Goblins are at worst malicious and at best mischievious. They often live in the woods but come into homes to play their tricks. James Witcomb Riley's poem for children, "Little Orphan Annie," plays on the fears that many children have of goblins and uses these fears to discipline children with the recurring threat "the gobble-uns'll git you ef you don't watch out!"

going crazy, fear of   Many individuals who have anxieties, fears, phobias, and panic attacks (see PANIC, PANIC ATTACKS, AND PANIC DISORDER) at times fear that they are going crazy. Their misinterpretation of their situation may be heightened if they do not have any support and understanding from relatives and friends or, particularly, if those close to them suggest that the phobic's feelings are "all in the mind." When individuals fear going crazy, usually they are referring to a severe mental disorder known as schizophrenia. However, most individuals who have phobias, anxieties, panic attacks, depression, and OBSESSIVE-COMPULSIVE DISORDERS are not schizophrenic, and when an individual understands the nature of his or her psychological problem, he or she will have less fear of going crazy. Schizophrenia is a major mental disorder characterized by such severe symptoms as disjointed thoughts and speech, sometimes extending to babbling, delusions, or strange beliefs (for example, that one is receiving messages from outer space), and hallucinations (for example, hearing voices). Schizophrenia usually begins gradually and not suddenly (such as during a panic attack). Schizophrenia is often genetic, and in some people, no amount of anxieties or stress will cause the disorder. People who become schizophrenic usually will show some mild symptoms for most of their lives, such as unusual or bizarre thoughts or speech. Schizophrenia usually first appears in the late teens to early 20s. Individuals who are in therapy for their fears, phobias, and anxieties can be fairly certain that they are not likely to become schizophrenic because they would have been so diagnosed during examination, interviews, and testing. At a more symbolic level, the fear of going crazy is a fear of becoming disconnected from reality and other people and living in an isolated or alienated state.

good news   Fear of hearing good news is known as euphobia. Those who have this fear may fear that the good news will not last, that they do not deserve to have good fortune, or that they should have some guilt about the news. Some who fear good news fear that bad news may follow, some fear success. Fear of good news may be related to a fear of gaiety or happiness.

grief reaction   This feeling of loss and anxiety that an individual experiences when a crucial bond is disrupted is often followed by depression. There is a higher death and illness risk for individuals for a year after they lose a spouse. Through the exposure approach of guided mourning, the bereaved may be led to reduce avoidance of cues reminiscent of the deceased.

Grief is a type of suffering, a symptom of bereavement and loss, experienced physically, emotionally, and psychologically. Grief may be synonymous with sorrow, the emotion that accompanies mourning. Individuals who experience grief may have sensations characteristic of emotional disorders such as ANXIETY, INSOMNIA, depression, loss of appetite, and preoccupation with the lost party. As a result of a classic study following the 1942 Cocoanut Grove nightclub fire in Boston, five normal stages of grief reaction were defined as: initial shock, intense sadness, withdrawal from the environment, protest of the loss, and finally a gradual resolution of the loss. Elisabeth Kübler-Ross (b. 1926) Swiss-American physician and author of *On Death and Dying* (1969), identified the stages of emotion experienced after the death of a loved one as: denial, anger, bargaining, depression, and acceptance. Most grieving persons will experience these stages or others similar. All stages of mourning are a normal and necessary component to grief resolution.

growing old, fear of   Fear of growing old is known as gerascophobia. This is a fear shared by many middle-aged people who fear being alone as they age, deteriorate physically and mentally, and lose control, and become a burden to their children or others to care for and possibly support. Some fear losing their memory; others fear losing control of bodily functions and being embarrassed by their dependence on others.

Many fear the financial costs of care in a nursing home, if that type of care should be needed. More specific fears related to growing old are fear of ALZHEIMER'S DISEASE, fear of HEART ATTACK, and certain disease phobias, such as fear of diabetes, which is more prevalent in older people.

guilt   An aversive feeling that an individual experiences as a consequence of an action or in anticipation of performing the behavior, guilt is felt following commission of an act and omission of an acceptable course of action. Guilt is a form of anxiety. Along with guilt, an individual anticipates punishment; when he or she projects guilt onto others, he or she also anticipates their punishment. Some individuals believe, possibly unconsciously, that they have "sinned," and they fear God will attack and punish them. Guilt keeps individuals trapped because they blame themselves or others. Severe or abnormal guilt feelings may result in depression and or chronic anxieties (see ANXIETY). Individuals who have obsessive-compulsive neuroses often feel the need to scrutinize their conduct and may have a compulsion to confess to therapists or clergy. Some individuals commit suicide out of profound guilt feelings over events for which death seems to be the only appropriate restitution. Guilt is a way to hold onto the past and to produce self-condemnation, which keeps the individual under the control of his or her ego and supports a view that he or she is unlovable.

gymnophobia   Fear of naked bodies is called gymnophobia.

H

hair fears Fear of hair is known as trichophobia or chaetophobia. The most frequently occurring fear regarding hair is baldness or loss of hair. Also, some individuals fear having the hair on their head touched, pulled, brushed, combed, or washed. Some fear that they will grow bald unless their hair is untouched; other individuals fear the sight of a hair on clothing (their own or the hair of others), on the table, or on a sink. There are those who fear body hair on themselves or on others, and others who fear white or grey hair on themselves or others. As with many fears, hair fear is a conditioned response or a generalized response.

Fear of having a haircut Fear of having a haircut arises from a number of causes including a fear of sitting confined in the barber or beautician's chair, a feeling of being out of control while the barber or beautician is working with a scissors or razor, or a fear of injury from these implements. Some who have agoraphobia fear going out to get a haircut; others fear being seen by others while they are having a haircut or fear being judged and compared unfavorably with others as they sit on the chair. Fear of having a haircut is related to many phobias, including agoraphobia, social phobia, and fear of blood and injury.

Fear of hair disease Fear of hair disease is known as chaetophobia. The most common hair disorder is thinning hair or baldness. Hair loss in men is largely due to male-pattern baldness; thinning hair in women is most often due to female-pattern baldness. Most other losses of hair are temporary such as those following illness or as a result of certain drug therapy. Normal regrowth usually resumes in most cases.

Some fear unusual hair conditions, one of which is called trichorrhexis, in which the hair shaft may alter, bulge, and narrow; the hair tends to split at regular intervals. The cause of this condition is not known, and there is no cure for it. Some people fear having too oily or too dry hair.

Some hair-related problems involve the scalp. Such conditions include dandruff, psoriasis, seborrheic dermatitis, inflammation of the hair follicles (folliculitis), and ringworm. Some fear these conditions because, particularly in the case of dandruff, they are socially noticeable. An individual who has any tendency toward social phobia may use dandruff as an excuse to avoid social situations.

hallucinations Feelings that a person is seeing, hearing, smelling, tasting, or feeling something that is really not there, hallucinations are sources of anxiety because these perceptions cannot be reinforced by any-one else. Hallucinations may be disturbing to sufferers as well as those who are trying to understand what they are feeling.

Hallucinations sometimes occur as a reaction to certain medications, to high fevers, and to serious illnesses. They also occur in some severe mental disorders, such as schizophrenia.

Reactions to hallucinogens Hallucinogens are drugs and agents that produce profound distortions to one's senses of sight, sound, smell, and touch, as well as to the senses of direction, time, and distance. Although some individuals may resort to hallucinogens for relief from stress, there are no acceptable medical uses for hallucinogens.

People may experience a "high" associated with use of hallucinogens which may last as long as eight hours. However, there are aftereffects, including acute ANXIETY, restlessness, and sleeplessness. Long after the hallucinogen is eliminated from the body, the user may experience "flashbacks," which are fragmentary reoccurrences of hallucinogenic effects.

Hallucinogens occur naturally but are primarily created synthetically. The most common hallucinogens are LSD (lysergic acid diethylamide, mescaline, peyote, psilocybin mushrooms, MDMA 3,4-methylene-dioxymethamphetamine, and phencyclidine PCP.

hand-wringing   Hand-wringing is usually a symptom of anxiety and uncertainty. Individuals who constantly wring their hands may have dif-ficulty in making decisions and seem to be expressing physically a worry or concern that they do not express verbally. For many, wringing the hands as though they were constantly washing them or squeezing out a cloth may become an unconscious habit. Some individuals start wring-ing their hands when faced with a stressful situation, while others may do it at any time. Handwringers tend to be worriers and consider all pos-sibilities of a situation before taking any action. Such individuals are often are meticulous about what they do, sometimes to the point of being compulsive.

haphephobia   This fear of being touched is also known as haptephobia and aphephobia.

happiness, fear of   Fear of happiness or fear of gaiety is known as cherophobia. This fear may be related to a fear of hearing good news or even a fear of success.

hardiness   *Hardiness* is a term coined by Salvatore Maddi, Ph.D. (a Uni-versity of Chicago psychologist), relating to stress-buffering characteristics of people who stay healthy. People with hardiness are able to withstand significant levels of stress without becoming ill; those who are more helpless than hardy develop more illnesses, both mental and physical.

headaches   Headaches include pains in the head from the outer linings of the brain and from the scalp and its blood vessels and muscles; headaches occur due to tension in or stretching of these structures. They are a source of anxiety because of their discomfort and unpredictability and may be caused by a reaction to stressful situations as well as to overindulgence in alcohol, extreme fatigue, and certain infections. Headaches are fairly common in depression, sleep disorders, and in individuals who have many anxieties (see ANXIETY) as well as those suffering from BOREDOM.

Types of Headaches   *Tension or muscle contraction headaches,* caused by tightening in the muscles of the face, neck, and scalp, may result from stress or poor posture; they may last for days or weeks and can cause variable degrees of discomfort. About 90 percent of all headaches are classified as tension headaches.

Cluster headaches. The term refers to the characteristic grouping in a series of attacks; the pain is generally very intense and severe and is almost always one-sided; during a series, the pain remains on the same side. In a new series, it can occur on the opposite side. Cluster headaches are not associated with gastrointestinal disturbances or sensitivity to light that typically accompany other vascular headaches, such as migraine.

Temporomandibular joint (TMJ) headaches cause a dull ache in and around the ear that gets worse when one chews, talks, or yawns. Sufferers may hear a clicking sound on opening the mouth and feel soreness in the jaw muscles. Stress, a poor bite, or grinding of the teeth may bring on the headache.

Caffeine headaches occur in some individuals who drink too much caffeine in coffee, tea, and soft drinks. Some people can relieve their symptoms by eliminating drinks containing caffeine from their diet. Others, however, who drink large quantities of the liquids and stop abruptly may suffer caffeine withdrawal symptoms, including headaches, irritability, depression, and sometimes nausea; relief may occur with ingestion of a caffeinated beverage.

Migraine headaches   Migraine or vascular headaches are characterized by the throbbing sensation that occurs when blood vessels in the head dilate or swell. Migraine is often a debilitating disease that occurs in periodic attacks, with each attack lasting from four to 72 hours. Symptoms may include intense pain, often associated with nausea, vomiting, appetite loss, and an unusual sensitivity to light and/or sound. Migraines generally start on either side of the head and usually remain one-sided.

Of the 23 million American migraine sufferers, 60 percent are women. Men and women between the ages of 35 and 45 years of age suffer most from migraine headaches, according to a study reported in the *Journal of the American Medical Association* (December 31, 1991). More than three-fourths of migraine sufferers come from families in which other members have the same disorder. The *JAMA* researchers reported that 8.7 million females and 2.6 million males suffer from migraine headache with moderate to severe disability. Of these, 3.4 million females and 1.1 million males experience one or more attacks per month.

Common migraine headaches start unexpectedly, while a *classic* migraine is usually preceded by a warning symptom known as an aura, which occurs five to 30 minutes prior to the headache. Typically, the aura includes HALLUCINATIONS of jagged light or color, speech impairment, perception of strange odors, confusion, and tingling or numbness in the face or limbs.

Why migraine headaches produce anxiety   Because migraine headaches usually recur, sufferers become concerned that an attack will happen at an unfortuitous time, such as on the day of a graduation, a wedding, or important appointment. Migraine headaches often begin during a period of time filled with anxieties, such as during adolescence or menopause (see MENOPAUSE, FEAR OF) or around the time of a DIVORCE or death of a mate. When a physician diagnoses headaches, the individual's anxieties and COPING styles will be considered.

Migraine headaches, which often occur in members of the same family, may result from a predisposing genetic biochemical abnormality. Also, personality traits may play a role in determining who gets migraines. Although there is no typical personality associated with these headaches, some migraine sufferers have characteristics of compulsivity and perfection.

Emotional tension and stress may lead to migraine attacks because under extreme stress, the arteries of the head and those reaching the brain draw tightly together and restrict the flow of blood. This in turn may result in a shortage of oxygen to the brain. When blood vessels dilate or stretch, a greater amount of blood passes through, putting more pressure on the pain-sensitive nerves in and close to the walls of the arteries.

Common migraine triggers   In a susceptible person, the migraine trigger might be something seen, smelled, heard, eaten, or experienced; it may be one particular trigger or a combination of factors.

Approximately 20 percent of all migraine sufferers have a sensitivity to a specific food or foods. Knowing that certain foods may trigger migraines is an additional source of stress. Many individuals find that certain foods (such as cheese, chocolate, and red wine) containing a substance known as tyramine trigger migraine attacks. Sodium nitrite, a

---

COMMON MIGRAINE TRIGGERS

- Dietary habits (see detailed listing following)
- Environmental factors, such as weather, bright lights, glare, or noise
- Emotional factors, such as depression, anxiety, resentment or fatigue
- Activity, such as motion from riding in a car or airplane, lack of sleep, too much sleep, eyestrain, and a fall or head injury
- Hormonal, such as menstrual cycle, oral contraceptives or estrogen supplements
- Medications, such as overuse of over-the-counter pain relievers and some prescription medications

---

DIETARY FACTORS: POSSIBLE MIGRAINE ATTACK TRIGGERS

- Caffeinated foods and drinks: coffee, tea, chocolate, cocoa, colas/soft drinks
- Alcohol, especially red wine, vermouth, champagne, beer
- Dairy products: aged cheeses, sour cream, whole milk, buttermilk, yogurt, ice cream
- Breads: sourdough, fresh yeast, and some types of cereals
- Vegetables: some types of beans (broad, Italian, lima, lentil, fava, soy), sauerkraut, onions, peas
- Snacks: nuts, peanuts, peanut butter, pickles, seeds, sesame
- Meats: organ meats, salted meats, dried meats, cured meats, smoked fish, meats with nitrites (such as hot dogs, sausages, lunch meat)
- Fruits: most citrus fruits, bananas, avocados, figs, raisins, papaya, passion fruit, red plums, raspberries, plantains, pineapples
- Monosodium glutamate (MSG), a flavor enhancer often used by restaurants and also in seasoned salt, instant foods, canned soup, frozen dinners, pizza, potato chips
- Soups, particularly those containing MSG; soups made from bouillon cubes
- Desserts: chocolate, licorice, molasses, cakes/cookies made with yeast
- Seasonings and flavorings such as soy sauce, some spices, garlic powder, onion powder, salt, meat tenderizers, marinades
- Hunger; missing meals, fasting, dieting

---

preservative used in ham, hot dogs, and many other sausages, is a trigger for some people. Although some migraine researchers have recommended that all migraine sufferers avoid these foods, only about 30 percent of people who have migraine headaches experience this reaction to some foods. Not eating or missing meals can cause low blood sugar levels, which are also a migraine trigger.

Identifying and avoiding the triggers that cause headaches is the one of the most significant management techniques for controlling headache frequency and stress.

Sexually related headaches   Some individuals have headaches related to sexual activity. Such persons do not use the headache to avoid sexual activity but actually do endure discomfort before, during, or after sexual intercourse. Nevertheless, the headaches become involved in a cycle of anxiety and apprehension. Sex-related headaches may include three types: muscle contraction (tension) headaches, benign orgasmic headaches, and malignant coital headaches. Muscle contraction headaches cause dull, aching pains on both sides of the head and are relatively brief. More men than women experience these because many couples use positions during intercourse in which the man is more active, typically above his partner with his head and neck unsupported. In women, muscle contraction headaches can be influenced by premenstrual hormonal changes.

Benign orgasmic headaches are intense, short headaches associated with rises in blood pressure (see BLOOD PRESSURE, FEAR OF HIGH) during sexual arousal and orgasm. These headaches usually occur in individuals who also suffer from migraine headaches. They may be brought on by alcohol and or certain medications.

Malignant coital headaches are caused by fluid escaping through a defect in a person's spinal cord sheath, which widens during sexual intercourse. Some individuals have these headaches only while participating in sexual activity when standing and or sitting, but not when reclining.

Sex-related headaches are associated more often with extramarital sexual relations than intercourse between married partners. The anxiety and guilt caused by having a sexual relationship with someone other than a spouse may be the most significant reason for these headaches.

heart attack, anxiety following   Individuals who have a heart attack (myocardial infarction) are likely to have some anxiety afterward. As many as one-third of these people may require some psychotherapeutic help to relieve emotional stress.

The anxiety that individuals experience during and after a heart attack often follows a pattern. On initial symptoms of a heart attack, a person may, although recognizing the symptoms, deny them. Unfortunately, such denial often delays life-saving medical treatment. Educating individuals known to have coronary artery disease, as well as educating their friends and family, is an important step toward convincing heart attack victims to seek prompt medical attention.

Once in the emergency ward, a heart attack victim often experiences much confusion, as well as fear and anxiety. At this point, treatment to minimize these feelings may be limited to a medical explanation of what is happening, plus medications to relieve physical pain. Four emotional responses are fairly common after a person has been admitted to a coronary care unit: (1) anxiety, (2) denial, (3) depression, and (4) coping. Initially, the person is anxious and fearful of death, the unknown, and pain (see PAIN, FEAR OF). As he or she begins to feel better, the individual may resort to denial, often even requesting to leave the hospital. Shortly thereafter, the individual realizes the implications of the heart attack and shows signs of depression. Following this, usually by about the fifth day in the hospital, the person is more secure and begins to return to methods of coping that are typical of persons who have coronary-prone (often referred to as type A) behavior. Both drugs and nonpharmacologic treatment are often used to relieve anxiety and depression at this point for heart attack victims. Anxiety, especially if left untreated, can bring about serious arrhythmias (variations in heartbeat). Most commonly, when medication is prescribed for anxiety or depression, it is in the form of a BENZODIAZEPINE, such as ALPRAZOLAM (Xanax). Psychotherapeutic intervention or counselling may be used to help people adapt to new requirements in lifestyle—such as diet, giving up smoking, and management of stress (see STRESS MANAGEMENT) resulting from type A behavior. Sexual counseling may also be of help to the heart attack victim and spouse who have anxieties about resuming sexual activity.

heart attack, fear of   Fear of heart attack is known as anginophobia. *Heart attack* is the common term for a coronary occlusion. In a heart attack, one of the coronary arteries becomes blocked. The condition may or may not result in a myocardial infarction (heart attack) depending on the extent of the damage to the surrounding muscle.

heart, anxiety and the   There have been indications of interrelationships between anxieties and the heart since the earliest recordings of humankind's physical and psychological symptoms. Ancient Egyptians regarded the heart as central in psychosomatic relationships. When the modern scientific view began in the early 19th century, one of the first English language textbooks on cardiology discussed the subject of palpitation. Some diagnostic features were described, such as the "occasional nature" of the symptoms, and their accompaniments of dyspepsia, hypochondriasis, and hysteria. A description of the hypochondriacal implications of the syndrome are still of significance:

> There are few afflictions which excite more alarm and anxiety in the mind of the patient than this. He fancies himself doomed to become a martyr to organic diseases of the heart, of the horrors of which he has an

exaggerated idea; it is the more difficult to divest him of this impression because the nervous state which gives rise to his complaint imparts a fanciful gloomy and desponding tone to his imagination. (Hope, J. *A Treatise on the Disease of the Heart and Great Vessels Comprising a New View of the Physiology of the Heart's Action According to which the Physical Signs are Explained* London: Churchill, 1832.)

During the French Revolution and the Italian civil wars, the heart syndrome was viewed as a result of the moral and physical circumstances of modern times. In 1870, a surgeon described the causes rather than the symptoms of "soldier's heart" by saying that functional heart disorder was more common in the army than in both the navy and the police, and he endorsed the causal significance of tight uniforms and equipment. On the civilian side, the *British Medical Journal of 1958* presented information on chest pain in women that could not be explained by intercostal neuralgia or herpes zoster. Symptoms were described as: (1) disorders of the nervous system, various pains, spasms, fits both hysterical, and globus; (2) disorders of circulation, variability of temperatures, irregularity of pulse, palpitations of the heart; (3) derangements of abdominal vicera, vomiting and constipation, and (4) disorders of the reproductive system.

heartburn   Heartburn is a burning sensation in the upper part of the abdomen or under the breastbone. It is a cause of stress for many people who may fear that it is related to heart disease. Heartburn is also a symptom of anxiety because it can be brought on by nervousness or overeating. The burning sensation is actually associated with the esophagus, a muscular tube that connects the throat with the stomach. The tube passes behind the breastbone alongside the heart, which is why irritation or inflammation here is known as heartburn.

Heartburn and distress in the digestive tract is frequently a response to emotional stress. Tense, nervous people who worry about their jobs and family problems often complain of "acid indigestion" and heartburn. The list of foods that disagree with heartburn sufferers includes just about anything a person would want to eat. When things go smoothly for these people, everything agrees with them. When they are upset or frustrated, nothing does. Heartburn usually starts slowly, about an hour or so after they have eaten a heavy or spicy meal. The pain can sometimes be quite intense and may last a few hours.

Coping with heartburn   In some cases, the pain is due to irritation (esophagitis) from hydrochloric acid in the stomach juice that has backed up into the esophagus; relaxation of the valve between the stomach and the esophagus is one cause of esophagitis. Hiatus hernia, in which part of the stomach slips up into the chest, is another. This type of heartburn is often brought on by lying down, especially after overeating. It may be helped by raising the head of the bed, by avoiding certain foods, especially sweets, and by a low-fat, low-calorie diet.

People whose heartburn is brought on by stress and emotional factors may not have abnormal amounts of hydrochloric acid in their stomachs. They are probably oversensitive to normal acidity, just as they may overreact to the ordinary stressors of daily life. Adequate rest and RELAXATION and occasional use of antacids may be helpful. Individuals who suffer frequent heartburn should be checked by a physician. If there are no medical problems, a change in mental attitude toward the stressors in the individual's life should be considered. Relaxation training and medication may be helpful.

TIPS FOR RELIEVING THE ANXIETIES OF HEARTBURN

- Avoid certain foods that are spicy, acidic, tomato based, or fatty, such as sausages, chocolate, tomatoes, and citrus fruits.
- Avoid alcohol, tea, colas, and coffee, even decaffeinated.
- Eat moderate amounts of food to avoid overfilling your stomach.
- Stop or at least cut back on smoking.
- Don't try to exercise immediately after eating before lying down.
- Elevate the head of your bed or use extra pillows to raise the level of your head above your feet.
- Avoid tight belts and other restrictive clothing.
- Learn relaxation techniques.
- If none of these help, see your doctor.

---

heart rate in emotion   Strong emotion, such as fear or anxiety, can increase the rate of the heartbeat through sympathetic impulses (arousal system). Parasympathetic reflexes (calming system) resulting from increased blood pressure during emotion also can alter the heart rate. A strong parasympathetic reflex can slow the heart rate to a point at which it may appear on the verge of stopping. Although most phobic individuals experience rapid heartbeat when exposed to their phobic stimulus, those who fear blood often experience a slower heartbeat.

heaven, fear of   Fear of heaven is known as uranophobia or ouranophobia. Some people fear the idea that they will be judged after life and assigned either the rewards of heaven or the punishment of hell (see HELL, FEAR OF). Religious skeptics and radical thinkers object on social and ethical grounds to what they consider to be the carrot-in-front-of-the-donkey aspect of a belief in heaven. The prospect of heaven serves as a disciplinary element to promote good behavior and to encourage the feeling that inequities and injustices must be suffered patiently and passively in this life with a reward in the next. Some object to the pleasureable, delightful quality of heaven on the grounds that this image of paradise appeals to man's baser, more hedonistic qualities.

hedonophobia   A fear of feeling pleasure, this term is also used to mean fear of travel.

heights, fear of   Fear of heights is known as acrophobia, altophobia, hypsophobia, and hypsiphobia. It is a very common phobia, especially in its milder forms. Those who have phobias of heights emphasize that their visual space is important. They will not be able to go down a flight of stairs if they can see the open stairwell, will be frightened looking out of a high window that stretches from floor to ceiling but not if the window's bottom is at or covered to waist level or higher, and they have difficulty crossing bridges on foot because of proximity of the edge but may be able to do so in a car. Sometimes, fear of heights is related to an acute fear of falling (which is innate). Babies usually begin to be wary of heights some time after starting to crawl. Walking, like crawling, also enhances their fear of heights.

Fear of heights, classified as a specific phobia, is not usually associated with other psychiatric symptoms or disorders, such as depression. The heights-phobic person is no more or less anxious than anyone else until exposed to heights, but then he or she becomes overwhelmingly uncomfortable and fearful, sometimes having symptoms associated with a panic attack, such as palpitations, sweating, dizziness, and difficulty breathing. A person who fears heights can also fear just thinking about the possibility of possible confrontation with this phobic stimulus.

Fear of heights is sometimes associated with a fear of airplanes and flying, although the height is only one element in the complex reaction that leads to fear of flying in an airplane. Fear of heights is sometimes involved in many related fears, such as bicycles, skiing, amusement rides, tall building, stairs, bridges, and freeways.

hell, fear of   Fear of hell is known as hadephobia, stigiophobia, and stygiophobia. Individuals have feared hell for thousands of years before Christianity. Egyptian writings contain some indication of a belief in judgment and punishment after death. The early Greeks believed in an afterlife that was a shadowy realm where almost all of the dead were fated to go, and Plato's writings of the fourth century B.C. indicate a growing fear of punishment after death. The original Jewish concept of the afterlife was *Sheol*, a dark place removed from God that was everyone's fate after death. Gradually, the concept of punishment for a sinful life after death began to enter Judaism partly to rationalize inequities in this life and partly because Jews wished to think of their oppressors as suffering after death. At this point the image of writhing in flames became part of the fearful description of punishment in the underworld. *Gehenna*, the term for the place of torment in Judaism, was adapted from the name of the flaming rubbish dump of Jerusalem. Later, Christians produced elaborate descriptions of hell in art and literature as well as religious writings, and these increased fears of hell.

The addition of the devil and his orders of demons as residents of hell provided a rationalization for the theological dilemma of explaining the presence of evil in a world ruled by a loving God.

The fire and brimstone image of hell has decreased in the 20th century. More common fears are either of annihilation after death or that God's mercy will extend to all regardless of their conduct in life on Earth.

helplessness   Learned helplessness is an experience of fear and indecision and a sense of not being able to influence the external world personally. Freud used the term *psychic helplessness* to describe the experience during the birth process when respiratory and other physiological changes occur; he believed that this psychic helplessness state led to later anxieties. Freud also believed that the baby's helplessness and dependence on the mother created frustration, which in turn led to an inability to cope with later tension. During the 1970s, psychologist Martin Seligman (b. 1942) developed the concept and coined the term *learned helplessness* to describe an individual's dependence on another. Many phobic individuals have characteristics of learned helplessness, particularly agoraphobics, who cannot go away from home without someone accompanying them.

hematophobia   This fear of blood or the sight of blood is also known as hemophobia.

hemophilia   Sufferers from hemophilia have their own fears and may produce fearful feelings in those who are aware of their condition and who witness bleeding episodes. Hemophiliacs are rarely female. Because the disease is hereditary and recessive in females, the mother may fear and or feel guilty about passing the disease to her child. Parents of hemophiliacs may be excessively protective toward their hemophiliac child. The child may react by being fearful of all physical activity or by rebelling against reasonable limitations and putting himself or herself in danger. Siblings of hemophiliacs may be overprotective or jealous of the extra attention given to their brother or sister. Teachers or other adults

An obsessive feeling about horses is the subject of Peter Shaffer's play, *Equus*. Filled with shame because horses (to whom he attributes divine qualities) have watched his first sexual encounter, a young man blinds them with a spike. The drama, based on an actual incident, follows the relationship between the boy and his psychiatrist as they piece together the reasons for the boy's attack on the horses.

hospitals, fear of   Fear of hospitals is known as nosocomephobia. Some people fear hospitals because they fear contamination by germs that they believe are prevalent around hospitals; being ill, having pain, and being out of control of their lives; doctors, nurses, and other health care providers; and injury and seeing their own blood or the blood of others. Some people become anxious on seeing individuals who are ill or recovering from surgery.

Many who fear visiting others in hospitals are fearful about their own death. Visiting a hospital, where a certain number of patients die every day, reminds the anxious individual of his or her own mortality. Visiting an ill person makes many individuals anxious because as the visitor, one does not know what to talk about and is afraid to ask about the patient's condition for fear of hearing about pain and suffering.

Another fear of hospitals stems from their impersonal aspects; many individuals fear being a patient because hospital patients become known by their injuries or their conditions rather than their names. Strangers must provide very personal care and invade what many individuals view as personal bodily privacy.

Fears of hospitals can be overcome, to some extent, by visiting a local hospital while feeling well, taking a guided tour, and developing a better understanding of what services various hospitals provide for the community. Systematic desensitization also may be helpful.

humanistic psychology   This approach to psychology centers on the individual and his or her personal experience. Humanistic psychology opposes Freudian psychology, which hold that sexual drive is the sole motivating force, and behaviorial psychology, which explains human behavior as the product of a multiplicity of organismic and environmental relationships, each of which in turn dominates the others at certain times. In humanistic psychology, emphasis is on human qualities such as choice, creativity, valuation, and self-realization; meaningfulness is the key to selection of problems for study, and therapists oppose primary emphasis on objectivity at the expense of significance. The ultimate concern of humanistic psychology is the development of the each person's inherent potential. According to humanistic psychologists, a person has a hierarchy of many needs, beginning with physiological needs, safety, love and "belongingness"; esteem needs; esthetic needs; the need to know and understand; and ending in the essential need for self-actualization. The American Association for Humanistic Psychology was founded in 1962 by Abraham Maslow, Kurt Goldstein, Rollo May, Carl Rogers, and others.

humor, fear of   Humor has been studied by psychologists as a form of human behavior and does have some relationship to fears and anxieties. Humor is feared by some individuals who view laughing at rather than with someone as a form of attack. Belittling, sarcastic, or derisive remarks are high on the list of fear producers for individuals who are socially insecure or socially phobic. Laughter can be disturbing if it is an indication that sincere remarks are not being taken sincerely. Laughter and a light joking attitude also may be objectionable and manipulative when used to convince someone that he or she is not being a good sport about a truly negative, distressing situation. Insincere laughter that is used to flatter and gain social or professional favor often causes tensions. Laughter may also promote rifts and misunderstandings between social and ethnic groups because what may be funny in one culture and language may not even be amusing in another.

humor, use in therapy   Humor can be a useful way of releasing tension, dispelling anxieties, and momentarily relieving depression during therapy sessions because it promotes an individual's hopeful feelings about himself. If an individual can laugh during a therapy session, he will probably be more inclined to open up and reveal more about himself. Humor has known properties of healing. A therapist can employ humor as exaggeration or as a way of adding emphasis: Using a technique called paradoxical therapy, a therapist gives the individual perspective on his or her problems by exaggerating them until they become funny. With a similar exaggeration technique, a therapist assigns the individual a certain time of day to be anxious, depressed, or jealous. Often the silliness of the situation helps to alleviate the individual's distressed feelings. Humor can be used with individuals who are depressed or angry but who will not admit to their true feelings. Thus humor allows the therapist to explore without generating resistance. Because humorous remarks and stories have layers of meaning, such stories can at times be used to reach into the individual's unconscious.

Humor as anxiety relief   Humor serves to relieve the pressures of anxiety and stress in many ways. Comedians have indicated that they entered the profession because it affords an emotional release and a way of attracting positive attention. The simple absurdity and irrationality of humor is a welcome relief in the usual orderly, serious process of living. If some humor can be found in a negative situation, such as a setback at work or a minor accident, the victim can laugh about it, relax momentarily, and then pick up the pieces instead of uninterruptedly sustaining the stress of the situation. Because of the element of detachment inherent in humor, humor can reduce the stress of an ambitious person trying to reach a goal. Thus having a sense of humor allows the highly motivated person to be objective about the amount of effort and sacrifice necessary to reach the top.

Humor also provides a sense of freedom from political and social constraints. If a powerful figure or government program can be viewed as amusing, the stressful sense of autocratic control is reduced. Studies have shown that brainwashing is impossible as long as the victim retains his ability to laugh. Humor also affords relief from anxieties related to social situations. A witticism can cover complaints and awkward situations that would cause hostility or tension if approached directly.

Shared humor is also a great reliever of anxiety in stressful group situations such as delayed trains. Humor also relieves the stress that can result from boredom. When there seems nothing left to talk about, familiar topics can be made new by the use of humor.

hurricanes   Fear of hurricanes is known as lilapsophobia. Those who fear hurricanes will stay indoors with windows, shades, and shutters closed during any period of time in which hurricanes are possible. Some will leave the area and remain in another geographic location for fear of being in the path of a hurricane. Some who fear hurricanes fear not only the destruction of property that occurs but also a threat to their physical safety. Some fear that they might die as a result of the hurricane.

hydrophobophobia   Fear of rabies is called hydrophobophobia.

hyperthyroidism   Too much thyroid hormone in the body's system—hyperthyroidism, or thyroid overactivity—increases the body's ability to convert foods, vitamins, and minerals into secretions, tissues, energy, and heat. Hyperthyroidism is one of the most common problems of the endocrine glands. Some symptoms of hyperthyroidism are similar to some ANXIETY disorders, including an excess of energy, restlessness, nervousness, anxiety, headaches, sweating, and shaky, uncoordinated movements. A hyperthyroid individual may have difficulty sleeping at night and may experience wide changes in mood, varying from very happy to very depressed. An overactive thyroid gland can increase the body's basal metabolic rate (the use of oxygen while resting) from 60 to 100 percent or more. An individual who has hyperthyroidism burns up food rapidly so that appetite may become ravenous at the same time that weight loss occurs. There may be muscle weakness, loss of calcium, and diarrhea or loose bowels. A hyperthyroid individual has a rapid heartbeat, and, in severe cases, congestive heart failure can occur because blood cannot be pumped out of a heart chamber fast enough and collects there. Hyperthyroidism is a condition that requires medical attention, and once diagnosed, close monitoring of treatment.

hyperventilation   Very rapid and deep breathing, and a feeling of shortness of breath that can bring on high levels of ANXIETY, hyperventilation causes a reduction in level of carbon dioxide in the blood, which in turn can lead to feelings of numbness, tingling of the hands, dizziness, muscle spasms, and fainting. Individuals who are anxious or aroused begin to breath in a rapid deep manner with shallow exhalations. Gasping may occur. Although they have the sensation of shortness of breath, they are actually overbreathing. Sometimes this experience is accompanied by a feeling of constriction or pain in the chest.

The symptoms of hyperventilation and hyperventilation syndrome are frightening, and sufferers may fear that they are having a heart attack or that they will die. Some agoraphobics experience hyperventilation when they attempt to leave home or even think of going out, particularly unaccompanied by a companion upon whom they depend for security. Hyperventilation, or overbreathing, is also a common symptom among phobics when they face (or even think about) their phobic stimuli; for example, height phobics may hyperventilate when they think about looking out from the top of a tall building.

Hyperventilation is more common in women than in men, and usually occurs in individuals who are nervous, tense, or having an anxiety or panic attack. Repeated attacks of hyperventilation may occur, but once the individual recognizes that the hyperventilation syndrome is a reaction to anxiety and not a disease itself, the attacks may become fewer or stop because the panic component will be somewhat reduced.

An individual who hyperventilates can help himself by understanding what happens during an attack. By voluntarily hyperventilating (about 50 deep breaths while lying down) and reproducing the symptoms felt during an anxiety attack, the sufferer will see that the symptoms do not indicate a heart attack or a "nervous breakdown." When the fear is reduced, hyperventilation during an anxious time may decrease.

Hyperventilation may also be a response to severe pain, particularly abdominal pain. When there is doubt about the cause of hyperventilation, the sufferer should be examined by a physician.

hypnosis   A form of focused attention in which the individual becomes relatively open to receiving new information and exploring the mind-body relationship, hypnosis is not in itself a "therapy" but can be a useful supplement to an appropriate anxiety reduction therapy. Under hypnosis, the individual is in a trancelike state resembling sleep, during which he or she will be more susceptible to suggestion than during the "normal waking" state. Although there are theories, no one knows exactly what the trance-state represents physiologically or psychologically. Any susceptible individual may experience one or more of many hypnotic phenomena, including sensory, motor and psychological changes, such as an ability to alter perceptions, capacity to dissociate, amnesia for part or all of the hypnotic experience, a tendency to compulsively comply with suggestions given during the hypnotic state, and a willingness to accept logical incongruities.

There are two types of hypnosis: One is directive or authoritative hypnosis, in which the individual is ordered to give up a symptom, such as a phobic behavior. The second is cathartic hypnosis, in which the individual searches for hidden memories.

Hypnosis is a relatively safe procedure when used by a competent therapist, who is specially trained in hypnosis. Practitioners do not have to be medical doctors.

Although some people fear that under hypnosis they will do something that they would not do under conscious circumstances, it is generally thought that hypnotized individuals cannot be coerced into actions that go against their values and beliefs.

Most hypnosis is used to help relieve symptoms. Some therapists teach individuals to self-hypnotize themselves; other therapists prefer to have repeated sessions during which suggestions are given, behavior is supported, and therapeutic gains are rewarded.

Many individuals who have forms of anxiety and phobias are hypnotizable. People can learn to put themselves into the trance state to relax and dissociate psychological and body tension. This can be particularly helpful for those who have specific or simple phobias or performance anxiety. The trance experience can be used to induce physical relaxation in the face of the anxiety-provoking stimulus and to help an individual prepare for an anxiety-producing encounter by focusing on aspects of the experience that are less anxiety provoking. Individuals who fear flying in an airplane, for example, can prepare themselves for flight by going into the trance state, thinking about the flight and themselves in the plane, and viewing the plane as an extension of their body, just as a bicycle or car is an extension of their body that enables them to get from one place to another more quickly. Individuals learn to restructure flying from an experience of being trapped in the plane into one of using the plane for their own benefit. They can also choose to enter the self-hypnotic trance state repeatedly during the trip, especially at stressful times, such as take-offs and landings. Hypnosis may also be helpful in conjunction with exposure therapy for simple phobias.

Hypnosis is useful in a variety of pain conditions, such as headache and dentistry. Individuals can be hypnotized to begin their relaxation techniques when they feel a headache coming on. It has been used in dentistry with fearful patients. The technique enables such individuals to have necessary care performed without use of drugs and the side effects from them.

It is sometimes helpful to induce hypnosis as an adjunct in psychotherapy to help an individual intensify memories or to relive aspects of the past. However, only individuals who are highly hypnotizable are capable of such regression. Age regression and/or recall can be accomplished with hypnosis when the therapist, usually a psychiatrist, wishes a subject to return to any age in his or her childhood and react as he did then. Regressed to the state of an infant, the individual will go through sucking motions; regressed to age two, he or she will draw a crude picture as he or she did at that age and will react to frustrations as he did then. With this method, childhood traumas that might have led to phobic behavior in adulthood but have been consciously forgotten can be uncovered.

hypochondriasis   This preoccupation with the fear of having, or the belief that one has, a serious disease is based on the individual's interpretation of physical signs or sensations. This is sometimes referred to as hypochondriacal neurosis. A thorough physical examination does not support the diagnosis of any physical disorder that can account for the physical signs or sensations or for the individual's unwarranted interpretation of them, although a coexisting physical disorder may be present. The unwarranted fear or belief of having a disease persists despite medical reassurance, but it is not of delusional intensity in that the person can acknowledge the possibility that he or she may be exaggerating the extent of the feared disease or that there may be no disease at all.

The preoccupation may be with bodily functions, such as heartbeat, sweating, or digestion, or with minor physical abnormalities, such as a small sore or an occasional cough. The individual interprets these sensations or signs as evidence of a serious disease. The feared disease or diseases may involve several body systems at different times or simultaneously. Alternatively, there may be preoccupation with a specific organ or a single disease, as in cardiac neurosis, in which the individual fears or believes that he or she has heart disease.

Individuals with hypochondriasis frequently show signs of anxiety, depressed mood, and obsessive-compulsive personality traits. The most common age of onset is between 20 and 30 years, and it seems equally common in males and females.

hypoglycemia A reduced level of glucose in the blood, hypoglycemia can produce extreme nervousness, trembling, hallucinations, and many characteristic symptoms of anxiety states. Hypoglycemia was thought to be the medical basis for many anxiety disorders, but research has indicated that true hypoglycemia seldom occurs in anxiety disorders. Some individuals with known blood sugar level abnormalities fear reactions to their body's own chemistry. In normal individuals, lowering of blood sugars is performed by the body's insulin, which is produced by the islets of Langerhans in the pancreas. In an individual who has diabetes, the insulin is lacking or is incapable of transporting glucose across cell walls for utilization; in other cases, excessive amounts of insulin may be produced so that blood sugar is almost depleted. If glucose levels fall below certain limits, insufficient amounts are available in the blood for transport to the brain. Unconsciousness can result from too little insulin or too much insulin. It is difficult to tell the difference between the two cases, but the acetone smell on the breath and deep, heavy, rapid breathing are present only in diabetic coma.

hypothalamus A part of the brain responsible for emotional control, thirst, temperature, and certain endocrine functions, the hypothalamus is the lower part of the thalamus and relays stimuli for most sense organs (except olfactory). It is an endocrine gland.

hypothyroidism This condition causes production of hormones by the thyroid gland to be below normal or to be unable to keep pace with the body's temporary extra needs. In severe hypothyroidism, the individual may become absentminded, disinterested, and often alternately anxious, nervous, and complacent. Nearly every vital process of the body is affected by the main thyroid hormone, thyroxine. A shortage of this hormone will result in a slowdown of all bodily processes, mental, emotional, and physical, until the hormone is replaced in drug form. Temporary thyroid deficiency can occur during certain periods when the body needs larger amounts of thyroid hormone than usual, such as puberty or menopause.

hypsiphobia Hypsiphobia is a fear of heights.

imperfection, fear of   Fear of imperfection is known as atelophobia. Some individuals who have OBSESSIVE-COMPULSIVE DISORDER fear that they are not doing everything "right" or that they will make some error in their daily routines unless they check and recheck. Many phobias stem from a fear of being imperfect. Many individuals are unduly concerned with what others think of them and hence develop a phobia of imperfection. Fears of imperfection occur when talking on the telephone, going for a job interview, writing in front of others, eating in front of others, or speaking in public.

inferiority complex   Originally, this was a term used by Austrian psychiatrist Alfred Adler (1870–1937) to describe the cluster of ideas and feelings that arise in reaction to the sense of "organ" inferiority; now it is a popular term for a general sense of inadequacy that accompanies depression or a mood disorder in which the individual feels a low sense of self-esteem and low self-worth. The opposite of the inferiority complex is a superiority complex; individuals who have bipolar disorder or MANIC-DEPRESSIVE DISORDER often exhibit a superiority complex while they are in the manic phase of their illness.

inhibition   Inhibition is an inner restraint that keeps an individual from following through on feelings or thoughts, such as anger or lust. It may be caused by real or imagined fear of the consequences of expression. Individuals who have inhibitions in specific areas may experience increased ANXIETY when confronted with the feared object or situation. Inhibitions often lead to SHYNESS; some social phobics have many inhibitions and consequently avoid many situations in which they feel uncomfortable.

injection phobias   Fear of injections is known as trypanophobia. A fear of injection may be one reason many individuals fear doctors and dentists. Many individuals say that their fear of dentists arises from fear of injection of local anesthetic. Usually, fear of injections begins before age 10 or 11 and diminishes with age. Some who fear acupuncture do so because they fear needles.

Some who fear donating blood or having blood transfusions also fear injection. Injection phobias include fear of vaccination and fear of inoculation and immunizations.

insanity, fear of   Fear of insanity is known as dementophobia, lyssophobia, and maniaphobia.

insects, fear of   Fear of insects is known as acarophobia and entomophobia. Some individuals are so afraid of insects that they seal off their windows, vacuum and sweep twice a day, and feel uncomfortable outside their "cleansed" environment. There is no instinctual basis or symbolism for fear of insects.

insight   A special kind of understanding of a situation, in therapy the term implies depth and suddenness of understanding, for example, the origins of one's PHOBIA or ANXIETY. Insight means seeing beneath the surface of one's behavior or ideas: In cognitive insight, an individual understands a relationship between cause and effect and achieves new ways to solve behavioral problems; in emotional insight, one gains new awareness about feelings, motives, and relationships. In PSYCHOANALYSIS, insight is an awareness of the relationship between past experience and current behavior, particularly with regard to UNCONSCIOUS conflicts brought into the conscious. In all therapies, insight involves accepting the conceptual system of the therapist to a large extent. Insight therapies are not effective for anxiety disorders and are not the treatment of choice.

insomnia   Insomnia is an inability to sleep or to stay asleep. Some individuals fear insomnia; for others, insomnia is a symptom of other disorders—it is a frequent symptom of individuals who have anxieties (see ANXIETY). Many moderately or severely depressed individuals complain of fitful sleep with early morning wakening; however, some depressed individuals sleep more than normal. Many people suffer from temporary insomnia when faced with a particular situation that causes them anxiety or great excitement, but there are also chronic insomniacs.

There are four main categories of insomnia: (1) Light sleep insomnia, characterized by an overabundance of light sleep and less or an inadequate amount of deep sleep; (2) Sleep awakening insomnia, in which the individual wakes up repeatedly during the night and spends at least 30 minutes trying to go back to sleep; (3) Sleep onset insomnia, in which the individual has trouble initially falling asleep; and (4) early termination insomnia, in which the individual awakens after less than six hours and cannot go back to sleep at all.

Behavior treatment for insomnia has been effective in eliminating sleep disturbance within a relatively brief therapy duration. Behavioral therapists try to build an association between bed and sleep, and the individual who cannot sleep is asked to get out of bed until sleep is possible. Modification of cognitions (e.g., excessive worries) is often necessary, as well as training in relaxation (which is used preceding attempts to sleep).

in vivo desensitization   This is a technique for treating phobias in real-life situations, as opposed to work in a laboratory or in imagination. Phobic individuals are led through the actual situations that arouse their anxieties (see ANXIETY) with the goal of learning to relax in the presence of anxiety-causing stimuli. Whenever it is possible to use it, this is the more effective form of desensitization therapy. Also known as in vivo therapy.

in vivo therapy   *In vivo* literally means "real life." This is the preferred form of desensitization, as contrasted with imaginal psychotherapies using images. In vivo desensitization was used by U.S. behavioral psychiatrist Joseph Wolpe (1915–97), who then developed imaginal sensations as a more convenient tool in some situations.

irritable bowel syndrome   In this chronic gastrointestinal condition, the individual experiences abdominal discomfort or pain and a change in bowel habits, such as cramping, diarrhea, or constipation without weight loss or gastrointestinal disease. Some physicians say that the condition is of "nervous" origin and have described irritable bowel syndrome patients as neurasthenics. Among individuals who have irritable bowel syndrome, many have ANXIETY and depression. Conversely, functional gastrointestinal complaints are so common in individuals who have anxiety disorders that gastrointestinal distress has been included as a symptom of panic disorder in the American Psychiatric Association's *Diagnostic and Statistical Manual of Mental Disorders* (4th ed.). In both conditions, onset most often occurs in young and middle-aged adults. Both affect predominantly women, are associated with a variety of complaints, appear to be familial, and are often chronic conditions. In research studies, many individuals found relief from both irritable bowel syndrome and panic symptoms with antipanic therapy. Panic disorder and irritable bowel syndrome both improved with benzodiazepines (see BENZODIAZEPINES) and tricyclic antidepressants. Researchers hypothesize that gastrointestinal symptoms experienced by some individuals may be symptoms of panic disorder (see PANIC, PANIC ATTACKS, AND PANIC DISORDER) or may be irritable bowel syndrome worsened by a coexisting anxiety disorder. Panic disorder patients often report one particular symptom, such as diarrhea or DIZZINESS, as particularly troublesome and seek a specialist to treat that particular symptom.

J

jealousy   Fear of jealousy is known as zelophobia. Jealousy is an emotion that includes feelings of loss of self-esteem, envy, hostility, and self-blame. Jealousy frequently first appears at the age of two or three when a new child arrives in the family. There may be hostile feelings toward the newborn because he or she is getting more attention. In adulthood, many types of jealousy persist.

In the more extreme types it may take the form of a paranoid delusion. Many people have observed jealousy in others and may develop a fear of becoming jealous.

jumping (from both high and low places)   Fear of jumping from both high and low places is known as catapedaphobia. This fear may be related to fear of heights, a fear of falling, or a fear of being injured.

K

kissing, fear of Fear and anxieties about kissing range from feelings of social awkwardness, to rejection, to concern about disease. The AIDS (acquired immunodeficiency syndrome) epidemic during the 1980s has made actresses and actors fearful of engaging in the intimate kissing required in many films. Kissing is endowed with an element of performance anxiety for young people who may be more strongly motivated by a desire to appear adept and sophisticated than by genuine romance or passion. Kissing in social rather than romantic situations also creates a certain type of anxiety and confusion because there is such a variation in method and expectations in different ethnic and social groups. Kissing is also an unpleasant prospect for some people because of a strong but seldom freely expressed social fear: bad breath.

knees, fear of Fear of knees is known as genuphobia. Although this fear seems quite unnatural to most people, sufferers feel equally perturbed. However, fears related to parts of the body do develop just as fear of other objects develops. These fears, while rare, are treated with a behavioral, desensitization approach, with a high degree of success.

knives, fear of Fear of knives is known as aichmophobia. Individuals who are phobic about knives usually are also phobic about various objects with points, such as letter openers, spears, and daggers. This fear may interfere with eating because sufferers will avoid using knives or placing knives on a table.

L

laughter, fear of   Fear of laughter is known as gelophobia. This fear may be related to other fears, such as fear of gaiety, or cheerfulness, or good news.

lavatories, public, fear of   Fear of public lavatories is common. Many individuals fear urinating or moving their bowels in a place where another person might be aware of what they are doing. Some fear contracting a disease from a toilet seat or from a towel or sink in a public lavatory. Some fear producing odors themselves, and others fear encountering odors in public lavatories. Some individuals have an inability to pass urine or move their bowels in a place other than their bathroom at home. With the advent of AIDS (acquired immunodeficiency syndrome), fear of public lavatories has increased in incidence.

learning theory   Learning theory is the study of the circumstances under which habits are formed or eliminated; it is the framework of behavior therapy and behavior modification. Learning theory is a set of principles that seek to explain how behavior is modified in response to changes in the individual's environment. Behavior therapies used to treat individuals who have anxieties and phobias are derived from the learning principles developed by Pavlov, Thorndike, Watson, Tolman, Hull, Skinner, Wolpe, and others, whose work contributed to the theory of conditioning, motivation, and habit formation. Learning theory is put into use in the form of BEHAVIOR MODIFICATION; BEHAVIOR THERAPY; classical conditioning; and conditioning.

libido   *Libido* is Sigmund Freud's (1856–1939) term for the drives of the sexual instinct, love-object seeking, and pleasure. In many phobic and anxiety disorders as well as affective disorders, particularly depression, there is a reduction of libido. The word is derived from the Latin words for "desire, lust." He believed that the libido was one of two vital human instincts, the drive toward self-preservation and the drive toward sexual gratification. Freud suggested that when an individual represses libido because of social pressures, continued repression leads to changes in personality and to neuroses, such as anxieties (see ANXIETY) and PHOBIAS. Later, Freud gradually broadened the concept to include all expressions of love and pleasure. Swiss psychologist Carl Gustav Jung (1875–1961) expanded Freud's original concept to apply the term to the general life force which provides energy for all types of activities, including sexual, social, cultural, and creative.

lightning, fear of   Fear of lightning is known as astraphobia, astropophobia, and keraunophobia. Many people fear lightning so much that they will not go outdoors on days when lighting is predicted. When rain is forecast, many even call the weather bureau to check for the possibility of lightning. During a storm that includes lightning, many take refuge in a closet or in bed, feeling safer in an enclosed place. Fear of lightning is related to fear of storms in general, and many who fear lightning also fear thunder and noise.

Some individuals acquire the fear of lightning from observing their parents or grandparents. Others have experienced traumatic incidents in connection with lightning or thunderstorms.

Fears of specific natural phenomena, such as lightning, have been treated successfully in many cases with exposure therapy.

lithium carbonate   A drug used in treating MANIC-DEPRESSIVE DISORDER, lithium acts by altering the metabolism of NOREPINEPHRINE in the brain. Lithium preparations are used routinely to treat manic and hypomanic individuals and to prevent attacks in individuals who have recurrent affective disorders. These attacks include both manic and depressive episodes in bipolar individuals, episodes of mania in the recurrently manic patients, and depressive attacks in the unipolar (only depressed) patients.

Historical background   During the 19th century, lithium salts were known as important constituents of some spa waters to which many medicinal properties were ascribed. In the 1940s, lithium salts were used as a taste substitute for sodium chloride for cardiac patients on salt-free diets. When severe side effects and some deaths were reported, its use was stopped. Then, in the late 1940s, researchers in Australia discovered that lithium had certain tranquilizing properties. In later experiments, lithium safely quieted manic patients to whom it was administered. However, because of the known toxicity of lithium, there was little interest in it for almost a decade. In the 1950s and 1960s, several studies in Europe led to the acceptance of lithium into European and English psychiatric practices as a highly effective and safe treatment for manic-depressive illness. Lithium was accepted into U.S. practice during the 1970s after the need for careful monitoring of blood levels to overcome side effects was understood.

lockiophobia   Fear of childbirth is called lockiophobia.

locus of control   This concept attempts to explain why some people behave the way they do and why some have more anxieties than others. An individual with an "internal" locus of control believes that whatever happens in his or her life is the direct result of his or her own actions and that he or she has some control over these events and behaviors. A person who believes that God, destiny, or outside forces determine fate is said to have an "external" locus of control; people who have an external locus of control are more likely to develop anxieties. Most people are not entirely internalists or externalists but feel more or less in control of their lives. An individual's belief about his or her locus of control affects his or her behavior, emotional condition, and manner of dealing with anxieties. The concept was developed in the late 1960s.

lonely, fear of being   Fear of being lonely is known as monophobia. This fear seems to increase with age, as an individual sees friends and loved ones dying and anticipates having few contemporaries around. Fear of loneliness is compounded by the fear of illness.

long waits, fear of   Some agoraphobics fear long waits, such as for buses and trains. This fear may prevent them from going out. In some cases, agoraphobics develop such a feeling of panic while waiting for a bus or train that when it finally arrives, they cannot board. However, if there is no wait, they can get on without anxiety.

looking ridiculous, fear of   This social phobia includes such specific fears as those of shaking, blushing, sweating, fainting, vomiting, performing in front of an audience, entering a room, and looking inappropriate or unattractive—for example, those who will not swim because they think they look ridiculous in a swimsuit.

Some fear that their hands will tremble while writing a check or handling money in front of someone else; fear of shaking may prevent a secretary from typing or a teacher from writing on the blackboard. In such cases, the phobics fear that their hands or heads might shake; in reality, these fears rarely materialize. However, individuals who have such tremors as those of Parkinson's disease—who shake vigorously and unconsciously—usually do not fear doing anything in public despite their regular shaking.

Generally, people who fear looking ridiculous have fewer positive and more negative thoughts and consider themselves awkward and less skillful. This fear is treated in the same ways social phobias and shyness are treated, specifically with behavior modification, cognitive modification, and other therapies aimed at improving the individual's self-esteem.

losing control, fear of   Many phobic individuals avoid their feared situations because they fear losing control; for example, during a panic attack, some people fear that they might become totally paralyzed and not be able to move, or that they will not know what they are doing and will embarrass themselves or others in some way. Some agoraphobics who experience panic attacks have this fear.

This feeling occurs because during intense anxiety the entire body becomes prepared for action and escape. This "fight or flight" response often makes people feel confused and distracted; however, individuals in such situations are still able to think and function normally. In fact, others rarely notice another individual experiencing a panic attack.

lost, fear of being   Fear of being lost is common among children as well as adults. In childhood, this fear is reinforced by such fairy tales as *Hansel and Gretel*, in which the children lose their way in the forest. Fear of being lost is a fear of being out of control of one's destiny and may be related to fears of the dark, of animals, of injury, and of being far from safety and may prevent individuals from visiting certain areas in major cities, from visiting the cities themselves, or from driving their cars in certain areas or on unfamiliar roads. Those who do not speak the language of the country in which they consider traveling may fear being lost and not being able to communicate well enough to ask for directions.

love, fear of   Fear of love is known as philophobia. Love is a complex emotion that is comprised of trust, respect, acceptance, strong affection, feelings of tenderness, pleasurable sensations in the presence of the love object, and devotion to his or her well-being. As an emotion, love takes many forms, such as concern for one's fellow humans, responsibility for the welfare of a child, sexual attraction and excitement, and self-esteem and self acceptance.

lying, fear of   Fear of lying is known as mythophobia. Many individuals fear lying because they fear being caught in a lie and being punished. Lying—making false statements with conscious intent to deceive—may be considered nonpathological or pathological. When adults or children seek to avoid punishment or to save others from distress; these nonpathological lies are sometimes referred to as white lies; pathological lying is a major characteristic of an antisocial personality and may be a symptom of many psychophysiological disorders due to guilt and fear reactions. The lie detector (polygraph) is based on physiological reactions.

M

magic, fear of   Fear of magic is primarily concerned with the fear of and desire for supraconscious power and striving for connection with a greater power. Magicians do not consider themselves capable of working miracles but of using the powers of their minds and their knowledge of the laws and secrets of nature as a way of exerting control over nature and human events. Some magicians believe that a person is a miniature replica of God and capable of expanding his or her powers accordingly, not in the rational path of progress provided by science but by ascending a hierarchy of mysterious secrets; this process is an individual matter and cannot be taught.

Prehistoric cave paintings indicate that early peoples believed in and feared magic. The Egyptians, the Greeks, and the Romans combined magical beliefs and practices with their religious observances. Early Christians successfully claimed the superior power of their magic to gain pagan converts. For a time, Christianity rejected magic, but the medieval church revived it claiming the power to exert a certain degree of control over God's will and the course of events. During the Reformation, Protestants branded as superstitions the use of holy water and belief in the intercession of the saints.

The power of black magic, to a certain extent, may be a self-fulfilling prophecy. An individual who is cursed by a person he or she believes to be a witch or magician may become mentally or physically ill from sheer anxiety.

mania   See MANIC-DEPRESSIVE DISORDER.

manic-depressive disorder   Manic depression, or manic-depressive disorder, also known as bipolar illness, is the most distinct and dramatic of the depressive or affective disorders (mood disorders). Unlike major depression, which can occur at any age, manic-depressive disorder generally strikes before the age of 35; nearly one in 100 persons will suffer from the disorder at some time in their lives.

What distinguishes bipolar illness from other depressive disorders is that the individual swings from depression to mania, generally with periods of normal moods in between the two extremes. Some patients, however, cycle from mania to depression and back within a few days and without a period of normal mood. People with this condition are called rapid cyclers. Many people who have manic depression also have phobias, but phobias may come and go during the cycles.

When an individual experiences a manic phase, he or she will feel a sudden onset of elation or euphoria that increases in a matter of days to a serious impairment. Symptoms of the manic phase include a mood that is excessively good, euphoric, or expansive; the individual feels "on top of the world," and not even bad news will change his or her happiness. The mood is way out of bounds, given the individual's personality.

A manic lacks judgment and will express unwarranted optimism. Self-confidence reaches the point of grandiose delusions in which the person thinks he or she has a special connection with God, celebrities, or political leaders. He or she may think that nothing, not even the laws of gravity, can stop him or her from accomplishing any task. As a result, he may think he can even step off a building or out of a moving car without being hurt.

Other symptoms are hyperactivity and excessive plans or participation in numerous activities that have good chances for painful results. The manic becomes so enthusiastic about activities or involvements that he fails to recognize that he hasn't enough time in the day for all of them; for example, he may book several meetings, parties, deadlines, and other activities in a single day, thinking he can make all of them on time. Added to the expansive mood, mania also can result in reckless driving, spending sprees, foolish business investments, or sexual behavior that is unusual for the person.

The manic person's thoughts race uncontrollably. When the person talks, his or her words come out in a nonstop rush of ideas that abruptly change from topic to topic. In its severe form, the loud, rapid speech is hard to interpret because the individual's thought processes have become so totally disorganized and incoherent.

The manic will experience a decreased need for sleep, allowing him or her to go with little or no sleep for days without feeling tired. The manic will also experience distractibility in which his or her attention is easily diverted to inconsequential or unimportant details. At times, the manic will become suddenly irritable, enraged, or PARANOID when his grandiose plans are thwarted or his excessive social overtures are rebuffed.

many things, fear of   Fear of many things is known as polyphobia. Individuals who are very anxious often have many phobias, some of which may be related, such as fear of precipices, fear of heights, and fear of looking up at tall buildings. Others have unrelated fears, such as fear of water and fear of dogs.

masturbation   Sexual self-gratification without a partner which until recently, many people considered harmful. Many young people were told that masturbation would lead to many consequences, ranging from acne to impotence. Because of the taboo against masturbation, many people became fearful and anxious about the practice. The more morally restrictive the culture or the environment in which people live, the more likely they are to develop fear and guilt about masturbation. Now it is recognized that masturbation is almost a universal practice before sexual maturity is reached and is a frequent practice in older age when a sexual partner is not available. In U.S. zoologist and sexologist Alfred Kinsey's (1894–1956) research in the late 1940s, more than 90 percent of men reported masturbatory experiences in their adolescence. In the early 1980s, results of a research project by Shere Hite (b. 1942), an American cultural anthropologist, on female sexuality indicated that about 82 percent of American women masturbate. In most cases, men masturbate their penis and women the clitoris by hand.

mathematics anxiety   An individual's anxiety about mathematics can be broken down into three main components: numerical anxiety, mathematical-test anxiety, and abstraction anxiety. Numerical anxiety involves the practical application of mathematics and numbers to one's everyday concerns (real-life "story problems")—items such as personal budgeting, timetables, counting change, and even odds for betting at a horse race). Nearly everyone in an academic setting has experienced some degree of anxiety about mathematical tests—from multiplication flash cards to a pop quiz in a calculus class. The third component, abstraction anxiety, is concerned with an individual's anxiety when confronted with methods of abstract mathematical reasoning involving mathematical schemas, theorems and proofs, or symbols and letters in place of numbers.

Questionnaires and anxiety scales can help to refine an approach to diminish or eradicate an individual's mathematics fears.

meditation   Meditation is a learned technique to relieve stress involving deep RELAXATION brought on by focusing attention on a particular sound or image and breathing deeply. One directs thoughts away from work, family, relationships, and the environment. During meditation, the heart rate, blood pressure, and oxygen-consumption rate decreases; temperature of the extremities rises; and muscles relax.

Meditation also has been shown to reduce a number of medical symptoms and improve health-related attitudes and behaviors; for example, people with chronic obstructive pulmonary disease (COPD) who practiced meditation reduced the frequency and severity of episodes of shortness of breath and numbers of visits to emergency rooms. People with heart disease, hypertension, cancer, diabetes, and chronic pain (see PAIN, FEAR OF) have reported feeling more self-confident, more in CONTROL in their lives, and better able to manage stress after mastering the meditation technique. Meditation has been used successfully by individuals who have panic attacks and panic disorder (see PANIC, PANIC ATTACKS, AND PANIC DISORDER).

Meditation may bring out increased efficiency by eliminating unnecessary expenditures of energy. Individuals who practice meditation sometimes report a beneficial surge of energy marked by increased physical stamina, increased productivity on the job, the end of writer's or artist's "block," or the release of previously unsuspected creative potential.

Learning to meditate Meditation is a very self-disciplined routine and a way to learn more about one's own thoughts and feelings. Simple procedures can be learned easily. The basics include sitting in a quiet room with eyes closed and breathing deeply and rhythmically with attention focused on the breath. Also, there may be a focus on either a special word, or mantra, such as *peace* which one repeats over and over again, or on steadily watching an object, such as a candle flame for a 20-minute period once or more daily.

Meditation relies on the close links between mind and body. When one meditates, the alpha brainwaves indicate that the body is relaxed and free from physical tension and mental strain. BIOFEEDBACK monitoring has indicated that meditation encourages the brain to produce an evenly balanced pattern of alpha and theta brain-wave rhythms. This means that the body is relaxed and the mind is calm, yet alert. The "relaxation response" sets in, which is the opposite of the physical tension that results from stress.

Individuals who meditate frequently report that they are more aware of their own opinions after beginning to meditate. They are not as easily influenced by others as they were previously and can arrive at decisions more quickly and easily. They may before more self-assertive and more able to stand up for their own rights effectively. Additionally, researchers have shown that the meditating person may become less irritable in his or her interpersonal relationships within a relatively short period of time after beginning meditation.

Types of meditation vary Modern meditation techniques are derived from spiritual practices in Eastern cultures dating back more than 2,000 years. Traditionally, the benefits of the techniques have been defined as spiritual in nature, and meditation has constituted a part of many religious practices. In the latter part of the 20th century, however, simple forms of meditation have been used for stress management with excellent results. Contributing to the rising interest is the fact that these meditation techniques are related to biofeedback (which also emphasize a delicately attuned awareness of inner processes) and to muscle relaxation and visualization techniques used in BEHAVIOR THERAPY.

There are two basic types of meditation: *concentration* and *insight.* Concentration types, such as TRANSCENDENTAL MEDITATION, often use a special sound or silently repeated phrase to focus attention and screen out extraneous thoughts or stimuli. *Insight-oriented meditations,* such as *mindfulness meditation,* accepts thoughts and feelings that arise from moment to moment as objects of attention and acceptance. The goal of mindfulness is an increased awareness of what is happening in one's mind and body right now. Recognition and acceptance of present reality provides the basis for changes of attitudes and conditions.

melancholia   A term used throughout history to denote a severe form of depression, *melancholia* derives from the Greek prefix *melas,* meaning black. In a state of melancholia, the individual feels loss of interest or pleasure in all or almost all activities, has low self-esteem, and is preoccupied with self-reproaches and regrets.

memory loss, fear of   Older adults often fear memory loss as something that is inevitable. Health care professionals use the term *age-associated memory impairment* to describe those minor glitches in memory that affect older adults' experience. Rather than remaining anxious and dwelling on this, many individuals find that written reminders, such as lists, and repeating names or other information aloud helps relieve these fears. Studies of older people actually find little memory loss but some decreases in psychomotor speed.

menopause, fear of   Some women fear menopause, or the cessation of the menses. Some women fear that they will become unattractive to men at the time when they are no longer able to bear children. They fear having hot flashes and other symptoms of menopause, such as vaginal dryness, depression, and dry skin. Treatments involving use of estrogen replacement can alleviate many of the uncomfortable symptoms of menopause. Advances in estrogen products have made them safer to use with fewer side effects. Fewer women fear menopause than in earlier generations because women now have longer life expectancies and anticipate satisfying lives after menopause. The average age for menopause in the United States is 50–51; in the United Kingdom it is 49 years 9 months.

menstruation, fear of   Fear of menstruation is known as menophobia. Some uninformed young women may fear menstruation because they have not learned about their bodies and sexuality. Because blood flow is usually a signal of physical injury and is a common fear of young children, adolescent girls may become alarmed at the first sight of monthly bleeding with the onset of menstruation at puberty. Some women who fear menstruation reflect the anxiety felt by their mothers and generations of women before them: they feel shame if men around them know they are menstruating, resent men for not having to endure menstruation, and dread the repetition of what they regard as unpleasantness.

Historically, some men have had fears of menstruating women. Some men—especially those who have blood phobia—fear castration by having intercourse with a menstruating woman. They fear that menstrual blood should have formed the body of a child and that it is therefore charged with potent and dangerous energy. Some men fear that menstruation is a punishment for sexual activity; others who fear menstruation are jealous of women's reproductive process; still other, fear that women have cosmic power because of the connection of menstruation with the powerful rhythms of nature, such as the moon, the sun, and the tides.

In some cultures, largely as a result of men's fears of them, menstruating women were excluded from society during their periods and excluded from contact with religious people or ceremonies. Over centuries, women's fears regarding menstruation have included the notion that sexual intercourse during menstruation is harmful to both men and women's health, that deformed children result from intercourse at this time, and that intercourse during menstruation is a sin against God; there has also been an assumption that women are not sexually aroused during menstruation.

Fears of menstruation can be overcome with appropriate information and reassurance that monthly periods are normal and part of female development. Notions that many people have that women are "unclean" during menstruation should be dismissed.

meteors, fear of   Superstitions and traditional beliefs associate meteors, also known as falling stars, with death and bad luck. Meteors are chunks of matter from outer space, probably pieces of disintegrated comets that burn when they enter Earth's atmosphere. Meteorites are the remainders of meteors that are not completely destroyed by their blazing fall to Earth.

Asian tribes thought meteors were disembodied souls, some believing optimistically that they carried treasure, others that their purpose in coming to Earth was to feed on the blood of the living. A Native American belief links meteors with the moon; seeing a meteor was thought to cause one's face to become pockmarked like the surface of the moon.

Meteors also are feared because they can cause injury. A meteor may weigh more than 2,000 pounds and a shower may consist of 100,000 stones. There are unsubstantiated reports of human deaths caused by meteors from periods before the early 20th century. Meteorites have fallen through the roofs of houses and animals have been killed by them.

mice, fear of   Fear of mice is known as suriphobia or musiphobia. Some people fear mice because they are considered to carry dirt and filth, because they can hide in small places, and because they destroy stored food and leave droppings around homes and stores. Some who fear mice have fainted at the sight of a mouse or run at the sight of one, or at least jumped away to avoid contact with them.

milieu therapy   Behavior change procedures that attempt to make the total environment conducive to psychological improvement. Milieu therapy is useful in treating some agoraphobics and their families. Although this form of therapy began as an approach to a large number of patients in a hospital ward, the term is now used in many different settings to generically describe environmental intervention, mainly in a generic sense.

Minnesota Multiphasic Personality Inventory (MMPI)   A self-rating questionnaire to determine personality types. The MMPI may be of some use to therapists in helping anxious or phobic individuals. The MMPI was developed by Starke Rosecrans Hathaway (1903–84), a U.S. psychologist, and John Charnley McKinley (1891–1950), a U.S. psychiatrist, in 1942. Results of the questionnaire point toward nine personality scales: hypochondria, depression, hysteria, psychopathic deviate, masculine-feminine interest, paranoia, psychasthenia, schizophrenia, and hypomania. The subject of the test indicates agreement or disagreement with 550 statements; results are scored by an examiner or by computer to determine the individual's personality profile as well as any tendency to fake responses. The MMPI is widely used in clinical research.

mirroring   A BEHAVIOR MODIFICATION technique in which an individual sees himself portrayed by another person, usually the therapist, thereby acquiring a better idea of how he or she is viewed by others. Mirroring is used in helping some people overcome SOCIAL PHOBIAS. It is especially helpful in desensitizing a person to speech phobias.

mirrors, fear of   Fear of mirrors is known as catoptrophobia, eisotrophobia, and spectrophobia. Many modern fears of mirrors are based on ancient fears and superstitions about reflections.

The earliest-known looking glasses, or mirrors, were the still waters of lakes and pools. Primitive people believed that when a person saw his or her own image in a pool or any other reflective surface, this was not a mere reflection but the person's soul returning the gaze. The notion that the soul could be separated from the body without causing death and that it was sometimes visible as a reflection or a shadow was widespread in early times and appears in many well-known folktales. As long as the separated spirit was unharmed, the person whose body normally contained it was safe, but if it was injured in any way, misfortune, evil, and very often death would follow.

The broken reflection of the human image has long been interpreted as a symbol of disaster. Many people fear seeing a broken or distorted image of themselves because they view distortion as a sign of disintegration or of impending trouble and even death. Ancient Greeks considered it an omen of death to dream of seeing one's reflection in the water because the water spirits might drag the soul into the dark depths below, leaving its owner to perish.

Some people fear breaking mirrors because they believe it brings seven years of bad luck or a misfortune of a particular kind, such as the loss of a close friend or a death in the house. Another superstition prohibits a child of less than a year from seeing its likeness in a mirror because to do so would cause it to languish, stunt its growth, or bring about an early death. The custom of veiling mirrors after a death is partly due to the fear that whoever sees his or her reflection then will die soon after or, if not he or she, then someone else in the house. Brides have been warned not to look at themselves in their wedding clothes, lest something happen to prevent the marriage. However, after the ceremony, it is considered lucky for the married couple to look at themselves together in the mirror. Actors fear looking into a mirror over another's shoulder. They fear seeing two reflections together, because doing so will bring bad luck to the one overlooked. Some individuals who have dysmorphobia (a fear that part of their body is misshapen) fear looking in mirrors because seeing their reflection provokes anxiety.

mitral valve prolapse (MVP)   In this heart defect, which sometimes has been linked with anxiety, the mitral valve does not close sufficiently, and blood is forced back into the atrium as well as through the aortic valve. About 40 percent of normal adults have MVP. The condition can lead to a feeling of palpitations, anxiety, and difficult breathing. Research to study the relationship between anxiety disorders and mitral valve prolapse has unequivocally demonstrated that MVP is not a precursor, a cause, or even related to panic and agoraphobia. Although there is some symptom overlap, the overwhelming majority of MVP reactors do not develop panic or anxiety. However, individuals who have an anatomic vulnerability of their mitral valves may develop prolapse as a result of increased demands placed on their cardiovascular systems by anxiety.

modeling   Modeling is the acquisition of behavior by observation of a real or symbolic model. Acquisition can occur in one observation if the individual identifies with or is attracted to the model. Modeling or observational learning may be produced by stories, television, or movies, or direct observation (e.g., of a parent or friend). It is also possible to acquire emotional responses through observation: in this case, the model would be displaying emotional reactions in a particular stimulus situation, such as the ocean or showers. Many people, for example, developed fears of swimming in the ocean after seeing the movie *Jaws*. Likewise, people developed fears of taking showers alone after seeing the Hitchcock thriller, *Psycho*. Behavior theorists make a distinction between acquisition (which occurs through observation) and performance (which requires repeated trials, reinforcement, etc., and is affected by the individual's learning history). In other words, people might acquire fear through observation, but whether they avoid the situation and consequently become phobic might depend on other factors, such as reinforcement.

money, fear of   Fear of money is known as chrematophobia. Money can help an individual maintain esteem. Fear of loss of money represents a fear of losing the external validation of one's worth provided by money. After the Great Depression, many people committed suicide because they viewed lack of money as a loss of self-worth.

monoamineoxidase inhibitors (MAOIs)   A class of antidepressant drugs (used to treat depression), MAOIs reduce excessive emotional fluctuations and may stabilize brain chemistry by inhibiting the action of the enzyme monoamine oxidase, which in turn inactivates NOREPINEPHRINE. When more norepinephrine becomes available in the sympathetic nervous system, mood is elevated. (See AFFECTIVE DISORDERS.)

monotony, fear of   Fear of monotony is a fear of sameness or unchanging situations and consequently has been called homophobia. (This term has also been applied to fear of homosexuality.) This may be related to a fear of boredom and a fear of time, known as chronophobia. Interestingly, monotony—or lack of stimulation—can trigger anxiety in agoraphobic individuals susceptible to react to lack of stimulation.

mood   A mood is a sustained or pervasive emotion that markedly colors the individual's perception of the world. Examples of moods include depression, anxiety, anger, or elation. Moods may be of significance in diagnosing anxieties and phobias, and therapists discuss moods with individuals who seek help for such problems. Following are some terms used to describe moods:

Dysphoric: An unpleasant mood, such as depression, anxiety, or irritability.

Elevated: A mood that is more cheerful than normal. It does not imply pathology (as in manic-depressive illness).

Euphoric: An exaggerated feeling of well-being. Euphoria occurs in manic-depressive disorder. As a technical term, *euphoria* implies a pathological, or diseased, mood. Whereas an individual with a normally elevated mood may describe himself or herself as being in "good spirits," "very happy," or "cheerful," the euphoric person is like to exclaim that he or she is "on top of the world," "up in the clouds," or "high."

Euthymic: A mood in the "normal" range, which implies the absence of depressed or elated mood.

Irritable: Internalized feeling of tension associated with being easily annoyed and provoked to anger. (See also AFFECTIVE DISORDERS.)

Moon, fear of   Fear of the Moon is known as selenophobia. The effects of the Moon on human behavior, especially as causing insanity, have been noted for centuries. The word *lunatic,* coined by the physician Paracelcus in the Middle Ages, derives from the Latin word for "moon." In some countries there is a fear that the man in the Moon is the biblical Cain, accounting for the observation that as the Moon becomes fuller and stronger, human behavior becomes more violent and erratic. People who are mentally unstable are thought to be particularly affected by the Moon. Although scientific proof is lacking, professionals such as nurses, police, and firefighters who deal with large numbers of people in emergency situations report an upsurge in activity and more extreme behavior at the time of the full moon.

Ancient Greeks and other cultures believed that the rays of the Moon contained damaging power that could be collected by witches and magicians and used for their own evil purposes.

The observation that the Moon's cycles parallel those of a woman's body led to the belief in some cultures that the Moon was a lecherous man who ravished and caused abortive or abnormal pregnancies each month. Other cultures identified the Moon with a feminine emotional influence. In medieval Europe, the Roman moon goddess Diana became the patroness of witches.

Many fear-inducing superstitions are connected with the Moon; for example, a full moon on Christmas prophecies a poor harvest; on Sunday, bad luck. A red moon foretells murder or war. Sleeping in the moonlight is thought to produce a twisted face.

Fear of the Moon is often related to fear of the night or situations that might occur at a full moon, such as a manifestation of seeing darkness or emptiness or being out at night, not looking at pictures of the Moon, and sometimes even anxiety at seeing circles or circular objects that resemble the shape of the Moon.

motion, fear of   Fear of motion is known as kinesophobia. Persons may fear motion for many reasons: they may fear the motion of race cars and roller coaster rides because of the danger involved; plane, train, car, or other vehicular motion because they fear motion sickness; physical discomfort that they have previously experienced; having a lack of control over what may happen during the movement experience; and looking at or being in a whirlpool. Individuals who have balance problems or inner-ear disorders may have a greater fear of motion because of their reduced ability to accommodate to it physically; some who fear movement are startled by sudden changes, such as a loss of support, changes in altitude in an airplane, or being plunged into darkness. Infants and young children may react with fear when they see a live or toy animal rushing toward them. Movement also means increases in stimulation and for anxiety-prone individuals, stimulation that can be a trigger for anxiety.

motivation   Motivation is the force or energy that causes individuals to behave in a particular manner and may include satisfaction of basic drives, such as hunger, thirst, or sex, or desire for praise, power, money, or success. Anxiety or fear may act as motivation for fight or flight, causing the anxious individual either to stand up to the feared stimulus or to flee from it. Anxiety may motivate very different behaviors in different individuals, depending on their underlying personality structure.

moving, fear of   Fear of moving is known as tropophobia. This fear may be related to a fear of newness or of new things. A move from one home to another brings with it the anxiety of facing the unknown, and people anticipating a move fear the possibilities of hidden defects in a house or apartment, noisy or disagreeable neighbors. The sheer number of details and responsibilities in moving and the necessity of focusing energy on one project may be physically as well as mentally exhausting. Seeing their parents faced with unaccustomed anxieties and fears, children may sense the uneasiness and become anxious themselves.

A move that involves a complete change of location can cause many anxieties as the sense of the familiar vanishes. Differing customs, a change from rural to urban living or vice versa, or change of climate, may create difficulties including unexpected expenses. Activities that formerly were almost automatic, such as going to the grocery store, the library, or getting a haircut, take more time and investigation in a new place. Children feel lonely and depressed after leaving friends and abandoning group activities such as sports and clubs in which they had created a place for themselves. Anxiety can arise from newness and from the emergence of these adverse feelings.

The reasons for moving may create anxieties. Some moves are made for negative reasons, such as death in the family, divorce, or a reduced economic situation. Even though the move may be an advantage to one member of the family, others may feel dragged along and become resentful and anxious.

mugging, fear of   Mugging is a realistic contemporary fear that many people have because victims are confronted unexpectedly and suffer physical harm as well as losing possessions. Fear of being mugged leads many people to avoid wearing expensive, attention-getting clothes or jewelry on the street; in major cities, some individuals have been known to change their clothes before riding the subway, putting on clothes that "disguise" their mission as a business person or a partygoer. They carry their "good clothes" in a plain paper bag so that they will not be the victim of a thief. Some individuals may carry this avoidance response to an extreme.

music, fear of   Fear of music is known as musicophobia and melophobia. Music phobics usually fear only one type of music, such as organ music, which may have unpleasant associations for the individual. Historically, music has created a number of social fears and has been subjected to censorship; for example, operas hinting at revolution were censored in 19th-century Europe as were music of Jewish composers in Nazi Germany and music expressing subjectivity or individuality in Soviet Russia. Social and religious leaders have objected to jazz because of its association with sensuous dancing and because of its development in lower-class dance halls, which served as contact points for prostitutes. Jazz was particularly looked down upon by white southerners because of its origin in black culture, and some blacks attempting to rise in a white world have rejected it. Similarly, many have objected to and feared rock music for its associations with developed objectionable associations with commercialization, violence, sex, unbridled primitive energies, and drugs. Folk music became associated with radical, left-wing political movements, which frequently labeled subversive in the United States in the 1930s and '40s and again in the '60s and '70s.

music as anxiety therapy   Since antiquity, benefits of music as a soother of anxieties have been known. Music probably has powers to relieve anxieties because it involves nonverbal communication and fills physiological and psychological needs for pattern, form, and sensory stimulation. Music is a way to make the external environment more appealing and acceptable to the individual. Music can provide a focus for therapeutic activity and can motivate and reinforce participation in therapy.

In Greek mythology, Apollo was god of both medicine and music; Apollo's son, Aesculapius, god of medicine, was said to cure diseases of the mind by using music and song; the Greek philosopher Plato believed that music affected the emotions and could influence the individual's character. In the Bible, David played his harp to relieve King Saul's melancholy (depression). Music was used during the Middle Ages to exhaust crowds of people suffering from mass hysteria (probably because the music encouraged them to keep on dancing until exhaustion). Shakespeare made reference to the healing powers of music in his plays.

The first book in English on the subject was *Medicina Musica,* written by Richard Browne, an apothecary in the early 1700s. In the book, music was said to "soothe the turbulent affections" and calm "maniacal patients who did not respond to other remedies."

During the 19th century, music therapy in the form of brass bands and concerts was used for patients with all the then-identified mental disorders, including anxiety. In the 20th century, particularly during World War II, many U.S. psychiatric hospitals used active music-therapy programs. The National Association for Music Therapy (NAMT) was organized in 1950 and, in 1954, recommended a curriculum for preparation of music therapists. Subsequently, organizations of music therapists were formed in England, Europe, South America, and Australia.

Contemporary music therapists use music and musical activities to bring about desirable changes in an individual's behavior and help the individual adjust to the environment.

myctophobia   Fear of darkness is called myctophobia.

nail-biting   Nail-biting is a difficult habit to break. In spite of the stereotype of the nervous nail-biter, nail-biting does not correlate with specific personality qualities. However, many children as well as adults bite their nails when affected by anxiety or stress.

With some people, nail-biting continues because it is a routine and unconscious habit without a seemly underlying cause. Many people are embarrassed and only bite their nails when no one is around to see them .A somewhat universal habit, nail-biting, which has no relationship to sex, race, or intelligence, usually starts in childhood after the age of three and frequently ends in adolescence when peer pressure and personal grooming become important. About 20–25 percent of adults remain nail-biters. More women than men seek help to break the habit.

There seems to be a slight hereditary tendency to nail-biting, but, because family members are prone to mimic each others' habits, this is hard to establish. It seems, however, that a nail-biting parent is likely to have trouble correcting a nail-biting child.

narcolepsy, fear of   Some individuals fear sleep attacks, known as narcolepsy. An individual who has narcolepsy may fall asleep suddenly and involuntarily without warning. Sleep attacks appear to be triggered by strong emotions and may be accompanied by visual or auditory hallucinations at the onset. The attacks may occur up to several times per day and often include the type of muscle paralysis common in REM sleep. Individuals who have narcolepsy may experience increased anxiety throughout the day due to their inability to control their actions.

narrowness, fear of   Fear of narrowness, known as anginaphobia, may relate to a fear of being in narrow places, viewing scenery from a narrow vantage point, or of having any narrowing of the body, such as a narrowing of the arteries. The fear may also relate to fear of being in a tunnel and fear of crossing a bridge.

Fear of narrow places is known as stenophobia. This fear is related to the fear of narrowness and may be related to a fear of enclosed places, such as occurs in claustrophobia. Some who fear narrow places also fear being in tunnels, riding on escalators, moving walks at airports, and bridges.

nausea   Nausea, a common symptom of ANXIETY and anxiety disorders, is experienced as a feeling of sickness in the stomach and a feeling that one wants to vomit. Nausea may be accompanied by DIZZINESS or lightheadedness, sweating (see SWEATING, FEAR OF), and muscular weakness, may accompany anxiety attacks, and can appear either as a precursor to or at the onset of an actual bout with anxiety. It may occur on contact with a food that is associated with an anxiety-producing experience from childhood, or in response to certain odors and may be involved with many specific phobias, such as SOCIAL PHOBIAS, PERFORMANCE ANXIETY, sports anxiety, and examination anxiety. Many individuals experience nausea before an important appointment, before job interviews, before speaking in public, before playing an important game, and before taking tests, whether academic or a type of physical examination. Various forms of BEHAVIOR THERAPY are used to help individuals overcome nausea that does not have physical causes.

needles, fear of   Fear of needles is known as belonephobia. Some fear being pricked by a sewing needle; others fear injections by hypodermic needles. Many individuals fear dentists because they fear an injection of an analgesic substance with a needle; others fear needles because needles have been strongly implicated in the transmission of AIDS.

Because of fear of needles, some individuals are reluctant to donate blood. Some fear having or seeing a blood transfusion because of their needle fear.

Individuals who have a phobia of needles should, if possible, advise any health care professionals who treat them of their fear; for example, if a dentist knows that a patient has a phobia of needles, he or she will ask the patient to relax first or to look away and will keep the needle out of the patient's view rather than provoke a panic attack or make the patient scream or faint. Exposure therapy has been effective in successfully treating many individuals who fear needles.

nervous   An informal term indicating a state of tension, apprehension, and restlessness, nervousness is a form of anxiety. The term comes from Freud's theory that neurological weaknesses (neurasthenias) developed as a result of unconscious conflicts.

nervous breakdown   This obsolete but once popular term referred to any one or more of a variety of mental health disorders in an acute phase. It is a type of collapse during which the individual has lost ability to function at his or her previous level of adjustment. Some phobic individuals fear a nervous breakdown when their fears increase or when they have a panic attack. Anxiety disorders do not lead to more serious debilitating forms of mental illness.

nervous system   This is an informal term for the AUTONOMIC NERVOUS SYSTEM.

neurosis   An obsolete term used interchangeably with *neurotic disorder* (also considered obsolete), a neurosis is a mental condition characterized by anxiety, fears, obsessive thoughts, compulsive acts, dissociation, and depression. Neuroses are considered exaggerated, unconscious ways of coping with internal conflicts. The symptoms are distressing and unacceptable to the individual. The more current term for neurosis is *anxiety disorder*.

neurotic disorders   This obsolete diagnostic term has now been replaced by several terms including *anxiety disorders*. The term *neurotic disorders* comes from psychoanalytic theory and was used in the first diagnostic systems.

neurotransmitters   Chemical substances that are important in transferring nerve impulses from one cell to another, neurotransmitters are released at nerve fiber endings to help a nerve impulse across the gap between neurons. At least 30 different substances are known, produced in systems that link various parts of the brain. Several neurotransmitters are involved with fear and anxiety, particularly serotonin, acetycholine, and dopamine.

newness, fear of   Fear of newness or of anything new is known as neophobia. Individuals who have this fear tend to have fairly routine lives, avoid doing new things, going to new places, or perhaps even wearing new clothes. This fear is related to a fear of change, fear of traveling, and fear of moving.

night, fear of   Fear of night, known as noctiphobia or nyctophobia, is related to fear of the unknown or of the dark. Night fear is common in young children. Children may fear the night because they fear separation from their parents, being alone, or imaginary monsters and demons; adults may fear the night for more realistic reasons, such as burglars (who operate under cover of darkness), fear of becoming lost in the dark, or fear of driving a car during the dark hours. Some who fear night fear sleep (see SLEEP, FEAR OF), dreaming, or having NIGHT TERRORS. Some people fear sleepwalking (see SLEEPWALKING, FEAR OF) or sleeptalking; others fear going to bed at night for fear that they will not wake up in the morning. People who fear the night usually begin to avoid their fear by going home as dark nears. Night to many primitive people symbolized death, the color black, and unknown forces.

nightmare   Frightening dreams during the night, nightmares resemble phobias in that they are unpleasant stimuli that individuals avoid thinking or talking about in detail. Those who have had a nightmare awaken with a vivid memory of the dream and a deep sense of ANXIETY. Those who suffer from nightmares often tend to have other forms of sleep disorders and high scores on the Taylor Manifest Anxiety Scale. Children as well as adults fear nightmares that leave them with acute feelings of extreme anxiety, terror, or helplessness. Normal children may have an occasional nightmare after an alarming experience, but constant nightmares may reflect more deep-rooted anxieties or emotional conflicts.

In some cases, nightmares may be the expressions of waking fears, such as bridges or heights (see BRIDGES, FEAR OF, and HEIGHTS, FEAR OF) and can be reduced by gradual exposure to the frightening stimuli. Exposure therapy, which helps phobias, also eases nightmares when applied as rehearsal relief.

Recurrent nightmares are a pronounced feature of acute and chronic POSTTRAUMATIC STRESS DISORDER which often follows massive trauma and can persist for many years. Fantasy flooding, a form of behavioral therapy, has helped Vietnam veterans and victims of physical and sexual assault. Other sufferers of PTSD have improved with fantasy desensitization, and battle dreams have been reported to fade after the individual talks about them.

night terror   A nightmare, sometimes containing a phobic object or situation, from which the dreamer, usually a child, awakens screaming with fright, the terror may continues for up to 15 minutes while the child is in a state of semiconsciousness. He or she may scream or talk loudly and show intense fear. The child may appear to be asleep or in a trance, may be difficult to awaken, may be sitting up, or may be walking around or lying in bed thrashing about. If the child is wakened, he or she cannot recall what was frightening him or her. Night terrors can make parents anxious. Most children outgrow these episodes without treatment. The Latin name for night terrors is *pavor nocturnus.*

noise, fear of   Fear of noise is known as acousticophobia or ligyrophobia. Noise PHOBIA goes beyond just being startled by loud noises: the individual reacts with fear because he feels that the environment is in control of him and he is powerless to stop it. Some individuals fear specific noises, such as sonic booms, whistling, or balloons popping; those with the latter fear avoid going to birthday parties. Some fears of noises may be related to POSTTRAUMATIC STRESS DISORDER; for example, soldiers who have been in battle may fear loud noises later on. Individuals who have been involved in serious automobile accidents may recall only the noise of the impact and fear loud noises later on. Behavior therapy can be helpful to such individuals.

norepinephrine   A hormone and neurotransmitter to the nervous system, also known as noradrenaline, norepinephrine is found in circuits that control arousal, wakefulness, eating, learning, and memory. It can be either excitatory or inhibitory—its actions include increased pulse and blood pressure. Disturbances in the level of norepinephrine in the brain may be associated with depression and manic states. One viewpoint suggests that depression is the result of too little norepinephrine (and too much leads to mania); another viewpoint suggests that depression results from too little SEROTONIN, another neurotransmitter. There are receptors in the central and sympathetic nervous systems that are sensitive to norepinephrine or substances that mimic its actions. Some receptors accept agents that mimic or inhibit norepinephrinelike qualities. Norepinephrine is a strong vasoconstrictor.

nosebleeds, fear of   Fear of nosebleeds is known as epistaxiophobia. Some blood phobics become fearful when they see anyone else having a nosebleed. For some of these individuals, the sight of blood lowers blood pressure, reduces breathing rate, and induces a feeling of weakness or even a fainting spell. Others fear having nosebleeds themselves, which may be related to a fear of more serious disease or even fear of bleeding to death. Nosebleeds may have many causes. Among the most common causes of nosebleed are physical injuries to the nose, dryness of the nasal lining, picking at nasal passage with the fingernails, or too forceful blowing of the nose. However, persistent or recurring bleeding from the nose may be a symptom of a systemic disease, such as high blood pressure, or of an infection in the nasal passages.

nosophobia   Fear of disease is known as nosophobia.

nostophobia   Fear of returning home is known as nostophobia.

novelty, fear of   Fear of novelty is known as cainophobia, cainotophobia, kainophobia, kainotophobia, neophobia, and centophobia. For some, novelty implies greater danger, and the strange and the unfamiliar provoke fear in many individuals. Individuals who fear novelty tend to have repetitive patterns in their lives: they do not move often, usually live in the same place for a long time, keep the same job, and wear the same clothes. They tend to take vacations in the same places each year to avoid the novelty of something different. They tend to resist change of any sort.

nuclear weapons, fear of   Fear of nuclear weapons is known as nucleomitophobia. The same term applies to fear of atomic energy. This is a 20th-century fear related to the development of atomic and nuclear power. The fear is based on a feeling by individuals that they have no control over the fate of the world and that nuclear weapons can kill off all of human life and civilization. This fear is also related to a fear of death and a fear of the apocalypse, or the end of the world.

numbers, fear of   Fear of numbers is known as numerophobia. Some individuals have fears of particular numbers, such as 13, others fear working with numbers, such as doing mathematics.

People who fear the modern tendency to give everything a number instead of a name fear namelessness and anonymity.

numbers, fear of specific   Some numbers, historically, have been feared, while some are considered lucky; for example, the numbers 3 and 7, while generally considered to be lucky, also have their unfortunate side. For good or evil, some events are thought to occur in threes; therefore, if two misfortunes occur, some fear that a third is sure to follow. The "seven-year-itch" concept is an outgrowth of the idea that every seventh year of life is considered critical. Sixty-three is thought to be a dangerous age, according to common beliefs, but an individual who survives that year is destined for a long life.

Distinguished persons, such as Napoleon, J. Paul Getty, and Herbert Hoover thought it important to avoid having 13 at a dinner table. Franklin Delano Roosevelt went to great lengths to avoid beginning a trip on the 13th of the month. Fear of the number 13 is the most prevalent vestige of a belief in the mysterious power of numbers that originated in Pythagorean philosophy of antiquity. Ideas about the evil inherent in the number 13 specifically stem from Nordic mythology and the number in attendance at the Last Supper. According to modern numerology, 4 is also considered to be an unlucky number.

In reaction to the common fear of the number 13, in 1882, 13 men in New York founded the Thirteen Club and dedicated themselves to such practices as walking under ladders and spilling salt at their dinners.

numerophobia   This is a fear of numbers.

O

obsessions These are insistent, unwanted thoughts that recur despite active resistance against their intrusion; for example, a mother may be plagued by urges to strangle her baby while it sleeps. The word *obsession* is derived from the Latin word *obsidere*, meaning "to besiege." Individuals who have obsessions usually also have compulsive rituals that they feel compelled to repeat against their will, for example, checking and rechecking that the lights are turned off before leaving home.

obsessive-compulsive disorder (OCD) Obsessions are persistent, intense, senseless, worrisome, and often repugnant ideas, thoughts, images, or impulses that involuntarily invade consciousness. The automatic nature of these recurrent thoughts makes them difficult for the individual to ignore or retrain successfully. Furthermore, there is a strong emotional component that affects frequency and intensity.

Compulsions are repetitive and seemingly purposeful acts that result from the obsessions. The individual performs certain acts according to certain rules or in a stereotyped way to prevent or avoid aversive consequences. However, the compulsive act is not connected in a realistic way with what it is designed to produce or prevent and is usually clearly excessive. Although the individual may recognize the senselessness of the behavior and does not derive pleasure from carrying out the activity, doing so may provide a release of tension.

Common obsessions are repetitive thoughts of violence, contamination, and doubt. The most common compulsions involve hand-washing, cleaning, counting, checking, touching, repeating, avoiding, slowing, striving for completeness, and being meticulous. Checking and cleaning are the two major forms of compulsive behaviors.

Depression and ANXIETY are often associated with obsessive-compulsive disorder (and vice versa). There may be a phobic avoidance of situations that involve the content of the obsessions, such as contamination or dirt.

Obsessive-compulsives fear LOSING CONTROL. The obsessive-compulsive seems to need structures and ridigity more than others. He or she usually checks, filters, and censors all ingoing and outgoing stimuli. Obsessive-compulsives rarely drink alcohol excessively because they fear becoming out of control while under the influence. Further, they endeavor to extend their sense of control to their immediate environment, and some try to force family and close friends into ritualistic patterns.

In addition to fearing loss of control, obsessive-compulsives fear uncertainty. They are constantly in doubt about how their behaviors will influence their environment and activities and constantly ask for reassurance from others. Because of the fear of uncertainty and the need for reassurance, they are somewhat resistant to any form of medication. When medicated, they resist the effects of a drug, which takes more effort in control, with the net result that they become more anxious.

Imagery is an important part of obsessive-compulsive disorder and its treatment. Commonly, there are obsessional images, compulsive images, disaster images, and disruptive images. The disaster image has been well suited for a habituation training approach. The disaster image is a secondary event arising from an obsession or a compulsive urge and serves to increase the anxiety and distress of the individual. In many cases, content of disaster images is of future disasters and catastrophes. Habituation training to these images may prove to be helpful in treating individuals whose symptoms include this particular type of image. Researchers have found that imaginal exposure to feared disasters, when used in combination with response prevention procedures, leads to better long-term outcomes. The anxiety caused by an obsession is partially the result of its unwantedness and intrusiveness. When the individual can gain mastery or control over it, such anxiety can be alleviated.

odonophobia   Fear of teeth is known as odonophobia.

odors, fear of certain   Fear of particular odors is known as chromophobia, chromatophobia, olfactophobia, and osmophobia. Individuals may develop fears of certain odors because of traumatic experiences, associations with fearful situations or objects, or for many other reasons. Some fear odors of foods in general or those of particular foods. Usually, the phobic individual reacts to particular smells, such as types of foods, perfumes and stale odors, and becomes anxious in the presence of these odors. Some fear body odors from themselves or others; others fear odors in nature, such as flowers, trees, grasses, or molds.

Benjamin Rush (1745–1813), U.S. physician and author, commented on "the odor phobia":

> The odor phobia is a very frequent disease with all classes of people. There are few men or women to whom smells of some kind are not disagreeable. Old cheese has often produced paleness and tremor in a full fed guest. There are odors from certain flowers that produce the same effects: hence it is not altogether a figure to say, that there are persons who 'die of a rose in aromatic pain.'

Oedipus complex   Attachment of the child to the parent of the opposite sex, accompanied by envious and aggressive feelings toward the parent of the same sex. These feelings are largely repressed or made UNCONSCIOUS because of the fear of displeasure or punishment by the parent of the same sex. Many individuals have PHOBIAS and anxieties (see ANXIETY) resulting from an unresolved Oedipus complex. The Oedipus complex, originally described by Sigmund Freud (1856–1939), is a crucial component of Freudian psychology. It derives from the Greek myth of Oedipus who unwittingly killed his father and married his mother. In its original use, the term applied only to the boy or man in his relationship with his mother. The term *Electra complex* applied to girls and women and their relationships with their fathers.

one's own voice   Fear of one's own voice is known as phonophobia. Some individuals fear hearing their own voice on a recording or in an echo. Some fear that their voice does not project a powerful image, and thus fear of one's own voice may be related to a fear of public speaking, speaking over the telephone, and speaking out loud in social situations.

one thing, fear of   Fear of one thing is known as monophobia. Many individuals who have SPECIFIC PHOBIAS, such as fear of dogs or fear of thunderstorms, have fear of only one thing. Some individuals who have SOCIAL PHOBIAS also fear only one thing, such as public speaking or entering a crowded room.

operant conditioning   A method of learning, operant conditioning involves the strengthening or weakening of some aspect of a response (for example its form, frequency, intensity, etc.) based on the presentation of consequences. The two basic forms of operant learning are contingency management and operant shaping. Contingency management involves the manipulation of existing stimuli that precede or signal the behavior (such as taking cookies out of the cupboard to stop a child from climbing and opening the cupboard) or the manipulation of stimuli that follow it as consequences (reinforcement or punishment). Shaping involves selective reinforcement for approximation to a particular behavior until the final behavior is emitted.

The term was coined by Burrhus Frederic Skinner, a U.S. psychologist (1904–90), who applied understanding of operant conditioning to psychotherapy, language, learning, educational methods and cultural analysis. The principles of operant conditioning have been the basis for programs that successfully treat a wide range of human behavior problems, habit problems, and behavioral deficiencies and that elicit and maintain new behavior development. Operant conditioning researchers have applied this methodology to study in the development and treatment of behavioral and cognitive manifestations of anxiety.

opinions, fear of others'   Fear of others' opinions is known as allodoxaphohia. Individuals who fear criticism or ridicule fear opinions of others. Some social phobics have this fear.

opposite sex, fear of   Fear of the opposite sex is known as sexophobia. Some individuals fear those of the opposite sex in business and/or social situations. For some this fear may be a fear of sexual activity, a fear of a mother, a fear of a father, or a repressed feeling of sexual desire toward the parent of the opposite sex. The fear seems unrelated to the development of homosexuality.

orderliness (as a ritual)   Some individuals, out of fear, feel compelled to organize and arrange objects in a particular way, such as items on a desk or on a kitchen counter. They become fearful and upset if anyone moves an item or attempts to interfere with their compulsion. The fear of disorder and disarray is known as ataxiophobia.

outer space, fear of   Fear of outer space is known as spacephobia. This fear is based on a fear of the unknown. People has fearfully wondered for years if there is life in the alien, totally dark, soundless and airless environment known as outer space. Discovery of the immensity and shape of the universe, the possibilities of other universes, and theories about black holes, white holes, and "worm holes" that might connect one universe to another are disturbing because they are difficult concepts to comprehend. Scholarly theologians have interpreted these findings in light of their beliefs, but many people find these matters not only incomprehensible but somewhat frightening.

P

pain, anxiety and depression in   ANXIETY or depression are rarely the only causes of pain; both can make pain seem worse. Most people with pain have some emotional reaction to it: some feel depressed, worried, or easily discouraged when they have pain; some feel out of control, hopeless, or helpless; others feel alone or embarrassed, inadequate, angry, or frightened.

Anxiety or depression that accompany the pain of illness or injury may be caused by problems other than pain; for example, one may have concerns over family or friends while one is ill, spiritual problems, or difficulties with insurance or money because of illness.

Fatigue can intensify pain. If one is tired, one may not be able to cope with pain as well as when one is rested. Some individuals who have chronic pain fear fatigue or fear getting too tired to cope with their painful condition.

pain, fear of   Fear of pain is known as algophobia, odynesphobia, and odynophobia. Pain is a sensation that hurts enough to make one uncomfortable; it may be mild distress or severe discomfort, acute or chronic. Acute pain is usually severe and lasts a relatively short time; chronic pain may be mild or severe and is present to some degree for long periods of time. Pain is often a signal that body tissue is being damaged in some way. Pain can only be defined by the person who is feeling it; it cannot be verified by someone else.

Humanity has suffered and feared pain since the beginning of time. Although a wide variety of drugs are now available to ease pain, pain is still a fearful subject, and the prospect of having pain makes people anxious. Fear of pain is evidenced by avoidance of potentially painful situations such as visits to doctors or dentists and dislike or avoidance of hospitals, rehabilitation centers. The phobic individual's reaction is usually anticipatory and often not the result of any traumatic event in his or her life. This phobia is a good example of how reactions become sensitized and expanded by cognitive processes that operate during avoidance.

Some people find pain very difficult to explain. The fact that they cannot explain it to their doctor or others around them contributes to their anxiety and feelings of tension.

panic, panic attacks, and panic disorder   Panic attacks strike some individuals with little warning and for no apparent reason. Panic and panic attacks are characterized by an abrupt surge of anxiety with a feeling of impending doom that quickly peaks. Panic may be elicited by particular stimuli or by thinking about it. Also, it may occur unpredictably and spontaneously without any cues. A panic attack is not like ordinary anxiety and nervousness that most people feel before a job interview or giving a speech. Symptoms of a panic attack include light headedness, dizziness, rubbery legs, difficult breathing, a racing, palpitating heart, and choking and tingling sensations.

The word *panic* is derived from the name for the god whom the Greeks worshiped as their god of flocks, herds, pastures, and fields—Pan. The Greek word for "all" is also *pan.* People were dependent on Pan to make the flocks fertile; Pan—himself was a lustful creature and known for an ability to reproduce—had the shape of a goat; a goat could traverse fields and dart through herds of cattle. This goat god loved to scare people: he would dart out of the woods and frighten passersby, often in dark forests and at night and would make eerie noises. The fright he created was known as panic. Later, Pan fell out of favor because the Christian church portrayed the devil with the goat god's features; his two horns symbolized the philosophy of devil worship.

Nearly all severe phobics (except some blood and food phobics) have phobic panic, making it difficult to classify phobias according to the presence of panic. During phobic panic, nearly all phobics feel changes in heart rate, tense muscles, and sweaty palms.

panphobia   Also known as panophobia, pantophobia, and pamphobia, panphobia is a fear of anything and everything. It may be a form of anxiety rather than a true phobia.

paper, fear of   Fear of paper, which is classified as a simple phobia because it is a fear of one thing, is known as papyrophobia. This fear may include touching paper, seeing paper, being cut by the edge of paper, or even thinking about paper. Fear of paper may extend to wrapping paper, wallpaper, or drawing paper. It may be a fear of the paper itself or of writing or printing on paper. See PHOBIA; SPECIFIC PHOBIAS.

paradoxical intention   In this technique that is used to treat phobias, the phobic individual is instructed to think strongly and imagine himself or herself in his or her phobic situation or facing the feared object. The individual is asked to magnify his or her fear reactions, such as rapid breathing in an actual phobic situation.

Paradoxical intention is based on an understanding of the effects of anticipatory anxiety and the self-fulfilling prophecy. The goal of paradoxical intention is to teach individuals that they can control symptoms instead of allowing symptoms to control them, that they can reverse the instinctive avoidance of the feared object, situation, or event, and that they can break the cycle through which anticipatory anxiety produces symptoms.

paranoid   Paranoid relates to a mental disorder that is characterized primarily by delusions. Paranoid delusions may include grandiosity or persecution. The word comes from the Greek word meaning "derangement" or "madness." In psychiatric terms, paranoid ideation is thinking in less than delusional proportions, involving suspiciousness or the belief that one is being harassed, persecuted, or unfairly treated. In some instances the term is used when the therapist is unsure of whether the disturbances are actually delusional. There are some aspects of paranoid thinking in agoraphobia and other phobic syndromes in which the individual wrongly believes that he is being watched or observed.

parasites, fear of   Fear of parasites is known as parasitophobia or phthiriophobia. This fear may extend to any tiny organism such as a virus, bacterium, or fungus that lives in or on another organism (the host) and at some time in its life takes all or part of its nourishment from the host. Some people fear that they may become infested with parasites but do not believe that they are currently infested. Some who believe that they are hosting parasites, pick, scratch, and tear their skin out of fear of the damage the parasites will do until they develop sores. They may display bits of skin as examples of the parasites.

Fears of parasites are not totally unfounded, as some parasites are harmful to one's health and cause a disease. Parasites may exist in the intestinal tract, where they have access to predigested food; hookworms and tapeworms are examples. Parasites elsewhere in the body can damage cells, block organ ducts, cause toxic or allergic reactions, and stimulate the host's tissue to a point where abnormal growths are formed.

penis fear   Fear of penises is known as phallophobia. These fears usually relate to anxiety regarding social judgment about the size of one's penis or social embarrassment about having an erection in public.

performance anxiety   Performance anxiety, or stage fright, is a form of SOCIAL PHOBIA that is a persistent, irrational fear of exposure to scrutiny in certain situations, particularly public speaking and musical, dramatic, or other types of performances. Some musicians are more prone to anxiety than performers in other disciplines because musicians have spent many years practicing by themselves, away from people. Actors, however, even though they train with other people, still may experience extreme performance anxiety when they appear before the public.

Some individuals experience performance anxiety in activities that are not scrutinized by the public, such as doing mechanical work or taking tests. Individuals who have this fear worry about doing something over which they might become embarrassed or humiliated. They tend to catastrophize, or worry about what might happen in the worst possible cases. Catastrophizing thoughts might include "I think I'm going to faint," "I don't think I will be able to get through to the end without cracking up," "I'm almost sure to make a dreadful mistake, and that will ruin everything," Some individuals fear personal odors from themselves; other individuals fear personal odors from others.

phallic stage   In psychoanalysis, the phallic stage is the third stage of psychosexual development, usually between ages three and six, when the child first focuses sexual feeling on the genital organs and masturbation becomes a source of pleasure. According to Sigmund Freud (1856–1939), the penis becomes the center of attention for both boys and girls. During the phallic phase or stage, the boy experiences sexual fantasies toward his mother and rivalry toward his father, both of which he eventually gives up due to castration fear. Similarly, the girl experiences sexual fantasies toward the father and hostility toward the mother, due to rivalry and blaming her for being deprived of the penis, but gives up these feelings when she becomes afraid of losing the love of both parents. According to the U.S. psychoanalyst Erik Erikson (1902–   ), if the child does not successfully advance out of the phallic stage into the genital stage, he or she experiences guilt and role fixation or inhibition, leading to later anxieties.

phallic symbol   In psychoanalysis, any object that resembles or represents the penis becomes a phallic symbol. Structures that are longer than they are wide may be symbolic of the penis in dreams or in daily life. Examples include trees, skyscrapers, cigars, pencils, snakes, flutes and other musical instruments such as clarinets or trombones, motorcycles, airplanes, hammers, and many other similarly shaped objects.

phobia   A phobia is an irrational, intense fear of a person, object, situation, sensation, experience, thought, or stimulus event that is not shared by the consensual community and is thus out of proportion to any real danger. The individual cannot easily explain or understand the phobia, has no voluntary control over the anxiety response, and seeks to avoid the dreaded situation or stimulus. Phobias are classified as specific phobias, social phobias, and agoraphobia. Some individuals have more than one type of phobia. All phobias cannot be neatly classified because phobias of almost any situation can occur and may be associated with almost any other psychological symptom. However, when phobias occur as the dominant symptom, the condition is called a phobic state, a phobic reaction, or a phobic disorder.

phobic anxiety   A response of mind and body that the individual experiences only in the actual or imagined presence of the feared object, person, or situation is called phobic anxiety. There may be a sudden onset of intense apprehension and terror, feelings of unsteadiness, of unreality, impending doom, dying, going crazy, or doing something uncontrolled. Also, there may be shortness of breath, sensations of choking and smothering, chest pain or discomfort, hot or cold flashes, faintness, and trembling. Behavioral theories emphasize the conditioned associative learning that produces a bond between triggering stimuli and the response of anxiety.

photographed, fear of being   The fear of being photographed, common in certain traditional ethnic groups such as Native American and gypsies, is an extension of the belief that an individual's soul exists in his or her reflection. Being photographed puts the subject in the power of the photographer and may cause harm or even death.

Modern believers in magic and witchcraft have even more to fear from being photographed. Twentieth-century wizards and sorcerers have adapted and intensified the practice of using a doll to injure someone by attaching a photograph of the victim to the doll.

photophobia   Photophobia is a fear of light. More commonly, however, the term for photophobia refers to an organically determined hypersensitivity to light that results in severe pain and tearing in the eyes when the individual is exposed to light. This may occur during many acute infectious diseases.

phronemophobia   Fear of thinking is termed *phronemophobia*.

placebo   A preparation containing the form of treatment but not the substance—that is, a pretense of treatment without the actual ingredients being there—a placebo may be prescribed or administered to cause the phobic individual to believe he or she is receiving treatment. Placebo effects include the psychologic and physiologic benefits as well as undesirable reactions that reflect the individual's expectations. For example, if the individual believes that a medication will reduce anxiety, it probably will.

Placebos also influence the effects of psychotherapy; for example, research in psychotherapy includes placebo groups in the research design to determine the proportion of people who recover just because they think they are receiving a treatment. Surprisingly, depending on the research method and types of treatment presented, between 30 and 70 percent of people will significantly improve with just placebo treatment. Similar results have been obtained in drug research.

These results suggest that a powerful internal and personal energy is available to people who "suffer" from mental disorders that can produce positive change and growth.

plants, fear of   Fear of plants is known as botanophobia. Some fear plants because they believe that plants consume oxygen needed by humans; some fear the allergies and skin rashes plants cause; others fear plants because of personal associations. There is an old superstition about leaving flowers in the rooms of sick persons at night: flowers and plants, according to this superstition, were the hiding places for evil spirits who at night, under cover of darkness, would take possession of the sick person and inflict harm.

pleasure, fear of   Fear of pleasure is known as hedonophobia. Some individuals who have guilt feelings about themselves fear enjoying themselves, and hence fear pleasure. Some cannot enjoy an activity or event themselves because others less fortunate than they cannot do what they are doing.

poetry, fear of   Fear of poetry is known as metrophobia. Some individuals have fearful and even aversive feelings about poetry because of its basic nature and because of the way it is taught and analysed. In classical times, Spartans banned certain types of poetry because they thought it promoted effeminate and licentious behavior. The rhyme and figurative language of poetry is odd and distracting to some people. Frequently, poetry contains words, allusions and obscurely stated thoughts and feelings that are confusing or incomprehensible to people who lack a scholarly, academic background.

poetry as therapy for anxiety   Like MUSIC AS ANXIETY THERAPY, poetry therapy, the treatment of ANXIETY by the patient's reading or writing poetry, can help an anxious or fearful individual communicate feelings that he or she might not otherwise be able to express. Poetry helps the individual uncover and release emotions that previously may have been repressed, consciously or unconsciously, and thus reduce anxiety and fears. In reading poetry, the individual realizes that someone else feels as he or she does; he or she feels less alone with anxieties and fears. Making up poetry gives an individual a chance to express ideas in an indirect manner. Poetry therapy is used as an adjunct to other forms of therapy and can be used in group or individual therapy.

pointing the finger, fear of   Some individuals fear pointing at their own body to show a place that is diseased or weak and fear pointing at their own body when talking about where another person is diseased; the fear is that the pointing individual will suffer the same complaint in the same place.

A second fear regarding pointing the finger relates to pointing the finger at someone else. Children are taught not to point their finger at anyone. This notion goes back to early times when man worshiped the phallus, which was the source of life. People feared the outstretched finger as the image of the male organ, and thus the finger could prove equally productive in the creation of both good and evil. In primitive society, the phrase *to point the finger* became synonymous with killing a person.

police, fear of   Individuals who have a fear of police and police personnel may fear authority, punishment, or entrapment. It is usual for those who break the law to fear police because they probably fear being caught. Those who exceed the speed limit while driving fear being seen by a police officer because they may have to pay a fine for their violation or go to court to defend themselves. However, when an individual becomes very anxious every time he or she sees a uniformed police person, it may actually be a phobia that causes physiological effects such as rapid breathing, dizziness, and gastrointestinal symptoms. Some individuals who fear police fear that if they are apprehended, they will be subjected to extensive questioning and perhaps prison. Thus a fear of police may also be a fear of loss of control over one's own destiny.

pollution, fear of   Fear of environmental pollution may come from the fear of bad health effects brought on by exposure to polluted air or water. Anxiety may be increased by an individual's personal lack of control over his or her exposure to pollution and the inability to avoid the many pollutants founds in everyday life, such as exhaust from cars, wastes from industry, smoke from cigarettes, and toxins in drinking water. Some individuals deal with fears of pollution by using avoidance behavior, such as refusing to live in or travel to big cities, where pollution is more prevalent. Fear of air pollution may lead some individuals to develop agoraphobia.

polyphobia   Fear of many things is known as polyphobia. Many phobic individuals have more than one phobia and hence are polyphobic.

Positron Emission Tomography (PET)   Using this brain imaging technique, PET researchers can measure blood flow in areas of the brain that are thought to control panic and anxiety reactions. Differences in blood flow between the two hemispheres of the brain are probably connected with differences in metabolic rates and reflect differences in the activity levels of nerve cells of the two sides. PET is useful in assessing the amount of psychoactive drug in various parts of the brain, as well as physiological abnormalities.

postpartum anxiety Many women experience postpartum anxiety, depression after childbirth or delivery. Many women have "weepy" spells and feel somewhat "blue" at this time. Even though a woman may be elated with her new baby, some of the mild depression can be attributed to the letdown after months of eager anticipation. Also, a woman's anxiety may come about because she feels fearful of being a parent, fears being a failure as a parent, feels less loving toward her baby than she thinks she should, and feels less sexually attractive to her mate because her body has not regained its normal shape. The woman may also feel a loss of self-esteem if she has gone from a job outside the home into full-time motherhood. Because of the demands of the new baby, she may feel exhausted, overwhelmed with chores, deprived of sleep, and fear the chronic fatigue that seems to accompany her new status. Also, any tensions between the couple that existed before the birth of a baby may worsen after the baby's arrival in the household.

Hormonal changes after the birth of a baby may also affect a woman's mood; for example, rapidly plummeting estrogen and progesterone can lead to hot flashes and irritability, similar to the phenomena associated with menopause. Additionally, sleep deprivation caused by frequent waking during the night by the baby can lead to irritability and depression.

The degree to which a woman experiences postpartum depression also depends on her support system, including her husband, her family, and any additional caretaker for the baby. The baby's temperament may also affect her mood; for example, if the baby is colicky and cries frequently, she may become anxious and irritable, and if the baby is calm, she will feel like a better mother and experience less anxiety.

posttraumatic stress disorder (PTSD) PTSD, also once known as shell shock, battle fatigue, and war neurosis, affects hundreds of thousands of individuals who have survived the trauma of natural disasters such as earthquakers, accidental disasters such as airplane crashes, war, school shootings, crimes, and effects of abuse or neglect as children or adults. PTSD is not confined to war and catastrophy victims: there is growing concern that living in poverty, in ghettos, and in high crime areas can produce anxiety and panic as a form of PTSD.

Although its symptoms can occur soon after the event, PTSD often surfaces several months or even years later. Symptoms include repeated episodes of reexperiencing the traumatic event that can happen in sudden, vivid memories accompanied by very painful emotions that seem to have no cause. These emotions, often of grief, can also be of anger or intense fear. Individuals say these emotional experiences occur repeatedly, much like memories or dreams about the traumatic event. Panic attack (see PANIC, PANIC ATTACKS, AND PANIC DISORDER) and ANXIETY often result from PTSD experiences. The memory can be a flashback, a recollection so strong that the individual thinks he or she is actually experiencing the traumatic event again. When a person has a severe flashback, he or she is in a dissociative state, which sometimes can be mistaken for sleepwalking. Sometimes the reexperience occurs in NIGHTMARES that are powerful enough to awaken the person screaming in terror. Some individuals with PTSD develop insomnia in an attempt to avoid the dreaded dreams. At times, the reexperience comes as a sudden, painful rush of emotions.

These may result from the extreme fear they felt during the traumatic event that remained unresolved during other events in their lives. During the panic attack, their throats tighten, their breathing and heart rate increase, and they may feel dizzy and nauseated.

Avoidance behavior also occurs. This affects the individual's relationships with others because he or she often avoids close emotional ties with family, colleagues, and friends. At first the person feels numb, has diminished emotions and can complete only routine, mechanical activities. Later, when reexperience of the event begins, the individual alternates between the flood of emotions caused by the reexperience and the inability to feel or express emotions at all. Some individuals who have PTSD often say they cannot feel emotions, especially toward those to whom they are closest; if they can feel emotions, often they cannot express them. As the avoidance continues, the person seems to be bored, cold, or preoccupied.

Therapists can help individuals who have PTSD work through the trauma and pain. The goal is resolution of the conscious and unconscious conflicts that were thus created. Additionally, the individual works to build his or her self-esteem and self-control, develop a good and reasonable sense of personal accountability, and renew his or her sense of integrity and personal pride.

pregnancy, fear of   Some women fear becoming pregnant, not becoming pregnant, or pregnancy itself for a wide range of reasons. Some unmarried women fear conceiving and bearing a child out of wedlock. Some women, although married, do not want to be burdened with a child, some fear the pain of childbirth, and some fear that they might die during pregnancy or childbirth. Thus fears of pregnancy stem from both psychological and physical sources. Some women fear being taken over by their pregnancy, as if they had no other purpose than to produce a child. They fear feeling victimized by motherhood, as though the child inside them is a parasite. Although many women are delighted with the first fetal movement, some find it a frightening indication that they are harboring a separate life. Many women fear the interruption in their work and physical activity brought about by pregnancy. There is the fear in some women that their physical appearance while pregnant will become comical and that they will not be attractive to their husbands and to men in general. A pregnant woman sometimes extends this fear to a feeling that she will never return to her original physical appearance. Some women fear a loss of interest in sexual activity during pregnancy; others fear an increased interest in sexual activity.

Pregnant women often have intense dreams and fantasies about the child they are carrying. Some women fear that they are losing their minds. Mood swings during pregnancy, sometimes triggered by hormonal changes, disturb many women and their husbands. Well-meant advice and anecdotes from other women can also be a source of anxiety.

Many women become anxious and embarrassed by the physical symptoms associated with pregnancy: morning sickness, food cravings, frequent urination, water retention, bloating and swollen breasts are frequent complaints. First-time mothers fear that they may not be able to recognize the first movements of the fetus and as a result may fear that the baby is abnormal or dead. Although most mothers fear weight gain during pregnancy, others may feel that they are not gaining enough. Recent findings about the effects on the fetus of the mother's smoking and alcohol consumption have caused many pregnant women to abstain out of fear that they will have an unhealthy baby.

Clumsiness increases during the last months of pregnancy and, in addition to being unpleasant in itself, makes women fearful of accidents. Some men and women fear that intercourse during pregnancy will harm the fetus; others may feel uneasy during intercourse in the belief that the fetus is watching and aware of what they are doing.

premenstrual syndrome (PMS), fear of   Fear of the physical and mental symptoms of anxiety and tension is experienced by some women before getting their menstrual periods. Many women fear the discomfort associated with PMS, which may include water retention, tender breasts, headaches, body aches, food cravings, lethargy, and depression. Causes of premenstrual syndrome have not been determined and vary from woman to woman. The symptoms that occur several days before menstruation seem to be related to the interplay of hormones between ovulation and the beginning of menstruation.

Many fears about PMS are grounded in actual fact; some may be due to inhibitions and unpleasant associations. Sufferers from PMS sometimes fear that they are going crazy; other women resent the regular loss of several days a month to PMS; even nonsufferers dread the fact that a genuine emotional response or complaint may be chalked up to hormones. Because menstruation is not a subject that is discussed freely, many women feel isolated or misunderstood because they suffer in silence. Women are anxious and fearful about the possibility of hostile or even violent interaction with husbands, lovers, children, or employers because of PMS. Statistics on occupational and automobile accidents show that women are more likely to be clumsy, inattentive, and unable to judge distances just before their periods. Students fear that they may have to take an exam that will affect their scholastic records and ultimately their career at this time. Women fear that other occasions when they want to be at their best, such as employment interviews or athletic events, will fall just before menstruation. Because resistance to infection is lowered before the onset of menstruation, a woman has more reason to fear illness just before her period.

Until recently, the medical attitude that the discomfort of PMS was all in the mind has tended to increase rather than decrease anxiety. Attitudes are changing and PMS is a recognized physical condition, but there is still some reluctance to take it seriously. Although there is no single successful treatment for PMS, many doctors now regard it as a challenging problem in need of solution. A variety of treatments, such as hormones, vitamins, analgesics, and diuretics, have been tried with varying degrees of success.

prepared fears   This theory states that individuals may be biologically prepared to develop certain fears and less prepared to develop others. Humans may be prepared to develop conditioned fear responses to certain stimuli that once evoked danger in our evolutionary cycle. An ability to develop fear readily to these stimuli helped our ancestors avoid such stimuli and therefore survive. This theory helps explain the disproportionately high number of certain phobias, such as snakes and small animals.

Researchers who have tested the preparedness theory of fears and phobias say that prepared fears are easily acquired with as little as a single conditioning trial, that once developed they will be quite resistant to extinction, and that the prepared conditioned fear is not easily reduced by information for example, that spiders are not likely to be harmful.

primal therapy   A technique developed by Arthur Janov (1924–   ), a U.S. psychologist and author of *The Primal Scream*, primal therapy, also known as primal scream therapy, treats anxieties and phobias by encouraging the individual to relive basic or primal traumatic events and discharge painful emotions associated with them. Such events may have led to development of the anxieties and phobias and frequently involve feelings of abandonment or rejection experienced in infancy or early childhood. During therapy, the individual may cry, scream, or writhe in agony and later experience a sense of release and freedom from primal pain

primary gain   Primary gain is the basic internal psychological benefit that the individual derives from having a phobic condition, anxiety, or emotional illness. If the individual develops mental symptoms defensively in largely unconscious ways to cope with or to resolve unconscious conflicts, then the symptoms provide a relief to the individual's system by reducing conflict between UNCONSCIOUS and defensive forces. The need for such gain may be the reason why a phobic condition or emotional problem develops. In contrast, secondary gain is that which is obtained from a symptom of an illness or phobia that one already has. The term *primary gain* is derived from psychoanalytic and psychodynamic theories that emphasize the role of unconscious forces in ANXIETY.

progressive muscle relaxation   Progressive muscle relaxation (also known as progressive relaxation) is an anxiety management procedure in which individuals learn to make heightened observations of what goes on under their skin. They learn to control all of the skeletal muscles so that any portion can be systematically relaxed or tensed by choice.

First, there is recognition of subtle states of tension. When a muscle contracts (tenses), waves of neural impulses are generated and carried to the brain along neural pathways. This muscle-neural phenomenon is an observable sign of tension.

Next, having learned to identify the tension sensation, the individual learns to relax it. Relaxation is the elongation (lengthening) of skeletal muscle fibers, which then eliminates the tension sensation. This general procedure of identifying a local state of tension, relaxing it away, and making the contrast between the tension and ensuing relaxation is then applied to all of the major muscle groups.

As a technique for managing anxiety and stress, progressive relaxation is only effective when individuals have the ability to elongate their muscle fibers selectively on command. They can then exercise the self-control required for progressive relaxation and more rationally deal with the stressful situation.

projection   Unconsciously using this defense mechanism, the individual rejects ideas or thoughts that are emotionally unacceptable to the self and attributes (project) them to others. Interpersonally, this is called blame as well as projection. This mechanism is a common form of protection with children; unfortunately, it often remains in place into adulthood. The use of blame prevents the individual from making any significant personal changes. In phobias, an individual is projecting danger onto a neutral objects or situations.

propranolol   A drug within the family of medications known as BETA ADRENERGIC BLOCKING AGENTS, beta blocking agents, or beta blockers, propranolol is commonly used to treat high blood pressure, migraine headaches, angina, and some heart conditions. It is also used in some cases to reduce symptoms of anxiety, such as rapid heartbeat (tachycardia) and sweating, and general tension. Propranolol has been used successfully to help control symptoms of stage fright and fears of public speaking. Because it has few side effects, many tolerate it well. But there are some possible side effects, including dizziness, unusually slow pulse, insomnia, diarrhea, cold hands and feet, and numbness, and/or tingling of fingers or toes. Propranolol should not be taken by individuals who have chronic lung disease, asthma, diabetes, or certain heart diseases or by individuals who are severely depressed.

Propranolol and other beta blockers are sometimes prescribed for individuals who have mitral valve prolapse (MVP) and for individuals who fear having rapid heartbeat.

psychiatrist   Psychiatrists are physicians with an M.D. degree from a medical school who specialize in mental/emotional treatment and research. Some psychiatrists tend to view mental "disorders" as chemical or biological in their source and hence medical in nature.

By virtue of their medical degree, psychiatrists can prescribe medications and conduct medically defined procedures (such as electroconvulsive shock therapy) and can admit patients to hospitals.

psychoactive drug   This chemical compound has a psychological effect and alters mood or thought processes. A tranquilizer is an example of a psychoactive drug. Some psychoactive drugs are sometimes prescribed for individuals under treatment for phobias.

psychoanalysis   A therapy developed by Sigmund Freud (1856–1939) that stresses free association, dream analysis, transference, and the modification of defenses to allow the conscious expression of unconscious impulses, memories, emotions, experiences, and so on. Psychoanalytic theory has had a powerful impact on our culture, art, movies, literature, advertising, child-rearing practices, views of mental and emotional disorders, and therapy.

Anxiety was a key component of the therapy and the theory of human behavior. Psychoanalysis in theory was instrumental in developing anxiety as a diagnostic category.

psychodrama   A therapeutic technique in which individuals act out or watch others act out personal problems, including phobias and anxieties, psychodrama is a type of group therapy that evolved in Vienna in the early part of the 20th century. Individuals create their own plays that mirror their personal problems and conflicts. Psychodramatic methods are applicable to many types of phobic individuals and may be used by therapists to help individuals overcome specific phobias or general anxieties.

Psychoneuroimmunology (PNI)   Psychoneuroimmunology is a relatively new branch of science that studies the interrelationships among the mind (pyscho), the nervous system (neuro), and the immune system (immunology). The aim of this field is to investigate and document interrelationships between psychological factors and the immune and neuroendocrine systems. Research efforts include looking at effects of emotional stress on the immune system and health. In a general way, PNI seeks to understand the scientific basis of the mind-body connection.

Authors Locke and Colligan, in *The Healer Within*, explain that a premise of PNI is that the immune system does not operate in a biological vacuum but is sensitive to outside influences. PNI researchers speculate that there is a line of communication between the mind and cells that are the immune system. Tendrils of the brain's nerve tissues run through important sectors of the immune system, including the thymus gland, bone marrow, lymph nodes, and spleen. Hormones and NEUROTRANSMITTERS secreted by the brain have an affinity for immune cells. Also, certain states of mind and feelings can have strong biochemical results.

During the later 1980s and 1990s, researchers from various background were drawn to this new discipline. Social psychologists, experimental psychologists, psychiatrists, immunologists, neuroendocrinologists, neuroanatomists, biologists, oncologists, and epidemiologists among other specialists have all made contributions to PNI research. Together, they seek to explain the way the brain and mind contribute to illness or keep people healthy.

psychologist   In most states, a psychologist has a Ph.D. degree from a graduate program in psychology. After World War II, psychologists began to perform psychotherapy for "mental illness" (up until the 1950s, psychotherapy was claimed to be a medical procedure) and now possess all the privileges of a mental-health professional in the form of licensing, insurance reimbursement, hospital privileges, and expert-witness designation.

Psychology, like medicine, has many areas of specialization, including child, developmental, school, clinical, social, and industrial. The Ph.D. degree requires training in research skills. Clinical psychologists take further training in psychodiagnosis and psychotherapy and require supervision and an internship experience as does psychiatry.

psychology   The study of all behavior as part of the total life process, this includes the sequence of development, inherited and environmental factors, social interactions, conscious and unconscious mental processes, mental health and disorder, bodily systems associated with behavior, observation, testing and experimental study of behavior, and the application of psychological information to fields such as employment, education, and consumer behavior.

psychosexual anxieties   Psychosexual anxieties are disorders caused by mental attitudes about sexuality and physical conditions involving sexuality. Some anxieties are caused more by psychological attitudes; others come from physical aspects. Many psychosexual anxieties may have arisen because of new sexual freedoms that many individuals discovered in the latter decades of the 20th century. Sexual activity between men and women, unmarried as well as married, seemed to increase for a number of reasons: first, improved methods of contraception in the form of the birth control pill became available; second, previously known sexually transmitted (venereal) diseases, most notably syphilis and gonorrhea, were curable with penicillin and other drugs.

During the last two decades of the 20th century, an increasing number of new sexually transmitted diseases (STDs) appeared, causing psychosexual anxieties that differed from previously recognized generalized SEXUAL FEARS. For example, when an individual discovers, feel, or suspects a genital lesion, he or she may lose interest in sexual intercourse or at least restrain himself/herself for fear of infecting the partner. Another situation is the concern faced by the innocently infected partner of an individual with a sexually transmitted disease who has had intercourse outside a stable relationship. The innocent partner may realize the implications of the STD but may not want to face the reality of the diagnosis.

Under the stress of having a sexually transmitted disease, a person may become angry, anxious, or depressed. Anger may be directed at the physician consulted as well as at the person who transmitted the infection. Professionals in clinics specializing in sexually transmitted disease deal with this kind of anxiety by letting the individual voice these feelings and later by reassurance. In some individuals, anxiety is so severe that a short course of antianxiolytic medication is given.

GUILT and depression over a sexually transmitted disease is not uncommon. In some cases, antidepressant medications are given. Many conditions, such as genital herpes, pelvic inflammatory disease, acute epididymitis, and hepatitis B, may cause anger, anxiety, guilt, and depression.

Many individuals visit sexually transmitted disease clinics for checkups because they fear having acquired an STD. Some continue to believe or fear that they have contracted an infection in spite of extensive and frequent reassurance. Some of these individuals may have delusions of venereal disease, which are fixed ideas that the individual cannot be talked out of (found in schizophrenic disorders, psychotic depression, and monosymptomatic delusions) and phobias or obsessional fears. Individuals who have a fixed belief of venereal disease should be referred for psychotherapy.

psychosis   A psychosis is a severe mental disorder characterized by gross impairment in reality testing. A psychotic (one who has a psychosis) incorrectly evaluates the accuracy of his or her perceptions and thoughts and makes incorrect inferences about external reality, even in the face of contrary evidence. The term *psychotic* does not apply, however, to minor distortions of reality that involve matters of relative judgment; for example, a depressed individual who lacks self-esteem and underestimates his or her achievements would not be described as psychotic, whereas one who believes that he or she has caused a natural catastrophe would be so described.

psychotherapy   Psychotherapy is the treatment of PHOBIA, ANXIETY, or mental disorder through a corrective experience resulting from the interaction between a trained therapist and the individual.

R

rabies   A virus-produced disease that destroys the brain nerve cells in both humans and animals. Rabies is also called hydrophobia (also the name for fear of water); fear of rabies is known as cynophobia, kynophobia, and lyssophobia. Although the dog is the most common transmitter of rabies, many domestic and wild animals such as cats, wolves, foxes, raccoons, bats, horses, and skunks may also carry it.

People who fear rabies avoid outdoor activities such as hiking and camping. After a person has been bitten and infected by an animal carrying the virus, it usually takes 20 to 90 days for symptoms to develop. During the early part of the disease, the individual may be restless and anxious. The sight of water will produce throat spasms, pain, and fear of water. At this stage, convulsions and delirium may occur, and the disease is almost always fatal in two to 10 days. Immediate medical care after a dog or animal bite can be lifesaving. Cleansing of the bitten area removes much of the virus. Treatment consists of seven to 14 daily injections, depending on the severity of the exposure.

radiation, fear of   Fear of radiation is known as radiophobia. Some individuals fear harmful health effects from radiation. They fear that overexposure to rays may cause sterility, mutations, and damage to internal organs. These are legitimate fears, but if carried to extremes or in the absence of radiation, these are phobias. Some individuals fear radiation from emissions from color television sets, as well as from nuclear bombs.

Radiation has many beneficial characteristics that phobics overlook. Radioactivity in the form of X rays has been used for many years to diagnose and treat people for many injuries and diseases. Use of radiation has expanded to the use of radioisotopes to trace metabolic systems in the body and to the direct use of rays to treat cancer. Many elements including radium and radioactive cobalt are used to produce radiation for diagnostic and therapeutic purposes.

rationalization   The individual uses rationalization, a defense mechanism, as an unconscious way to attempt to justify or make consciously tolerable by plausible means feelings, behavior, or motives that otherwise would be intolerable. Rationalization differs from conscious evasion.

Rat Man, case of   In a well-documented case, Sigmund Freud (1856–1939) treated a young man who was tormented by anxieties and thoughts of harm to others and to himself. His most horrifying thoughts were of a form of torture involving rats eating at the anus being applied to his father and the woman he loved. Probing further, Freud found that the death of the man's father had occurred after he had imagined his death. Freud thought that the young man had developed a belief in what he termed *omnipotence of thought*, a feeling that thinking about an occurrence could magically bring it about.

reality therapy   A form of behavior modification therapy, reality therapy tries to help the individual get more closely in touch with the real world around him by providing assistance in learning new ways of fulfilling needs in real-life situations, such as managing anxieties and phobias. The method was developed by William Glasser, (b. 1925) a Los Angeles psychiatrist, along with Dr. G. Leonard Harrington (b. 1916). In reality therapy, the individual is treated not as a patient with a disease stemming from some past crisis but rather as someone needing guidance in facing the present conditions of his reality. Attention is directed to both present and future behavior with little emphasis on the past.

reciprocal inhibition, law of   A principle based on the logical and physiological fact that two opposing emotions cannot be experienced at the same time, useful in combating many fears and emotions. For example, soldiers forget their fear when they are angry during combat. Many persons overcome the fear of flying by focusing on the pleasure they will derive during their good time at the end of the flight. Those who have elevator phobia, manage to take the elevator up to their place of work because they enjoy thinking about what they will buy with their paycheck.

The term was introduced by Joseph Wolpe (1915–97) a pioneering psychiatrist in the use of behavior therapy. Wolpe's original book, *Psychotherapy by Reciprocal Inhibition,* lead to the practical use of behavioral techniques with adults and children and accelerated the growth of behavior therapy. The principle of reciprocal inhibition is the basis of such widely diverse techniques as systematic desensitization (relaxation is the incompatible response to anxiety), assertive training (assertion is incompatible with fear and inhibition), and sexual responsiveness (treatment of impotence by introducing gradual sexual arousal to inhibit performance anxiety).

reflexology   Reflexology is a form of body therapy based on the theory that every part of the body has a direct line of communication to a reference point on the foot, the hand, and the ear. By massaging these reference points, professional reflexologists say they can help the corresponding body parts to heal. Through improved circulation, elimination of toxic by-products, and overall reduction of anxieties, the body responds and functions better because it is more relaxed.

regression   Reversion to behavior appropriate during an earlier developmental stage, regression is a defense mechanism that the individual uses when threatened with anxiety-producing situations or internal conflicts. The regression may be general and longstanding, or it may be temporary and situation specific. Individuals may react with earlier behaviors, such as fear, crying, thumb sucking, or temper tantrums to gain attention or to force others to solve their problems. In working with phobic individuals, some therapists may encourage regression to determine the initial cause of the individual's phobic behavior. In psychoanalysis, regression is encouraged so that analyst and analysand can get in touch with the past. Individuals are also encouraged to regress in certain types of group therapy, such as primal therapy and rebirthing.

reinforcement   A procedure to change the likelihood or frequency of a phobic response or fearful behavior pattern, reinforcement increases the strength of a conditioning or other learning process. In classical conditioning, reinforcement is the repeated association of the conditioned stimulus with the unconditioned stimulus. In operant conditioning, reinforcement refers to the reward given after a correct response that strengthens the response or the punishment given after an incorrect response that weakens that response.

rejection, fear of   Fear of rejection, part of most social phobias, is a fear of being socially excluded or criticized, which would produce considerable emotional pain and self-degradation. The avoidance of social situations may take obvious forms such as extreme SHYNESS, avoidance of meeting new people, or fear of parties and crowds and may also take more subtle forms by the avoidance of elevators and freeways. Individuals with extreme fear of rejection generally have a low sense of self-esteem.

relaxation   Relaxation is a feeling of freedom from anxiety and tension. Internal conflicts and disturbing feelings of stress are absent. Relaxation also refers to the return of a muscle to its normal state after a period of contraction.

People who are very tense and anxious can learn to relax using relaxation training, a form of BEHAVIOR THERAPY or alternative therapy. Relaxation techniques are methods used to release muscular tension unconsciously and to achieve a sense of mental calm. Historically, relaxation techniques have included MEDITATION, TAI CHI CHUAN, massage therapy, YOGA, music (see MUSIC AS ANXIETY THERAPY), and aromatherapy. More modern developments include PROGRESSIVE MUSCLE RELAXATION, HYPNOSIS, BIOFEEDBACK, and aerobic exercise.

Many of these techniques were developed to help people cope with anxieties brought on by the challenges of life. They are different approaches to relieving stress by bringing about generalized physical as well as mental relaxation. Relaxation techniques have in common the production of the relaxation response as one of their stress and anxiety relieving actions. Additionally, relaxation may counter some of the immunosuppressing effects of anxieties and may actually enhance the activity of the immune system.

Relaxation training programs are commonly used in conjunction with more standard forms of therapy for many chronic diseases. The mind-body connection between relaxation and ill health has been demonstrated in many conditions. Some of the physiological changes that occur during relaxation include decreased oxygen consumption, decreased heart and respiratory rates, diminished muscle tension, and shift toward slower brain wave patterns.

the relaxation response   In the 1970s, Herbert Benson, M.D. (1935–), a cardiologist at Harvard Medical School, studied the relationship between stress and hypertension. In stressful situations, the body undergoes several changes, including rise in blood pressure and pulse rate and faster breathing. Dr. Benson reasoned that if stress could bring about this reaction, another factor might be able to turn it off. He studied practitioners of TRANSCENDENTAL MEDITATION (TM) and found that once into their meditative states, some individuals could willfully reduce their pulse rate, blood pressure, and breathing rate. Dr. Benson named this the relaxation response. He explained this procedure in his book (written with Miriam Z. Klipper) *The Relaxation Response* (1976).

Relaxation applications   Relaxation training can be particularly useful for individuals who have "white-coat hypertension," which means that their blood pressure is high only when facing certain specifically anxiety-producing situations, such as having a medical examination or visiting a dentist. It can also help reduce hostility and anger, which in turn affect the body and the individual's physical responses to stress. Anxieties can lead to panic attacks, nausea, or gastrointestinal problems.

There are many applications of relaxation training to help individuals learn control over their mental state and body and in treating conditions as diverse as high blood pressure, cardiac arrhythmia, chronic pain, insomnia, premenstrual syndrome, and side effects of cancer treatments.

Relaxation training is an important part of childbirth classes to help women cope with the pain of labor.

In a training program, individuals are instructed to move through the muscle groups of the body, making the tense and then completely relaxed. Through repetitions of this procedure, individuals learn how to be in voluntary control of their feelings of tension and relaxation. Some therapists provide individuals with instructional audiotapes for use during practice; other therapists go through the procedure repeatedly with their clients.

To determine the effectiveness of relaxation training, some therapists use biofeedback as an indicator of an individual's degree of relaxation and absence of anxiety.

repeating (as a ritual)   Many individuals, out of fear of not doing an act correctly or sufficiently, become compulsive and ritualistic about repeating certain activities; for example, an individual may repeat stirring a cup of coffee a fixed number of times or washing a glass a number or times. About 40 percent of those who have OBSESSIVE-COMPULSIVE DISORDER experience repeating as a ritual.

See RITUAL.

repression   A defense mechanism by which one pushes impulses and thoughts into the unconscious is called repression.

resistance   An individual's efforts to obstruct the process of therapy, resistance, a basic concept in psychoanalysis, led Sigmund Freud (1856–1939) to develop his fundamental rule of free association, the need for neutrality on the part of the therapist, and recognition that the unconscious could be reached only by indirect methods. Freud viewed resistance primarily as the ego's efforts to prevent unconscious material from coming into the conscious; later, he considered resistance as a defense mechanism.

Other therapeutic disciplines regard resistance in different ways; for example, behavior therapists view resistance from a social learning point of view. Some behavior therapists explain both repression and resistance in terms of avoidance learning. When certain thoughts are repeatedly associated with painful experiences, such as situations that produced anxieties or fears, they become aversive. Strategic therapists and social-influence theorists design strategies to overcome the individual's resistance to the therapist, to the process of treatment, and to the loss of symptoms.

respondent conditioning   Also known as classical conditioning or Pavlovian conditioning, respondent conditioning is the eliciting of a response by a stimulus that usually does not elicit that response through association with another stimulus that regularly elicits that response. The response (salivation or a change in heart rate) is one that is brought about by the autonomic nervous system. A previously neutral stimulus is repeatedly presented just before an unconditioned stimulus that normally elicits that response. When the response subsequently occurs in the presence of the previously neutral stimulus, it is called a conditioned response; the previously neutral stimulus is considered to be a conditioned stimulus.

risk taking, fear of   Fear of taking risks includes fears of gambling, of making decisions, of making errors, and of new things. People who fear taking risks prefer the security of known places and situations. Such individuals may fear losing control by taking risks. Those who fear losing money, for example, avoid risky investments such as the stock market.

ritual   A distorted or elaborate activity that an individual repeats as part of a daily routine. Individuals who have obsessive-compulsive disorders commonly include some rituals in their routine, for example, frequent hand-washing or constant checking. Some individuals seek treatment to free themselves of the rituals, even though keeping up with the ritualistic behavior relieves their anxieties to some extent.

There are, of course, also rituals of daily life which are not indications of abnormalities and may actually have benefits in relieving anxieties. This type of ritual has been defined as "a symbol that is acted out" and "an agreed upon pattern of movement." Such rituals are part of social, educational, religious, and athletic events. Rituals such as the use of good manners serve a positive social purpose as protection from aggressive, antisocial behavior. Religious rituals reduce feelings of guilt because of their cleansing, purifying quality. Rites of passage rituals, such as the engagement and marriage ceremony, provide a way to reduce the anxieties inherent in passing from one cycle of life to another. Funeral rites provide companionship for the survivors and an organized way to behave at a time of grief and crisis. As rituals tend to be traditional, they also satisfy a need many people feel for a sense of continuity with the past and an avoidance of newness. Rituals make use of unique clothing and objects and exaggerated, repetitious, or unusual language to intensify communication, to focus the attention of leader and participants, and to exclude outside distractions.

Rituals may also promote fear and anxiety. Individuals may feel inhibited or anxious about conforming to certain types of rigid group-behavior patterns. Rituals that have become empty and meaningless or that are observed too rigidly may promote disaffection and disillusionment in individuals who perceive them as either time wasting or tension producing.

role-playing A technique used in psychotherapy in which the client acts according to a role that is not his or her own, role-playing is used in a variety of ways; for example, it can help a therapist determine how anxious or phobic individuals react to certain important social roles and how they see themselves in social situations. Role-playing can help the individual gain insight into the conduct of others. It can also help the individual gain catharsis, or release from phobic or other anxiety symptoms.

rolfing A deep massage technique. Rolfing is named for its originator, Ida Rolf (1896–1979), a biochemist who worked extensively at the Esalen Institute in California. Rolfing is based on the theory that muscle massage will relieve both physical and psychic pain because the body is the source for memories of experience. It is one of many body therapies used to help treat individuals who have anxieties and phobias.

Rorschach test A psychological test developed by Swiss psychiatrist Hermann Rorschach (1884–1922), it is also referred to as the inkblot test. An individual taking the test is encouraged to disclose conscious and unconscious personality traits and emotional conflicts by associating inkblots with objects, things, and situations.

rumination The act of persistently being excessively anxious about, worrying about, thinking about, and pondering one concern for an inordinate period of time, ruminations produce anxiety and are repetitive, intrusive thoughts or OBSESSIONS about some aspect of one's life, such as fear of contamination, fear of harming others, or fear of not doing certain tasks correctly. The thoughts may be evoked by external cues or may come out of the blue. Ruminations impair concentration and are hard to drive out of one's mind. Rumination is a common symptom of OBSESSIVE-COMPULSIVE DISORDER.

S

sacred things, fear of Fear of sacred things is known as heirophobia and includes holy or religious objects. The individual suffering from such a fear would avoid churches, shrines, museums, and so on where particular objects are displayed. Often, this fear is quite specific, involving "holy" people or objects (such as crosses) that evoke anxiety.

sarmassophobia Fear of love play is termed *sarmassophobia*.

Satan, fear of Fear of Satan is known as satanophobia. People fear manifestations of satanic interests, such as symbols, rituals, and possibly unknown destructive forces. The name *Satan* derives from the ancient Hebrew word for "devil." Early men believed that the harmful forces of nature were demons and evil spirits, and they blamed such demons for all their troubles. In the Old Testament, Satan is not God's opponent; rather, he searches out the sins of men and accuses humanity before God. In the Apocrypha, Satan is the author of all evil and rules over a host of angels. In the New Testament, other names for Satan are *devil, enemy,* and *Beelzebub*. In the Middle Ages, Satan usually was represented with horns, a tail, and cloven hoofs.

"scared stiff" During extreme fear, many people become "scared stiff" or "frozen with fear." These terms refer to a paralyzed conscious state with abrupt onset and end. This type of fear reaction has been reported by survivors of attacks by wild animals, shell-shocked soldiers, and rape victims. Characteristics of being frozen with fear include an inability to move (tonic immobility), body shaking, an inability to scream or call out, numbness or insensitivity to pain, and sensations of feeling cold. This term also refers to an involuntary erection that may occur under intense fear.

schizophrenia This mental illness displays characteristic psychotic symptoms involving withdrawal from reality, delusions, hallucinations, and disturbances in affect and form of thought. The word *schizoprenia* is derived from the New Latin terms for "split mind" (*schizo* + *phrenia*). Schizophrenia begins gradually, creating inner turmoil, and symptoms worsen to become severe distortions in perception, speech, and thought.
  Symptoms include some of the following:

• Paranoid delusions, which are unshakable personal thoughts that convince the individual that others are plotting against him or her (delu-

sions of persecution)
- Delusions that one's thoughts are "broadcast" outside one's head so others can hear them
- Delusions that outside forces are controlling thoughts, inserting them into the individual's head, or removing them from the individual's mind (delusions of influence)
- Hallucinations in which voices threaten, insult, or command the victim. Hallucinations may occur less commonly in any of the senses.
- Emotions that are blunted or inappropriate to the situation, such as laughing or smiling inappropriately.

Treatment generally combines therapies because the disease is so complex. Antipsychotic medications usually relieve the hallucinations and delusions. Psychotherapy helps victims understand their disease and assists in learning to distinguish reality from distorted perceptions. Family therapy helps spouses, parents, or siblings learn about the disease and helps the individual live in the community. Family therapies seem to be crucial to successful treatment.

Much of the progress in treating schizophrenia results from medications.

Aside from the pain the individual suffers, the other real tragedy of schizophrenia is the effect on families. Often family members are burdened with a stubborn, confused, and marginally socialized young adult schizophrenic who, though not capable of independent life, is able to attend school part time, drive a car, and meet people. Family members find themselves in the position of caretakers, often intervening at acute episodes when crises occur.

school phobia   School phobia is known as scolionophobia. School phobia is an exaggerated fear of going to school or, more correctly, of leaving home or parents (separation fear). Although many children show anxiety about school at one time or another, school phobics show frequent or long-standing fear and refusal to go to school.

In some individuals, school phobia develops from fears connected either with the school or the home. Some may have an irrational dread of some aspect of the school situation, such as fear of a teacher, principal, a classmate, or examinations. For most, however, the school phobia may be part of a separation anxiety syndrome.

Not all school refusal is due to separation anxiety. Some children have very specific, identifiable fears relating to school, and when these are determined and confronted, specific avenues may be taken to make the child more comfortable about attending school; for example, being bullied on the school bus, being teased about appearance or clothing, reciting in class, undressing in front of other children for gym, and going to the bathroom without privacy may be contributory factors to school phobia.

screen memory   A screen memory is one that the individual consciously tolerates to cover up a related remembrance that would be emotionally painful if recalled. Apparently, these memories are repressed or suppressed due to their painful or frightening nature and emerge only when the anxiety begins to lessen.

scriptophobia   This fear of writing in public, a social phobia, prevents many individuals from being able to write checks, use bank cards, or vote. When scriptophobics anticipate having to be seen writing, they experience physiological symptoms of heart palpitations, shortness of breath, trembling hands, sweating, and dizziness. Financial transactions have to be preplanned so that purchases can be made with cash (e.g., at grocery stores) or so that others do not see the individual writing (such as filling out deposits at home). Many rely on others to handle all financial matters involving writing. Some scriptophobics can cope better with writing in public when a trusted friend or relative is with them.

Many scriptophobic individuals also have other social anxieties, especially if they think they are being watched while doing some tasks and are afraid of doing something wrong, looking funny (by shaking or trembling), and becoming embarrassed. Scriptophobia represents a generalized fear of negative evaluation by others. Scriptophobia has been treated successfully with behavior therapy, graded exposure, and cognitive restructuring.

seasonal affective disorder (SAD)   Seasonal affective disorder (SAD) is a syndrome characterized by severe seasonal mood swings. Typically, SAD sufferers become clinically depressed with the approach of winter. In addition to gaining weight, oversleeping, and feeling listless, they feel anxious and irritable, withdraw socially, and lose interest in sex. As spring approaches, depression subsides and behavior returns to normal.

Researchers suspect that there may be a genetic factor involved in SAD because more than two-thirds of those with the syndrome have a close relative with a mood disorder. The role of the absence or presence of light in seasonal mood shifts is unclear. One theory attributes the disorder to a disturbance in the body's natural clock, resulting in an abnormal production of melatonin, a hormone manufactured in the brain, and serotonin, a chemical that helps transmit nerve impulses.

Light therapy, in which the individual is exposed to artificial light with five to 10 times the intensity of indoor lighting, has helped some SAD sufferers.

secondary gain   A secondary gain is an obvious advantage that an individual gains from his or her phobia or anxiety disorder. Family and friends may be more protective and more attentive and may release the individual from responsibility; for example, agoraphobics experience secondary gains of having someone willing to accompany them outdoors and to do errands and other chores for them.

sedative   A substance, such as a drug or herb, that relieves nervousness, anxiety, or irritability, sometimes to the point of inducing sleep, sedative acts by depressing the central nervous system. The degree of sedation depends on the agent, the size of dose, the method of administration (for example, oral or intravenous), and the physical and mental condition of the individual. A sedative used as a relaxant in small doses may be used to induce sleep with larger doses. Barbiturates are common examples of sedative drugs used in this way.

self efficacy (SE)   Self-efficacy (SE) is the concept that one can perform adequately; it is also called self-confidence. This concept as it relates to phobias and anxieties was researched during the 1970s by Albert Bandura (b. 1925), a U.S. psychologist at Stanford University. SE measures how likely one believes one would be to succeed if one attempted a task. Such a rating can be used before, during, or after treatment for phobias. The SE rating correlates highly with performance in a behavioral test just after the rating. In phobics asked to rate SE concerning a phobic task, SE is low before treatment and rises after individuals improve with exposure treatment.

SE at the end of treatment may be the major mediator of fear reduction. However, a better way to increase SE is by exposure, the same procedure that reduces fear. In experiments, SE correlated highly not only with performance of a frightening task, but also with the fear expected during it. In one experiment with 50 snake-phobic students, most refused to try to hold the snake because they were frightened, not because they felt inept. They were certain that they could hold the snake if they really "had to." If a task is frightening, SE reflects an individual's willingness (rather than ability) to do it. When willingness rises, there is less anticipated fear.

SE can predict psychological changes achieved by different modes of treatment. Expectations of personal efficacy determine whether coping behavior will begin, how much effort will be expended, and how long it will be sustained in the face of aversive experiences. Persistence in activities that are subjectively threatening but in fact are relatively safe produces, through experiences of mastery, further enhancement of self-efficacy and corresponding reductions in defensive behavior.

Individuals derive expectations of self-efficacy from four main sources: performance accomplishments, vicarious experience, verbal persuasion, and physiological states. The more dependable the experiential sources, the greater the changes in perceived self-efficacy.

self-esteem   Self-esteem is the positive light in which one regards one's self. Many studies have been done on the effects of degree of self-esteem on psychological state. Early studies showed that negative stressors contribute to low self-esteem, and more recent work connects ANXIETY to low self-esteem because it too is a negative stressor; for example, test-taking anxiety could lead to a lower self-esteem because the anxious person worries about performance on a test. This may lead the person to question his or her abilities and look at him- or herself in a negative light.

Generally, individuals who have high self-esteem tend to be less anxious than those who have low self-esteem.

self-fulfilling prophecy   This is a belief that helps bring about its own fulfillment; for example, a feared event sometimes is brought about by predicting that it will happen. A student may worry that he or she will be extremely anxious during an examination or performance and will fail. The expectation plays a part in the result. On the other hand, self-fulfilling prophecy can work in a positive way; for example, in therapy, the phobic individual's expectation that the therapist will be helpful enables him or her to benefit from the therapeutic situation. The mystics talk about this phenomenon as the "law of manifestation."

self-help   Self-help means exactly what it says—to help one's self. Therapists want their clients to be able to function independently and, therefore, must teach some self-management techniques to those willing and able to use them. Self-help can be helpful for a number of psychological disturbances; for example, it is widely used by phobics who need to control their reactions to a particular stimulus. A therapist might teach the individual how to relax and breathe deeply when confronted with the object. Once mastered, the individual can do this independently, eliminating the need for constant outside support. Highly anxious people are trained to help themselves by repeating calming statements or by inducing previously practiced states of tranquility.

One form of self-help is known as focusing, in which the individual learns how to establish the problem in his or her mind, to feel the problem, and to let the answer form in consciousness. In this way, people learn to function more independently.

There are a number of questionnaires available for individuals to use on a self-help basis. From these questionnaires, an individual

---

SAMPLE ITEMS FROM THE SEX ANXIETY INVENTORY

Sex:

    a. Can cause as much anxiety as pleasure.

    b. On the whole is good and enjoyable.

I feel nervous:

    a. About initiating sexual relations.

    b. About nothing when it comes to members of the opposite sex.

When I awake from sexual dreams:

    a. I feel pleasant and relaxed.

    b. I feel tense.

When I meet someone I'm attracted to:

    a. I get to know him or her.

    b. I feel nervous.

Source. From Ronald M. Doctor, Ph.D., and Ada P. Khan, Ph.D., *Encyclopedia of Phobias, Fears, and Anxieties,* 2d ed. (New York: Facts On File, 2000).

---

can form some idea of how severe their fear of phobia actually is. The Fear Questionnaire and the Sex Anxiety Inventory are examples of such questionnaires. The Obsessive-Compulsive Self-Test can help an individual determine which activities of daily living are compulsive or ritualistic.

self-rating scales   Measurements of phobic reactions as reported by the phobic individuals themselves, self-rating scales or questionnaires are used by researchers and therapists, often to assess the extent of the phobia and also to measure the success of therapy after therapy is underway and perhaps again after therapy has been concluded. Self-rating scales are particularly useful in working with agoraphobic individuals, as those people are fearful of many varied situations. Scales have been devised for individuals to indicate, for example, on rating from 0 to 8, "how much" they "would avoid" or "would not avoid" certain situations. Likewise, questionnaires are used to assess fears relating to agoraphobia which might include traveling alone by bus or train, walking alone in busy streets, going into crowded stores, going alone far from home, and being in large open places. Although there is some controversy among researchers regarding the usefulness of self-rating scales because of their lack of specificity, most agree that the scales have a place when used in combination with other assessment techniques that sample behavior and physiological reactions directly.

semen, fear of   Fear of semen is known as spermophobia, or spermatophobia. This reaction is usually a variation of "germ" or contamination fears of obsessive-compulsive individuals.

serotonin
A neurotransmitter substance found in the central nervous system, blood, nerve cells, and other tissues. The substance was identified during the 1950s as 5-hydroxytryptamine (5-HT); it is also known as hydroxytryptamine. Serotonin is derived from tryptophan, an essential amino acid widely distributed through the body and in the brain. Serotonin functions as a smooth-muscle stimulator and constrictor of blood vessels. Serotonin is involved in circuits that influence sleep and emotional arousal, and is indirectly involved in the psychobiology of depression. One theory suggests low levels of serotonin as a factor in causing depression. Some antidepressant drugs increase the levels of serotonin and norepinephrine, another neurotransmitter.

sexual fears   Fears in human love life impair sexual responding so that erotic responses to partners are weakened. Common fears of women include fearing that their vaginas are too tight for insertion of their partners' penises, that they will experience pain during intercourse, and that they will not experience orgasm as often as they desire.

Common fears of men include that they will not have an erection, that they cannot maintain an erection long enough during intercourse to achieve orgasm, that they maintain an erection but do not ejaculate, and that they ejaculate sooner than desired.

There are many causes for sexual fears and anxieties. In males, inadequate sexual performance is often due to fear of the same (either through self-judgment "observer" effect—or perceived rejection or criticism of the partner). Anxiety may either prevent or weaken erection or more commonly lead to premature ejaculation. Thus a vicious cycle of fear, failure, and then the development of more fear. Fear has these effects only if it is stronger than the sexual excitation. In females, sexual fear may be caused by many things, ranging from the sight of a penis to fear of penetration, to the belief that she will be punished for indulging in sexual pleasure; some men share this latter fear. The term *frigidity* often applied to women's sexual inadequacies. Frigidity, in actuality, covers situations from a complete inability to be aroused, to a failure to reach a climax even when sexual excitement is very high. When a woman has a general inhibition of sexual response, it is often caused by anxiety. Some sexual fears may have origins in relatively trivial situations, such as having been frightened in the act of masturbation, or more serious ones, such as a history of sexual molestation.

Treatment of sexual fears depends on the severity of the fear, the extent to which it interferes with one's functioning, and on the perceived cause of the fear. Sexual anxieties are treated with many therapies, including behavior therapy, in which techniques including desensitization are used.

Paraphilias are various sexual deviations that involve sexual arousal by uncommon or bizarre stimuli. Fetishes are one form of paraphilia. A fetishist is almost always a male, and he derives sexual arousal by some inanimate object—such as women's shoes or underwear—or some specific nongenital part of a person, such as locks of hair, feet, ankles, or fingers. Transvestism (cross-sex dressing), incest, pedophilia (sexual gratification through physical and sexual contact with prepubertal children), voyeurism (peeping), and exhibitionism (exposure of genitals) are common forms of paraphilias.

Psychoanalytic theory generally considers the paraphilias as defensive functions that ward off castration anxiety about normal sexual behavior. These views have been challenged by learning theorists who prefer a theory of stimulus association as explanatory.

sexually transmitted diseases (STDS), fear of   Many people fear sexually transmitted diseases (STDs) because such diseases cause discomfort, may lead to infertility, and may be life threatening. Sexually transmitted diseases affect both men and women and are generally transmitted during sexual intercourse. Historically, syphilis and gonorrhea have been well known; they were referred to as venereal diseases long before the term *STD* was coined during the latter part of the 20th century.

There are several STDs that are feared because they became notably widespread during and after the 1980s. These include herpes, chlamydia, hepatitis B, as well as pubic lice, genital warts, and other vaginal infections. Syphilis and gonorrhea are still prevalent and, some sources say, on the increase due to the upswing in other concurrent STDs.

Acquired Immunodeficiency Syndrome (AIDS)   This is one of the most dread diseases ever identified. Each year, new therapies are developed, but as of 2000 there is no cure and no vaccine for prevention. It is a debilitating disease that leads to many opportunistic infections, many types of cancer, and in many cases, death. It is caused by the HIV (human immunodeficiency virus) virus. In April 2000, President Clinton declared the spread of AIDS internationally as a threat to U.S. national security.

Because AIDS is transmitted through exchange of bodily fluids, including blood, drug users who share needles, persons receiving or donating blood, and health-care workers may all be subject to anxiety surrounding the disease. With proper precautions, risk to health-care workers, hemophiliacs, and persons receiving blood transfusion is minimal and risk to blood donors is virtually nonexistent.

The epidemic was recognized between 1981–84. Many people discovered their illness for the first time in the emergency room when an AIDS-defining condition was diagnosed. Before 1986, HIV testing was not generally available except to a few people enrolled in research studies.

The drug AZT has been available since 1987. Other new and powerful treatments for opportunistic infections were subsequently approved. Thus the treatment of infections and cancers has become more sophisticated and more effective during the latter part of the 1980s, and during the 1990s, contributing to a more positive outlook for persons who have AIDS.

shyness   Shyness is a symptom of social anxiety, related to a fear of being unfavorably evaluated by others. Shyness can be observed in several ways. Physically, the shy person may blush and perspire. Emotionally, he or she may feel anxious and insecure. The shy person may think that no one wants to talk to him or her or that no one likes him or her. A shy person's behavior may actually help to discourage social intercourse because shy people tend to keep their heads down and even avoid eye contact with others. Shyness may bring on a lack of social relationships or a distorted view of social relationships, causing the shy person to feel the anxieties of loneliness and emotional unfulfillment.

Shyness may be related to social phobia; social phobia involves fear of scrutiny from other people and leads to gaze aversion and avoidance of eating, drinking, blushing, speaking, writing, or eliminating in their presence.

Almost everyone experiences shyness at some time, especially "situational shyness," which arises in such uncomfortable social situations as meeting new people or going for a job interview. The term *dispositional shyness* describes a pervasive personality trait that can be long lasting or correlated to a particular stage of life, especially adolescence.

Shyness may be handled in different ways, depending on the individual's personal system of defense mechanisms. Although it may cause some persons to withdraw and become quiet in social situations (introversion), shyness may encourage others to behave more aggressively in public, trying to cover up their shyness by being "the life of the party" (extroversion).

It is not uncommon for extroverted shy people to become performers or public figures, handling their shyness by keeping themselves in controlled, structured situations, performing well-rehearsed roles in familiar situations.

sick role   The protected position that an individual who is anxious, phobic, or considered not well assumes or is put in by family and friends, the sick role may give the individual so labeled the advantages of attention and support, emotional and financial, that he or she might not otherwise have. The individual in the sick role may not be motivated to improve because he or she fears removal of attention (a powerful reinforcer). Some individuals who have agoraphobia are encouraged in the sick role because their families do chores and errands for them, enabling the phobic individuals to perpetuate their agoraphobic (avoidance) tendencies. The sick role may have positive effects on a family in that it causes family members to become more cohesive.

skin conductance   Certain anxiety-inducing, stressful, or pleasant stimuli change the electrical resistance of the skin, particularly the skin on the palms or other areas without hair. The response is produced by unconscious activity of the sweat glands. This effect is known as galvanic skin response (GSR), electrodermal response (EDR), and psychogalvanic reflex (PGR).

sleep, fear of   Fear of sleep is known as hypnophobia. Fear of sleep may be common in individuals suffering from sleep disorders, such as nightmares, sleep talking, sleepwalking, and especially narcolepsy. Fear of sleep may be related to the individual's feeling of a loss of control of his actions if he or she falls asleep. The fear may also be related to a fear of death, as the person may fear not waking up.

sleep, function of   Sleep is an activity that causes many people anxieties as well as fears. Some individuals become anxious if they do not sleep enough; others become anxious that they sleep too much. Some have difficulty getting to sleep, and some have difficulty staying asleep; others have difficulty waking up. Sleep disorders are common in many individuals who have anxiety disorders. Those who have depression may have difficulty sleeping or may sleep too much. For many individuals, physical conditions that make them uncomfortable or anxious also interfere with adequate and satisfying sleep. In some people, sleep may be used as an escape for problems and tensions present during waking hours. Lack of adequate sleep may make one feel nervous and jumpy, affect judgment and decision-making abilities, and slow reaction times.

Sleep is a necessary activity that provides a restorative function. During sleep, daily bodily functions such as digestion and waste removal have a chance to rest and recharge. An evolutionary theory regarding sleep suggests that sleep originally allowed humans and animals to conserve energy during the dark hours when it was less practical to hunt for food and harder to escape from danger.

The average adult needs about eight hours of sleep per 24 hours; the need for sleep seems to decrease as the person ages. Individual sleep patterns vary, however, and may be affected by anxiety. An average person may go through his or her sleep cycle about four to six times each night. A sleep cycle consists of stages (known as Stages I, II, III and IV) in a cycle lasting about 90 minutes, followed by a period of rapid eye movement (REM) sleep for about 10 minutes. With each cycle, REM periods lengthen. During the last cycle, REM sleep may last for 30 to 60 minutes. Dreaming is most likely to occur during REM sleep. This period is characterized by extensive muscular inhibition; most of the voluntary muscles in the body take on a paralyzed state, and there are bursts of rapid movements of the eye under the closed eyelid, as if the person were watching something occurring in front of him or her.

sleepwalking, fear of   Sleepwalking (somnambulism) episodes occur most often in children ages 9–12 although they may happen at any age in a child's or adult's life. Estimates are that as many as 20 percent of the population has experienced sleepwalking at least once. Individuals who walk during sleep will usually perform some familiar or ritualistic activities such as dressing, going to the kitchen for something to eat, or entering their car. In very unusual cases, persons have been known to board trains and wake up hundred of miles away from home.

Sleepwalking may run in families and may also be related to other sleep disturbances such as sleeptalking and night terrors. An unpleasant or dangerous experience while sleepwalking may lead an individual to a fear of the disorder and may also cause increased anxiety concerning sleeping in general.

slips of the tongue, fear of   Many individuals fear slips of the tongue, or saying one thing when they mean to say something else. Fear of making such slips is based on the interpretation given to these remarks by Sigmund Freud (1856–1939) and are known as Freudian slips. It was through the study of slips of the tongue and dreams that Freud formulated his theory of psychic functioning. The Freudian view is that the speaker said exactly what he or she really meant to say. These slips may be the emergence of an unconscious wish or a failure to repress the unconscious desire. Everyone interchanges words frequently, usually without any meaning, but for some social phobics who fear being heard talking or fear talking with others, this fear is enough to keep them away from social situations. Slips of the tongue often happen when a person is distracted or preoccupied with some stressful situation.

slowness compulsive   Slowness compulsive describes a symptom of obsessive-compulsive disorder in which individuals take a very long time to do everyday actions. It may take these people several hours to bathe, dress, and eat breakfast. When they go out, it may take a long time for them to cross a street because they check and recheck traffic in all directions before they step off the curb.

smoking, fear of   Smoking of cigarettes, pipes, and cigars is most often feared because of its negative health effects on the smoker. Negative health effects have also been attributed to "secondhand smoke," or the sidestream smoke from the smoker's materials that others unwillingly inhale.

Although smoking oneself or being near another who is smoking may cause anxiety, many individuals use smoking itself as a means of relieving tension. Smokers often cite the act as a "nervous habit," providing oral gratification and giving them "something to do with their hands." Smokers who are addicted to the nicotine in tobacco need to smoke to relieve the anxiety caused by their withdrawal between cigarettes. Fear of becoming addicted to smoking may keep some individuals from ever starting to smoke.

smothering, fear of   Fear of smothering is known as pnigophobia. Smothering to phobic individuals may mean having their air supply cut off in a closed, crowded space, such as an elevator, in which they fear that there may not be enough air for everyone to breathe. Also, such individuals may fear having their faces covered with blankets, masks for anesthesia, or other items that may interfere with their breathing.

snakes, fear of   Fear of snakes is known as ophidiophobia, ophiophobia, ophiciophobia, and herpetophobia. Fear of snakes is a nearly universal fear among humans as well as animals. Many people fear snakes because of their fangs and the possibility of receiving a fatal snakebite. Many people cannot tell a poisonous snake from a nonpoisonous one, and so they fear any snakebite. Also, many people consider snakes slimy and therefore disgusting.

Some fears of snakes are realistic. In the United States and Europe, poisonous snakes include the Eastern diamond-back rattlesnake, the Western diamond-back rattlesnake, and the European viper (adder).

There is evidence that the vast majority of people who fear snakes have had no direct contact with them. This would suggest a genetic trigger or possibly cultural attitudes that condition the reaction.

In psychoanalysis, the snake is a symbol for the penis and is identified with sexual energies. The snake symbol appears frequently in dreams and in primitive rites and art productions in which it may represent life.

In psychological, symbolic terms, snakes represent life energy itself. For this reason, snakes carry multivalencies—guardians of life, health, wisdom, immortality, and mystery as well as destruction; illness; temptation; and the principle of will (potentially) inherent in all worldly things. Furthermore, the snake is also seen as a symbol of transformation; for example, the ancient Mayan myth tells of the snake (nature principle) climbing the tree, leaping, and catching the bird (spirit principle) to become transformed into a "winged serpent."

snow, fear of　Fear of snow is known as chionophobia. Because snow is associated with the harshness and sterility of winter, it has come to symbolize death, poverty, and suffering. In the myths of some cultures, the end of the world is predicted to occur in winter, preceded by a barrage of snow. In folktales, snow has been personified as a beautiful, alluring woman who leads her victims to their doom.

There are realistic reasons for fear of snow. Snow causes falls, traffic accidents, and collapsing roofs. Blizzards can create drifts as high as 30 feet. Victims of a white-out during a snowstorm suffer from loss of balance and sense of direction because snow blurs the horizon and landscape and cancels shadows. Avalanches, which may travel at speeds of 50 miles per hour, cause death and destruction not only because of the actual weight and force of the snow but also because of sudden air pressure changes preceding and following. The sudden melting of large amounts of snow may create destructive floods.

social phobia　The fear of being evaluated, criticized, censured, embarrassed, or in some way punished in social settings by the reactions of others, social phobias are the most common phobias. Social phobics fear acting or looking stupid, and thus they avoid doing many activities of daily life when and where they can be seen by others. Social phobias include eating, drinking, speaking, urinating, blushing, or vomiting in the presence of others. Social phobics fear that their hands will tremble or shake as they eat or write and tend to avoid restaurants, banks, and other public places. They often avert their eyes when talking to another person. Some social phobics have been known to cross the street to avoid greeting someone they know. Social phobics are fearful of attending parties, particularly with people they do not know.

Many social phobics have had lifelong shyness and introverted habits. Usually social phobias begin after puberty and peak in the late teens and are equally common among men and women. Many agoraphobics have social phobias, and many social phobics have minor agoraphobic symptoms.

sounds, fear of　Fear of sounds, known as acousticophobia, may relate to specific sounds, sound in general, or noise. Parents become anxious when they hear cries of fear or pain from their infants. Many people become fearful when they hear others screaming in agony or panic (for example, hearing children cry after receiving shots or the cries of women in labor). The sound of buzzing bees arouses fear in many people.

speaking, fear of Fear of speaking, a social phobia known as laliophobia, may be related to a fear of speaking out loud, a fear of speaking over the telephone, or a fear that one may use the wrong words, have an ineffective tone of voice, or sound powerless. Other fears related to speaking include hearing the sound of one's own voice and stuttering. Public speaking is one of the most prevalent fears among adults.

speaking aloud, fear of Fear of speaking out loud is known as phonophobia. This fear may be related to the fear of hearing one's own voice, of stuttering, or of having a poor voice quality. Muteness and aphonia (inability to speak louder than a whisper) may result as traces of avoidance.

specific phobias Specific phobias are phobias that are restricted to only one situation or object, such as darkness, heights, elevators, closed spaces, or animals. Agoraphobics often have fears of closed places, but that does not mean that all persons who fear closed places are agoraphobic. The gender incidence of specific phobias is approximately equal except that animal phobics are largely women. Onset of specific phobias varies from early childhood to old age. The exceptions are animal and blood phobias, which tend to begin in early childhood.

Most specific phobias are treated successfully by exposure therapy.

speed, fear of Fear of speed known as tacophobia, may relate to fear of driving fast, walking fast, or doing any sport activity fast, such as skating or bicycling. The fear may related to a fear of motion.

spiders Fear of spiders is known as arachnophobia or arachenophobia. Spider phobia, like other insect phobias, tends to be stimulus specific in that the frightened person will usually respond to particular characteristics over others. Common stimulus properties that trigger anxiety are size, color, and texture of the spider. Individuals who have severe spider phobia have to fumigate their homes regularly, wash all fruits and vegetables completely, and check incoming bags and other receptacles where spiders might hide. They are usually unable to picnic, unable to stay in strange hotels or houses, and generally must maintain a strong vigilance outside. The exact incidence of spider phobias is not known, but clinically it is not one of the more common phobias.

Spiders have many symbolic meanings such as a sinister face, evil, death and life, and the feminine mode. Spider phobics, however, are not responding to the symbolic qualities.

The fear of spiders may be almost instinctive, a case of what scientists call "prepared learning"; for example, the sight of a spider triggers a rapid heartbeat and the "fight or flight" response that might have served to protect us thousands or more years ago. In response to this fear, most people's brains manufacture and release into the bloodstream natural tranquilizers called endorphins, natural painkillers that temper the fear and allow the majority of people to react calmly to the sight of the spider. A failure to release endorphins may be the cause of excessive fear of spiders.

sports anxiety   Although sports and athletic games give many people satisfaction and relief from stress, for many others, sports lead to anxieties, fears, and avoidance. An example is a young child involved in a highly organized team sport (often known in the United States as little league) in which his parents have much interest invested—almost to the point of vicariously playing on the field while watching their children. Such a child may become fearful of losing the game and not pleasing the parents, being ridiculed, or being rejected. Fears that develop in this way may remain with a person into adult life.

Adults who wish to excel in their chosen sport but do not may suffer frustration and anxiety because of lack of ability and fear of embarrassment when they are watched by others. Some who fear losing may avoid the sport, even though it was once a source of great personal satisfaction.

Some sports participants have the same feelings of anxiety before a game or a match as speakers and performers; physical symptoms include "butterflies" in the stomach, gastrointestinal upset, vomiting, headache, lightheadedness, and dizziness. Usually these symptoms subside entirely as soon as the participant begins his or her activity. For some, this "nervous anticipation" becomes part of the routine of getting ready for the sport.

Practical anxieties relating to sports include fears of injury, such as fear of injuring a limb and not being able to play or fear of injury during a game such as football in which the risks of being thrown to the ground and trampled are great. There are specific fears within every sport: in tennis, a player may fear being hit in the eye with a ball; in hockey, there may be a fear of being hit with a puck. When the fear leads to avoidance of the sport, the fear becomes a phobia. Mild fear may actually be helpful and may encourage the player to use caution and to react quickly and effectively.

Other fears associated with sports include fear of crowds, fear of noise, and fear of motion.

stage fright   A fear of speaking or performing to an audience is a common social anxiety. Stage fright is also known as topophobia, or performance anxiety. This is a type of panic that affects people in many kinds of situations where they are being evaluated, such as making a speech, playing a musical instrument, or even attending a social affair. Stage fright is related to a fear of making a mistake in front of others, looking foolish, uncertain, and so on. Actors, politicians, executives, and others who regularly are in the spotlight often are afflicted. Some anxiety is natural and may even enhance performance because anxiety pumps more adrenaline into the body's system, making one more alert and motivated. However, when the pressure becomes extreme, the effects on physical and emotional well-being can be destructive. Migraine headaches, skin and gastrointestinal problems, hot and cold flashes, and hypertension can be typical reactions. As anxiety mounts, the individual may become increasingly involved with overcoming it, which depletes energy to think, concentrate, and be creative. When the anxiety becomes worse, it can become a phobia. The phobic person may then avoid any situation that might provoke fears.

A typical treatment program gradually reintroduces phobics to stressful situations to help them gain confidence and develop skills one step at a time as they learn to deal with the situation. The starting point is wherever each individual feels comfortable.

stairs, climbing, fear of   Fear of stairs is known as climacophobia. This fear may be related to fears of falling, injury, heights, or high places.

stars, fear of   Fear of stars is known as siderophobia. The fear that man's fate is written in the stars in ancient. Primitive man thought that gods made their home in the stars. The science of astrology, which began in Mesopotamia in the fifth century B.C., gave rise to the fear that human destiny was controlled by the heavenly bodies. In the Egyptian Hellenistic period, a complex set of writings described human subjection to the demonic powers of stars. An Egyptian scriptural text, "Poimandres," described how the soul could be saved and ascend to the highest heaven. These beliefs turned into the doctrine of Gnosticism, which portrayed Christ as the deliverer from the power of the stars and the star announcing his birth as the herald of a new order. Astrology continues to attract adherents.

state anxiety   A term used to differentiate types of anxiety, *state anxiety*, also called A-state, is a temporary and changing emotional state involving feelings of tension and apprehension and increased autonomic nervous system activity. It is a response to a specific situation that the individual perceives as threatening, but the response changes as the situation changes. Examples of state anxiety are the unpleasant feelings one experiences when taking an examination or facing a new and strange situation. When the situation is over or one becomes accustomed to it, the anxiety disappears. State anxiety may be contrasted with trait anxiety, an integral part of a personality which causes consistent anxiety.

steep places, fear of   Fear of steep places or cliffs, known as cremnophobia, may be related to fears of falling, injury, and heights, and a fear of looking at high places.

stimulus properties   In differentiating between fear and anxiety, some therapists describe fear and anxiety in terms of stimulus properties which include *identifiability, specificity*, and *predictability* of the source that brings on a response. Fear is considered a response to a clearly identifiable and circumscribed stimulus, whereas with anxiety although it is a similar response, the stimulus to which the individuals is responding is unclear, ambiguous, and/or pervasive. If a response occurs to a stimulus that is a realistic threat and therefore useful, it is said to be fear. Conversely, if a response is elicited by a stimulus that is not seen as a realistic or consensual threat and is therefore irrational and not useful, it is called anxiety. Another factor that differentiates fear from anxiety is the predictability of the source of the threat to which the individual responds. When an object or situation provides a signal of danger or threat and is therefore predictable, the state experienced is called fear; for example, the response of a person in the middle of a thunderstorm who worries about being struck by a lightning bolt would be considered fear because the stimulus is clearly identifiable and predictable and the threat is realistic.

storms, fear of   Many people fear storms that may involve lightning, thunder, rain, hail, or snow. Although most people do not fear personal injury from the storm, they do fear the unknown causes of the storm and the unknown consequences. Being near or in a storm leaves one feeling out of control. The power of the storm may overwhelm some people and thus make them fearful. Although some individuals become fearful during a storm, others have phobic reactions just at the suggestion of a storm or at the sight of little rain or a little snow. Some avoid going outdoors when any kind of storm is predicted. Sufferers may pull down their window shades or close the shutters on their house when they expect any kind of storm. Those who fear hurricanes or tornadoes may not venture outdoors even in seasons in which hurricanes or tornadoes never occur. Some individuals only fear storms when they have to be traveling through them, such as driving through a blizzard or riding on a train during a rainstorm. Some fear only one type of storm; others fear all types of storms.

Fears of lightning or thunder, rain, or snow, or storms in general are classified as simple or specific phobias.

strangers, fear of   The fear of unknown persons is known as xenophobia or zenophobia. The term refers to individuals as well as to entire groups of people, such as those from another country. Fear of strangers is normal in infants between six and 12 months old. The infant learns to recognize a familiar combination of forehead, eyes, and nose; this elicits the smile response, and this in turn elicits parental care. An unfamiliar face will frighten the infant and probably make him or her cry.

streets, fear of   Fear of streets is known as agyiophobia. Individuals who are fearful of streets may be afraid of being hit by a vehicle or may be afraid of crowds. Many agoraphobics are afraid of streets because they will be seen by others.

stress management   Appropriate management of stress in one's life is necessary to avoid anxieties. Stress, a feeling of being tired, jittery, nervous, or anxious, occurs when there are any demands upon an individual or changes in his or her life. Because people are social beings who interact daily with others and also face constant changes throughout the life cycle, stress is part of life.

Stress is an individualized physical and/or emotional response and may come from internal or external sources. The level of a person's tolerance for stress depends on his or her physiological condition, past experiences, perceptions of situations, and how he or she has learned to adapt. Examples of physical stresses are illness, excessive cold or heat, lack of sufficient oxygen, confinement, dietary insufficiencies, and trauma. Examples of emotional stresses are pressure, conflict, frustration, excessive emotions, and delayed satisfaction of needs. Emotional stress can occur when one is faced with making decisions or deadlines or after the loss of a loved one, which produces a major change in one's life. Death of a spouse is one of the most stressful situations an individual faces; next seems to be divorce and marital separation. Other highly stressful personal situations include personal injury or illness, marriage, being fired from a job, marital reconciliation, retirement, pregnancy, sex difficulties, business readjustments, changes in financial state, taking out a mortgage or loan for a major purchase, children leaving home, trouble with in-laws, change in residence or school or church, or change in sleeping or eating habits.

Individuals who are exposed to stress for long periods of time respond with what has been called the general adaptation syndrome (GAS). So named by Hans Selye, a Canadian endocrinologist (1907–82), the syndrome consists of an "alarm reaction," a "stage of resistance," and finally a "stage of exhaustion." The individual is alerted to stress, pauses to appraise it, and then attempts to make adjustments. When he or she realizes that he or she cannot adapt, his or her body may show damage or disease, or his or her personality may begin to disintegrate.

Stress causes certain changes in the structure and chemical composition of the body. The nervous system and the endocrine (hormonal) system are especially important in maintaining resistance during stress. Some studies indicate that many emotional disturbances and some common diseases such as high blood pressure, ulcers, HEADACHES, and asthma may be at least partly due to failure to adapt to stress.

When managed appropriately, stress can be useful. Stress is an adaptive mechanism that helps people ward off danger and solve problems. Many health care professionals have developed techniques and methods to help people cope with stress, using both older and more ancient methods, as well as new biophysiological and psychological methods. The best approach to solving stress-caused complications is to prevent the stress buildup in the first place. Some cultures have relatively well-defined methods of preventing the buildup of stress: in India, children at early ages are taught meditation, which, when used appropriately, seems to work well on the biophysiological system in reducing stress; in China, children as well as older adults practice TAI CHI CHUAN, a martial art and form of stylized, meditative exercise, characterized by methodically slow circular and stretching movements to balance bodily energy.

stuttering, fear of   Fear of stuttering is known as psellismophobia and laliophobia. The word *stammering* is used interchangeably with *stuttering* and refers to a nonfluency of speech. An individual who stutters has an interrupted flow of words, an inability to articulate certain sounds, or the repetitions of certain sounds. The speech pattern may be explosive, or there may be occasional hesitations. An individual's a speech difficulty may be aggravated by situations that arouse anxieties or fears of self-consciousness. Some individuals who have difficulties with speech may avoid certain situations, such as speaking aloud in a community meeting or going to social occasions, because they are fearful that they will stutter when they speak to others. Many forms of speech therapy help individuals overcome their stutters and their fears of stuttering. Also, behavior therapy can help individuals overcome anxieties and phobias about specific situations that bring on stuttering.

sublimation   A defense mechanism, individuals use sublimation unconsciously by diverting instinctual drives, such as sexual or aggressive drives that may be unacceptable, into personally and socially acceptable channels. Such channeling of energy may protect the individual from the anxiety that the original drive might produce and also usually brings the individual satisfactions, such as acceptance and recognition from others. An example of an individual who uses sublimation constructively is one who has exhibitionistic tendencies who becomes a choreographer. Although this term is used in psychoanalysis, it is also common in psychological vocabularies. The broader use of the term refers to the focusing of one's energy, frustration, anxiety, and so on on an activity that comes to dominate one's life; for example, an active achievement-oriented person might sublimate his or her energies into sports and fitness, working out, or competing on a regular basis.

success, fear of Some individuals have a fear of success that causes them anxieties while they are striving for an objective and after they achieve it. Fear of success is closely related to fear of failure. The individual who fears achieving success fears being a failure at another plateau or that he or she will not be able to fulfill expectations at the higher level. Some find that striving for success but not quite reaching it is tolerable, but when an anxious individual imagines himself or herself successful, the level of stress becomes intolerable and turns into a fear. Some who fear success fear that success will put them in another academic, social, or athletic class and that they will lose the friendship and comradeship of their peers or that they will not be conforming to their group if they are successful. Fear of success is related to a fear of RISK TAKING and criticism.

suffocation, fear of Fear of suffocation, or smothering, is known as pnigophobia. Suffocation means an inability of the body tissues to receive oxygen due to primary failure of the respiratory system to draw adequate amounts of air and oxygen into the lungs. Fears of suffocation may be related to many other fears such as being buried alive; being in a crowded room; being in an elevator, in a small, enclosed space, or even being in a bus, train, or airplane. Individuals who fear suffocation may actually have symptoms of suffocation, even though they are breathing in adequate air and oxygen. Symptoms of suffocation are dizziness, lethargy, drowsiness, and finally unconsciousness. If no oxygen is administered, there will first be brain damage and then death.

suicide, fear of A number of individuals who have anxieties and phobias fear that they will kill themselves. Some fear heights because they are afraid that they will feel compelled to jump from a high place; the same may be true of some bridge phobics and even some who fear flying in an airplane. Individuals whose parent or other relative committed suicide may fear that they will feel compelled to do so, too; however, suicide does not run in the family—it is an individual pattern.

Many who contemplate suicide have an overwhelming feeling of rejection and lack of love and affection in their lives. Individuals who commit suicide often suffer from depression and have deep feelings of hopelessness or helplessness. The attempt at suicide may be brought on by a wish for revenge against the world, for being reunited with an individual who has died, or for instilling guilt in a person who has rejected him or her. Some individuals make threats of suicide in an attempt to dominate and control a spouse or parent or to force favorable treatment. Studies reveal that the suicidal person gives many clues and warnings of his or her contemplated intentions. Although such individuals are often confused, alienated, and self-condemning, they are not mentally ill.

Sun and sunlight, fear of   Fear of the Sun and sunlight is known as heliophobia and phengophobia. Early people feared the Sun because they recognized it as a source of life and worshiped it as the supreme deity. They paid homage and brought offerings to the sun. They watched the Sun and its daily movement across the sky with awe, puzzlement, and terror. They were frightened by the sun's decrease of power in winter; they feared that the Sun might die and cause them to freeze to death. A solar eclipse caused the fear that the end of the world had come.

In modern times, the Sun is feared as a cause of cancer. Dermatologists and oncologists have repeatedly warned that excessive exposure to sunlight without appropriate covering or use of sunscreen puts people at great risk for developing skin cancers, some of which can be disfiguring or even fatal.

superego anxiety   Anxiety that occurs from the anticipation of feeling guilty is superego anxiety. Individuals are aware that if they violate their own moral standards, their superego or conscience will let them know by imposing (usually uncomfortable) feelings of guilt or shame. In thinking about the unpleasant guilt that they will experience after committing the act of transgression, the individuals may feel tense and anxious, possibly enough to prevent them from carrying out their planned actions.

supernatural, fears of   Belief in the supernatural with the accompanying fears and sense of terror has been common in many societies. Fears of the supernatural start in the child's vivid imagination and continue into later life; such fears are often associated with and prompted by religions, which use them as methods of discipline and social control. Natural disaster and misfortune, the behavior of wild animals, and the attempt to explain the fate of the soul after death contribute to fears of the super-natural.

As society becomes more scientific and rational and as beliefs in the supernatural decrease, stories of the supernatural have become more popular; the supernatural has become a popular subject for novels and films. Supernatural themes allow an escape from the relative security of modern life. Continuing interest in horror stories indicates that people have a capacity to enjoy being frightened. There is a communal quality about the horror story because a sense of shared terror brings people together and because children may fear the dark, monsters, and other frightening beings less when these creatures are organized into plots.

Interest in the supernatural has heightened in modern times around concerns of death; for example, the dying are isolated in hospitals and cared for by professionals at the time of death. In becoming less a part of life, death has become more remote and mysterious. In spite of modern skepticism, superstitions and half-beliefs linger. Frightening stories about the supernatural may be an acceptable way to express and contain these fears. Stories about supernatural, frightening situations may be a type of catharsis and drugless hallucinogen.

The study of death (thanatology) has become a legitimate area of science.

surgical operations (or surgical incisions), fear of   Fear of surgical operations is known as ergasiophobia or tomophobia. This fear may extend to any medical procedure that uses operations, instruments, and manipulation, especially cutting and suturing. An individual may be phobic about having an operation himself or herself or of hearing about someone else's operation. A fear of surgical operations may be related to fears of doctors, hospitals, or death. Some individuals have grown up with a fear of surgical operations because they are aware that an older member of their family or someone they knew died during surgery; they equate surgery with death from an early age. In recent years, knowledge about hospital-induced infections has caused many individuals to fear having anything to do with hospitals and surgery. Some individuals may fear particular types of surgery, such as hysterectomy.

swallowing, fear of   Fear of swallowing is known as phagophobia. Some individuals feel that they have a lump in their throat and find it difficult to swallow when they are very anxious. Muscles of the throat may actually go into spasm, and the individual may make some choking sounds. Fear of swallowing is a social phobia and may cause phobic individuals to avoid being seen while they are eating. The fear of swallowing is also related to the feeling of having a lump in the throat (*globus hystericus*).

sweating, fear of   Fear of sweating is a social phobia. Some individuals avoid crowds, being in close contact with others in elevators, and even eating in restaurants because they fear that they will sweat and look ridiculous. They may also worry about giving off an offensive odor and staining their clothing. They fear attracting attention to themselves. Some women who suffer from hot flashes fear that others will notice while they are having a hot flash. Many individuals have a low sense of self-esteem and worry that others will hold them in even less regard if they sweat at an unpredictable time. Social phobias, such as fear of sweating, are often treated successfully with behavior-modification techniques and exposure therapy.

swimming, fear of   Fear of swimming may be a social phobia in that many who fear swimming fear being seen in their bathing suits by others, fear criticism about their body shape, and fear that they may look ridiculous while swimming or approaching the pool or body of water. Fear of swimming may also come from a fear of water or a fear of drowning. Some fear being out of control if a wave or the undertow overtakes them while swimming in an ocean or large lake. Some individuals are comfortable standing in a pool or body of water but fear swimming; some can float or swim but fear putting their face in the water while they do so.

For many, a fear of swimming can be overcome by taking lessons and learning to use appropriate breathing techniques while in the water; for others, behavior-modification techniques may be effective.

symbolism, fear of   Fear of symbolism is known as symbolophobia. Many personal fears can be produced by phobic stimuli. Individuals may fear the symbols themselves with or without understanding their unconscious representation; for example, water has been viewed symbolically as a representation of the mind, and going underwater—the "deep dive," for example, in *Moby Dick*—is symbolic of going into the unconscious or going into the "dark side."

Carl Gustav Jung (1875–1961), to a greater degree than Sigmund Freud (1856–1939), explored the enduring and universal evolutionary aspects of symbols. Jung used the word *archetype* to designate universal symbols that possess constancy and efficiency and can force the way to psychic evolution. These ready-made systems of images are inherited and are powerful, instinctive guides to creative action and growth. The deeper significance of these archetypes are secret and require an opening to the beyond or unknown. Some archetypes are the mother, father, savant, warrior, and magician.

Freud viewed symbolism in dreams as important to understanding concealed unconscious wishes or conflicts. In the English school of psychoanalysis, also known as the Kleinian school, symbol formation was viewed as an essential prerequisite of early normal development. Investigations by Austrian psychoanalyst, Melanie Klein (1882–1960) led to an understanding of how symbolism helps the child construct an internal world at an early age. The infant's transference of interest from the subjective world to the outside world of external reality begins with symbols; for example, the baby regards objects as symbolizing others if there is some resemblance between them. The baby's fingers symbolize the breast when the breast is not available, and the symbol serves as a bridge to the actual object.

Behavior therapists acknowledge that symbolism distinguishes between radical objective theorists who are not interested in mediating processes and those who view cognitions and imagery as mediating between the stimulus and response in the behavioral sequence that governs human behavior. The development of language presupposes an ability to utilize symbols and symbolization.

sympathetic nervous system   One of two major divisions of the autonomic nervous system, the sympathetic nervous system prepares an individual for fighting, fleeing, action, or sexual climax. During a phobic reaction, the sympathetic nervous system becomes quickly activated and tends to excite or arouse one by speeding up the contractions of the blood vessels, slowing those of the intestines, and increasing the heartbeat to prepare the body for exertion, emotional stress, and extreme cold. The parasympathetic nervous system tends to depress many bodily functions. These two divisions of the autonomic nervous system coordinate to control bodily activities and respond appropriately to physical and psychological challenges. When an individual wants to be aroused (such as when fleeing from fear), the sympathetic system speeds up and the parasympathetic system slows down. When one wants to relax, the parasympathetic system increases its activities and the sympathetic system slows down.

The sympathetic nervous system consists of a group of 22 neural centers on or close to the spinal cord. From these 22 centers, fibers connect to all parts of the body, including the sweat gland and tiny blood vessels near the surface of the skin. When one is suddenly afraid, the sympathetic nervous system activates the following physiological responses:

- The heart pumps more blood to the brain and muscles and to the surface of the skin.
- Breathing becomes faster and harder.
- Blood sugar level becomes elevated.
- Digestion slows down.

- Skin perspires to remove waste products created by the exertion and to keep one cool.
- Pupils in the eyes open up to let in more light.

syndrome   A group of symptoms that occur together that constitute a recognizable condition, either physical or mental, a syndrome is also called a symptom complex or a disease entity; for example, the group of symptoms exhibited by agoraphobics is known as the agoraphobic syndrome. *Syndrome* is less specific than *disorder* or *disease,* which generally implies a specific cause or disease process.

systematic desensitization   This behavior therapy procedure is highly effective in the treatment of excessive emotional states such as anxiety and anger. It originated with U.S. behavioral psychiatrist Joseph Wolpe (1915–97) who used in vivo and imaginal desensitization with his patients and reported more than 80 percent recovery rates for a variety of anxiety, phobic, and emotional reactions.

The essence of systematic desensitization is the gradual exposure of an individual to components of a feared situation while he or she is relaxed. Systematic desensitization is the major treatment procedure for phobias and agoraphobia. Exposure may occur in imagination or self-visualization or in actuality (in vivo). Systematic desensitization is best applied with the help of a skilled therapist. Once relaxation skills are mastered (which takes five to six weeks), a hierarchy involving gradually more intimate (and reactive) triggering stimuli is developed, and imaginal or in vivo exposure is started. Systematic desensitization is a highly effective treatment method for simple phobias. The cure rate for simple phobias is about 80–85 percent within 12 to 15 sessions. Social phobias, agoraphobia, and panic require more patience, time, and skill in using systematic desensitization. These reactions also usually require in vivo exposure rather than imaginal to be effective.

T

tachycardia Rapid, intensive heartbeat, often associated with a fearsome situation or high levels of anxiety which occur during phobic attacks and panic attacks, tachycardia is not dangerous to the person's health but if persistent should be checked by a doctor. See ANXIETY; PANIC, PANIC ATTACKS, AND PANIC DISORDER.

tai chi chuan Tai chi chuan is a Chinese martial art and form of stylized, meditative exercise, characterized by methodically slow circular and stretching movements planned to rebalance bodily energy and possibly help to relieve anxieties. Practitioners of tai chi chuan usually perform their routines early in the morning to keep themselves more centered and relaxed during the day.

talking, fear of Fear of talking is known as glossophobia, laliophobia, lalophobia, and phonophobia. Fear of talking may be a social phobia in that the individual is afraid to speak up in a crowd, fears embarrassment, or fears saying something ridiculous or inappropriate. Also, fear of talking may relate to fear of hearing the sound of one's own voice or a fear of stuttering. Sometimes those who have a fear of talking out loud will resort to whispering as a way to communicate.

taste, fear of Fear of taste is known as geumaphobia, geumophobia, or geumatophobia. Individuals may fear certain tastes because of their associations with past experiences or situations that caused anxieties. The fear also may be generalized to other foods in the particular taste category; for example, a child who becomes nauseous after eating a lemon for the first time or who is always given lemons to eat by a feared authority figure may grow to associate lemon with discomfort and begin to fear not only this taste but any sour-tasting food.

There is a disorder known as gustatory agnosia, in which food becomes tasteless or even has a disgusting taste. Individuals who have this condition may also lose their ability to smell or may find that formerly pleasant odors are offensive. With an inability to smell, they may fear that they are unaware that they are eating or drinking something that formerly caused them anxieties.

tattoos, fear of Many individuals who fear tattoos do so because ornamental tattooing can produce tumors or because individuals may develop allergic skin reactions to some of the color pigment used. Those who fear contamination or infection may fear those problems from needles used in tattooing. The most common infections from needles are hepatitis and AIDS (acquired immunodeficiency syndrome). Some fear tattooing because it seems to be a permanent coloration of the skin. Because the pigment in a tattoo extends deep into the skin, its removal by any method is likely to leave a scar. Small tattoos can be removed by excision, leaving a small, minimal scar. Dermabrasion (skin planing) is also used to make the tattoo fainter.

Others may fear tattoos because the tattoos depict their phobic object, such as butterflies, lips, or the word *mother.*

technology, fear of   Fear of technology is known as technophobia. Many individuals fear technological devices in modern society; for example, some individuals look with fear on computers, highly technical telephone answering systems, and even videocassette recorders. Some individuals become very anxious when faced with a set of instructions that are supposed to be easy for the average individual to follow. Another aspect of technophobia is the fear that machines will be able to do what people do now. Fear of robots is part of this fear.

telephone, fear of the   Some individuals fear talking on the telephone. Others fear the ringing of a telephone, perhaps because they fear hearing bad news. Some are afraid to pick up the phone and answer it because they fear that they will say something that will be criticized by the listener. Some experience a great deal of anxiety if they have to pick up the telephone to inquire about a job, place an order, or make any kind of an inquiry. Some individuals feel that they are powerless when speaking to another person by telephone because when deprived of visual clues such as body language, they feel they cannot control the response they will get. Some express anxiety that they are intruding on the person they are calling and can never seem to find a "good" time to place their call. Others are fearful of using the telephone because doing so reminds them of overhearing conversations their parents had, of listening when they should not have been, or of hearing something specifically traumatic.

Individuals who have telephone phobia experience symptoms of nervous stomach and sweaty palms, which are typical anxiety reactions. Many telephone phobics are motivated to overcome their phobia because they realize that the telephone can be a bridge between themselves and someone about whom they care and between themselves and necessary services. Individuals who have overcome this phobia have suggested rehearsing the conversation before making the call, writing down what they want to say when they call, or standing up while speaking into the telephone. Behavior therapy techniques can be helpful for telephone phobics.

television, role of in phobias   Television can be a powerful source of observational learning for both children and adults. Children observe models of fearful behavior on television, such as people who are afraid of the dark and of harmless animals. Television presents many unrealistic and exaggerated situations in cartoon form that can frighten children, such as goblins, dragons, and vampires. Children may later think about these situations, dream about them, and even develop night terrors because of what they have seen. Crime programs make children as well as adults fearful of criminal attack; news programs that report murders, arson, and robberies reinforce the notion that these events are more frequent that they actually are.

test anxiety   Fear of taking tests is common among individuals of all ages, but it is particularly noticeable in students. Test anxiety may be related to a desire for perfectionism and fear of failure. Outside of academic settings, individuals face many test situations in everyday life, including tests for acquiring a driver's license, medical tests, and tests as part of employment applications. Desensitization programs have been used to treat test anxiety, with varying degrees of success.

testosterone   This male hormone is produced by the testes and stimulates development of male reproductive organs, including the prostate and secondary features such as the beard and bone and muscle growth. Testosterone stimulates the male sexual drive. Testosterone level usually decreases in men during ANXIETY and stress.

textures, fear of certain   Some people have aversions to fuzzy surfaces, such as certain carpets, tennis balls, peach skins, or the skins of kiwi fruit. Some avoid suede, velvet, corduroy or other fabrics, or shiny buttons. Usually, aversions to textures make the individual uncomfortable but do not elicit phobic reactions.

theaters, fear of   Fear of theaters is known as theatrophobia. Individuals who fear theaters may do so because they feel closed in and unable to get out easily. They may be agoraphobics and may also be afraid of crowds, suffocation, fire, or being far from a bathroom. Some people fear being in the center aisle of a theater and will not go unless they can be assured of an aisle seat. They may fear contamination from the seat or from the back of the seat. Some individuals who fear head lice fear that they will contract them while sitting in a theater seat (as well as in a bus or train).

theology, fear of   Fear of theology is known as theologicophobia. Some people fear theology because explanations of theological concepts are often made in specialized and obscure terms. Some believers with a mystical or personal approach to religion resent the scholarly application of theological thinking. Such individuals become anxious when they try to analyze and categorize religious ideas because the structured academic approach interferes with their personal sense of contact with God.

thirteen, fear of the number   Fear of the number 13 or of having 13 people at a table is known as tridecaphobia, tredecaphobia, and triskaidekaphobia. Individuals who fear the number 13 may fear any situation or event involving this number, such as a house number; the floor of a building, apartment, or office number; or the 13th day of the month. Because this is such a common fear, many buildings have omitted labeling the 13th floor as such. (Residents of the 13th floor are less anxious because they believe that they live on the 14th floor.)

thought stopping   This cognitive-behavior therapy technique was developed by Joseph Wolpe (1915–97). The therapist asks the phobic or anxious individual to recognize fear-producing thoughts. When the individual begins to verbalize or produces these undesirable thoughts, he or she is asked to interrupt them with an internal shout of *stop*. Eventually the individual learns to control and reduce the incidence of such thoughts. Thought stopping is also useful in treating smoking and sexual deviations.

thunderstorms, fear of   Fear of thunderstorms is known as astraphobia. Individuals who fear thunderstorms listen intently to weather forecasts and may call their local weather bureau with questions. Such individuals will avoid going outdoors when thunderstorms are predicted. Some phobics hide in a closet or under a bed during a thunderstorm; some become incontinent as a result of their fear. Some fear the noise of the thunder, and others fear injury or death.

tic   A tic is a frequent involuntary muscle spasm. A person with a tic is known as a tiquer. Tics can occur in any muscle group, but the ones most noticeable to others involve the facial muscles, such as the eyelids or the lips. Additionally, tics may also be vocal, involving sudden, uncontrollable, loud sounds. The individual who has a tic may not be aware of it until someone else points it out; on the other hand, once an individual knows that he or she has a tic, he or she may become very anxious and embarrassed about it and may even avoid people, becoming social phobic. Some people associate tics with nervousness and anxiety, and to some extent this is correct. Tics may disappear in time as the individual becomes more relaxed. Tics are treated with therapy to determine the conditions causing the anxiety and then with behavioral methods of relaxation training and SYSTEMATIC DESENSITIZATION. Tics are characteristic of Gilles de la Tourette syndrome, a disorder of the nervous system; they can also be brought about by certain drugs.

time, fear of   Fear of time is known as chronophobia. This fear relates to fear of time passing either too slowly or too rapidly, free time either too much or too little, or running out of time.

tobacco, fear of   Modern fears of tobacco are related to the evidence that smoking is a risk factor in the development of many types of cancer, lung diseases, and heart disease. Historically, in certain parts of Russia, the tobacco plant was feared because some individuals believed that it was inhabited by the devil.

tombs, fear of   The common fear of tombs relates to the fear of being buried alive, of suffocation, and of death.

tombstones, fear of   Fear of tombstones is known as placophobia. This fear is related to a fear of cemeteries and indirectly to a fear of death.

tophophobia   A fear of certain places, this term also refers to a fear of being on the stage, or stage fright.

tornadoes, fear of   Fear of tornadoes is known as lilapsophobia.

touched, fear of being   Fear of being touched is known as haphephobia, haptephobia, hapnophobia, aphephobia, haptophobia, and thixophobia. This fear may relate to a fear of contamination or to a sexual fear.

trait anxiety   A general, persistent pattern of responding with anxiety, trait anxiety resembles timidity and indicates a habitual tendency to be anxious over a long period of time in many situations. It is also known as A-trait. The person with a high A-trait perceives more situations as threatening than a person who is low in A-trait. Phobic individuals are high in A-trait. The term is used in research projects to differentiate between types of anxieties; for example, U.S. psychologist Charles Spielberger (1927–   ) has developed an instrument to measure A-trait vs. A-stage anxiety, A-trait anxiety being more situational and varied over time.

transactional analysis (TA)   A type of group therapy developed by Eric Berne, a Canadian-born U.S. psychoanalyst (1910–70), TA is based on his theory of personality structure. According to Berne, the personality is made up of three constructs: the parent, the adult, and the child, which correspond in a general way to Freud's superego, ego, and id. The parent ego state can be nurturing or critical ("I love you," "You should . . ."); the adult is practical and evaluative, taking in information and making rational decisions; and the child is primarily made up of feelings, either expressing them naturally as they occur or adaptively as they have been socialized.

In TA, group members make determined efforts to change their patterns of communications (or "transactions") with others, by engaging in "games" and role-playing scenarios that manipulate the way they choose to use their different ego states. Berne believed that transactions were frequently set up to satisfy only one person's needs, not allowing for mutual fulfillment. This unhealthy pattern can stem from an individual's fear of presenting his or her true self to another person and risking rejection.

Berne also stressed that each person is responsible for accepting himself or herself and his or her own feelings (I'm OK) and realizing that other people must do the same (You're OK). He believed that psychological disturbance would occur when the personality was inappropriately dominated by either the parent, the adult, or the child ego state.

The essence of TA therapy is to help the individual develop psychological independence and identity, marked by awareness of self and others, spontaneity, and intimacy in his or her lifestyle rather than the more common human coping attributes of manipulation and self-defeating behavior.

TA sees anxiety as the outcome of faulty lifestyle; hence the focus is on modification of lifestyle itself rather than specific symptoms; for example, Eric Berne, in his book about transactional analysis (*Games People Play*), did not make one reference to anxiety in the subject index.

transcendental meditation (TM)   TM is a type of meditation developed in the early 1960s by Maharishi Mahesh Yogi. Some individuals find relief from anxiety in TM. In TM, the individual sits quietly with eyes closed and focuses attention solely on the verbal repetition of a special sound or mantra. The person practicing TM usually spends about 20 minutes, twice a day, engaged in meditation. This process of focused attention should have the effect of taking the person's mind away from anxieties and worries, helping him or her to relax. TM claims benefits of reducing anxiety and aggression and possibly changing certain body states by slowing metabolism and heart rate and lowering blood pressure.

trauma   Real or imaginary incidents occur and affect the individual's later life and ability to cope with anxieties. Freud (1856–1939) believed that all neurotic illnesses were the result of early psychological trauma. The term *trauma* comes from the Greek word meaning "wound." In medicine, the word *trauma* refers to a violent shock or severe wound.

travel, fear of   Fear of travel is known as hedonophobia or hodophobia. Individuals who are afraid to travel are likely to be fearful of new things and new places; they may also have a fear of moving. Generally, agoraphobics fear traveling, as do some individuals who fear airplanes, trains, or moving vehicles.

trees, fear of   Fear of trees is known as dendrophobia. Individuals who fear trees may fear certain landscapes; being hit on the head with apples, acorns, or other falling objects; or blossoms or fruit from the trees. Some individuals fear seeing tress with leaves turning brown; this may represent a fear of death to them. In mythology and legends, trees were considered special, mysterious places because they gave shade and shelter; wood from trees enabled people to build fires, homes, and bridges, and the fruit of trees fed humans and animals. Trees were a link from earth to heaven, and tree worship was an early form of religion. The common practice to "touch wood" for luck is a carryover from tree worship. Early believers tried to summon friendly spirits by knocking on the trunks of the tree.

trembling, fear of   Fear of trembling is known as tremophobia. Individuals who fear trembling in themselves are afraid that others will notice and be critical or frightened. Some people who have trembling hands due to disease, such as Parkinson's, fear that if they are seen trembling they will appear helpless. People who fear trembling in others are afraid that the other individual may have a contagious disease or may act violently.

tricyclic drug   One of a group of antidepressants whose molecular structure is characterized by three fused rings, tricyclic drugs are effective primarily in alleviating endogenous depression. Imipramine, one of the tricyclic antidepressive drugs, has been used extensively for treatment of panic disorder. Although results are mixed, it does seem to be effective in the short run with a small percentage of people who have panic.

tuberculosis, fear of   Fear of tuberculosis is known as tuberculophobia, or phthisiophobia. Tuberculosis is an infectious disease that is caused by *Mycobacterium tuberculosis*, or the tubercle bacillus. Persons who have tuberculosis tend to cough, spreading moist particles of the TB germ into the air. Some of these particles continue floating in the air until they enter the respiratory passages of another person and find their way down to the lungs to cause common tuberculosis. The germ may remain dormant for many years before making the individual ill. The bacillus responsible for tuberculosis was identified in 1882, but it was not until 1944 that the drug, streptomycin, was found; it was effective against tuberculosis. Now that most forms of tuberculosis are treatable, the disease is not as feared as it once was, although it still occurs in some populations in the United States, particularly drug users and persons who have AIDS.

tyramine   A substance found in some foods that may contribute to causing headaches and may interfere with the effectiveness of certain antidepressant medications, tyramine affects the constriction or expansion of blood vessels. This reaction to certain foods occurs only in about 30 percent of people who have migraine headaches. Because there is no way to know whether an individual is in this sensitive group, physicians generally recommend that all migraine sufferers and individuals who take MAO (monoamine oxidase) inhibitors as mood elevators for depression avoid ripened cheeses, including cheddar, Emmentaler, Gruyere, Stilton, Brie, and Camembert (cottage, cream, and some processed cheeses are permitted); herring; chocolate; vinegar (except white vinegar); anything fermented, pickled, or marinated; sour cream; yogurt; nuts; peanut butter; seeds; pods of broad beans (lima, navy, pinto, garbanzo, and pea); any foods containing large amounts of monosodium glutamate (Oriental foods); onions; and canned figs.

U

UFOs, fear of   Individuals and groups of people often become anxious when they think they see unidentified flying objects (UFOs). Anxieties about sightings of UFOs are related to the times; for example, in the late 20th century when space travel became a reality, there was increased speculation about life on other planets, and some came to fear invasion by alien beings. However, in the Middle Ages, when dragon shapes were seen in the clouds or a fiery cross was sighted in the sky, people feared divine retribution. Fear of UFOs is an example of fear of the unknown because no one is sure where the UFOs are from or exactly what they are.

unconditional positive regard   A term used by client-centered therapists to denote the worth of the individual under treatment, unconditional positive regard is used interchangeably with the words *acceptance* and *prizing* and is viewed as necessary to promote effective psychotherapy. If a person is raised in a situation without unconditional positive regard, he or she is more likely to develop anxieties; for example, phobic individuals often come from families in which they received criticism (the opposite of unconditional positive regard).

unconscious, the   The designation given by Sigmund Freud (1856–1939) to a region of the psyche that comprises all mental functions and products of which the individual is unaware and which he or she cannot recognize of remember at will. The unconscious in its most simplistic form refers to the availability (or unavailability) of psychic material. Some individuals develop phobias because of unconscious memories.

urinating, fear of   Fear of urinating, called urophobia, can be a very embarrassing and debilitating fear that occurs more frequently in men than in women. Fear of urinating usually occurs when others are present when the person wants to or is actually urinating. Some men may be unable to urinate in front of any other person, and many waste time waiting at work and other places until the men's room becomes empty. Some women cannot urinate in any toilet except in their own home.

In its extreme form, the fear of urinating with another person nearby necessitates holding in urine through the working day until the home bathroom can be used. The victim often avoids parties, restaurants, and social gatherings that might involve long commitments of time. The fear usually develops as a form of social anxiety and is often traced to adolescent fears of public exposure and possible criticism, both of which are common in youth.

Some individuals fear that they might urinate when far from a toilet, wet themselves, and be seen by others. Such individuals may visit public toilets frequently and try to urinate so that they will not feel the urge far from a toilet. They may avoid social gatherings where no toilets are readily available. Individuals who become incontinent, or unable to control the flow of their urine, due to illness or injury fear odor and offending others. Urinary incontinence due to physical causes can be treated with medication, surgery, or commercially available adult diapers. Other fears relating to urination can be treated with psychotherapy and/or behavioral therapy quite effectively.

V

vaccination, fear of   Fear of vaccination is known as vacciniophobia. Some people fear vaccination because they fear injection (see INJECTION PHOBIAS), needles (see NEEDLES, FEAR OF) or devices that pierce the skin, or unwanted side effects from vaccination. Those who have illness phobia or fear of contamination may fear contamination from the inoculation device.

vacciniophobia   Fear of vaccination is called vacciniophobia.

vertigo, fear of   Fear of vertigo is known as illyngophobia. Vertigo is an anxiety response to a situation and is also the medical term that refers to DIZZINESS. Dizziness is a common symptom of many phobics, such as those who fear heights; looking over cliffs, bridges, and elevators; and riding in automobiles. Many agoraphobics experience dizziness when venturing out alone or to places they fear. Fear of dizziness is known as dinophobia.

Vertigo, or dizziness, may be caused by normal stimulation of the hair cells and other nerve endings in the vestibular (ear) apparatus. Wind or even loud noises can stimulate these tiny hair cells. When a phobic person looks over the top of a hill or down from the top of a tall building, the brain gets confused signals and may momentarily lose its sense of up and down, resulting in dizziness. One's sense of balance is also related to sight: There are nerve connections, coordinated by the brain, between the eye and the inner ear.

Individuals who experience vertigo because of phobias should sit, lie down, or brace themselves. Sitting with one's head between the one's legs is a good precaution if one thinks he or she may lose consciousness, but it may not stop the dizziness. Behavior therapies sometimes help individuals who experience dizziness because of phobic reactions.

vomiting, fear of   Fear of vomiting, known as emetophobia, is considered a social phobia. Some individuals who have this phobia fear that they might vomit in public or that they may see others vomiting, and so they avoid any situation that is remotely likely to provoke vomiting in themselves or in others, such as going on a boat or riding in a car.

Voodoo, fears in   Voodoo is a religion and set of related superstitions that include many different magical figures and frightening beliefs. Witches, sorcerers, medicine men, and priests all have their places in

Voodoo. At night, believers fear blood-sucking spirits called *loupgarous*. Noon is frightening too because the human shadow, which believers equate with the soul, disappears. The soul, called the *gros bon ange*, or "large good angel," is a fragile, easily disturbed link between the body and the conscience, the *ti bon ange*, or "good little angel." Magical spells aim at the soul in the culture of Haiti, where Voodoo was transplanted from African tribal beliefs. Any sort of enmity may be a source for possession by evil spirits that results in violent mental and physical symptoms.

Believers undertake initiation into Voodoo, a type of purified intentional form of possession, as a safeguard against calamity, a way to please ancestral spirits and a way to get the powerful Voodoo spirits known as *loa* on one's side. The initiation procedure is essentially a ritual death, a giving up of the soul, which is imagined to leave the body to be captured in a sacred vessel where it will be protected by the gods and safe from evildoers. The initiate is then considered to be a servant of the *loa*, reborn with a new name. The ceremony, during which the initiate learns the secrets and rites of Voodoo, is long and complex, lasting more than a month. At the end of this time, the initiate is called a *hounsi canzo*, the initiated spouse of the god. On the death of an initiate, a rite called *dessounin* releases his spirits into the water of death and again captures his soul in a sacred vessel to await resurrection.

A fear associated with Voodoo belief is the possibility of becoming a zombie, a walking corpse in the service of the person who has reanimated the corpse. The initiation and *dessounin* rituals are supposed to give some sort of assurance that the initiate's soul is safe from anyone with the magical powers to create a zombie.

W

waits, fear of long   Fear of long waits is known as macrophobia. Long waits are common in modern society; people are asked to wait on the telephone, in stores, at airports, and for each other. Many individuals become inpatient and anxious; some are so fearful of waiting that they will not frequent busy restaurants; they take scheduled transportation so that waits are predictable. This fear may be somewhat related to agoraphobia, in which individuals do not like to be away from a secure place for very long. Also, some individuals experience a feeling of being trapped while in line as they cannot leave easily and still maintain their place.

waking up, fear of not   Fear of not waking up may be related to a fear of death. Many individuals who fear going to bed or going to sleep have this fear. Fear of not waking up is somewhat common in physically ill and elderly persons and in individuals who have anxieties about death. This fear is related to fear of going to sleep.

walking, fear of   Fear of walking and/or standing upright is known as basiphobia, basistasiphobia, stasiphobia, and stasibasiphobia. The fear is often related to fear of falling, collapse, and death.

washing, fear of   Fear of washing is known as ablutophobia. Usually, this refers to fear of washing oneself or even of thinking of washing oneself. However, it also refers to a fear of viewing another individual washing himself or herself.

wasps, fear of   Fear of wasps is known as spheksophobia. Individuals who fear wasps often fear stings, pain, bees, or flying insects in general.

water, fear of   Fear of water is known as aquaphobia and also hydrophobia. Fear of water is related to a fear of drowning and a fear of death. In some aquaphobes, this fear extends to bathing, swimming, or seeing or imagining bodies of water or running water. Fear of water is a learned fear. By age three, children are ready to learn to swim, unless they become fearful of water, particularly deep water; some individuals who fear water may have had a traumatic experience in a pool or other body of water or may have been cautioned not to go near the water— some children of water phobics are taught at an early age to also be afraid of the water and consequently grow up fearful. Many individuals are phobic about going into water that is over their head, even though they know how to swim. Some fear putting their faces in the water and getting water up their nose; when this happens, they have a rapid heartbeat and breathe faster, often inhaling water, which further increases their anxiety. Some individuals avoid boat rides because they are afraid of falling out into deep water; others panic when flying in an airplane over water; for still others, fear of water may be related to a fear of landscape that includes a body of water. Former aquaphobics advise people who are afraid of water to take swimming lessons to become more comfortable in water and to learn to relax and breathe correctly.

waves, fear of   Fear of waves is known as cymophobia. This fear may be related to a fear of motion, of water, or of landscapes in which water and waves are prominent.

weakness, fear of   Fear of weakness is known as asthenophobia. Individuals fear weakness because they fear losing physical, emotional, social, or political control.

weight gain, fear of   Fear of gaining weight is known as obesophobia or pocrescophobia. Some individuals who fear gaining weight stop eating or eat very little, a condition known as anorexia nervosa that is found most often among teenage girls. Some individuals who fear gaining weight practice bulimia, or bingeing and purging, in which they gorge themselves and then induce vomiting. Fear of weight gain is related to concerns about one's body image and social fears.

weight loss, fear of   Fear of losing weight may be related to a fear of illness or a fear of death. Some individuals fear "losing themselves" or disappearing if they lose too much weight. Fear of losing weight may be related to a fear of being out of control of one's body.

wet dreams, fear of   Fear of wet dreams is known as oneirogmophobia. Wet dreams are nocturnal emissions from the penis while asleep. Some men fear wet dreams because of embarrassment that others might become aware of the problem. Nocturnal emissions are part of normal adolescent development and are brought about by accumulated normal tensions that find release during sleep.

"white-coat" hypertension   This term refers to high blood pressure caused by anxiety induced by visiting a doctor's office.

winged things, fear of   Many people fear such winged things as birds, bats, and flying insects because their quick, unpredictable movements simulate attack. Phobics react to this fear by keeping their houses closed to the point of discomfort, carrying umbrellas, and avoiding the out-of-doors and enclosed spaces where they might become trapped with a flying animal or insect.

witches and witchcraft, fear of   Historically, many individuals have feared witches and witchcraft because witches appear to be inherently evil and have mystical powers. Witches usually have been women, but male witches—warlocks—have also been feared. The term *witchcraft* derives from the Saxon word *Wicca*, a contraction of *witega*, a prophet or wise person. Beliefs that have led to persistent fears include the notions that witches can inflict misfortune and a state of demonic possession on their victims, fly through the air, become invisible, appear in spectral form as seductive women or men, eat human flesh, and have a mysterious link with animals. Some have believed that witches possessed the power of the evil eye and that they could change winds to adversely affect sailors, could cause the neighbor's wheat to rot, had power over certain animals, and could turn themselves into animals. Witches were believed to possess the power to make themselves invisible by means of magic given to them by the devil and of harming others by thrusting nails into a waxen image representing them. Other beliefs include notions that witches can be identified by marks on their bodies and by the use of tests and ordeals.

Beliefs in witches have persisted in part because such beliefs were a way to handle social strain and competition in primitive societies. Witchcraft provided a fear inducement for social control and promoted conformity within the society. It also explained misfortune; unlike other systems of metaphysical belief, this provided an opportunity for redress of wrongs. Beliefs in witches have also served a social and political purpose by punishing incompetent behavior and discouraging begging.

words, fear of   Fear of words is known as verbophobia or logophobia. This may be a fear of hearing words in general or of specific words. Those who have this fear become anxious even at the thought of certain words. Some individuals fear certain words because they fear that they will stammer or stutter when they try to say them.

worrying   Worrying is a common expression or symptom of ANXIETY. Persons troubled about a past, present, or future event may worry. Worrying is characterized by a feeling of uneasiness and mental discomfort; excessive or highly irrational worry may be a symptom of an anxiety disorder—individuals who have OBSESSIVE-COMPULSIVE DISORDER worry excessively. It is often worry that leads them to perform certain RITUALS such as repeated hand-washing or checking for locked doors. Individuals who have AGORAPHOBIA are commonly worriers, as are social phobics. Agoraphobics may worry that they will not be able to get to a secure place; social phobics may worry that they will be seen not looking their best or will find themselves in an embarrassing situation. Furthermore, anxiety sufferers almost always worry in anticipation of a situation in which they may experience anxiety.

Phobics and those who have obsessive-compulsive disorder differ in ways in which they worry. Phobics have persistent worries around one theme, such as their phobic object or situation, whereas obsessive-compulsives have repetitive worries that lead them to actions (such as checking repeatedly to see that the door is locked). Obsessive-compulsives worry about remote, abstract, and future consequences of contact with an evoking stimuli; phobics worry more about coming into contact with a specifically feared object or situation.

wrinkles, fear of getting   Fear of wrinkles or of getting wrinkles is known as rhytiphobia. The most feared wrinkles are those on the face, particularly around the eyes and the mouth. Wrinkles are feared because they are a sign of aging. Contemporary society places emphasis on youth as a standard of beauty, and many individuals, particularly women, fear losing their attractiveness because of wrinkles. Some who are so motivated seek reconstructive cosmetic surgery to remove wrinkles.

writing, fear of   Fear of writing is known as graphophobia. Some fear writing in public and having others observe as they write. They may fear criticism of their handwriting or of their posture while writing. Others fear writing anything at any time because they do not want to commit their ideas to paper for others to see. Fear of writing is a social phobia and can be treated with behavior modification therapy.

X

X rays   Fear of X rays is known as radiophobia. Many people refuse to have diagnostic X rays out of fear of harmful effects of radiation. This fear is becoming more prevalent as more people are aware of the possible effects of radiation. Dental X rays are part of routine dental examinations, and chest X rays are often part of routine physical examinations, particularly before admission to a hospital or before a surgical procedure.

Y

yoga Many individuals attempt to reduce anxieties through yoga, a system of beliefs and practices first described comprehensively in the third century B.C. Yoga is a way to balance energy and thus achieve relaxation and absence of anxiety and better functioning.

The most well-known form of yoga in the United States is Hatha yoga, which emphasizes physical well-being and mental concentration through stretching and breath control exercises.

Yoga proposes that the human ego produces attachments, dependencies, obsessions, and fantasies that in turn produce anxiety. Meditation reduces the effects of these anxiety-producing mental conditions, not by fighting them but by allowing the meditator to observe them in a state of detachment. Like other meditation techniques, yoga focuses on a higher level of consciousness than the ordinary waking state.

Yoga exercises and postures are based on the observation that an individual's mental state is reflected in his physical posture. Thus, exercises are intended to promote self awareness of the condition of the body. Stimulation of the spinal column and glands is thought to create a feeling of well-being. Concentration on breathing is central to yoga practice; breath control helps the individual conserve and focus energy.

Z

zelophobia Fear of jealousy is termed zelophobia.

Zen therapy Zen is one of many anxiety-reducing meditative techniques. Some individuals who begin Zen meditation are sufferers from depression who have not found help from other self-help techniques or therapy. Zen has been helpful to many individuals who have a strong sense of their own internal control. Meditation may be effective because extreme emotions produce a hypnotic, exclusive state of mind that meditation helps to break down. Meditation also helps the individual balance arousal, tranquility, and objective observation of behavior and thoughts.

Zen, derived from the Chinese word for meditation, emerged as a Buddhist movement in seventh-century China and evolved further as a Japanese practice. Two central concepts of Zen are the individual's ability to control his or her mind and the desirability of a state of detachment. An attitude common to the meditative techniques is that man's usual state of awareness is clouded and distorted with fantasies, emotions, and associations that produce many psychological problems and result from the lack of control of thought processes. Zen meditative techniques, or zazen, are intended to break through this distortion of perception. Zen meditation is practiced with the eyes open, the back upright and unsupported, the whole body in a firmly balanced position. The zazen technique may be a controlled method of breathing or concentration on a koan, a nonrational problem put to the meditator by a teacher. An example of a koan is the question: we know the sound of two hands clapping; what is the sound of one hand clapping? Meditators are to think about the koan but not to force themselves if their thoughts wander. They should simply observe their own thoughts in a detached state. The goal of this technique is a breakthrough in thought processes. A transcendental state of mind called satori, which is beyond thought and language, is the ultimate goal. A meditator who reaches this state is capable of accepting daily experience with a clear mind and without dwelling on the past or events, over which he or she has no control.

zoophobia Fear of animals is known as zoophobia.

PART III

READING LIST AND RESOURCES

READING LIST

Acquired immunodeficiency syndrome (AIDS)

Andre, Pierre. *People, Sex, HIV & AIDS: Social, Political, Philosophical and Moral Implications.* Huntington, W.Va.: University Press, 1995.

Banta, William F. *AIDS in the Workplace: Legal Questions and Practical Answers.* New York: Lexington Books, 1993.

Dispezio, Michael A. *The Science, Spread, and Therapy of HIV Disease: Everything You Need to Know But Had No Idea Who to Ask.* Shrewsbury, Mass.: ATL Press, 1998.

Donovan, Catherine A., and Elizabeth Stratton. "Changing Epidemiology of AIDS." *Canadian Family Physician* 40, no. 8 (August 1994): 1414ff.

Douglas, Paul Harding, and Laura Pinsky. *The Essential AIDS Fact Book.* New York: Pocket Books, 1996.

Epstein, Steven. *Impure Science: AIDS, Activism and the Politics of Knowledge.* Berkeley, Calif.: University of California Press, 1996.

Gifford, Allen. *Living Well With HIV & AIDS.* Palo Alto, Calif.: Bull Publishers, 1997.

Sirimarco, Elizabeth. *AIDS.* New York: M. Cavendish, 1994.

Storad, Conrad J. *Inside AIDS: HIV Attacks the Immune System.* Minneapolis: Lerner Publications Co., 1998.

Ward, Darrell E. *The AmFAR AIDS Handbook: The Complete Guide to Understanding HIV and AIDS.* New York: W.W. Norton, 1999.

Addictions (See also ALCOHOLISM; SMOKING.)

Bepko, Claudia, ed. *Feminism and Addiction.* New York: Haworth Press, 1991.

Carroll, Marilyn. *Cocaine and Crack.* Hillside, N.J.: Enslow Publishers, 1994.

Chopra, Deepak. *Overcoming Addictions: The Spiritual Solution.* New York: Harmony Books, 1997.

Ruden, Ronald A. *The Craving Brain: The Biobalance to Controlling Addictions.* New York: HarperCollins Publishers, 1997.

Agoraphobia (See also ANXIETY AND ANXIETY DISORDERS; PHOBIAS.)

Ballenger, James C., ed. *Biology of Agoraphobia.* Washington, D.C.: American Psychiatric Press, 1984.

Frampton, Muriel. *Agoraphobia: Coping with the World Outside.* Wellingstorough, Northamptonshire, Eng.: Turnstone Press, Ltd., 1984.

Goldstein, Alan J. *Overcoming Agoraphobia: Conquering Fear of the Outside World.* New York: Viking, 1987.

Paolino, Adele. *Agoraphobia: Are Panic and Phobias Psychological or Physical?* Winona, Minn.: Apollo Books, 1984.

Scrignar, Chester R. *From Panic to Peace of Mind: Overcoming Panic and Agoraphobia.* New Orleans, La.: Brunn Press, 1991.

Seagrave, Ann, and Faison Covington. *Free from Fears: A New Help For Anxiety, Panic and Agoraphobia.* New York: Poseidon Press, 1987.

Alcoholism

Barbour, Scott, ed. *Alcohol: Opposing Viewpoints.* San Diego: Greenhaven Press, 1998.

Berger, Gilda. *Alcoholism and the Family.* New York: F. Watts, 1993.

Dick, R. *New Light on Alcoholism.* Corte Madera, Calif.: Good Book Publishing, 1994.

Liehelt, Robert A. *Straight Talk About Alcoholism.* New York: Pharos Books, 1992.

Powter, Susan. *Sober—and Staying That Way: The Missing Link in the Cure for Alcoholism.* New York: Simon & Schuster, 1997.

Rosenberg, Maxine B. *Not My Family: Sharing the Truth About Alcoholism.* New York: Bradbury Press, 1988.

St. Clair, Harvey R. *Recognizing Alcoholism and Its Effects: A Mini-Guide.* New York: Karger, 1991.

Varley, Chris. *Alcoholism.* New York: M. Cavendish, 1994.

Alternative therapies (See COMPLEMENTARY THERAPIES; MIND/BODY CONNECTIONS.)

Alzheimer's disease

Davies, Helen D. *Alzheimer's: The Answers You Need.* Forest Knolls, Calif.: Elder Books, 1998.

Medina, John. *What You Need to Know About Alzheimer's.* Oakland, Calif.: New Harbinger, 1999.

Reekum, Robert van, Martine Simard, and Karl Farcnik. "Diagnosis of dementia and treatment of Alzheimer's disease." *Canadian Family Physician* 45 (April 1999): 945–952.

Warner, Mark L. *The Complete Guide to Alzheimer-Proofing Your Home.* West Lafayette, Ind.: Purdue University Press, 1998.

Anorexia nervosa (See EATING DISORDERS.)

Anxiety and anxiety disorders (See also PHOBIAS; OBSESSIVE-COMPULSIVE DISORDER; POSTTRAUMATIC STRESS DISORDER.)

Agras, M. W. *Panic: Facing Fears, Phobias, and Anxiety.* New York: W. H. Freeman, 1985.

Barlow, D. H. *Anxiety and Its Disorders: The Nature and Treatment of Anxiety and Panic.* New York: The Guilford Press, 1988.

Barlow, D. H., and J. A. Cerny. *The Psychological Treatment of Panic.* New York: The Guilford Press, 1988.

Barlow, D. H., and Michael Craske. *Mastery of Your Anxiety and Panic II.* Albany, N.Y.: Graywind Publications, 1994.

Bassett, Lucinda. *From Panic to Power.* New York: HarperCollins, 1995.

Beck, Aaron. *Anxieties and Phobias.* New York: Basic Books, 1985.

Bourne, Edmund J. *The Anxiety and Phobia Workbook.* Oakland, Calif.: New Harbinger, 1990.

Doctor, Ronald M., Ph.D., and Ada P. Kahn, Ph.D. *Encyclopedia of Phobias, Fears, and Anxieties.* 2d ed. New York: Facts On File, 2000.

Feniger, Mani. *Journey from Anxiety to Freedom: Moving Beyond Panic and Phobias and Learning to Trust Yourself.* Rocklin, Calif.: Prima Pub., 1997.

Gold, Mark S. *The Good News About Panic, Anxiety & Phobias.* New York: Bantam Books, 1990.

Gorman, J. M., M. R. Leibowitz, and D. F. Klein. *Panic Disorders and Agoraphobia.* Kalamazoo, Mich.: Current Concepts in Medicine, 1984.

Marks, Isaac Meyer. *Living with Fear.* New York: McGraw-Hill, 1980.

———. *Fears, Phobias, and Rituals: Panic, Anxiety, and Their Disorders.* New York, Oxford: Oxford University Press, 1987.

Nardo, Don. *Anxiety and Phobias.* New York: Chelsea House, 1992.

Ornstein, Robert, and David S. Sobel. "Calming Anxiety, Phobias and Panic." *Mental Medicine Update,* Vol. III, No. 3, 1994.

Ross, Jerilyn. *Triumph Over Fear: A Book of Help and Hope for People with Anxiety, Panic Attacks, and Phobias.* New York: Bantam Books, 1994.

Swedo, Susan, and H. L. Leonard. *It's Not All in Your Head.* New York: HarperCollins, 1996.

Warneke, Lorne. "Anxiety Disorders: Focus on Obsessive–Compulsive Disorder." *Canadian Family Physician,* Vol. 39, July 1993.

Arthritis

Brewerton, Derrick. *All About Arthritis: Past, Present, Future.* Cambridge, Mass.: Harvard University Press, 1992.

Cook, Allan R. *Arthritis Sourcebook.* Detroit: Omnigraphics, 1999.

Eisenstein, Phillis. *Overcoming the Pain of Inflammatory Arthritis.* Garden City Park, N.Y.: Avery Publishing Group, 1997.

Lorig, Kate. *Living a Healthy Life with Chronic Conditions: Self-management of Heart Disease, Arthritis, Stroke, Diabetes, Asthma, Bronchitis, Emphysema & Others.* Palo Alto, Calif.: Bull Publishing Company, 1994.

Lorig, Kate, and James Fries. *Arthritis Helpbook,* 3rd ed. Reading, Mass.: Addison-Wesley, 1990.

McCarty, Daniel J., and William J. Koopman, eds. *Arthritis and Allied Conditions: A Textbook of Rheumatology.* Philadelphia: Lea & Febiger, 1993.

Trien, Susan F., and David Pisetsky. *The Duke University Medical Center Book of Arthritis.* New York: Fawcett, 1992.

Asthma

Adams, Francis V. *The Asthma Sourcebook: Everything You Need to Know.* Los Angeles, Chicago: Lowell House, Contemporary Books, 1998.

Astor, Stephen. *What's New in Allergy and Asthma: New Developments and How They Help You Overcome Allergy and Asthma.* Mountain View, Calif.: Two A's Industries, 1996.

Firshein, Richard. *Reversing Asthma: Reduce Your Medications with This Revolutionary New Program.* New York: Warner Books, 1996.

Freedman, Michael R. *Living Well with Asthma.* New York: Guilford Press, 1998.

Hyde, Margaret O., and Elizabeth H. Forsyth. *Living with Asthma.* New York: Walker, 1995.

Stalmatski, Alexander. *Freedom from Asthma: The Revolutionary 5-Day Treatment for Healing Asthma With the Breath Connection Program.* New York: Three Rivers Press, 1999.

Attention deficit/hyperactivity disorder

Barkley, Russell. *Attention Deficit Hyperactivity Disorder: A Handbook for Diagnosis and Treatment.* New York: Guilford Press, 1990.
Connelly, Elizabeth Russell. *Conduct Unbecoming: Hyperactivity, Attention Deficit, and Disruptive Behavior Disorders.* Philadelphia: Chelsea House Publishers, 1999.
Hallowell, Edward M., and J. J. Ratey. *Driven to Distraction.* New York: Pantheon, 1994.
———. *Answers to Distraction.* New York: Pantheon, 1995.
Hartmann, Thom, and Janie Bowman, eds. *Think Fast! The ADD Experience.* Grass Valley, Calif.: Underwood Books, 1996.
Ingersoll, Barbara D. *Daredevils and Daydreamers: New Perspectives on Attention Deficit/Hyperactivity Disorder.* New York: Doubleday, 1998.
Sears, William. *The A.D.D. Book: New Understandings, New Approaches to Parenting Your Child.* Boston: Little Brown, 1998.
Silver, Larry B. *Dr. Larry Silver's Advice to Parents on Attention Deficit Hyperactivity Disorder.* New York: Times Books, 1999.
Umansky, Warren. *ADD: Helping Your Child.* New York: Warner Books, 1994.

Biofeedback

Basmajian, John V., ed. *Biofeedback: Principles and Practices for Clinicians.* Baltimore: Williams Wilkins, 1983.
Brown, Barbara. *Stress and the Art of Biofeedback.* New York: Harper & Row, 1977.
Olton, D. S., and A. R. Noonberg. *Biofeedback: Clinical Applications in Behavioral Medicine.* Englewood Cliffs, N.J.: Prentice-Hall, 1980.
Soroka, George F. *Twelve Steps to Biofeedback.* Demarest, N.J.: Ariel Starr Productions, 1998.

Blood and needle phobia

Hamilton, James G. "Needle Phobia: A Neglected Diagnosis." *The Journal of Family Practice* 41, no. 2, August 1995, 169–175.
Hellstrom, Kerstin, Jan Fellenius, and Lars-Goran Ost. "One Versus Five Sessions of Applied Tension in the Treatment of Blood Phobia." *Behavior Research Therapy* 34, no. 2 (1996): 101–112.
Kleinknecht, Ronald A., Robert M. Thorndike, and Marilyn M. Walls. "Factorial Dimensions and Correlates of Blood, Injury, Injection and Related Medical Fears: Cross Validation ot the Medical Fear Survey." *Behavior Research Therapy* 34, no. 4 (1996): 323–331.
Mavissakalina, Matig R., and Robert F. Prien, eds. "Blood Phobia" in *Long Term Treatments of Anxiety Disorders.* Washington, D.C.: American Psychiatric Press, Inc., 1996.

Cancer

Anderson, Greg. *Cancer: 50 Essential Things to Do.* New York: Plume, 1999.
Dollinger, Malin, Ernest H. Rosenbaum, and Greg Cable. *Everyone's Guide to Cancer Therapy.* Kansas City, Mo.: Andrews and McMeel, 1991.
Dreifuss-Kattan, Esther. *Cancer Stories; Creativity and Self-Repair.* Hillsdale, N.J.: Analytic Press, Inc., 1990.

Fiore, Neil A. *The Road Back to Health: Coping with the Emotional Aspects of Cancer,* rev.ed. Berkeley, Calif.: Celestial Arts, 1991.

Hersh, Stephen P. *Beyond Miracles: Living With Cancer: Inspirational and Practical Advice for Patients and Their Families.* Lincolnwood, Ill.: Contemporary Books, 1998.

McAllister, Robert M., S. T. Horowitz, and R. T. Gilden. *Cancer.* New York: Basic Books, 1993.

Sontag, Susan. *Illness as Metaphor and AIDS and its Metaphors.* New York: Doubleday, 1990.

Temoshok, Lydia and Henry Dreher. *The Type C Connection: The Behavioral Links to Cancer and Your Health.* New York: Random House, 1992.

Terkel, Susan Neiburg, and Marlene Lupiloff-Brass. *Understanding Cancer.* New York: F. Watts, 1993.

Childhood anxieties, fears and phobias

Eisen, Andrew R., Christopher A. Kearney, and Charles E. Schafer. *Clinical Handbook of Anxiety Disorders in Children and Adolescents.* Northvale, N.J.: Jason Aronson Inc., 1994.

Husain, Syed Arshad, Jyotsna Nair, William Holcomb et al. "Stress Reactions of Children and Adolescents in War and Siege Conditions." *American Journal of Psychiatry,* December 1998: 155–162.

King, Neville J., Viv Clowes-Hollins, and Thomas H. Ollendick. "The etiology of childhood dog phobia." *Behavior Research Therapy* 35, no. 1 (1997): 77.

Last, C. G., and C. C. Straus. "School Refusal and Anxiety-Disordered Children and Adolescence." *Journal of the American Academy of Childhood and Adolescent Pyschology* 29, 1990: 31–35.

Muris, Peter, Harald Merckelbach, and Ron Collaris. "Common Childhood Fears and Their Origins." *Behavior Research Therapy* 35, no. 10 (1997): 929–937.

Turecki, Stanley. *The Emotional Problems of Normal Children.* New York: Bantam, 1994.

Complementary therapies (See also MIND/BODY CONNECTIONS.)

Bensky, Dan, and Andres Gamble. *Chinese Herbal Medicine, Materia Medica.* Seattle, Wash.: Eastlands, 1986.

Bloomfield, Frena. *Chinese Beliefs.* London: Arrow Books, 1983.

Christi, Hakim. *The Traditional Healer's Handbook: A Classic Guide to the Medicine of Avicenna.* Rochester, Vt.: Healing Arts Press, 1991.

Eisenberg, David. *Encounters with Qi: Exploring Chinese Medicine.* New York: Norton, 1985.

Eisenberg, D., et al. "Unconventional Medicine in the United States: Prevalence, Costs, and Patterns of Use." *New England Journal of Medicine* 328 (1993): 246–252.

Facklam, Howard. *Alternative Medicine: Cures or Myths?* New York: Twenty-First Century Books, 1996.

Feldenkrais, Moshe. *Awareness Through Movement.* New York: Harper & Row, 1977.

Fradet, Brian. *Stress, Anxiety and Depression/The Natural Medicine Collective.* New York: Dell Publishing, 1995.

Frawley, David. *Ayurvedic Healing: A Comprehensive Guide.* Salt Lake City, Utah: Passage Press, 1989.

———— and Vasant Lad. *The Yoga of Herbs: An Ayurvedic Guide to Herbal Medicine.* Santa Fe., N. Mex.: Lotus Press, 1986.

Gordon, James S. *Manifesto for a New Medicine: Your Guide to Healing Partnerships and Wise Use of Alternative Therapies.* Reading, Mass.: Addison-Wesley Publishing Company, 1996.

Krieger, D. *Therapeutic Touch: How to Use Your Hands to Help or to Heal.* Englewood Cliffs, N.J.; Prentice Hall, 1979.

Lad, Dr. Vasant. *Ayurveda: The Science of Self-Healing—A Practical Guide.* Santa Fe, N. Mex.: Lotus Press, 1984.

McGill, Leonard. *The Chiropractor's Health Book: Simple Natural Exercises for Relieving Headaches, Tension and Back Pain.* New York: Crown Trade Paperbacks, 1995.

Morrison, Judith M. *The Book of Ayurveda.* New York: Fireside, 1995.

Morton, Mary, and Michael Morton. *5 Steps to Selecting the Best Alternative Medicine.* Novato, Calif.: New World Library, 1996.

Reid, Daniel. *The Complete Book of Chinese Health and Healing.* Boston: Shambhala, 1994.

Rondberg, Terry A. *Chiropractic First: The Fastest Growing Healthcare First . . . Before Drugs or Surgery.* Chandler, Ariz.: The Chiropractic Journal, 1996.

Ryman, Danielle. *Aromatherapy. The Complete Guide to Plant and Flower Essences for Health and Beauty.* New York: Bantam Books, 1991.

Sachs, Judith. *Nature's Prozac: Natural Therapies and Techniques to Rid Yourself of Anxiety, Depression, Panic Attacks & Stress.* Englewood Cliffs, N.J.: Prentice Hall, 1997.

Cross-cultural influences on phobias, fears, and anxieties

Friedman, Steven. *Cultural Issues in the Treatment of Anxiety.* New York: Guilford Press, 1997.

Pachter, Lee M. "Culture and Clinical Care: Folk Illness Beliefs and Behaviors and Their Implications for Health Care Delivery." *The Journal of the American Medical Association* 271, no. 9 (March 2, 1994): 690–694.

Dental fears

Getka, Eric J., and Carol R. Glass. "Behavioral and Cognitive-Behavioral Approaches to the Reduction of Dental Anxiety." *Behavior Therapy* 23 (1992): 433–448.

Jongh, Ad De, Peter Muris, Guusje Ter Horst et al. "One-session cognitive treatment of dental phobia: preparing dental phobics for treatment by restructuring negative cognitions." *Behavior Research Therapy* 33, no. 8 (1995): 947–954.

Walker, Edward A., Peter M. Milgrom, Philip Weinstein et al. "Assessing Abuse and Neglect and Dental Fear in Women." *The Journal of the American Dental Association* 127 (April 1998): 485–490.

Depression and manic-depressive disorder

Baskin, Valerie D. *When Words Are Not Enough: The Women's Prescription for Depression and Anxiety.* New York: Broadway Books, 1997.

Bloomfield, Harold H., and Peter McWilliams. *How to Heal Depression.* Los Angeles: Prelude Press, 1994.

Greist, John H., and James W. Jefferson. *Depression and Its Treatment: Help for the Nation's #1 Mental Problem,* rev. New York: Warner Books, 1992.

Healy, David. *The Anti-Depressant Era*. Cambridge, Mass.: Harvard University Press, 1997.

Kim, Henny H., ed. *Depression*. San Diego: Greenhaven Press, 1999.

Martin, Philip. *The Zen Path Through Depression*. San Francisco: HarperSanFrancisco, 1999.

Mondimore, Francis Mark. *Depression: The Mood Disease*. Baltimore: The Johns Hopkins University Press, 1993.

Quinn, Brian. *The Depression Sourcebook*. Los Angeles: Lowell House, 1997.

Reichenberg-Ullman, Judyth. *Prozac-free: Homeopathic Medications for Depression, Anxiety and Other Mental and Emotional Problems*. Rocklin, Calif.: Prima Health, 1999.

Robbins, Paul R. *Understanding Depression*. Jefferson, N.C.: McFarland & Co., 1993.

Rosen, David H. *Transforming Depression*. New York: G. P. Putnam's Sons, 1993.

Sanders, Pete. *Depression & Mental Health*. Brookfield, Conn.: Copper Beech Books, 1998.

Turkington, Carol. *Making the Prozac Decision: A Guide to Antidepressants*. Los Angeles: Contemporary Books, 1997.

Warneke, Lorne. "Management of Resistant Depression." *Canadian Family Physician* 42 (October 1996): 1973.

Whybrow, Peter C. *A Mood Apart: Depression, Mania and Other Afflictions of the Self*. New York: Basic Books, 1997.

Divorce (See MARRIAGE AND DIVORCE.)

Driving phobia

Ehlers, Anke, Stefan G. Hofmann, Christoph A. Herda et al. "Clinical Characteristics of Driving Phobia." *Journal of Anxiety Disorders* 8, no. 4 (1994): 323–339.

Eating disorders

Cassell, Dana K., and Donald H. Greaves, Ph.D. *Encyclopedia of Obesity and Eating Disorders*. 2d ed. New York: Facts On File, 2000.

Kinoy, Barbara P., ed. *Eating Disorders: New Directions in Treatment and Recovery*. New York: Columbia University Press, 1994.

Orbach, Susie. *Hunger Strike: An Anorexic's Struggle as a Metaphor for Our Age*. New York: Norton, 1986.

Sonder, Ben. *Eating Disorders: When Food Turns Against You*. New York: F. Watts, 1993.

Flying, fear of

Beckham, Jean C., Scott R. Vrana, Jack G. May et al. "Emotional Processing and Fear Measurement Synchrony as Indicators of Treatment Outome in Fear of Flying." *Journal of Behavior Therapy and Experimental Psychology* 21, no. 3 (1990): 153–162.

Brown, Duane. *Flying Without Fear*. Oakland, Calif.: New Harbinger Publications, 1996.

Hartman, Cherry. *The Fearless Flyer: How to Fly in Comfort and Without Trepidation*. Portland, Oreg.: Eighth Mountain Press, 1995.

McCarthy, Geoffrey W., and Kenneth D. Craig. "Flying Therapy for Flying Phobia." *Aviation, Space, and Environmental Medicine* 66, no. 12 (December 1995): 1179ff.

McNally, Richard J., and Christine E. Louro. "Fear of Flying in Agoraphobia and Simple Phobia: Distinguishing Features." *Journal of Anxiety Disorders* 6 (1992): 319–324.

Ost, Lars Goran, Mats Brandberg, and Tomas Alm. "One Versus Five Sessions of Exposure in the Treatment of Flying Phobia." *Behavior Research Therapy* 35, no. 11 (1997): 987–996.

Remington, John. *Avioanxiety Becomes Controlled: Now Fly Without Fear.* St. Louis, Mo.: Inner Marker to Growth, 1992.

Wilhelm, Frank H., and Walton T. Roth. "Clinical Characteristics of Flight Phobia." *Journal of Anxiety Disorders* 11, no. 3 (1997): 241–261.

Guided imagery (See also COMPLEMENTARY THERAPIES; MIND/BODY CONNECTIONS.)

Achterberg, Jeanne. *Imagery in Healing: Shamanism and Modern Medicine.* San Francisco, Calif.: Shambhala Publications, 1985.

Burns, David. *Feeling Good: The New Mood Therapy.* New York: Avon Books, 1992.

Epstein, Gerald. *Healing Visualizations, Creating Healing Through Imagery.* New York: Bantam Books, 1989.

Samuels, Michael. *Healing with the Mind's Eye.* New York: Random House, 1992.

Siegel, Bernie. *Love, Medicine and Miracles.* New York: Harper & Row, 1986.

———. *Peace, Love and Healing.* New York, Harper & Row, 1986.

Headaches

Blanchard, E. B., K. A. Appelbaum et al. "Placebo-controlled evaluation of abbreviated progressive muscle relaxation combined with cognitive therapy in the treatment of tension headache." *Journal of Consulting and Clinical Psychology* 58 (1990): 210–215.

Blanchard, E. B., N. L. Nicholson et al. "The role of regular home practice in the relaxation treatment of tension headache. *Journal of Consulting and Clinical Psychology* 59 (1991): 467–470.

Diamond, Seymour. *The Hormone Headache: New Ways to Prevent, Manage, and Treat Migraines and Other Headaches.* New York: Macmillan, 1995.

Finnigan, Jeffry. *Life Beyond Headaches.* Olympia, Wash.: Finnigan Clinic, 1999.

Hartnell, Agnes. *Migraine Headaches and the Foods You Eat: 200 Recipes for Relief.* Minneapolis: Chronimed, 1997.

Inlander, Charles B., and Porter Shimer. *Headaches: 47 Ways to Stop the Pain.* New York: Walker and Company, 1995.

Maas, Paula, and Deborah Mitchell. *The Natural Health Guide To Headache Relief: The Definitive Handbook of Natural Remedies For Treating Every Kind of Headache Pain.* New York: Pocket Books, 1997.

Minirth, Frank B., with Sandy Dengler. *The Headache Book.* Nashville, Tenn.: Nelson Publishers, 1994.

Solomon, Seymour, and Steven Fraccaro. *The Headache Book.* Yonkers, N.Y.: Consumer Reports Books, 1991.

Health, wellness, and stress

Benson, Herbert. *The Wellness Book: The Complete Guide to Maintaining Health and Treating Stress-Related Illness.* Secaucus, N. J.: Carol Publishing Group, 1992.

Bohm, David. *Wholeness and the Implicate Order.* London: Ark, 1980.

Campbell, Joseph. *The Inner Reaches of Outer Space.* New York: Alfred Van Der Marck, 1985.

Capra, Fritjof. *The Turning Point.* New York: Bantam, 1982.

Castenada, Carlos. *The Art of Dreaming.* New York: HarperCollins, 1993.

Dubos, Rene. *Mirage of Health.* New York: Anchor Books, 1959.

Hoffer, Eric. *The True Believer.* New York: Harper & Row, 1951.

Illich, Ivan. *Medical Nemesis: The Expropriation of Health.* New York: Pantheon, 1982.

Ornstein, Robert, and David Sobel. *The Healing Brain: Breakthrough Discoveries About How the Brain Keeps Us Healthy.* New York: Simon & Schuster, 1987.

Pelletier, Kenneth R. *Sound Mind, Sound Body: A Model for Lifelong Health.* New York: Simon & Schuster, 1994.

Peterson, Christopher, and Lisa M. Bossio. *Health and Optimism,* New York: Macmillan, 1991.

Strasburg, Kate, et al. *The Quest for Wholeness: An Annotated Bibliography in Patient-Centered Medicine.* Bolinas, Calif.: Commonweal, 1991.

Stutz, David, and Bernard Feder. *The Savvy Patient: How to Be an Active Participant in Your Medical Care.* Yonkers, N.Y.: Consumer Reports Books, 1990.

Weil, Andrew. *Eight Weeks to Optimum Health: Proven Program for Taking Full Advantage of Your Body's Healing Power.* New York: Alfred A. Knopf, 1997.

Williams, R. W., and V. Williams. *Anger Kills: 17 Strategies for Controlling the Hostility That Can Harm Your Health.* New York: Times Books, 1993.

Wolinsky, Stephen, *Quantum Consciousness: The Guide to Experiencing Quantum Psychology.* Norfolk, Conn.: Bramble Books, 1993.

Heart disease

Dembroski, T.M. et al. "Components of Hostility as Predictors of Sudden Death and Myocardial Infarction in the Multiple Risk Factor Intervention Trial." *Psychosomatic Medicine* 51 (1989): 514–522.

Kerman, D. Ariel. *The H.A.R.T. Program. Lower Your Blood Pressure Without Drugs.* New York: HarperCollins, 1992.

McGowan, Mary P. *Heart Fitness for Life: The Essential Guide to Preventing and Reversing Heart Disease.* New York: Oxford University Press, 1997.

Ornish, Dean. *Dr. Dean Ornish's Program for Reversing Heart Disease.* New York: Ballantine, 1992.

Sachs, Judith. *Natural Medicine for Heart Disease.* New York: Dell, 1997.

Skerritt, Paul W. "Anxiety and the heart—a historical review." *Psychological Medicine* 13 (1983): 17–25.

HIV (See ACQUIRED IMMUNODEFICIENCY SYNDROME.)

Holistic medicine (See COMPLEMENTARY THERAPIES; MIND/BODY CONNECTIONS.)

Hypnosis

Callahan, Jean. Hypnosis: Trick or Treatment?" *Health,* May 1997, pp. 52–58.

Caprio, Frank Samuel. *Healing Yourself With Self-Hypnosis.* Paramus, N.J.: Prentice Hall, 1998.

Erickson, M. H., and E. L. Rossi. *Hypnotherapy: An Exploratory Casebook.* New York: Irvington, 1979.

Hadley, Josie, and Carol Staudacher. *Hypnosis for Change.* Oakland, Calif.: New Harbinger Publications, Inc., 1996.

Haley, J. *Advanced Techniques of Hypnosis and Therapy: Selected Papers of Milton H. Erickson, M.D.* New York: Grune & Stratton, 1967.

Lankton, S. R., ed. *Ericksonian Hypnosis: Application, Preparation, and Research.* New York: Brunner/Mazel, 1988.

Immune system (See also PSYCHONEUROIMMUNOLOGY.)

Borysenko, M. "The Immune System: An Overview." *Annals of Behavioral Medicine* 9 (1987): 3–10.

Cohen, S., D. A. J. Tyrrell, and A. P. Smith. "Psychological Stress and Susceptibility to the Common Cold." *New England Journal of Medicine* 325 (1991): 606–612.

Herbert, Tracy B. "Stress and the immune system." *World Health,* March–April, 1994, pp. 4–5.

Locke, Steven, and Douglas Colligan. *The Healer Within.* New York: New American Library, 1986.

Marriage and divorce

Bray, James H. *Stepfamilies: Love, Marriage and Parenting in the First Decade.* New York: Broadway Books, 1998.

Briscoe, D. Stuart. *Marriage Matters! Growing Through the Differences and Surprises of Life Together.* Wheaton, Ill.: H. Shaw Publishers, 1994.

Conover, Kris. *Marriage Made Simple: Fifty Hints for Building Long-Lasting Love.* New York: Plume, 1999.

Gottman, John Mordechai. *Why Marriages Succeed or Fail: What You Can Learn From the Breakthrough Research to Make Your Marriage Last.* New York: Simon & Schuster, 1994.

Heyn, Dalma. *Marriage Shock: The Transformation of Women Into Wives.* New York: Villard, 1997.

Roleff, Tamara L., and Mary E. Williams, eds. *Marriage and Divorce.* San Diego: Greenhaven Press, 1997.

Simpson, Eileen B. *Late Love: A Celebration of Marriage after Fifty.* Boston: Houghton Mifflin, 1994.

Meditation (See also MINDFULNESS MEDITATION.)

Benson, Herbert. *The Relaxation Reponse.* New York: Avon Books, 1975.

———. *Beyond the Relaxation Response.* New York: Berkeley Press, 1985.

Borysenko, Joan, and J. Duscher. *On Wings of Light: Meditations for Awakening to the Source.* New York: Warner, 1992.

Chopra, Deepak. *Quantum Healing.* New York: Bantam, 1989.

———. *Creating Health: How to Wake Up the Body's Intelligence.* Boston: Houghton Mifflin, 1991.

———. *Unconditional Life.* New York: Bantam, 1992.

———. *Ageless Body, Timeless Mind.* New York: Crown, 1993.

———. *Creating Affluence: Wealth Consciousness in the Field of All Possibilities.* San Rafael, Calif.: New World Library, 1993.

Connor, Danny, with Michael Tse. *Qigong. Chinese Movement & Meditation for Health.* York Beach, Maine: Samuel Weiser, 1992.

Cousins, Norman. *The Healing Heart.* New York: Norton, 1983.

Denniston, Denish, and Peter McWilliams. *The TM Book: Transcendental Meditation, How to Enjoy the Rest of Your Life.* Allen Park, Mich.: Versemonger Press, 1975.

Dossey, L. *Space, Time and Medicine.* Boston: Shambhala, 1982.

———. *Meaning and Medicine: A Doctor's Tales of Breakthrough and Healing* New York: Bantam, 1991.

———. *Recovering the Soul.* New York: Bantam, 1989.

Dychtwald, K. *Bodymind.* Los Angeles: Tarcher, 1986.

Goleman, Daniel. *The Meditative Mind.* Los Angeles: Tarcher, 1988.

Levey, Daniel. *The Fine Arts of Relaxation, Concentration and Meditation.* London: Wisdom Publications, 1987.

Mahesh Yogi, Maharishi. *Science of Being and Art of Living: Transcendental Meditation.* New York: Meridian, 1995.

Nuernberger, Phil. *Freedom From Stress.* Honesdale, Pa.: The Himalayan International Institute of Yoga Science and Philosophy, 1985.

Trungpa, Chogyam. *Shambhala: The Sacred Path of the Warrior.* Boston: Shambhala, 1984.

Mindfulness meditation (insight meditation)

Goldstein, Joseph; and Jack Kornfield. *Seeking the Heart of Wisdom: The Path of Insight Meditation.* Boston: Shambhala, 1987.

Hanh, Thich Nhat. *Being Peace.* Berkeley, Calif.: Parallax Press, 1987.

———, *The Miracle of Mindfulness: A Manual of Meditation.* Boston: Beacon Press, 1976.

———. *The Sun My Heart.* Berkeley, Calif.: Parallax Press, 1988.

Kabat-Zinn, Jon. *Full Catastrophe Living: Using the Wisdom of Your Body and Mind to Face Stress, Pain and Illness.* New York: Delacorte Press, 1991.

———. *Wherever You Go, There You Are,* New York: Hyperion, 1994.

Levine, Stephen. *A Gradual Awakening.* Garden City, N.Y.: Anchor/Doubleday, 1979.

Suzuki, Shunryu. *Zen Mind, Beginner's Mind.* New York: Weatherhill, 1986.

Mind/body connections (See also COMPLEMENTARY THERAPIES; PSYCHONEUROIMMUNOLOGY.)

Benson, Herbert. *The Relaxation Reponse.* New York: Avon Books, 1975.

———. *Beyond the Relaxation Response.* New York: Berkeley Press, 1985.

Borysenko, Joan. *Minding the Body, Mending the Mind.* New York: Bantam, 1988.

———. *Guilt Is the Teacher, Love Is the Lesson.* New York: Warner, 1991.

Cannon, Walter. *The Wisdom of the Body.* New York: Norton, 1939.

Chopra, Deepak. *Perfect Health.* New York: Harmony Books, 1990.

———. *Quantum Healing: Exploring the Frontiers of Mind/Body Medicine.* New York: Bantam Books, 1989.

Cousins, Norman. *Head First: The Biology of Hope and the Healing Power of the Human Spirit.* New York: Viking Penguin, 1990.

———. *Anatomy of an Illness as Perceived by the Patient.* New York: Norton, 1979.

———. *The Healing Heart.* New York: Norton, 1983.

Dienstfrey, Harris. *Where the Mind Meets the Body.* New York: HarperCollins, 1991.

Dossey, Larry. *Space, Time and Medicine.* Boston: Shambhala, 1982.

Goleman, Daniel, and Joel Gurin, eds. *Mind Body Medicine: How to Use Your Mind For Better Health.* Yonkers, N.Y.: Consumer Reports Books, 1993.

Gordon, James S., et al. *Mind, Body and Health: Toward an Integral Medicine.* New York: Human Sciences Press, 1984.

Locke, Steven E., and Douglas Colligan. *The Healer Within: The New Medicine of Mind and Body.* New York: Dutton, 1986.

Moyers, B. *Healing and the Mind.* New York: Doubleday, 1993.

Ornstein, Robert, and David Sobel. *The Healing Brain.* New York: Simon & Schuster, 1988.

Pelletier, Kenneth R. *Mind as Healer, Mind as Slayer,* rev. ed. New York: Delacorte, 1992.

———. *Sound Mind, Sound Body: A New Model for Lifelong Health.* New York: Simon & Schuster, 1994.

———. *Holistic Medicine: From Stress to Optimum Health.* Magnolia, Mass.: Peter Smith, 1984.

Siegel, Bernie. *Love, Medicine and Miracles.* New York: Harper & Row, 1986.

———. *Peace, Love and Healing.* New York: Harper & Row, 1989.

Obsessive-Compulsive disorder (See also ANXIETY AND ANXIETY DISORDERS.)

Alper, Gerald. *The Puppeteers: Studies of Obsessive Control.* New York: Fromm International Publishing Corporation, 1994.

DeSilva, Padmal. *Obsessive-Compulsive Disorder: The Facts.* Oxford, New York: Oxford University Press, 1998.

Gravitz, Herbert L. *Obsessive Compulsive Disorder: New Help for the Family.* Santa Barbara, Calif.: Healing Visions Press, 1998.

Kahn, Ada P. "OCD Said to Be Underdiagnosed in Minority Population." *Psychiatric News* 26, no. 14 (July 19, 1991): 5.

Livingston, B. *Learning to Live With Obsessive Compulsive Disorder.* Milford, Conn.: OCD Foundation, 1989.

Rappaport, Judith. *The Boy Who Couldn't Stop Washing: The Experience and Treatment of Obsessive-Compulsive Disorder.* New York: Dutton, 1989.

Reyes, Karen. "Obsessive-Compulsive Disorder: There is Help." *Modern Maturity,* November–December 1995, p. 78.

Pain

Bogan, Meg. *The Path of Pain Control.* Boston: Houghton Mifflin, 1982.

Corey, David, with Stan Solomon. *Pain: Free Yourself for Life.* New York: NAL-Dutton, 1989.

Hardy, Paul A. J. *Chronic Pain Management: The Essentials.* London: Greenwich Medical Media, 1997.

Singh Khalsa, Dharma. *The Pain Cure: The Proven Medical Program That Helps End Your Chronic Pain.* New York: Warner Books, 1999.

Stacy, Charles B. et al. *The Fight Against Pain.* Yonkers, N.Y.: Consumer Reports Books, 1992.

Panic attacks and panic disorder (See ANXIETY AND ANXIETY DISORDERS.)

Performance anxiety

Dunkel, Stuart Edward. *The Audition Process: Anxiety Management and Coping Strategies.* Stuyvesant, N.Y.: Pendragon Press, 1989.

Moss, Robert. "Stage Fright Is Actors' Eternal Nemesis." *New York Times*, January 6, 1992, E2.

Salmon, P. G. "A Psychological Perspective on Musical Performance Anxiety: A Review of the Literature." *Medical Problems of Performing Artists* (March 1990): 2–11.

Salmon, Paul. *Notes From the Green Room: Coping With Stress and Anxiety in Musical Performance*. New York: Lexington Books, 1992.

Steptoe, A., and H. Fidler. "Stage Fright and Orchestral Musicians: A Study of Cognitive Behavioral Strategies and Performance Anxiety." *British Journal of Psychology* 78 (1987): 241–249.

Wesner, R. B., R. Noyes Jr., and T. L. Davis. "The Occurrence of Performance Anxiety Among Musicians." *Journal of Affective Disorders* 18 (1990): 177–185.

Pharmacological approach (See also DEPRESSION AND MANIC-DEPRESSIVE DISORDER; PHOBIAS; ANXIETY AND ANXIETY DISORDERS.)

Appleton, William S. *Prozac and the New Antidepressants: What You Need to Know About Prozac, Zoloft, Paxil, Luvox, Wellbutrin, Effexor, Serzone, and More*. New York: Plume, 1997.

Davidson, J. R. T., S. M. Ford, R. D. Smith, and N. L. S. Potts. "Long-term Treatment of Social Phobia Clonazapam," *Journal of Clinical Psychiatry* 52, no. 11 (1991 suppl.): 16–20.

Fieve, Ronald R. *Prozac*. New York: Avon, 1994.

Liebowitz, M. R., F. R. Schneier, E. Hollander et al. "Treatment of Social Phobia with Drugs Other Than Benzodiazepines." *Journal of Clinical Psychiatry* 52 (1991 suppl.): 10–15.

Monroe, Judy. *Antidepressants*. Springfield, N.J.: Enslow Publishers, 1997.

Turkington, Carol. *Making the Prozac Decision: A Guide to Antidepressants*. Los Angeles: Lowell House, 1997.

Wilkinson, Beth. *Drugs and Depression*. New York: Rosen Publishing Group, 1994.

Phobias (See also ANXIETY AND ANXIETY DISORDERS.)

Bourne, Edward. *The Anxiety & Phobia Workbook*. Oakland, Calif.: New Harbinger Publications, 1995.

Cheek, J. *Conquering Shyness*. New York: Dell Publishing, 1989.

Doctor, Ronald M., and Ada P. Kahn. *Encyclopedia of Phobias, Fears, and Anxieties*. New York: Facts On File, 1989.

DuPont, Robert L. *Phobia: A Comprehensive Summary of Modern Treatments*. New York: Brunner/Mazel, 1982.

Jampolsky, Gerald. *Love Is Letting Go of Fear*. New York: Bantam Books, 1979.

Marks, Isaac M. *Living with Fear*. New York: McGraw-Hill, 1980.

———. *Fears, Phobias, and Rituals*. Oxford: Oxford University Press, 1987.

Marshall, John R. *Social Phobia: From Shyness to Stage Fright*. New York: Basic Books, 1994.

Markway, B. G. et al. *Dying of Embarrassment: Help for Social Anxiety and Phobias*. Oakland, Calif.: New Harbinger, 1992.

Monroe, Judy. *Phobias: Everything You Wanted to Know, But Were Afraid to Ask*. Springfield, N.J.: Enslow Publishers, 1996.

Nardo, Don. *Anxiety and Phobias.* New York: Chelsea House, 1992.

Uhde, T. W., M. E. Tancer, B. Black, and T. M. Brown. "Phenomenology and Neurobiology of Social Phobias: Comparison with Panic Disorder." *Journal of Clinicago Psychology* 52 (November 1991): 31–40.

Zane, Manuel D., and Harry Milt. *Your Phobia.* Washington, D.C.: American Psychiatric Press, Inc., 1984.

Posttraumatic stress disorder (PTSD) (See also ANXIETY AND ANXIETY DISORDERS.)

Catherall, Donald Roy. *Back from the Brink: A Family Guide to Overcoming Traumatic Stress.* New York: Bantam Books, 1992.

Egendorf, A. *Healing from the War: Trauma and Transformation after Vietnam.* New York: Houghton Mifflin, 1985.

Eitinger, Leo, and Robert Krell, with Miriam Rieck. *The Psychological and Medical Effects of Concentration Camps and Related Persecutions on Survivors of the Holocaust.* Vancouver: University of British Columbia Press, 1985.

Eth, S., and R. S. Pynoos. *Post-Traumatic Stress Disorder in Children.* Washington, D.C.: American Psychiatric Press, Inc., 1985.

Herman, Judith. *Trauma and Recovery.* New York: Basic Books, 1992.

Lindy, Jacob D. *Vietnam: A Casebook.* New York: Brunner/Mazel, 1987.

Peterson, Kirtland C., Maurice F. Prout, and Robert A. Schwarz. *Post-traumatic Stress Disorder: Clinician's Guide.* New York: Plenum Press, 1991.

Porterfield, Kay Marie. *Straight Talk About Post-Traumatic Stress Disorder: Coping with the Aftermath of Trauma.* New York: Facts On File, 1996.

Sonnenberg, S. M., A. S. Blank, and J. A. Talbott, eds. *The Trauma of War: Stress and Recovery in Vietnam Veterans.* Washington, D.C.: American Psychiatric Press, 1985.

Van der Kolk, B. A., ed. *Post-Traumatic Stress Disorder: Psychological and Biological Sequelae.* Washington, D.C.: American Psychiatric Press, Inc. 1996.

Psychology, contemporary (See also COMPLEMENTARY THERAPIES; MIND/BODY CONNECTIONS; PSYCHONEUROIMMUNOLOGY.)

Berne, Eric. Games People Play. New York: Grove Press, 1964.

Borysenko, Joan. *Guilt Is the Teacher, Love Is the Lesson.* New York: Warner Books, 1990.

Bradshaw, John. *Bradshaw On: The Family.* Deerfield Beach, Fla.: Health Communications, Inc., 1988.

———. *Healing the Shame That Binds You.* Deerfield Beach, Fla.: Health Communications, Inc., 1988.

Cousins, Norman. *The Healing Heart.* New York: Avon Books, 1984.

Csikzentmihalyi, Mihaly. *Flow: The Psychology of Optimal Experience.* New York: HarperCollins Perennial, 1991.

Peck, M. Scott. *The Road Less Traveled.* New York: Simon & Schuster, 1978.

Wolinsky, Stephen H. *Trances People Live: Healing Approaches in Quantum Psychology.* Norfolk, Conn.: Bramble Co., 1991.

Psychoneuroimmunology

Ader, Rovert, D. Felton, and N. Cohen, eds. *Psychoneuroimmunology*, 2nd ed. San Diego: Academic Press, 1990.

Bohm, David. *Wholeness and the Implicate Order,* London: Routledge & Kegan Paul, 1980.

Cousins, Norman. *Anatomy of an Illness.* New York: Bantam Books, 1981.

Kiecolt-Glaser, J. K., and R. Glaser. "Psychoneuroimmunology: Can Psychological Interventions Modulate Immunity?" *Journal of Consulting and Clinical Psychology,* 60 (1992): 569–75.

Relaxation

Agras, W. S., C. B. Taylor, H. C. Kraemer, M. A. Southam, J. A. Schneider. "Relaxation training for essential hypertension at the work site: II. The poorly controlled hypertensive." *Psychosomatic Medicine* 49 (1987): 264–273.

Benson, Herbert. *The Relaxation Response.* New York: Avon Books, 1975.

———. *Beyond the Relaxation Response.* New York: Berkeley Press, 1985.

———. *Your Maximum Mind.* New York: Times Books, 1987.

Benson, Herbert, Eileen M. Stuart, and staff of the Mind/Body Medical Institute. *The Wellness Book: The Comprehensive Guide to Maintaining Health and Treating Stress-Related Illness.* New York: Carol, 1992.

Blumenfeld, Larry, ed. *The Big Book of Relaxation: Simple Techniques to Control the Excess Stress in Your Life.* Roslyn, N.Y.: Relaxation Company, 1994.

Davis, Martha, Elizabeth Robbins Eshelman, and Matthew McKay. *The Relaxation and Stress Reduction Workbook.* Oakland, Calif.: New Harbinger Publications, 1995.

Davis, M., and E. R. Eshelman, and M. McKay. *The Relaxation and Stress Reduction Workbook.* Oakland, Calif.: New Harbinger, 1995.

Self-esteem

Dobson, James C. *The New Hide and Seek: Building Self-Esteem in Your Child.* Grand Rapids, Mich.: Fleming H. Revell, 1999.

Hazelton, Deborah M. *Solving the Self-Esteem Puzzle.* Deerfield Beach, Fla.: Health, Communications, 1991.

Hillman, Carolynn. *Recovery of Your Self-Esteem.* New York: Simon & Schuster, 1992.

Johnson, Carol. *Self-Esteem Comes In All Sizes.* New York: Doubleday, 1995.

Kahn, Ada P., and Sheila Kimmel. *Empower Yourself: Every Woman's Guide to Self-Esteem.* New York: Avon Books, 1997.

Lindenfield, Gael. *Self-Esteem.* New York: Harper Paperbacks, 1997.

McKay, Matthew. *The Self-Esteem Companion: Simple Exercises to Help You Challenge Your Inner Critic and Celebrate Your Personal Strengths.* Oakland, Calif.: New Harbinger Publications, 1999.

Minchinton, Jerry. *Maximum Self-Esteem: The Handbook for Reclaiming Your Sense of Self-Worth.* Yanzant, Miss.: Arnford House Publishers, 1993.

Prato, Louis. *Be Your Own Best Friend: How to Achieve Greater Self-Esteem, Health, and Happiness.* New York: Berkeley Books, 1994.

Steinem, Gloria. *Revolution From Within: A Book of Self-Esteem.* Boston: Little, Brown and Co., 1992.

Smoking (See also ADDICTIONS.)

Buckley, Christopher. *Thank You for Smoking*. New York: Random House, 1994.
Liesges, Robert C., and Margaret DeBon. *How Women Can Finally Stop Smoking*. Alameda, Calif.: Hunter House, 1994.
Mowat, David L., Darlene Mecredy, Frank Lee et al. "Family Physicians and Smoking Cessation." *Canadian Family Physician* 42 (October 1996): 1946.
Rogers, Jacquelyn. *You Can Stop Smoking*. New York: Pocket Books, 1995.
Pietrusza, David. *Smoking*. San Diego: Lucent Books, 1997.
Sanders, Pete, and Steve Myers. *Smoking*. Brookfield, Conn.: Copper Beech Books, 1996.

Social phobias (See ANXIETY and ANXIETY DISORDERS; PHOBIAS.)

Social support, support groups, and self-help

Kahn, Ada P. "Psychosocial Support Influences Survival of Cancer Patient." *Psychiatric News*, October 1991.
Kreiner, Anna. *Everything You Need to Know About Creating Your Own Support System*. New York: The Rosen Publishing Group, 1996.
Pilisuk, Marc, and Susan H. Parks. *The Healing Web: Social Networks and Human Survival*, Hanover, N.H.: University Press of New England, 1986.
Spiegel, David. *Living Beyond Limits*. New York: Times Books, 1993.
White, Barbara J., and Edward J. Madara. *The Self-Help Sourcebook: Finding & Forming Mutual Aid Self-Help Groups*. Denville, N.J.: American Self-Help Clearinghouse, St. Clare's-Riverside Medical Center, 1992.

Spider phobia

Fredrikson, Mats, Peter Annas, and Gustav Wik. "Parental History, Aversive Exposure and the Development of Snake and Spider Phobia in Women." *Behavior Research Therapy* 35, no.1 (1997): 23–28.
Kindt, Merel, Jos F. Brosschot, and Peter Muris. "Spider Phobia Questionnaire for Children (SPQ-C): A Pyschometric Study and Normative Data." *Behavior Research Therapy* 34, no. 3 (1996): 277–282.
Kirkby, Kenneth C., Ross G. Menzies, Brett A. Daniels et al. "Aetiology of spider phobia: classificatory differences between two origins instruments." *Behavior Research Therapy* 33, no. 8 (1955): 955–958.
Ost, Lars-Goran. "One-Session Group Treatment of Spider Phobia." *Behavior Research Therapy* 34, no. 9 (1996): 707–715.

Stress and stress management

Brammer, L. M. *How to Cope with Life Transitions: The Challenge of Personal Change*. New York: Hemisphere Publishing, 1991.
Bridges, W. *Managing Transitions: Making the Most of Change*. Reading, Mass.: Wesley, 1991.
Colino, Stacey. "How to Find Your Stress Hot Spots." *McCalls's*, September 1994, p. 38.
Cuban, Barbara. "Getting the best of stress." *Diabetes Forecast*, June 1989, 43.
Eliot, Robert S. *From Stress to Strength: How to Lighten Your Load and Save Your Life*. New York: Bantam Books, 1994.

Faelten, Sharon, and David Diamond. *Take Control of Your Life: A Complete Guide to Stress Relief.* Emmaus, Pa.: Rodale Press, 1988.

Flint, Robert S. *From Stress to Strength: How to Lighten Your Load and Save Your Life.* New York: Bantam Books, 1994.

Gordon, James S. *Stress Management.* New York: Chelsea House Publishers, 1990.

Hafen, B. Q., K. J. Frandsen, K. J. Karren, and K. R. Hooker. *The Health Effects of Attitudes, Emotions and Relationships.* Provo, Utah: EMS Associates, 1992.

Kahn, Ada P. *The A–Z of Stress: A Sourcebook for Facing Everyday Challenges.* New York: Facts On File, Inc., 1998.

Lark, Susan M. *Anxiety and Stress: A Self-Help Program.* Los Altos, Calif.: Westchester Publishing Company, 1993.

Lehrer, Paul M., and Robert L. Woolfolk, eds. *Principles and Practice of Stress Management,* 2nd ed. New York: The Guilford Press, 1993.

Maddi, Salvatore, and Suzanne Kobasa. *The Hardy Executive: Health Under Stress.* Homewood, Ill.: Dow Jones-Irwin, 1984.

Miller, Lyle H., and Alma Dell Smith. *The Stress Solution: An Action Plan to Manage the Stress in Your Life.* New York: Pocket Books, 1993.

Ornish, Dean. *Stress, Diet, and Your Heart.* New York: Holt, Rinehart & Winston, 1983.

Padus, Emrika, ed. *The Complete Guide to Your Emotions and Your Health.* Emmaus, Pa.: Rodale Press, 1992.

Patel, Chandra. *The Complete Guide to Stress Management.* New York: Plenum Press, 1991.

Sapolsky, Robert M. *Why Zebras Don't Get Ulcers.* New York: W.H. Freeman & Company, 1994.

Seaward, Brian Luke. *Managing Stress: Principles and Strategies for Health and Wellbeing; Managing Stress: A Creative Journal.* Boston: Jones and Bartless Publishers, 1994.

Selye, Hans. *Stress Without Distress.* New York: Lippincott, 1974.

———. *The Stress of Life,* rev. ed. New York: McGraw Hill Book Company, 1978.

Snyder, Solomon H., ed. *Stress Management.* New York: Chelsea House Publishers, 1990.

Visualization (See GUIDED IMAGERY.)

Women

Berg, Barbara J. *The Crisis of the Working Mother.* New York: Summit Books, 1986.

Freudenberger, Herbert, and Gail North. *Women's Burnout: How to Spot It, How to Reverse It, and How to Prevent It.* Garden City, N.Y.: Doubleday & Company, Inc., 1985.

Kahn, Ada P. "Women and Stress." *Sacramento Medicine* 46, no. 9 (September 1995): 16–17.

Lerner, Harriet Goldhor. *The Dance of Anger.* New York: Harper & Row, 1985.

———. *The Dance of Intimacy.* New York: Harper & Row, 1989.

Long, B. C., and C. J. Haney, "Coping strategies for working women: Aerobic exercise and relaxation interventions." *Behavior Therapy* 19 (1988): 75–83.

Powell, J. Robin. *The Working Woman's Guide to Managing Stress.* Englewood Cliffs, N.J.: Prentice Hall, 1994.

Siress, Ruth Hermann. *Working Women's Communications Survival Guide: How to Present Your Ideas With Impact, Clarity, and Power and Get the Recognition You Deserve.* Englewood Cliffs, N.J.: Prentice Hall, 1994.

Weinstock, Lorna, and Eleanor Gilman. *Overcoming Panic Disorder: A Woman's Guide.* Chicago: Contemporary Books, 1998.

Witkin, Georgia. *The Female Stress Syndrome: How to Become Stress-Wise in the '90s.* New York: Newmarket Press, 1991.

Workplace

Adams, Scott. *The Dilbert Principle: A Cubicle's-Eye View of Bosses, Meetings, Management Fads and Other Workplace Afflictions.* New York: HarperBusiness, 1997.

Arrobe, Tanya. "Reducing the cost of stress: an organizational model" *Personnel Review* 19: (winter, 1990).

Brown, Stephanie. *The Hand Book: Preventing Computer Injury.* New York: Ergonomne, 1993.

Frankenhaeuser, Marianne. "The Psychophysiology of Workload, Stress, and Health: Comparison Between the Sexes." *Annals of Behavioral Medicine,* 13, no. 4: 197–204.

Karasek, Robert, and Tores Theorell. *Health Work: Stress, Productivity, and the Reconstruction of Working Life.* New York: Basic Books, 1990.

Leana, Carrie R., and Daniel C. Feldman. *Coping with Job Loss: How Individuals, Organizations and Communities Respond to Layoffs.* New York: Lexington Books, 1992.

Meyer, G. J. *Executive Blues: Down and Out in Corporate America.* New York: Franklin Square Press, 1997.

Murphy, Lawrence R. "Stress Management in Work Settings: A Critical Review of the Health Effects" *American Journal of Health Promotion* 11, no. 2 (November/December 1996).

Paulsen, Barbara. "Work and Play: A nation out of balance" *Health* 8, no. 6 (October 1994): 44–48.

Peterson, Michael. "Work, Corporate Culture, and Stress: Implications for Worksite Health Promotion." *American Journal of Health Behavior* 21, no. 4 (1997): 243–252.

Repetti, Rena, Karen Matthews, and Ingrid Waldron. "Employment and Women's Health," *American Psychologist* 44, no. 11 (November 1989): 1394–1401.

Rosch, Paul J. "Measuring Job Stress: Some Comments on Potential Pitfalls." *American Journal of Health Promotion* 11, no. 6 (July/August, 1997): 400–401.

Rosen, Robert. *The Healthy Company.* Los Angeles: Jeremy P. Tarcher, 1991.

Schnall, Peter L., Carl Pieper, and Joseph E. Schwartz. "The relationship between job strain, workplace disastolic blood pressure, and left ventricular mass index: results of a case-control study." *Journal of the American Medical Association* 263, no. 14 (April 11, 1990): 1929–1935.

Schor, Juliet. *The Overworked American: The Unexpected Decline of Leisure.* New York: Basic Books, 1991.

Shalowitz, Deborah. "Another health care headache: job stress could strain corporate budgets." *Business Insurance* 25, no. 20 (May 20, 1991): 3, 21–22.

Snyder, Don J. *The Cliff Walk: A Memoir of a Lost Job and a Found Life.* Boston: Little Brown, 1997.

Veninga, Robert L., and James P. Spradley. *The Work Stress Connection.* New York: Ballantine Books, 1981.

Walker, Cathy. "Workplace stress." *Canadian Dimension* 27, no. 4 (August 1993): 29.

Wolf, Stewart G., Jr., and Albert J. Finestone. *Occupational Stress.* Littleton, Mass.: PSG Publishing, 1986.

Worry

Hallowell, Edward M. *Worry: Controlling It and Using It Wisely.* New York: Random House, 1997.

Yoga

Devananda, Swami Vishnu. *The Swivananda Companion to Yoga.* New York: Fireside-Simon & Schuster, 1983.

Groves, Dawn, *Yoga for Busy People: Increase Energy and Reduce Stress in Minutes a Day.* Emeryville, Calif.: New World Library, 1995.

Iyengar, Geeta S., *Yoga: A Gem for Women.* Palo Alto, Calif.: Timeless Books, 1990.

Lad, Vasant, and David Frawley. *The Yoga of Herbs,* Santa Fe, N. Mex.: Lotus Press, 1986.

Taylor, Louise. *A Woman's Book of Yoga: A Journal for Health and Self-Discovery.* Boston: Charles F. Tuttle Company, 1993.

Terkel, Susan Neiburg. *Yoga Is for Me.* Minneapolis: Lerner Publications Company, 1987.

Vishnudevananda, Swami. *The Complete Illustrated Book of Yoga.* New York: Crown Publishers, Inc., Julian Press, Inc., 1960.

RESOURCES

Acupuncture (See
COMPLEMENTARY THERAPIES)

Addictions

American Society of Addiction
  Medicine
4601 N. Park Avenue Arcade
  (Suite 101)
Chevy Chase, MD 20815
(301) 656-3920
e-mail: usamoffice@aol.com

Center for Substance Abuse
  Prevention
5600 Fishers Lane, Rockwall II
Rockville, MD 20857
(301) 443-0365
http: www.nnadal@samhsa.gov

Cocaine Anonymous
3740 Overland Avenue (Suite H)
Los Angeles, CA 90034-6337
(310) 559-5833
http://www.ca.org

Debtors Anonymous
P.O. Box 920888
Needham, MA 02492
(781) 453-2743
http://www.debtorsanonymous.org

Gamblers Anonymous-
  International Service Office
P.O. Box 17173
Los Angeles, CA 90017
(213) 386-8789
http://gamblersanonymous.org

Marijuana Anonymous
P.O. Box 2912
Van Nuys, CA 91404
(800) 766-8779
http://www.marijuana-anonymous.org

Narcotics Anonymous
P.O. Box 9999
Van Nuys, CA 91409
(818) 773-9999
http://www.wsoinc.com

National Council on Problem
  Gambling
P.O. Box 9419
Washington, DC 20016
(410) 730-8008
http://www.ncpgambling.org

National Institute on Alcohol Abuse
  and Alcoholism
6000 Executive Boulevard Wilco
  Building
Bethesda, MD 20892-7003
(301) 496-4452
http://www.niaaa.nih.gov/

Substance Abuse and Mental Health
  Services Administration, Center for
  Mental Health Services
5600 Fishers Lane
Rockville, MD 20857
(800) 789-2647 or (301) 443-2792
http://www.samhsa.gov/cmhs/
  cmhs.html

Aging and Elder Care

Administration on Aging DHHS
330 Independence Avenue SW
Washington, DC 20201
(202) 401-4511 or (202) 619-0724
http://www.aoa.dhhs.gov

Aging Network Services
4400 East-West Highway (Suite 907)
Bethesda, MD 20814
(301) 657-4329
http://www.agingnets.com

Alliance for Aging Research
2021 K Street NW, Suite 305
Washington, DC 20006
(202) 293-2856
http://agingresearch.org

American Association of Retired
  Persons
601 E Street NW
Washington, DC 20049
(800) 424-3410
www://www.aarp.org

National Aging Information Center
330 Independence Avenue SW,
  Room 4656
Washington, DC 20201
(202) 619-7501
http://pr.aoa.dhhs.gov/naic

National Institute on Aging
31 Center Drive Building 31,
  Room 5C27
MSC 2292
Bethesda, MD 20892-2292
(301) 496-1752
http://www.nih.gov/nia/

Agoraphobia

Agoraphobics Anonymous
P.O. Box 43082
Upper Montclair, NJ 07043
(973) 783-0007

Agoraphobics Building Independent
  Lives, Inc. (ABIL)
3805 Cutshaw Avenue (Suite 415)
Richmond, VA 23240
(804) 353-3964
e-mail: abil1996@aol.com

Agoraphobics in Motion (AIM)
1719 Crooks Street
Royal Oak, MI 48067
(248) 547-0400

Anxiety Disorders Association of
  America (ADAA)
11900 Parklawn Drive (Suite 100)
Rockville, MD 20852
(301) 231-9350 or 231-9259
http://www.adaa.org

AIDS (acquired immunodeficiency syndrome) and HIV

AIDS Clinical Trials Information
  Service
P.O. Box 6421
Rockville, MD 20849-6421
(800) TRIALS-A
http://www.actis.org

AIDS Health Project
1930 Market Street
San Francisco, CA 94102
(415) 476-6430
http://www. ucsf-ahp.org

CDC National Prevention Information
  Network (NPIN)
P.O. Box 6003
Rockville, MD 20850
(800) 458-5231
http://www.cdcnpin.org

National AIDS Hotline: (800) 342-2437
TTY//TDD: (800) 243-7889
English Hotline: (800) 342-AIDS
Spanish Hotline: (800) 344-SIDA

National Association of People With
  AIDS (NAPWA)
(202) 898-0414
Hotline and TTY/TDD

Project Inform
National HIV Treatment Line
(800) 922-7422

Alcoholism

Al Anon/Alateen Family Group
  Headquarters, Inc.
1600 Corporate Landing Parkway
Virginia Beach, VA 23454-5617
(800) 344-2666
http://www.al-anon.alateen.org

Alcoholics Anonymous
A.A. World Services, Inc.
P.O. Box 459
New York, NY 10163
(212) 870-3400
www.alcoholics-anonymous.org

National Council on Alcoholism and
  Drug Dependence
12 West 21st Street
New York, NY 10010-6902
(212) 206-6770
http://www.ncadd.org

National Institute on Alcohol Abuse
  and Alcoholism
6000 Executive Boulevard—Wilco
  Building
Bethesda, MD 20892-7003
(301) 496-4452
http://www.niaaa.nih.gov

Alzheimer's disease

Alzheimer's Association
919 N. Michigan Ave (Suite 1000)
Chicago, IL 60611-1676
(800) 272-3900
http://www.alz.org

Alzheimer's Disease Education and
Referral Center
P.O. Box 8250
Silver Spring, MD 20907-82250
(301) 495-3311 or (800) 438-4380
http://www/alzheimers.org

Anxiety disorders

Anxiety Disorders Association of
America (ADAA)
11900 Parklawn Drive, Suite 100
Rockville, MD 20852-2624
(301) 231-9350 or 231-9259
http://www.adaa.org

Anxiety Disorders Institute
1 Dunwoody Park, Suite 112
Atlanta, GA 30338
(770) 395-6845

Anxiety & Phobia Clinic
Davis Avenue at Port Road
White Plains, NY 10601
(914) 681-1038
http://www.phobia-anxiety.com

Council on Anxiety Disorders
Route 1, Box 1364
Clarkesville, GA 30523
(706) 947-3854
mailto:slvau@stc.net

TERRAP Programs
932 Evelyn Street
Menlo Park, CA 94025
(800) 2-PHOBIA

Attention deficit disorders

Attention Deficit Information Network
(ADIN)
475 Hillside Avenue
Needham, MA 02194
(781) 455-9895
http://www.addinfonetwork.com

Children and Adults with Attention
Deficit Disorders
8181 Professional Place, Suite 201
Landover, MD 20785
(800) 233-4050
http://www.chadd.org

National Attention Deficit Disorders
Association
P.O. Box 972
Mentor, OH 44061

(800) 487-2282
http://www.add.org

Body therapies

American Massage Therapy Association
820 Davis Street, Suite 100
Evanston, IL 60201-4444
(847) 864-0123
http://www.amtamassage.org

Inside Move, Inc.
4509 Interlake Avenue
North Seattle, WA 98103
(425) 778-6042

Feldendrais Guild of North America
3611 Southwest Hood Avenue,
Suite 100
Portland, OR 97201
(800) 775-2118
http://www.feldendrais.com

The Rolf Institute
P.O. Box 1868
Boulder, CO 80306
(303) 449-5903
http://www.Rolfinstitute@Quadzilla.
apple.com

Cancer

American Cancer Society
1599 Clifton Rd., NE
Atlanta, GA 30329
(404) 320-3333 or (800) 227-2345
http://www.cancer.org

Cancer Information Clearinghouse
(NCI/OCC)
Bldg. 31, Room 10A18
9000 Rockville Pike
Bethesda, MD 21205
(301) 496-5583
http://www.cis.nci.nih.gov

National Cancer Institute
9000 Rockville Pike
Bethesda, MD 20982
(800) 4CANCER or (800) 422-6237
http://www.nci.nih.gov

Sloane Kettering Institute for Cancer
Research
1275 York Avenue
New York, NY 10021
(212) 639-2000
http://www.mskwc.org

Susan G. Komen Breast Cancer
  Foundation
5005 LBJ, Suite 370
Dallas, TX 75244
(214) 450-1777
http://www.breastcancerinfo.com

Y-Me National Breast Cancer
  Organization
212 W. Van Buren Street
Chicago, IL 86807
(312) 986-8338
http://www.y-me.org

Chronic fatigue syndrome

The CFIDS Association of
  America Inc.
P.O. Box 2203398
Charlotte, NC 29222-0398
(800) 442-3437
http://www.cfids.org

National Chronic Fatigue Syndrome
  and Fibromyalgia Association
P.O. Box 18426
Kansas City, KS 64133
(816) 313-2000
e-mail: keal55A@prodigy.com

Complementary therapies

The Academy for Guided Imagery
P.O. Box 2070
Mill Valley, CA 94942
(800) 726-2070
http://www.interactiveimagery.com

American Art Therapy Association
1202 Allanson Road
Mundelein, IL 60060
(847) 949-6064
http://arttherapy.org

American Association of Naturopathic
  Physicians
P.O. Box 20386
Seattle, WA 98102
(206) 323-7610
http://www.naturopathic.org

American Association of Oriental
  Medicine
433 Front Street
Catasauqua, PA 18032
(610) 266-1433
http://www.aaom.org

American Chiropractic Association
1701 Clarendon Boulevard
Arlington, VA 22209
(703) 276-8800
http://www.amerchiro.org

Association of Applied Psychology and
  Biofeedback
10200 W. 44th Avenue (#304)
Wheat Ridge, CO 80033
(303) 422-8436
http://www.aapb.org

Ayurvedic Institute
P.O. Box 23445
Albuquerque, NM 97192-1445
(505) 291-9698

Chopra Center for Well Being
7630 Fay Avenue
La Jolla, CA 92037
(858) 551-7788
http://www.chopra.com

The Herb Research Foundation
1007 Pearl Street (Suite 200)
Boulder, CO 80302
(303) 449-2265
http://www.herbs.org/herbs/

International Foundation for
  Homeopathy
2366 Eastlake Avenue E, #301
Edmonds, WA 98020
(206) 776-4147
http://www.healthy.net/ifh

Mind-Body Medical Institute
New Deaconess Hospital
Harvard Medical School
185 Pilgrim Road
Cambridge, MA 02215
(617) 632-9530
http://www.mindbody.harvard.edu

National Academy of Acupuncture &
  Oriental Medicine
P.O. Box 62
Tarrytown, NY 10591
(914) 332-4576

National Center for Complementary
  and Alternative Medicine
National Institutes of Health
6120 Executive Boulevard (Suite 450)
Rockville, MD 20892-9904
http://nccam.nih.gov

National Center for Homeopathy
801 North Fairfax Street (Suite 306)
Alexandria, VA 22314
(703) 548-7790
http://www.homeopathic, org

National Dance Association
1900 Association Drive
Reston, VA 22091
(703) 476-3436
http://www.aahperd.org/nda.html

Sharp Institute for Human Potential
  and Mind/Body Medicine
8010 Frost Street (Suite 300)
San Diego, CA 92123
(800) 82-SHARP

Cults

Cult Hotline and Clinic
1651 Third Avenue
New York, NY 10028
(212) 632-4640
http://www.jbfcs.org

Task Force on Cults
711 Third Avenue, 12th Floor
New York, NY 10017
(212) 983-4977
http://www.tforce.org

Dental fears

American Dental Association
211 East Chicago Avenue
Chicago, IL 60611
(312) 440-2500
http://www.members.aol.com/adaa/
  index,html

Depression

Depression After Delivery
P.O. Box 278
Belle Meade, NJ 08502
(800) 944-4773 or (215) 295-3994
http://infotrail.com/dad/dad.html

Depression and Related Affective
  Disorders Association
Meyer 3-181
600 North Wolfe Street
Baltimore, MD 21287-7381
(202) 955-5800 or (410) 955-4647
http://www.med.jhu.edu/drada

Foundation for Depression and Manic
  Depression
24 E. 81st Street
New York, NY 10028
(212) 772-3400

National Depressive and Manic
  Depressive Association
730 N. Franklin Street (Suite 501)
Chicago, IL 60610-3526
(312) 642-0049 or (800) 826-3632
http://www.ndmda.org

National Foundation for Depressive
  Illness
P.O. Box 2257
New York, NY 10116
(800) 248-4344
http://www.depression.org

Domestic violence

Batterers Anonymous
1269 N.E. Street
San Bernardino, CA 92405
(714) 355-1100
e-mail: jmgoff@genesisnetwork.net

National Council on Child Abuse and
  Family Violence
1155 Connecticut Avenue NW
Washington, DC 20036
(202) 429-6695
e-mail: nccafv@aol.com

Dreams

Association for the Study of Dreams
6728 Old McLean Village Drive
McLean, VA 22101-3906
(703) 556-0618
http://www.ASDreams.org

Community Dream Sharing Network
P.O. Box 8032
Hicksville, NY 11802
(516) 735-1969 or (516) 796-9455

Eating disorders

American Anorexia Bulimia Association
165 W. 46th Street (Suite 1008)
New York, NY 10036
(212) 575-6200
http://www.members.aol.com/AmAnBu

Anorexia Nervosa and Related Eating
  Disorders
P.O. Box 5102
Eugene, OR 97405
(503) 344-1144
http:www.anred.com

BASH (Bulimia Anorexia Self Help)
c/o Deaconess Hospital
6150 Oakland Avenue
St. Louis, MO 63139
(314) 768-3061

National Association of Anorexia
  Nervosa and Associated Disorders
P.O. Box 7
Highland Park, IL 60035
(847) 831-3438
http://192.131.22.19/health/nhic/data/
  hr0200/hr0204.html

Flying, fear of

Fly Without Fear
310 Madison Avenue
New York, NY 10017
(212) 697-7666

The Institute for Psychology of
  Air Travel
551 Boylston Street, Suite 202
Boston, MA 02116
(617) 437-1811
e-mail: InsPsyAirT@aol.com

Grief

Bereavement and Loss Center of
  New York
170 East 83rd Street
New York, NY 10028
(212) 879-5655

Theos (groups in the U.S. and Canada
  for widowed people)
322 Boulevard of the Allies, Suite 105
Pittsburgh, PA 15222-1919
(412) 471-7779

Headaches

American Association for the Study
  of Headache
19 Mantua Road
Mt. Royal, NJ 08061
(609) 423-0043
http://www.aash.org

National Headache Foundation
5252 N. Western Avenue
Chicago, IL 60625
(773) 878-7715
http://www.headaches.org

Heart disease

American Heart Association
7320 Greenville Avenue
Dallas, TX 75231
(214) 373-6300
http://www.americanheart.org

National Heart, Lung and Blood
  Institute
9000 Rockville Pike
Bethesda, MD 20892
(301) 496-4236
http://www.nhlbi.nih.gov

Humor

International Laughter Society
16000 Glen Una Drive
Los Gatos, CA 95030
(408) 354-3456
e-mail: yesferrari@juno.com

Hypnosis

American Society of Clinical Hypnosis
33 W. Grand Avenue, Suite 402
Chicago, IL 60610
(312) 645-9810

International Society for Medical and
  Psychological Hypnosis
1991 Broadway (18B)
New York, NY 10023
(212) 874-5290

Learning disabilities

Learning Disabilities Association of
  America
4156 Library Road
Pittsburgh, PA 15234
(412) 341-1515
http://www.danatl.org

Marriage and family

American Association for Marriage
  and Family Therapy
1133 15th Street NW (Suite 300)
Washington, DC 20005-2710

(202) 452-0109
http://www.aamft.org

Center for the Family in
  Transition
P.O. Box 157
Corte Madera, CA 94976
(415) 924-5750

Stepfamily Association of
  America
215 Centennial Mall (Suite 212)
Lincoln, NE 68508
(800) 735-0329

Mental health

American Psychiatric Association
1400 K Street NW
Washington, DC 20005
(202) 692-6850
http://www.psych.org/address.html

National Alliance for the Mentally Ill
200 N. Glebe Road, Suite 1015
Arlington, VA 22203-3754
(703) 524-7600 or (800) 950-6264
http://www.nami.org

National Institute of Mental Health
  Neuroscience Center
6001 Executive Boulevard
Bethesda, MD 20892-9669
(301) 443-3673
http://www.nimh@nih.gov

National Mental Health
  Association
1021 Prince Street
Alexandria, VA 22314-2971
(800) 969-6642 or (703) 684-7722
http://www.nmha.org

Mental health: children and adolescents

American Academy of Child and
  Adolescent Psychiatry
3615 Wisconsin Avenue NW
Washington, DC 20016-3007
(202) 966-7300
http://www.aacap.org

National Committee on Youth
  Suicide Prevention
666 Fifth Avenue, 13th Floor
New York, NY 10103

Mental retardation

American Association on Mental
  Retardation
444 N. Capitol Street NW, Suite 846
Washington, DC 20001
(202) 387-1968
www.aamr.org

Association for Retarded Citizens
  (ARC)
P.O. Box 6109
Arlington, TX 76005
(817) 640-0204
e-mail: thearc@metronet.com

National Down Syndrome Society
141 5th Avenue
New York, NY 10010
(212) 460-9330
http://www.ndss.org

Obsessive-compulsive disorder

Obsessive Compulsive Foundation
P.O. Box 70
Milford, CT 06460-0070
(203) 878-5669 Ext. 16
http://pages.prodigy.cn.alwillen/ocf.
  html

Phobias

Anxiety Disorders Association of
  America (ADAA)
11900 Parklawn Drive (Suite 100)
Rockville, MD 20852
(301) 231-9350 or 231-9259
http://www.adaa.org

National Mental Health Association
1021 Prince Street
Alexandria, VA 22314-2971
(703) 684-7722
http:www.nmha.org

Phobics Anonymous
P.O. Box 1180
Palm Springs, CA 92263

Special Interest Group on Phobias and
  Related Anxiety Disorders (SIGPRA)
245 E. 87th Street
New York, NY 10028
(212) 860-5560
http://www.cyberpsych.org/anxsig.
  htm

Posttraumatic stress disorder

Anxiety Disorders Association of
America (ADAA)
11900 Parklawn Drive (Suite 100)
Rockville, MD 20852
(301) 231-9350 or 231-9259
http://www.adaa.org

National Association of Veterans
Administration Chiefs of
Psychiatry
54th Street and 48th Avenue
Minneapolis, MN 55417
(612) 725-6767

U.S. Veterans Administration
Mental Health and Behavioral
Sciences Services
810 Vermont Avenue NW,
Room 915
Washington, DC 20410
(410) 687-8567

Self-help and support groups

National Self-Help Clearinghouse
25 W. 43rd Street (Room 620)
New York, NY 10036
(212) 642-2944 or (212) 354-8525
http://www.selfhelpweb.org

Recovery, Inc.
802 N. Dearborn Street
Chicago, IL 60610
(312) 337-5661
http://www.recovery-inc.com

Sexually transmitted diseases

American Academy of
Dermatology
P.O. Box 4014
930 N. Meacham Road
Schaumburg, IL 60168-4014
(947) 330-0230
http://www.aad.org

American Social Health Association
P.O. Box 13827
Research Triangle Park, NC 27709
(919) 361-2742
http://sunsite.unc.edu/ASHA

The Herpes Resource Center
260 Sheridan Avenue, Suite 307
Palo Alto, CA 94306
(800) 227-8922 or (415) 328-7710

National VD Hotline
American Social Health Association
(800) 227-8922
http://www.ashastd.org

SIECUS (Sexuality Information and
Education Council of the U.S.)
130 W. 42nd Street, Suite 2500
New York, NY 10036
(212) 819-9770
http://www.siecus.org

Sleep

American Sleep Apnea Association
1424 K Street NW, Suite 302
Washington, DC 20005
(202) 293-3650
http://www.sleepapnea.org

American Sleep Disorders
Association
6301 Bandel Road, Suite 101
Rochester, MN 55901
(507) 287-6006
http://www.asda.org

Narcolepsy Network
277 Fairfield Road, Suite 310B
Fairfield, NJ 07004
(973) 276-0115
http://www.websciences.org

National Sleep Foundation
729 15th Street NW, Floor 4
Washington, DC 20005
(202) 347-3471
http://www.sleepfoundation.org

Social phobia/social anxiety

Social Phobia/Social Anxiety
Association
5025 N. Central Avenue (#421)
Phoenix, AZ 85012
http://www.socialphobia.org

Suicide

American Association of
Suicidology
4201 Connecticut Avenue, NW, Suite
310
Washington, DC 20008
(202) 237-2280
http://www.cyberpsych.org/aas/index.
html

American Foundation for
  Suicide Prevention
120 Wall Street, 22nd Floor
New York, NY 10005
(888) 333-AFSP or (212) 363-3500
http://www.afsp.org

Volunteerism

Volunteer Management Associates
320 South Cedar Brook Road
Boulder, CO 80304
(303) 447-0558 or (800) 944-1470
www.volunteermanagement.com

INDEX

Page numbers in boldface indicate A to Z article titles

A

abuse 75, 143, 220
acceptance **99**, 269
accidents, fear of **99**
acculturation, fear of **99**
acetycholine 205
acquired immunodeficiency syndrome.
    See AIDS
acrophobia 48–49, **99–100**, 172, 173. *See
    also* heights, fear of
acupressure **100**, 129
acupuncture 88, **100–101**, 129, 181
Adaptation to Life (Vaillant) 139
addiction, fear of **101**. *See also* codepen-
    dency
ADHD **111**
Adler, Alfred 181
adolescents
    autonomy 113
    depression in 81, 82
    fear of menstruation 194–95
    migraine headaches 164
    wet dreams 274
adrenaline **101**, 112–13
adverse drug reactions **101**
affect 102
affective disorders **102–3**, 198–99
afterlife. *See* heaven, fear of; hell, fear of
    aggression **103–4**
aging-related fears
    of Alzheimer's disease 105
    of being alone 122
    books as anxiety relief for 129
    of forgetting 151
    geropsychiatry for 94–95
    of getting wrinkles 276
    of growing old 160
    of loneliness 188
    of memory loss 194
    of not waking up 273
agoraphobia 4, 6, 56–64, **104**
    ambivalence in 106
    anger suppression in 107
    behavior therapy for 119
    biological basis for 61–62
    boredom as anxiety factor in 130
    codependency 136
    cycle of 57

depression linked with 60, 102
effects of 58
fear of being alone and 105, 122
fear of boredom and 130
fear of flying and 149
fear of long waits and 188
inception of 58–59
milieu therapy for 196
pharmacological therapy for 63, 105
self-rating scales 241
symptoms of 59–60
treatments for 62–63
worrying and 276
AIDS-related fears
    of blood transfusions 127
    hemophilia and 172
    of kissing 185
    of needles 204
    of public lavatories 186
    of sexually transmitted diseases
        243–44
    of tattoos 262
ailurophia **104**. *See also* black cats, fear of;
    cats, fear of
alcoholism **104–5** 114, 119, 136
alone, fear of being **105**
    as autophobia 113
alprazolam (Xanax) 63, **105**, 109, 150, 167
alternative therapies. *See* complementary
    therapies; mind/body connection
altophobia **105**. *See also* heights, fear of
Alzheimer, Alois 105
Alzheimer's disease **105**, 106, 151, 160
ambivalence **105–6**
American Association for Humanistic
    Psychology 175
amnesia, fear of **106**
amphetamines **106**
"Angel of the Bridge, The" (Cheever) 131
anger **106–7**, 138, 260
angst **107**
animal phobias 45
    as zoophobia 279
    See also specific animals
anniversary reaction **107**
anorexia nervosa 128, 144–45, 274
anorgasmia (anorgasmy) **107**
antianxiety drugs 40, 63, 64, **107**